Modern
GERMAN
Grammar

Routledge Modern Grammars

Series concept and development – Sarah Butler

Other books in the series:

Modern German Grammar Workbook

Modern French Grammar
Modern Italian Grammar
Modern Spanish Grammar

Modern
GERMAN
Grammar

A practical guide

**Bill Dodd, Christine Eckhard-Black,
John Klapper, Ruth Whittle**

London and New York

First published 1996 by Routledge
11 New Fetter Lane, London EC4P 4EE

Simultaneously published in the USA and Canada
by Routledge
29 West 35th Street, New York, NY 10001

© 1996 Bill Dodd, Christine Eckhard-Black, John Klapper, Ruth Whittle

Typeset in Utopia by Solidus (Bristol) Limited
Printed and bound in Great Britain by
TJ Press Ltd, Padstow, Cornwall

British Library Cataloguing in Publication Data
A catalogue record for this book is available from the British Library

Library of Congress Cataloguing in Publication Data
Modern German Grammar : a practical guide/Bill Dodd [et al.].
    1. German language – Grammar.   2. German language – Textbooks for
    foreign speakers – English.   I. Dodd, Bill.
    PF3112.M55   1996
    438.2 '421—dc20   95–35096

ISBN 0-415-09847-5 (hbk)
ISBN 0-415 09848-3 (pbk)

Contents

Part B Functions

Introduction

Modern German Grammar: A Practical Guide is an innovative reference grammar designed to be used with modern approaches to teaching and learning German as a foreign language. The book addresses learners' practical needs by combining a detailed description of the grammatical structures of German with a 'functional' approach to language. By functions we mean the specific uses to which we can put language in order to communicate effectively in particular situations: e.g. apologizing, accepting or declining an invitation, expressing regret, voicing an opinion or casting doubt on something.

The book is intended for all those who have a basic knowledge of German, including undergraduates taking German as a major or minor part of their studies, as well as intermediate and advanced students in both schools and adult education. It will also prove an invaluable resource for teachers seeking back-up to syllabuses organized around functions, or designers of German language courses and syllabuses in all sectors of education.

Before using the book the reader is advised to refer to pp. 4–5 on 'How to use this book'. There are two main parts. Part A (sections 1–59) provides a detailed description of the structures of modern German, and is in this respect quite close to being a 'traditional' grammar. The explanations given in Part A are supported by a detailed glossary of grammatical terms which assumes no previous grammatical training. In contrast, the larger Part B (sections 60–121), focuses on functions, explaining and illustrating the appropriate use of German in particular contexts, the specific ideas the learner wishes to express and the concrete situations in which he or she is likely to wish to use them.

There is a comprehensive index at the back of the book. This is a very important section as the detailed entries on functions, structures and grammatical terminology allow the reader to approach the language in more than one way: he or she can either look up how to express a particular function or seek information on how a certain aspect of the language works. Having located the required function (e.g. 'Attracting attention in a dangerous situation' **90.1**B), the learner is referred to relevant structures in Part A (e.g. 'Use of subjunctive II'). This approach avoids the difficulties learners have with traditional grammars where, faced with expressing something in German, they frequently do not know which structure(s) they need to look up. In this book, the grammatical structures needed to perform the function successfully are highlighted in Part B and can be checked more fully in Part A. An extensive system of cross-references within and between the two major parts of the book provides further information which the user may find helpful, especially when consulting individual functions.

A key factor in a book of this kind is the description of register. The term register denotes the relationship between a speaker or writer and the person he or she is speaking or writing to. The degree of formality or informality which characterizes their communication is determined by their respective ages, by how intimately they are acquainted and by their status, i.e. their respective professional or social standing. While there are numerous gradations on the register scale between the two extremes of formality and informality, in this book it is assumed that, unless otherwise stated, the language being described belongs to a standard, neutral, educated and polite register which is neither excessively formal nor excessively informal. Only those expressions which clearly stand out from this general polite usage have been marked for register. Expressions marked as 'informal' are examples of casual or colloquial usage; this can include slang or vulgar terms, but the latter are always indicated separately. Language marked as 'formal' denotes official or literary language which may have an archaic ring to it or may be restricted to use in written German.

Readers should note that the spellings in the book, in particular the use of ß, are based on conventional usage. A number of significant reforms to German orthography have recently been proposed by an international conference of experts from the major German-speaking countries in Europe, and in the near future many of these may be accepted by the governments of Germany, Austria and Switzerland. These proposed changes are summarized in section **59.6**A.

We have adopted the following conventions:

- within an English sentence bold type is used for German text, and single speech marks for English translations, e.g. **ein*laden** 'to invite'
- as the above example shows, an asterisk indicates a separable prefix to a verb
- the slash symbol (/) indicates an alternative word or expression
- **-r, -e, -s** denote **der, die, das** respectively
- noun plurals are indicated via brackets, e.g. **(e)** or **(en)**
- the following abbreviations are used:

> **etw.** = **etwas**
> **jmd.** = **jemand**
> **jmdn.** = **jemanden**
> **jmdm.** = **jemandem**
> **jmds.** = **jemandes**

nom = nominative
acc = accusative
dat = dative
gen = genitive
sb. = somebody
sth. = something.

How to use this book

Functional heading	# XIII *Transactions: getting things done*
General function	**90** *Attracting attention*
Cross-reference to related function	(See also **61.1**B on 'Making initial contact')
Specific function	**90.1** **Attracting attention in a dangerous situation**
German illustrations with English translations	**Hilfe!** Help **Hallo!** Hello!
Note on meaning/ usage	(**Hallo!** is not necessarily understood as a request for rescue but as a casual greeting. Only when shouted out with a prolonged *a* does it mean a call for help in dire circumstances.) (See also **60.2a**B)
Cross-reference to grammatical explanation in Part B	**Achtung!** Beware!/Watch out!
	90.2 Attracting someone's attention when he or she is busy
	Darf ich mal kurz stören. (polite) May I interrupt you for a moment. **Entschuldigen Sie bitte**. (polite) Excuse me, please. **Hallo, Sie da!/He, Sie da!** (rude)
	Requests for attention using the Subjunctive II are particularly polite though not deferential (see **39.2b**A).
Cross-reference to grammatical explanation in Part A	***Dürfte** ich mal kurz stören.* If I might interrupt you for a moment. **Wenn Sie einen Moment Zeit für mich hätten**. If you could spare me a moment.
Bold italic to highlight feature under discussion	
	90.3 Turning one's attention to somebody
Sub-division of specific function	(a) In order to help
	Ja, bitte? Yes? (How can I help you?) **Worum handelt es sich?** (formal) What is it about?

Information on register (pointing to "Darf ich mal kurz stören / Entschuldigen Sie bitte / Hallo, Sie da" block)

Index shows where to find various functions

Box summarizes main expressions and structure presented in the section

Indicates dative of person

68 *Expressing apologies and regret*

The most common expressions include:

jmdm. leid tun 'to be sorry'
sich (= acc) **bei jmdm. entschuldigen** 'to apologize to sb.'
Shows case — **etw. mit etw.** (= dat) **entschuldigen** 'to excuse sth. with sth.'
Indicates dative of thing **sich bei jmdm. entschuldigen lassen** 'to send one's apologies to sb.'
Indicates accusative of person **jmdn. bei jmdm. entschuldigen** 'to convey sb.'s apologies to sb.'
sich (= dat) – **jmdm. verzeihen** 'to forgive oneself/sb.'

68.1 **Apologizing and seeking forgiveness**
(a) To say sorry for a slight mishap or some minor misdemeanour a simple
Verzeihung! or **Entschuldigung!** 'sorry' will suffice:

> **Entschuldigung, falsch verbunden.**
> I'm sorry I've got the wrong number. (on the telephone)
> **Verzeihung, ich habe mich verwählt.**
> I'm sorry I've dialled the wrong number.

Information on register

Tut mir leid, short for **es tut mir leid** (see **68.1b**B), is also used in this sense. In German
border regions with France, in particular, the form **Pardon!** (pronounced as in French)
Note on cultural aspects may well be heard, while in informal spoken German **Sorry!** is now frequently heard,
although it tends to be a lot more superficial than in English and it should not be used
for a genuine apology.

(b) The expression **leid tun** is very commonly used to convey apologies and regret,
Indicates alternative forms often with an adverb for reinforcement. Note that the verb is always used impersonally
(see **19.7**A for impersonal verbs).

> **Es tut mir furchtbar/aufrichtig leid, daß ich das Buch schon wieder
> vergessen habe.**
> I am terribly/sincerely sorry for having forgotten the book again.
> **Es tut uns sehr/wirklich leid, daß ihr nicht mitkommen könnt.**
> We are very/really sorry that you can't come with us.
> (See also **113.3**B on 'Disappointment'.)

Cross reference to related function

Glossary

accusative object also known as the direct object, denotes the person or thing the action of the verb is being done to, and is in the accusative case in German: **Sie kaufte** *den Rock* 'She bought the skirt'.

adjective describes a noun. It can be a simple description such as **rot** 'red', **langweilig** 'boring', or it can be a possessive such as **mein** 'my', **unser** 'our', **Ihr** 'your': **Das ist ein** *schöner* **Anzug** 'That's a nice suit'. **Hast du** *meine* **Jacke gesehen?** 'Have you seen my jacket?'.

adjectival noun a noun derived from an adjective, which has the usual adjective endings: **der Angestellte** '(male) employee', **die Angestellte** '(female) employee', **die Angestellten** 'employees'.

adverb indicates e.g. the manner in which something is done. It can consist of one word or a phrase: **schnell** 'quickly', **schlecht** 'badly', **am Abend** 'in the evening', **in der Schule** 'at school'.

auxiliary verb used in combination with the past participle to form tenses and the passive. The German auxiliaries are **haben, sein** and **werden**: *Habt* **ihr es schon gemacht?** 'Have you already done it?' **Er** *ist* **noch nicht angekommen** 'He has not arrived yet.' **Sie** *wurden* **in der Stadt gesehen** 'They were seen in town.'

case the function of nouns or pronouns in a German sentence is shown by a change in their form or that of the determiners and adjectives used with them. The nominative indicates the subject of the verb, the accusative indicates the accusative/direct object, the dative indicates the dative/indirect object, and the genitive indicates possession or the relationship between nouns. Prepositions also require certain cases to be used. See **16–21**A.

clause sub-section of a sentence containing a verb. The main clause is that part of a sentence which does not depend on any other element in the sentence for its meaning. The subordinate clause depends on another clause, i.e. it cannot stand alone, and is usually introduced by a conjunction: **Er weiß doch schon,** *daß ich krank bin* 'He already knows that I'm ill'. Here the section in bold italics is the subordinate clause, while what precedes it is the main clause. A relative clause is a subordinate clause introduced by a relative pronoun (usually **der/die/das**) and relates back to a preceding noun or pronoun: **Das ist die Schule,** *die wir früher besuchten* 'That is the school we used to go to'.

completion of the verb the phrase or phrases which complete the meaning of the verb, such as accusative and dative objects or prepositional phrases: **Er klopfte** *an der Tür* 'He knocked on the door'. **Sie gab** *ihrer Freundin das Buch* 'She gave her friend the book'.

compound noun a noun formed by joining together two or more words: **das Büro** 'office', **die Maschine** 'machine', **die Büromaschine** 'office machine'.

conditional the form **würde** is the Subjunctive II form of the verb **werden** and is sometimes referred to as the conditional tense, even though it is not strictly a tense. It is frequently used in conditional sentences, so called because they suggest some condition applies to the meaning of the main clause. The subordinate clause in a conditional sentence very often begins with the conjunction **wenn** 'if': **Wenn es heute nicht regnete, würden wir im Garten arbeiten** 'If it weren't raining today, we would work in the garden'. Another type of conditional sentence with **wenn** and the present tense of the verb in both clauses denotes an open or real condition: **Wenn sie heute abend kommt, gehen wir ins Kino** 'If she comes this evening, we'll go to the cinema'.

conjugation the changing of a verb's person, number, tense or mood to indicate different meanings or grammatical functions: **Ich gehe, du gehst, sie ging, er ginge**, etc.

conjunction a word that links clauses: e.g. **daß, obwohl, weil, aber, und.**

dative object also known as the indirect object, it usually denotes a person or thing indirectly involved in the action of the verb. In English it comes before the accusative/direct object or after 'to'/'for'; in German it is always in the dative case: **Sie zeigte** *ihrem Bruder* **das neue Auto** 'She showed *her brother* the new car'/'She showed the new car *to her brother*'. **Er hat es** *dir* **gekauft** 'He bought it *for you*'.

declension the changing of a noun's case and number (singular/plural) to indicate different meanings or grammatical functions.

determiner a function word preceding a noun. Determiners include definite articles (**der, die, das** 'the'), indefinite articles (**ein** 'a', **kein** 'not a'), possessive adjectives (**mein** 'my', **unser** 'our'), demonstratives (**dieser** 'this', **jener** 'that'), indefinites (**mancher** 'some', **viele** 'many').

finite verb the one verb in a clause which has a subject and can be either singular or plural, in the present or past tense, in contrast to participles and infinitives which are the non-finite parts of the verb: **Wir** *sind* **nach Paris geflogen** 'We flew to Paris'. *Schwimmst* **du noch am Wochenende?** 'Do you still go swimming at the weekend?'.

gender a means of classifying nouns grammatically through the different forms of the determiners which precede them: *Der* **Mann/** *das* **Haus.** *Dieser* **Mann/** *diese* **Frau.** In *keinem* Dorf/in *keiner* Stadt. German has three genders – masculine, feminine and neuter. In most cases grammatical gender is not based on natural gender.

imperative mood the form of the verb used to express commands: *Bring* mir das Buch 'Bring me the book'. *Gehen Sie* nach Hause! 'Go home!'. *Kommt* mal her, Kinder 'Come here, children'. See also Indicative Mood and Subjunctive Mood.

indicative mood the form of the verb used to make unconditional statements or to ask questions: Die Arbeit *war* schon am Montag fertig 'The work was finished on Monday'. *Wohnen* Sie hier in der Nähe? 'Do you live near here?' See also imperative mood and subjunctive mood.

infinitive the form of the verb found in a dictionary: arbeiten 'to work'. The infinitive is also used in particular constructions, e.g. with a modal verb: Wir müssen jetzt *arbeiten* 'We have to work now'.

inseparable verb a verb with an inseparable prefix: vergeben 'to forgive'. The past participle does not begin with ge-: Ich habe dich *vergeben* 'I have forgiven you'.

intransitive verb a verb which needs only a subject to form a basic sentence: Sie schläft 'She is asleep'.

irregular verb a verb which changes its stem in the du and the er/sie/es forms of the present tense, e.g. geben 'to give': ich gebe, du g*i*bst, er g*i*bt.

modal particles words which signal the speaker's attitude towards what he or she is saying and help to involve the listener in what is being said. There is often no direct English equivalent: Das hast du *ja* selber gesagt 'You said that yourself (after all)'.

modal verb a verb which can be used with another verb to modify the kind of statement being made: Ich kaufe es 'I buy it' can be modified to Ich *will* es kaufen 'I want to buy it', Ich *muß* es kaufen 'I have to buy it', etc.

noun a word which names things, processes or concepts. In written German all nouns begin with a capital letter: der Brief 'letter', die Tiefe 'depth', das Schreiben '(act of) writing'. All nouns in German have a gender.

object (of the verb) the person or thing affected by the action of the verb, as distinct from the person or thing responsible for the action. See accusative object and dative object.

orthography the conventions for correct spelling and punctuation.

participle a non-finite form of a verb. The present participle is usually an adjective: führend 'leading'. The past participle is used in forming various tenses and signals the completion of an action: Er wird es *gemacht* haben 'He will have done it'. The past participle can also have an adjectival sense: berühmt 'famous'.

passive voice a grammatical construction in which the person or thing affected by the action of a verb appears as the subject of the sentence. For example, the sentence **Er hat den Brief geschrieben** 'He has written the letter' can be expressed in the passive as **Der Brief ist (von ihm) geschrieben worden** 'The letter has been written (by him)'.

preposition a word that typically describes where things are in time and space. German prepositions always put the noun or pronoun into a case other than the nominative: **unter dem Tisch** 'under the table', **für mich** 'for me'.

prepositional verb a verb that forms an idiomatic unit with a particular preposition: **glauben an** (+ acc) 'to believe in sb. or sth.'

pronoun a word that stands in for and refers to a noun. There are personal pronouns: e.g. **er**, which means 'he' when referring to a noun like **der Abteilungsleiter** 'head of department', and 'it' when referring to a noun like **der Computer** 'computer'. Relative pronouns introduce relative clauses: **Das ist eine Frage,** *die* **mich interessiert** 'That is a question which interests me'. The possessive pronouns **meiner, meine, meins; deiner, deine, deins**, etc. correspond to 'mine', 'yours', etc. Demonstrative pronouns point to something specific: **dieses Spiel** 'this game', **jene Frau** 'that woman'. Informally **der/die/das** also act as demonstrative pronouns: *Den* **haben wir heute nicht gesehen** 'We haven't seen him today'.

reflexive verb a verb that is used with a reflexive pronoun to indicate that the subject and the object of the verb are identical: **Ich rasiere mich** 'I shave'. Some German verbs can only be used reflexively: **Ich befinde mich in Bonn** 'I am in Bonn'.

reported speech a way of showing that the words used by the speaker or the writer are someone else's. German uses a subjunctive form of the verb for this: e.g. an original sentence such as **Ich bin krank** 'I am ill' can be reported as **Er sagte, er** *sei* **krank** 'He said he was ill'.

separable verb a verb with a (stressed) separable prefix which appears separately from the main part of the verb in some structures: **Der Zug** *kam* **pünktlich** *an* 'The train arrived on time'.

strong verb a verb which undergoes a change to its stem in forming the simple past: **wir singen** 'we sing', **wir s**a**ngen** 'we sang'.

subject (of the verb) usually a noun or pronoun which denotes the person or thing doing the action expressed by the verb. The subject agrees with the verb in number: **Die Maschine läuft** 'The machine is running', **Die Maschinen laufen** 'The machines are running'.

subjunctive mood a form of the verb used to express an action, process or state which is not actually in existence at the time of speaking. The subjunctive is mainly used in reported speech and in conditional sentences such as **Ich** *könnte* **morgen kommen**

(**, wenn du Zeit hast**) 'I could come tomorrow (if you have time)'. See also indicative mood.

tense a finite form of the verb which usually expresses whether the action takes place in the present, past or future. German has six tense forms. See **33.3**A and **34**A.

transitive verb strictly, a verb which can have an accusative object: **Ich verstehe dich** 'I understand you'.

verbal prefix a prefix added to a verb in order to create a new verb with a different meaning. Verbal prefixes may be separable (**an*kommen** 'to arrive') or inseparable (**vergeben** 'to forgive'). A few verbal prefixes can be separable or inseparable, with a distinction in meaning: See **36**A.

PART A

Structures

I Letters and sounds

Sections 1–4 provide a reference guide to the correspondences between letters and the sounds they represent in German. Approximate versions of German pronunciation are given in square brackets. A stressed syllable is shown in italic. (See also **59.6**A on proposed spelling reforms)

1 Vowels

1.1 The quality of a vowel depends on whether it is stressed or unstressed (see **4**A). In unstressed syllables vowels tend towards the neutral sound found in the unstressed syllables of English 'farmer', 'armour', 'along'.

1.2 The relationship between written vowels and spoken syllables is different in English and German in one important respect: 'dame' is one syllable in English, but **Dame** (lady) is two syllables in German: [*da:*-me].

1.3 German vowels are pronounced either short or long. In this section, a vowel which is pronounced long is followed by a colon [:]. A doubled consonant following a vowel indicates that the vowel is short (**Lamm** [lam] 'lamb'); an **h** following a vowel indicates that the vowel is long (**lahm** [la:m] 'lame'). German vowels are also much 'purer' than English vowels, which tend to be slight glides (see **2**A). The quality of German vowels is typically close to northern English pronunciation.

1.4 The letters and sounds for vowels are as follows:

a   Short, like the vowel in (northern) English 'ham': **Kamm, Lamm**.
Long, like the vowel in English 'harm': **kam, lahm**.

ä/e These represent the same set of sounds. Short, like the first vowel in English 'enter': **Essen, Ämter**. Long, it has no equivalent in English. **Esel** ([*e:*zel] 'donkey') almost rhymes with 'hazel' but without the vowel glide of English.

ee   This is always pronounced long: **Tee** ([te:] 'tea') rhymes with 'hay' but without the vowel glide of English.

i   Short, like the vowel in English 'it': **List** ([list] 'cunning')

ie   As a single syllable, this is always pronounced long, like the vowel in English 'eat': **liest** ([li:st] 'reads'). But see also **4.3**A.

o   Short, like the vowel in English 'off': **offen** ([*o*fen] open). Long, like the vowel in English 'oaf', but without the vowel glide of English: **Ofen** ([*o*:fen] 'oven').

ö   Short [ö], it has no near equivalent in English: **können** ([*kö*nen] 'be able to'). Long [ö:], like the vowel in English 'urn', but with the tongue further forward, the lips rounded and without the glide of English: **Söhne** ([*zö*:ne] 'sons').

u   Short [u], like the vowel in English 'pull': **Pulli** ([*pu*li] 'pullover'). Long [u:], like the vowel in English 'tool': **Puder** ([*pu*:der] 'powder').

ü/y   These represent the same set of sounds as produced by performing English 'ee' in 'green' and pursing the lips. This produces a front vowel sound with rounded lips, long in **grün** ([grü:n] 'green') and **typisch** ([*tü*:pish] 'typical'); short in **Küsse** ([*kü*se] 'kisses').

j   This is pronounced 'y' in German: **Juli** ([*yu*:li] 'July').

1.5 Where umlauted vowels (**ä, ö, ü**) mark grammatical changes, e.g. in forming the plural of a noun or the subjunctive of a verb, the umlauted vowel has the same length as the vowel it replaces: both short in **Kamm, Kämme** ([kam] [*ke*me] 'comb', 'combs'); both long in **kam, käme** ([ka:m] [*ke*:me] 'came', 'would come'). An umlaut basically takes a vowel produced at the back of the mouth [**a a: o o: u u:**] and moves it to the front of the mouth [**e e: ö ö: ü ü:**] but with the lips shaped as they were for the back vowel.

2   *Diphthongs*

2.1 Diphthongs are vowel glides. The tongue 'glides' from one position to another as the sound is produced.

au   Like English 'ow' in 'how now'. The vowel in German **braun** is very like the vowel in English 'brown'.

ai/ei Both pronounced like the glide in English 'ice' (German **Eis**).

äu/eu Both these combinations of letters represent the sound 'oi': **Mäuse** ([*moi*ze] 'mice'); **Europa** ([oi*ro*:pa] 'Europe').'

Note that **äu** is the umlauted form of the back vowel glide **au**: **Haus** ([haus] 'house'), **Häuser** ([*hoi*zer] 'houses').

2.2 In German, **ei** is always pronounced 'eye', and **ie** is always pronounced 'ee'. Thus, saying the second letter of the pair always produces the correct sound for English speakers: **Wein** ([vain] 'wine') sounds like English 'vine'. **Bier** ([bi:r] 'beer') sounds like English 'beer'.

2.3 Most English vowels have a slight tendency to be pronounced as glides, i.e. the tongue moves from one position to another nearby. However, most German vowels are pronounced with the tongue held in a constant position.

3 Consonants

3.1 German has one consonant letter not found in English: **ß**. Called 'sharp s' or 's-tset', this letter is always pronounced voiceless, i.e. as in 'hiss' as opposed to 'his'. It is always written instead of double -**s** (**ss**) when followed by a consonant and at the end of a word, irrespective of whether it is preceded by a long or a short vowel. Thus **Maß** ([ma:s] 'measure') has a long vowel and **Haß** ([has] 'hatred') has a short vowel (but see **59.6**A). Between vowels in the middle of a word, however, the choice of **ß** or **ss** depends on the length of the preceding vowel. A long vowel is followed by **ß**, a short vowel by **ss**: **Maßes** ([*ma:*ses] genitive of **Maß**), **Hasses** ([*ha*ses] genitive of **Haß**). That is to say, when **ß** is written between vowels it shows that the preceding vowel is long. Thus:

Long:	**Maße** [*ma:*se]	**Füße** [*fü:*se]	**stoße** [*shto:*se]	**Stöße** [*shtö:*se]
Short:	**Masse** [*ma*se]	**Flüsse** [*flü*se]	**Sprosse** [*shpro*se]	**Schlösser** [*shlö*ser]

3.2 Most consonants are pronounced as they are in English, with the following principal exceptions:

b, d These are pronounced 'p' and 't' respectively when at the end of a word or syllable: **ab** ([ap] 'away'), **Rad** ([ra:t] 'wheel').

ch (a) This is pronounced hard, midway between 'k' and 'h' (as in Scots English 'loch') when it follows a back vowel (**a, a:, o, o:, u, u:** and **au**): **Bach** ([bakh] 'stream'), **Loch** ([lokh] 'hole'), **Buch** ([bu:kh] 'book'), **Bauch** ([baukh] 'stomach').

(b) This is pronounced soft, rather like 'sh' (but halfway between English 'sh' and the above sound) when it follows a consonant or a front vowel [**i, i:, e, e:, ä, ä:, ö, ö:, ü, ü:** and **äu, eu, ai, ei**]: **Milch** ([milch] 'milk'), **Löcher** ([*lö*cher] 'holes'), **Bücher** ([*bü:*cher] 'books'), **Bäche** ([*be*che] 'streams'), **Bäuche** ([*boi*che] 'stomachs'). It is the first sound in the English word 'huge'.

ig	The **g** is pronounced like soft **ch** (see above) when at the end of a word or syllable. In some parts of Germany it is, however, pronounced 'k' in these positions: **billig** ([*bil*lich, *bil*lik] 'cheap').
ng	The **g** is never pronounced in German. Like English 'singer'.
st, sp	These are pronounced 'sht', 'shp' at the beginning of a word or syllable: **Stuttgart** [*shtut*gart], **Spiel** ([shpi:l] 'game'). (In some parts of Germany, e.g. in Hamburg, these are pronounced without the 'sh' sound: [*stut*gart] [spi:l].)
s	This is pronounced 'z' preceding a vowel: **so** [zo:], **versammeln** ([fer*za*meln] 'gather'), but is pronounced as an 's' in some words imported from English: **sexy** [*se*ksi], **Suzy** [*su:*zi].
z	This is pronounced 'ts', also at the beginning of a word or syllable: **Skizze** ([*ski*tse] 'sketch'), **zu** ([tsu:] 'to'), **hinzu** ([hin*tsu:*] 'in addition'), **zusammen** ([tsu*za*men] 'together').
v	This is usually pronounced 'f' at the beginning of words and syllables: **viel** ([fi:l] 'a lot'); and at the end of words: **brav** ([bra:f] 'well-behaved').
w	This is pronounced 'v' at the beginning of words and syllables: **weil** ([vail] 'because').
sch	This is pronounced 'sh': **Schule** ([*shu:*le] 'school').
qu	This is pronounced 'kv': **quer** ([kve:r] 'diagonal').
-age	At the end of some nouns imported from French, this has a French pronunciation, but it is pronounced with two syllables, the first one of which carries the stress: **Garage** [gar*a:zh*e].
-tion	At the end of a word this is pronounced as two syllables, the last one of which carries the stress: **Inflation** [inflatsi-*o:n*]. This may be pronounced faster, almost as a single syllable: [infla-*tsyo:n*].

Any consonant clusters not listed above are pronounced in full. For example: **Knie** ([kni:] 'knee'), **Pfad** ([pfa:t] 'path'), **Psychologie** ([**psücholo*gi:***] 'psychology').

4 *Stress*

4.1 It is only in stressed syllables that vowels have their full value.

4.2 Many words which look like English words have a different stress: **Student** [shtu*dent*], **Altar** [al*ta:r*], **Hierarchie** [hi:ra:r*chi:*], **Diskothek** [disko*te:k*].

4.3 **ie** is usually pronounced as a single syllable, but in some nouns and adjectives imported from other languages **ie** is pronounced as two syllables [i:-e]: **Familie**

([fa*mi:*li-e] 'family'). Sometimes the second of these syllables carries the main stress in the word: **hygienisch** ([hügi*e:*nish] 'hygienic').

4.4 Where two vowels meet at an internal boundary in a word they are not pronounced as a single sound but remain in separate syllables, e.g. **geehrt** ([ge-*e:rt*] 'honoured'), **geimpft** ([ge*imft*] 'inoculated'), **beeilen** ([be-*ai*len] 'hurry').

II Word order

Although German certainly has several strict rules on word order, the order in which words appear in a sentence does not by itself determine meaning. The rules which follow therefore need to be considered alongside the case system (see **16–21**A).

5 Simple sentences and main clauses

5.1

A simple sentence is a statement that contains no questions or direct commands (see **41**A on imperatives). The basic rule to remember about word order in simple sentences or main clauses is that the finite verb is always 'second idea' (see **5.2**A). The finite verb is the one verb which can be either singular or plural, in the present or past tense:

> **Sie *spielen* mit meiner kleinen Schwester.**
> They are playing with my little sister.

> **Mein Mann *schwimmt* jeden Tag mindestens 500 Meter.**
> My husband swims at least 500 metres every day.

spielen and **schwimmt** are the finite verbs here.

There can be only one finite verb in each German sentence; infinitives and past participles, for example, are not finite verbs:

> **Sie *werden* wohl erst nachts ankommen.**
> You'll probably not arrive until night-time.

> **Wir *hatten* den Film schon gesehen.**
> We had already seen the film.

Here **werden** and **hatten** are the finite verbs.

(For exceptions to the 'verb second' rule, see **7.2**A on direct questions, **7.3**A on commands, and **58.3**A on informal conversational responses)

5.2

The verb's second position applies even when some element other than the subject stands in first position. This other element can be:

(a) One or more adverbs or adverbial phrases:

> ***Morgen* wird es schon zu spät sein.**
> Tomorrow it will be too late.

> ***Letzten Samstag gegen drei Uhr nachts* starb er an einem Herzinfarkt.**
> He died of a heart attack at about 3a.m. last Saturday.

> ***Vor zwei Wochen* kaufte ich mir ein neues Auto.**
> Two weeks ago I bought myself a new car.

(b) A noun phrase:

> ***Diesen alten VW* kaufst du?!**
> You're buying that old VW?!

(c) A pronoun:

> ***Uns* war das Haus zu teuer.**
> The house was too expensive for us.

(d) A nominative noun or phrase complementing the verbs **sein, werden** or **bleiben**:

> ***Ein berühmter Politiker* ist er bestimmt nicht geworden.**
> He certainly didn't become a famous politician.

(e) An infinitive or infinitive phrase:

> ***Fernsehen* kannst du ja später; zuerst mußt du aber die Hausaufgaben machen.**
> You can watch television later. First you must do your homework.

> ***Um Mißverständnissen vorzubeugen,* sollten Sie ihn sofort anrufen.**
> To avoid any misunderstanding you ought to phone him at once.

(f) A past participle:

> ***Unterschrieben* ist der Vertrag allerdings noch nicht.**
> The contract has not, however, been signed yet.

(g) An adverb and some other part of speech together:

> ***Dadurch freilich* wurden all unsere Pläne zunichte gemacht.**
> Admittedly that ruined all our plans.

(h) A subordinate clause: see **8.1–8.2**A below.

5.3 Introductory words such as the following are not considered first ideas:

> **ja** 'yes'
> **nein** 'no'
> **also** 'therefore'
> **so** 'thus'
> **nun** 'now/well'
> **na** 'well'
> **ach** 'oh'
> **das heißt** 'that is, i.e.'
> **im Gegenteil** 'on the contrary'
> **wissen Sie/weißt du** 'you know'
> **sehen Sie/siehst du** 'you see'
> **verstehen Sie/verstehst du** 'you understand'
> **wie gesagt** 'as I say'
> **mit anderen Worten** 'in other words'
> **unter uns gesagt** 'between you and me'

Note that each of these is followed by a comma:

> **Ja, ich komme um acht vorbei.**
> Yes, I'll call in at eight o'clock.
>
> **Das heißt, Sie sind die ganze Woche verreist?**
> That means you're away all week?

5.4 The usual position for past participles, or for infinitives dependent on modals (see **35**A) or the verb **werden**, is at the end of the clause or sentence (but see also **58.4**A):

> **Das habe ich ihm schon öfters *gesagt.***
> I've often told him that.
>
> **Könntest du nicht bis Dienstag *bleiben*?**
> Couldn't you stay until Tuesday?

An infinitive dependent on a finite verb (see **5.1**A) precedes a past participle at the end of a sentence. This applies particularly to modal verbs which, when used in combination with other verbs, employ the infinitive as the past participle:

> **Er hat es nicht *machen* dürfen** (compare: **er hat es nicht gemacht**).
> He wasn't allowed to do it (he hasn't done it).

In passive constructions (see **40**A) the past participle precedes **werden**:

> **Muß der Vertrag heute noch *unterschrieben werden*?**
> Does the contract have to be signed today?

5.5 Separable prefixes (see **36**A) are placed in final position:

> **Er steht immer um sieben Uhr *auf*.**
> He always gets up at seven o'clock.

6 Two main clauses

6.1 In a sentence with two or more main clauses linked by the co-ordinating conjunctions **aber, denn, oder, sondern, und**, the finite verb (see **5.1**A) is always the second element in each clause:

> **Rudi *fiel* auf den Boden, und Peter *lachte* laut.**
> Rudi fell on the floor and Peter laughed loudly.

6.2 If the subjects of such clauses are the same, the second subject may be omitted:

> **Wir spielten jeden Tag Fußball oder (wir) gingen spazieren.**
> We played football or went for a walk every day.

6.3 If the second clause has another element in first position, the subject must be included:

> **Ich wusch mich, dann *ging* ich in die Küche.**
> I had a wash, then I went into the kitchen.

As this example shows, the 'finite verb second' rule also applies following the conjunction **dann** which is not to be confused with the co-ordinating conjunction **denn**.

(See **59.5**A for the use of commas in German clauses)

7 Direct questions and commands

7.1 After interrogative words, such as **wer, was, wie, warum, wo, wann, womit, wovon**, etc., the verb retains second position:

> **Wo *sind* meine Schuhe?**
> Where are my shoes?

> **Warum *hat* er es dir denn nicht gesagt?**
> Why didn't he tell you then?

> **Worüber *ärgert* er sich so?**
> What's he so annoyed about?

7.2

With all other direct questions, however, the finite verb is the first element in the sentence:

> **_Ist_ er immer noch nicht angekommen?**
> Has he still not arrived?

7.3

In direct commands and suggestions/exhortations the finite verb is again always first element:

> **_Gehen_ Sie sofort nach Hause!**
> Go home at once!

> **_Zieh_ doch den Mantel aus!**
> Take your coat off.

> **_Vergessen_ wir das!**
> Let's just forget about it.

(See **41**A for imperatives)

8   *Subordinate clauses*

8.1

A subordinate clause is one which requires another, main, clause to make it fully meaningful. For example:

> **Ich habe mich geärgert, weil er so spät gekommen ist.**
> I was annoyed that he arrived so late.

weil er so spät gekommen ist is the subordinate clause which cannot stand on its own without the preceding main clause **ich habe mich geärgert**.

A subordinate clause is separated by a comma from the main clause.

8.2

The finite verb (see **5.1**A) in subordinate clauses is almost always in final position (but see **58.4**A), and main and subordinate clauses are linked by a subordinating conjunction such as **daß** ('that'):

> **Wir wußten nicht, _daß_ er die Arbeit schon gemacht _hatte_.**
> We didn't know that he had already done the work.

The finite verb thus follows the past participle in a subordinate clause.

8.3 Other common subordinating conjunctions include:

> **als** 'when' (one occasion in the past)
> **bevor** 'before'
> **bis** 'until'
> **da** 'since', 'because'
> **damit** 'so that'
> **nachdem** 'after'
> **ob** 'whether'
> **obgleich/obwohl** 'although'
> **ohne daß/ohne. . . zu** 'without'
> **sobald** 'as soon as'
> **so daß** 'so that as a result'
> **seit/seitdem** 'since' (of time)
> **solange** 'as long as'
> **um . . . zu** 'in order to'
> **während** 'while'
> **weil** 'because'
> **wenn** 'if', 'whenever'

> **Uli ging gestern abend in die Kneipe,** *obwohl* **er kein Geld** *hatte.*
> Uli went to the pub yesterday evening even though he didn't have any money. .

> **Ich warte hier,** *bis* **ich mit meiner Tochter gesprochen** *habe.*
> I'll wait here until I've spoken to my daughter.

> *Weil* **es heute** *regnet,* **dürfen wir nicht draußen spielen.**
> We cannot play outside today because it's raining.

8.4 Sometimes the conjunction **daß** may be omitted. On such occasions the verb does not go to the end of the clause:

> **Ich glaube, daß er gestern krank** *war.*
> BUT **Ich glaube,** *er war* **gestern krank.**
> I think he was ill yesterday.

8.5 Quite often the subordinate clause comes before the main clause. Where this happens, the subordinate clause is the first idea and the verb in the main clause retains second position:

> **Da wir nun mitten in einer Großstadt wohnen,** *gehen wir* **selten wandern.**
> Since we now live in the centre of a city we rarely go walking.

> **Wenn er mir morgen das Buch gibt,** *sage ich* **dir Bescheid.**
> If he gives me the book tomorrow, I'll let you know.

In this second example **wenn** can be omitted from the subordinate clause by putting the verb first:

> *Gibt* **er mir morgen das Buch, sage ich dir Bescheid.**

8.6 When modal verbs (see **35**A) are used in subordinate clauses in tenses other than the present and simple past, two or three verbs may be grouped together at the end of the clause. If this happens, the finite verb (usually **haben** but also in the future tense **werden**) is placed in front of the other verbs:

> **Ich bin sicher, daß wir uns die Reise nächstes Jahr** *werden* **leisten können.**
> I am sure we will be able to afford the trip next year.

> **Sie schreibt, daß sie die ganze Arbeit allein** *hat* **machen müssen.**
> She writes to say she has had to do all the work herself.

> **Wenn er uns wirklich** *hätte* **sehen wollen, wäre er wohl ein bißchen früher aufgestanden, oder?**
> If he'd really wanted to see us, he'd have got up a little earlier, don't you think?

> **Bist du sicher, daß die neue Regelung** *hat* **eingeführt werden müssen?**
> Are you sure the new regulation had to be introduced?

If **lassen** is used with another modal verb, there may (exceptionally) be three infinitives at the end of the clause:

> **Meinst du, daß ich die Umzugskosten von der Firma hätte bezahlen lassen können?**
> Do you think I could have got the firm to pay the removal costs?

8.7 (a) Infinitive clauses (that is, clauses containing verbs preceded by **zu**) are usually placed outside the main clause:

> **Ich habe versucht,** *das Buch zu lesen.*
> I've tried to read the book.

> **Ich habe aufgehört** *zu rauchen.*
> I have given up smoking.

Note, in the first example, that extended infinitive clauses are separated from the main clause by a comma, while in short infinitive phrases such as the second the comma is omitted.

(See also **42.3f**A for verb completion by an infinitive clause with **zu**)

(b) With separable verbs a dependent infinitive (see **5.4**A) is normally placed outside the main clause; only occasionally is it found enclosed:

> **Er hörte auf** *zu singen.*
> OR (less commonly and only with short infinitive clauses) **Er hörte** *zu singen* **auf.**
> He stopped singing.

N.B. If **als** or **wie** are used in a comparison, they are usually placed after the finite verb:

> **Du weißt ja, daß er schneller läuft** *als ich.*
> You know he can run faster than I can.

> **Der Lehrer sagte, daß mein Aufsatz genauso gut war** *wie Manfreds.*
> The teacher said my essay was just as good as Manfred's.

9   Indirect questions

When the interrogative adverbs (**wann**, **wo**, **wie**, etc.), pronouns (**wer**, **wessen**), adjective (**welcher**) and determiner (**was für ein**) introduce an indirect question, the finite verb must go to the end of the clause:

> **Wir fragten ihn,** *wie lange* **er bleiben** *möchte.*
> We asked him how long he would like to stay.

> **Meine Mutter möchte wissen,** *wer* **am Wochenende dorthin***fährt.*
> My mother would like to know who's going there at the weekend.

> **Bitte sagen Sie mir,** *welche* **Kollegen diesen Kurs schon besucht** *haben.*
> Please tell me which colleagues have been on this course.

10   Relative clauses

10.1

These are subordinate clauses which relate back to a noun, noun phrase, pronoun or determiner (see **24.1c**A) in the main clause. They are introduced by an appropriate form of the relative pronoun (**der**, **die**, **das** or plural **die**). The relative pronoun sends the finite verb (see **5.1**A) to the end of the clause, and must agree in number and gender with the noun or phrase it refers to. (In the plural, of course, it only needs to agree in number.) The case of the relative pronoun is decided by its role in the subordinate clause:

Structures

Haben Sie den Mann gesehen, *der* **das Paket abgeholt hat?**
Did you see the man who picked up the package?

Die Frau, *der* **ich diesen Auftrag gegeben habe, arbeitet schon lange bei uns.**
The woman I gave this job to has been working for us for a long time.

10.2 The relative pronouns decline like the definite articles (see **22.2**A) with the exception of the masculine and neuter genitive singular (**dessen**), the feminine genitive singular (**deren**), the genitive plural (**deren**) and the dative plural (**denen**):

Dieses Unternehmen, *dessen* **Arbeiter schon öfters gestreikt haben, hat große finanzielle Probleme.**
This firm, whose workers have often been on strike, has serious financial problems.

10.3 Relative pronouns are sometimes preceded by a preposition. Here the case of the pronoun is determined by the preposition, and the finite verb is still placed at the end of the clause:

Kennst du die Mädchen, *mit denen* **Elke spielt?**
Do you know the girls Elke is playing with?

Das alte Gebäude, *in dem* **wir arbeiten, wird gerade umgebaut.**
The old building which we work in is at present being renovated.

10.4 As the last example shows, the relative clause is usually placed within the main clause immediately after the item(s) it refers to. Occasionally, however, lengthy relative clauses may follow the main clause:

Sie kann nun jeden Tag mit ihrem Mann verbringen, der nach zehn schwierigen Monaten in Brasilien endlich nach Hause gekommen ist.
She can now spend every day with her husband, who has finally returned home after ten difficult months in Brazil.

10.5 When it refers back to one of the following, 'which' is conveyed by **was** and the finite verb is again sent to the end of the clause:

(a) A neuter indefinite:

alles 'everything'
einiges 'some things'
etwas 'something'
folgendes 'the following'

manches 'many things'
nichts 'nothing'
vieles 'lots'
weniges 'few things'

Alles, was **ich hier mache, ist falsch.**
Everything I do here is wrong.

Following **etwas, das** may also be used.

(b) The demonstrative **das** 'that':

Ich bin mit *dem, was* **er uns anbietet, gar nicht zufrieden.**
I'm not at all pleased with what he's offering us.

(c) An indefinite neuter adjective, e.g. **das Schlimmste** 'the worst thing', **das Erste** 'the first thing', **das Neue** 'the new (thing)':

Ist das wirklich *das Beste, was* **er bieten kann?**
Is that really the best he can offer?

(d) The whole of a preceding clause:

Sie behauptet, sie habe das Haus um neun Uhr verlassen, *was* **nicht stimmen kann.**
She claims to have left the house at nine, which cannot be true.

11 *Order of adverbials*

11.1

The normal word order in a sentence with several adverbs is time–manner–place:

Sie hat gestern (TIME) **in der Kirche** (PLACE) **gesungen.**
She sang in church yesterday.

Ich fahre manchmal (TIME) **mit dem Fahrrad** (MANNER) **zur Arbeit** (PLACE).
I sometimes go to work on my bike.

N.B. Adverbs of attitude are placed before all other adverbs:

Du fährst doch (ATTITUDE) **nicht jeden Tag** (TIME) **mit dem Fahrrad** (MANNER) **zur Arbeit** (PLACE), **oder?**
You don't go to work on your bike every day, do you?

11.2 Unless it is placed in initial position, the adverb follows all pronouns:

> **Meine Frau schenkte mir *zu Weihnachten* diesen Pulli.**
> My wife gave me this jumper for Christmas.

> **Meine Frau schenkte ihn mir *zu Weihnachten*.**
> My wife gave me it for Christmas.

11.3 Adverbs are placed between dative (also called indirect) and accusative (also known as direct) noun objects:

> **Er warf dem Mädchen *plötzlich* einen letzten Blick zu und verschwand.**
> He suddenly threw the girl a final glance and disappeared.

11.4 Adverbs are placed before any adjectives:

> **Meinem Großvater geht es *nach der Operation wesentlich* besser.**
> My grandfather is much better after his operation.

12 Noun and pronoun objects

12.1 When both objects are nouns, the dative precedes the accusative:

> **Sie gab *ihrer Freundin* das Kleid.**
> She gave her friend the dress.

12.2 When both objects are personal pronouns, the accusative precedes the dative:

> **Sie gab *es* ihr.**
> She gave her it.

12.3 When one object is a noun and the other a personal pronoun, the pronoun comes first, regardless of case:

> **Sie gab *es* ihrer Freundin.**
> She gave it to her friend.

> **Sie gab *ihr* das Kleid.**
> She gave her the dress.

Note that when a noun in the accusative is placed in initial position for the purpose of emphasis the accusative precedes the dative, and when a dative pronoun is similarly emphasized the dative precedes the accusative:

> **Das Kleid wollte sie ihrer Freundin nicht geben.**
> She didn't want to give her friend the dress.

> **Uns hat sie es nicht gegeben.**
> She didn't give it to us.

12.4 In direct questions, the object pronoun (here a dative) normally comes before the subject:

> **Wie hat *Ihnen der Rotwein* geschmeckt?**
> (How) did you like the red wine?

With two pronoun objects the noun subject tends to come first:

> **Deshalb wollte *der Vorarbeiter es ihnen* nicht glauben.**
> That's why the foreman would not believe them.

Note also that personal pronouns come before demonstrative pronouns:

> **1945 war *uns das* noch nicht klar geworden.**
> In 1945 that was still not clear to us.

12.5 Nouns and pronouns are normally placed before adjectives which take the dative:

> **Ich bin *Ihnen* sehr dankbar.**
> I'm very grateful to you.

> **Du siehst *deinem Vater* sehr ähnlich.**
> You look very much like your father.

13 *Position of* nicht

13.1 The general rule is that **nicht** comes immediately before the individual element which it negates:

> **Das Essen hat sie *nicht für uns* vorbereitet.**
> It wasn't for us that she made the meal.

> **Das ist doch *nicht dein* Schlüssel.**
> That's not your key.

13.2 It is important to note that **nicht** precedes all elements which complete the sense of the verb:

> **Stell die heiße Tasse *nicht auf den Tisch.***
> Don't put the hot cup on the table.

> **Sie meint, ich soll mich *nicht darüber* ärgern.**
> She says I shouldn't get annoyed about it.

> **Er ist heute *nicht nach London* gefahren.**
> He hasn't gone to London today.

Note in the third example that if stress is placed on **London**, the implication is that he travelled somewhere other than London. More explicitly this would be:

> **Er ist nicht nach London gefahren, sondern nach Paris.**
> It's Paris he's gone to, not London.

> **Er ist dorthin nicht gefahren, sondern geflogen.**
> He didn't drive there, he flew.

13.3 If **nicht** negates a whole clause, it is placed after any objects or adverbials but before adverbs of manner:

> **Er ist gestern wegen des starken Verkehrs *nicht früh genug* angekommen.**
> He didn't arrive early enough yesterday because of the heavy traffic.

14 *Position of reflexive pronouns*

14.1 The reflexive pronouns (**mich/mir, dich/dir, sich, uns, euch**) are placed immediately after the finite verb in a main clause:

> **Er schaute *sich* dann die Bücher an.**
> He then had a look at the books.

> **Setzt *euch* einen Augenblick.**
> Have a seat for a moment.

14.2 When some element other than the subject is in initial position in a main clause, the reflexive pronoun is placed after a pronoun subject, but it can be placed before or after a noun subject:

> **Dann schaute *er sich* die Bücher an.**
> Then he had a look at the books.

> **Dann schaute *sich Wolfgang* die Bücher an.**
> OR **Dann schaute *Wolfgang sich* die Bücher an.**
> Then Wolfgang had a look at the books.

14.3

In a subordinate clause this word order still applies:

> **Ich wußte nicht, ob *sie sich* schon kennengelernt hatten.**
> I didn't know whether they had already met.

> **Ich wußte nicht, ob *sich die Studenten* schon kennengelernt hatten.**
> I didn't know whether the students had already met.

14.4

In infinitive phrases the reflexive pronoun is placed at the head of its clause:

> **Es ist ja ganz interessant, *sich* mit ihm über seine Jugendtage in Deutschland zu unterhalten.**
> It's really interesting talking to him about his youth in Germany.

15 *Flexible word order and emphasis*

In spite of the above rules there is more flexibility to word order in German than in English. This flexibility allows for subtle shifts of emphasis and shades of meaning.

15.1

First position

As seen in **5.2**A, the first element in a sentence can be one of a wide range of parts of speech.

(a) This first element is the item which the speaker/writer wishes to explain or elaborate on:

> ***Die Regierung* hat ihre neuen Reformen nicht durchsetzen können.**
> The government was unable to carry through its new reforms.

(This communicates something about the government.)

> ***Den alten Mann* hat er im Garten gefunden.**
> He found the old man in the garden.

(This conveys something about the old man.)

> ***In seiner Wohnung* ist die Heizung kaputt.**
> The heating has broken down in his apartment.

(This tells us something about his flat.)

> ***Nach den Ferien* werde ich das Haus streichen.**
> I shall paint the house after the holidays.

(Here we learn what will happen after the holidays.)

(b) The first element is unlikely to contain new information as it usually either refers back to something mentioned before or hints at information which is already familiar:

> *Abgesehen von den üblichen Schwierigkeiten an der Grenze* **war die Reise nach Moskau ein großer Erfolg.**
> Apart from the usual difficulties at the border the trip to Moscow was a great success.

(The new element here is the success of the trip; the difficulties are already well known.)

> *In fast allen diesen Städten* **leidet die Bevölkerung unter den Folgen der Luftverschmutzung.**
> In almost all these towns the population is suffering from the effects of air pollution.

(The towns are familiar because they have been referred to before – what is new is the information on pollution.)

(c) The use of the dummy subject **es** (see **42.3g**A) helps to emphasize the subject when it is this element which conveys new or significant information:

> **Es fehlten** *vierzehn Bücher.*
> Fourteen books were missing.

> **Es besteht ja** *die Gefahr, daß* **er die Wahl verlieren könnte.**
> There is, of course, a danger that he might lose the election.

(d) This principle of familiar or shared information coming first can result in some emphatic formulations. This is especially the case when infinitives or past participles come first:

> *Sprechen* **will ich ihn nicht. Ich möchte ihm nur diesen Brief geben.**
> I don't want to *talk* to him, I would just like to give him this letter.

> *Gesehen* **habe ich sie nicht, nur gehört.**
> I didn't *see* her, I just heard her.

Here the speaker uses this word order to contrast what is expected or assumed (i.e. talking to him, seeing her) with what is actually the case.

15.2 Final position

(a) Elements can be placed at the end of a sentence for the purposes of emphasis:

> **Heute abend sah mich zum Glück** *keiner.*
> Fortunately no one saw me this evening.

The resultant style is often quite formal:

> **Nach vielen erfolgreichen Jahren als Personalleiter der Firma tritt nun in den Ruhestand unser alter Freund und langjähriger Kollege *Willi Ruttkamp*.**
>
> After many successful years as the firm's Personnel Director our old friend and long-time colleague Willi Ruttkamp is now retiring.

The same emphasis can be applied to elements that complete the verb:

> **Nach langem Streben und Warten wurde Emil Hauptmann in seiner alten Heimatstadt endlich *Bürgermeister*.**
>
> After much effort and having waited for so long Emil Hauptmann finally became mayor in his old home town.

(b) This practice may sometimes override accepted rules such as the indirect object preceding the direct object:

> **Wir zeigten unsere Arbeit den Besuchern aus Japan.**
>
> We showed the visitors from Japan our work.

Here the people being shown the work are considered more important than the work itself. In a subordinate clause this final position excludes any infinitives, finite verbs or separable prefixes. Thus in the following two examples the phrases in italics are being emphasized:

> **Es war klar, daß auf uns *etwas ganz Unangenehmes* wartete.**
>
> It was clear something very unpleasant awaited us.

> **Sie hat ihre Eltern *dem neuen Direktor* vorgestellt.**
>
> She introduced her parents to the new head teacher.

(c) The flexibility of German word order is reflected in the three possible variations on the last sentence. Apart from the neutral **Sie hat dem neuen Direktor ihre Eltern vorgestellt**, the following are also possible: **Dem neuen Direktor hat sie ihre Eltern vorgestellt**, with its mild emphasis on **Eltern** as the people of particular interest to whom she introduced the head-teacher; and **Ihre Eltern hat sie dem neuen Direktor vorgestellt**, with its slight emphasis on **Direktor** as the person of particular interest to whom she introduced her parents.

III The case system

16 The cases

Although English retains a few examples of its earlier case system an English word's grammatical role is usually determined by its position in the sentence. Thus, the meaning of the sentence 'The dog bit the man' is changed entirely by swapping the position of the two nouns to give: 'The man bit the dog'.

In German, the case system is more fully developed and allows a slightly more flexible approach to subject-object word order. Thus, the first of the above sentences could be quite accurately translated as: *Den* Mann biß *der* Hund; and the second as: *Den* Hund biß *der* Mann. This use of case endings on articles, and also on nouns, pronouns and adjectives to indicate the role these words play in a sentence, depends on a system of four distinct grammatical cases (the nominative, accusative, dative and genitive). Each of these has a number of clearly defined functions.

(For an overview of the various case endings see **22.2**A and **22.3**A on the article, **28.1d**A and **28.2a**A on noun declensions, **30–32**A on pronouns and **44–46**A on adjective endings)

17 The nominative

This is the form in which nouns are presented in reference books and in which they need to be learnt. The nominative is used:

17.1 For the subject of the finite verb (see **5.1**A on finite verbs):

> *Der Bundespräsident* ist nach Washington geflogen.
> The German president has flown to Washington.

> **Heute morgen hat** *dein japanischer Freund* **angerufen.**
> Your Japanese friend phoned this morning.

17.2 Following the verbs **bleiben**, **heißen**, **scheinen**, **sein**, **werden** and, in the passive (see **40**A), **nennen**:

> **Mein Nachbar ist *ein bekannter Schriftsteller*.**
> My neighbour is a well-known writer.

> **Er wurde bald *ein verläßlicher Kollege*.**
> He soon became a reliable colleague.

> **Sie blieb *meine beste Freundin*.**
> She remained my best friend.

> **Ich wurde von meinen Lehrern immer *ein Faulenzer* genannt.**
> I was always called a lazy-bones by my teachers.

17.3 For nouns and pronouns independent of a verb, as in exclamations or when addressing people:

> **Ach, der alte Schuft!**
> The old rascal!

> **Du frecher Junge!**
> You naughty boy!

> **Eine ganz schön stürmische Überfahrt, nicht?**
> It's a really stormy crossing, isn't it?

18 The accusative

The accusative is used:

18.1 To indicate the direct or, as it is sometimes called, accusative object:

> **Sie zeigte uns *den großen Garten*.**
> She showed us the large garden.

> **Er suchte *den empfohlenen Rotwein*.**
> He looked for the red wine that had been recommended.

18.2 After the prepositions **bis**, **durch**, **für**, **gegen**, **ohne**, **um** and **wider**:

> **Das machst du aber *ohne mich*.**
> You can do that on your own (lit. without me).

Wir sind *durch einen langen Tunnel* gefahren.
We drove through a long tunnel.

Wir liefen *um den Sportplatz* herum.
We ran around the sports ground.

18.3 After the prepositions **an, auf, hinter, in, neben, über, unter, vor** and **zwischen** when motion *towards* the following noun or pronoun is implied. Compare this with the dative (see **19.5**A) which denotes position:

Sie setzte sich *vor die Tür*. (Compare the dative **Sie saß *vor der Tür*.**)
She sat down in front of the door. (She was sitting in front of the door.)

Sie setzten sich *neben ihre Freunde*. (**Sie saßen *neben ihren Freunden*.**)
They sat down next to their friends. (They were sitting next to their friends.)

Soll ich das Plakat *an die Wand* hängen? (**Das Plakat hängt *an der Wand*.**)
Should I hang the poster on the wall? (The poster is/hangs on the wall.)

N.B. The preposition **entlang** follows the noun in the accusative case:

Gehen Sie *die Hauptstraße entlang*.
Go along the main street.

Notice the abbreviated prepositional forms:

an + das = ans
in + das = ins
auf + das = aufs
um + das = ums

Also, but usually only in spoken German: **durchs, fürs, gegens, hinters, nebens, übers, unters** and **vors**.

18.4 To indicate a particular point in time or a length of time in phrases without a preposition:

***Letzten Samstag* war das Wetter ganz furchtbar.**
The weather last Saturday was really terrible.

***Einen Augenblick*, bitte.**
Just a moment, please.

Wir wollten noch *einen Tag* bleiben.
We wanted to stay another day.

> *Die ganze Woche* **ging er nicht zur Arbeit.**
> He didn't go to work all week.

But note the exception in the genitive **eines Tages** 'one day':

> **Eines Tages möchte ich nach Australien fahren.**
> I'd like to go to Australia one day.

18.5 To denote direction or distance with motion verbs:

> **Sie lief** *die Treppe* **hinauf.**
> She ran up the stairs.

> **Ich wohne nur** *einen Kilometer* **von der Schule entfernt.**
> I live only one kilometre from school.

18.6 For adverbial expressions of measurement or value:

> **Er wiegt schon** *einen Zentner.*
> He already weighs 100 pounds.

> **Trier ist** *eine Reise* **wert.**
> Trier is worth a visit (lit. trip).

18.7 In wishes and greetings:

> **Herzlichen Glückwunsch!**
> Many congratulations!

> **Guten Tag.**
> Hello/good day.

18.8 The verbs **kosten**, **lehren** and **nennen** require two accusative objects:

> **Sie nannte** *ihn ihren Liebling.*
> She called him her darling.

> **Das kostet** *ihn eine Menge Geld.*
> That will cost him a lot of money.

> **Sie lehrte** *das Kind das Alphabet.*
> She taught the child the alphabet.

19 The dative

The dative case is employed widely in both spoken and written German. It is used:

19.1 To convey the indirect or dative object, expressed in English by word order (i.e. indirect object first) or by 'to':

> **Sie zeigte *uns* den neuen Rock.**
> She showed us the new skirt./She showed the new skirt to us.

> **Er hat *seinen Kollegen* das Problem erklärt.**
> He explained the problem to his colleagues.

> **Ich gab es *meinem Bruder*.**
> I gave it to my brother.

19.2 For the so-called dative of advantage, i.e. to indicate the person for whom the action of the verb is done:

> **Kauf *mir* bitte etwas zu lesen.**
> Please buy me something to read.

> **Kannst du *uns* die Tür aufmachen?**
> Can you open the door for us?

> **Zieh *ihr* bitte den Mantel an.**
> Help her on with her coat, please.

Note that with reflexive verbs the pronoun may be omitted:

> **Du hast (dir) das Gesicht noch nicht gewaschen.**
> You haven't washed your face yet.

19.3 For the dative of disadvantage, usually indicating something unpleasant:

> **Die Behörden haben *ihr* das Kind weggenommen.**
> The authorities have taken the child away from her.

> **Er hat *mir* den Geldbeutel gestohlen.**
> He's stolen my purse.

> **Die Sonne scheint *ihm* in die Augen.**
> The sun is shining in his eyes.

19.4 — After certain prepositions:

> **ab** 'from, as from'
> **aus** 'out of'
> **außer** 'apart from'
> **bei** 'by/near/with'
> **gemäß** 'in accordance with'
> **laut** 'according to'
> **mit** 'with'
> **nach** 'after'
> **seit** 'since'
> **von** 'from/of'
> **zu** 'to'

> *Außer uns und unseren Freunden* **wurde niemand eingeladen.**
> No one else was invited apart from us and our friends.

> **Sie liefen** *aus der Wohnung.*
> They ran out of the flat.

> **Ich wohne** *bei meinen Eltern.*
> I live with my parents.

> **Wir fahren** *mit dem Auto.*
> We travel by car.

> *Zu welchem Zweck* **wurde dies eingeführt?**
> For what purpose was this introduced?

> *Nach dem Frühstück* **putze ich mir immer die Zähne.**
> After breakfast I always brush my teeth.

The prepositions **entgegen** 'against/contrary to' and **gegenüber** 'opposite' usually follow the noun, as does **nach** in the sense of 'according to':

> **Sie wohnt** *dem Stadion* **gegenüber.**
> She lives opposite the stadium.

> *Meiner Meinung nach* **ist das falsch.**
> In my opinion that's wrong.

19.5 — After certain prepositions when rest or movement *at* a place is implied. This includes:

> **an** 'on/at/by'
> **auf** 'on' (a horizontal surface)
> **hinter** 'behind'
> **in** 'in'

neben 'near/next to'
über 'over/above'
unter 'under/among'
vor 'in front of'
zwischen 'between'

Das Bild hing *über dem Bett.*
The picture was hanging over the bed.
(Compare **Er hängte das Bild** *über das Bett.*
He hung the picture over the bed.)

Ich saß zwischen *meinem Bruder und seiner Frau.*
I was sitting between my brother and his wife.
(Compare **Ich setzte mich** *zwischen meinen Bruder und seine Frau.*
I sat down between my brother and his wife.)

Jeden Sonntag gehen wir *auf dem Schulgelände* **spazieren.**
We go for a walk in the school grounds every Sunday.
(Compare **Ich gehe gerade mit dem Hund** *aufs Schulgelände.*
I'm just going (in)to the school grounds with the dog.)

Notice the abbreviated prepositional forms:

an + dem = am
bei + dem = beim
in + dem = im
von + dem = vom
zu + dem = zum
zu + der = zur

19.6

With several verbs, the vast majority of which only ever have a dative object. The most common include:

ähneln 'to resemble'
antworten 'to answer'
begegnen 'to meet'
danken 'to thank'
dienen 'to serve'
drohen 'to threaten'
entsprechen 'to correspond to'
folgen 'to follow'
gehorchen 'to obey'
gelten 'to be meant for/aimed at'
genügen 'to suffice'

geschehen 'to happen to'
glauben 'to believe'
gleichen 'to be like'
gratulieren 'to congratulate'
helfen 'to help'
kündigen 'to dismiss (sb.)/give (sb. their) notice'
sich nähern 'to approach'
nutzen/nützen 'to be of use'
passen 'to fit/to suit'
passieren 'to happen to'
schaden 'to harm'
trauen 'to trust'
vertrauen 'to have trust in'
vorkommen 'to seem to'

Ich habe *ihm* nicht geantwortet.
I didn't answer him.

Die Atmosphäre kam *uns* ein bißchen seltsam vor.
The atmosphere seemed a little strange to us.

Wann ist das denn *Ihren Freunden* passiert?
When did it happen to your friends?

Sie näherten sich *dem Gebäude*.
They approached the building.

Der Chef hat *meinem ältesten Kollegen* gestern gekündigt.
The boss gave my eldest colleague his notice yesterday.

19.7 With a number of verbs which either have an **es** as their subject and/or whose dative object corresponds to the subject of the equivalent English sentence. They include:

auffallen 'to strike/occur to'
einfallen 'to occur to'
fehlen 'to be missing'
gefallen 'to like'
gehören 'to belong to'
gelingen 'to succeed'
leidtun 'to be sorry'
schmecken 'to taste (good)'
wehtun 'to hurt'

Es tut *uns* leid, daß du nicht kommen kannst.
We're sorry that you cannot come.

Ist es *euch* gelungen, das Problem zu lösen?
Did you succeed in solving the problem?

Das Stück hat *ihr* gar nicht gefallen.
She didn't like the play at all.

Mir tut der Arm weh.
My arm is hurting.

Hat *den Kindern* der Kuchen geschmeckt?
Did the children like the cake?

19.8 With verbs prefixed by **bei-**, **ent-**, **entgegen-**, **nach-**, **wider-** or **zu-**:

Der Dieb lief *uns* entgegen.
The thief ran towards us.

Hast du schon wieder *dem Lehrer* widersprochen?
Did you contradict the teacher again?

Sie ist *ihrer Mutter* nachgelaufen.
She's run after her mother.

Ich stimme *dem Plan* zu.
I agree with/to the plan.

Er ist *den Grünen* beigetreten.
He's joined the Green Party.

19.9 With a large number of adjectives combined with **sein** or **werden**. To denote an excess or a sufficiency of a certain quality, appropriate adjectives may be preceded by **zu** or **genug** respectively:

Ihm war immer noch schlecht/übel/unwohl.
He was still feeling bad/ill/unwell.

Dem Alten wurde plötzlich schwindlig.
The old man suddenly began to feel dizzy.

Das wird *uns* ja ganz nützlich/schädlich sein.
That will be quite useful/harmful to us.

Es ist *mir* ja gleich/egal.
I don't care about it.

Ich bin *Ihrem Kollegen* sehr dankbar.
I am very grateful to your colleague.

Das britische Klima ist *uns* zu unzuverläßig.
The British climate is too unreliable for us.

***Den Kindern* ist es zu heiß/kalt.**
It is too hot/cold for the children.

Der Wein ist *meinem Mann* zu süß.
The wine is too sweet for my husband's taste.

Ist *Ihnen* das Essen noch warm genug?
Is the food still warm enough for you?

The dative with **zu** and **genug** are often replaced by **für** + accusative:

Das Essen ist für mich zu salzig.
The food is too salty for me.

20 *The genitive*

The genitive case is nowadays less common in spoken German where the use of prepositions tends to be preferred. Thus, 'Mr Zeiler's old car' would more likely be **das alte Auto von Herrn Zeiler** than **das alte Auto des Herrn Zeiler**. In the written language, however, the genitive is still very widely used. The normal position for the genitive in modern German is after the noun it relates to. It is used:

20.1

To denote possession:

Die neue Wohnung *meiner* Schwester ist ganz schön.
My sister's new flat is really nice.

Kennst du *Helmuts* Freundin? (OR **die Freundin von Helmut**)
Do you know Helmut's girlfriend?

Wart ihr schon in *Herrn Schmidts* Büro? (OR **das Büro von Herrn Schmidt**)
Have you been in Mr Schmidt's office?

Ich fahre mit *Frau Schmidts* Auto. (OR **dem Auto von Frau Schmidt**)
I'll go in Mrs/Ms Schmidt's car.

Das Schloß *der Habsburger* finde ich häßlich.
I think the Habsburgs' castle is ugly.

Ich liebe die Schlösser *Frankreichs/Frankreichs* Schlösser.
I love French castles.

20.2 After collective nouns or nouns denoting proportion:

> **Er hat eine große Sammlung *deutscher Bierdeckel*.**
> He has a large collection of German beer mats.

> **Ich unterrichte eine Klasse *vierzehnjähriger Jungen*.**
> I teach a class of fourteen-year-old boys.

> **Die Hälfte *des Geldes* ist schon weg.**
> Half the money has already gone.

The preposition **von** tends to be used more frequently in spoken German to convey quantity (see also **21.5**A):

> **eine große Anzahl *von Arbeitslosen***
> a large number of unemployed

20.3 With some adjectives, the most common of which are:

> **bewußt** 'aware of'
> **fähig** 'capable of'
> **gewiß** 'certain of'
> **schuldig** 'guilty of'
> **sicher** 'assured/sure of'
> **voll** 'full of'

> **Unser Projekt ist nun *des Erfolges* sicher.**
> Our project is now assured of success.

> **Ich bin mir *des Problems* bewußt.**
> I am aware of the problem.

> **Er ist *des Mordes* einfach nicht fähig.**
> He's simply not capable of murder.

20.4 With a small number of verbs. The more common include:

> **anklagen** (with accusative and genitive object) 'to accuse (someone) of'
> **bedürfen** 'to be in need of'
> **gedenken** 'to remember/commemorate'
> **sich bedienen** 'to make use of'
> **sich entsinnen** 'to remember'
> **sich erfreuen** 'to enjoy'
> **sich rühmen** 'to boast of'
> **sich schämen** 'to be ashamed of'

sich vergewissern 'to make sure about/of'
versichern (with accusative and genitive object) 'to assure'

Wir bedürfen *Ihrer Unterstützung.*
We need your support.

Ich schämte mich *meiner Feigheit.*
I was ashamed of my cowardice.

Sie sollten sich *der finanziellen Lage* der Firma vergewissern.
You ought to make sure about the firm's financial position.

20.5 Following the verb **sein** in a number of set expressions:

Wir sind *der Meinung/ der Auffassung, daß...*
We are of the opinion that ...

Er ist *der Ansicht,* daß wir es falsch gemacht haben.
He is of the opinion that we have done it wrong.

Sie war *schlechter/guter Laune.*
She was in a bad/good mood.

20.6 In set adverbial expressions:

meines Wissens 'to my knowledge'
meines Erachtens 'in my judgement/opinion'
letzten Endes 'after all'
allen Ernstes 'in all seriousness'
eines Tages 'one day'

20.7 After the following prepositions:

angesichts 'in view of'
(an)statt 'instead of'
anstelle 'in place of'
aufgrund 'on the strength of'
außerhalb 'outside of'
beiderseits 'on both sides of'
diesseits 'this side of'
infolge 'as a consequence of'
inmitten 'in the middle of'
innerhalb 'within'
jenseits 'on the far side of'

> **oberhalb** 'above'
> **trotz** 'in spite of'
> **um... willen** 'for the sake of'
> **unterhalb** 'beneath'
> **unweit** 'not far from'
> **während** 'during'
> **wegen** 'because of'

(an)statt, **trotz**, **während** and **wegen** can also be used with the dative, especially in spoken German.

In the spoken language, **außerhalb**, **innerhalb**, **oberhalb**, **unterhalb** and **unweit** are very often replaced by another preposition or used with **von** and the dative.

jenseits is nowadays normally replaced by **hinter** + dative.

21 *Apposition*

A noun placed after another in order to expand on or qualify its meaning is in apposition to the first noun. In German, the noun in apposition is always in the same case as the one it refers to:

> **Das ist mein Freund, *der* Polizist.**
> That's my friend the policeman.

> **Haben Sie schon meinen Freund, *den Polizisten*, kennengelernt?**
> Have you met my friend the policeman?

> **Könnten Sie bitte meinem Freund, *dem Polizisten*, helfen?**
> Could you please help my friend the policeman?

> **Das ist die Wohnung meines Freundes, *des Polizisten*.**
> That is the flat of my friend the policeman.

Note that the noun in apposition is separated from the rest of the sentence by commas. However, titles of books, films, plays, etc. which are in apposition to a noun that describes them do not have the same case as the latter and are not separated by commas:

> **Kennst du den Film 'Der Mann im Schatten'?**
> Do you know the film 'The Man in the Shadow'?

> **Das kommt im Stück 'Die Drei Schwestern' mehrmals vor.**
> That occurs several times in the play 'The Three Sisters'.

21.2

Apposition also applies in noun phrases denoting measurements and quantities, where English uses 'of':

> **Ein Glas *kalte Milch*, bitte.**
> A glass of cold milk, please.

> **Eine Tasse *indischen Tee*, bitte.**
> A cup of Indian tea, please.

> **Haben Sie meine Tasche mit den zwei Dosen *grünen Bohnen* gesehen?**
> Have you seen my bag with the two tins of green beans?

21.3

Following a numeral or some other expression of amount, masculine and neuter nouns denoting measurement, quantity or value are only used in the singular:

> **Bringen Sie uns zwei *Glas* Bier, bitte.**
> Bring us two beers, please (lit. two glasses of beer).

> **Bei 35 *Grad* Hitze bleibe ich in der Wohnung.**
> When it's 35 degrees (lit. of heat), I stay indoors.

Feminine nouns (other than **Mark**), however, use plural forms:

> **Sechs *Flaschen* Weißwein.**
> Six bottles of white wine.

> BUT **Das kostet sechzehn Mark.**
> That costs sixteen marks.

21.4

With place names, German has no equivalent of English 'of':

> **Wir studieren an der *Universität Marburg*.**
> We're studying at the University of Marburg.

> **Kennen Sie die *Stadt Donaueschingen*?**
> Do you know the town of Donaueschingen?

21.5

When the nouns **das Dutzend** 'dozen', **das Hundert** 'hundred', **die Million** 'million' and **die Milliarde** 'billion' are preceded by another numeral, the noun they relate to is in apposition:

> **Wir haben jetzt fast drei Millionen *Arbeitslose*.**
> We now have nearly three million unemployed.

> **Er ist mit zwei Dutzend *spanischen Apfelsinen* nach Hause gekommen.**
> He came home with two dozen Spanish oranges.

Structures

But if these nouns do not have a preceding numeral in the plural, **von** is used:

> **Tausende** *von* **Leuten kamen zur Kundgebung.**
> Thousands of people came to the demonstration.

> **Wir haben Millionen** *von* **Ameisen gesehen.**
> We saw millions of ants.

21.6   Apposition is also seen with **als** 'than' and **wie** 'as' in comparisons:

> *Er* **ist genauso alt wie** *ich.*
> He's just as old as I am.

> *Der* **läuft doch viel schneller als** *du.*
> He can run a lot faster than you.

> *Er* **ist viel fleißiger als** *mein Bruder.*
> He's a lot more hard-working than my brother.

> **Sie kennt** *ihn* **länger als** *mich.*
> She's known him longer than she has me.

IV Nouns

22 The article

22.1

Just as English employs two different articles, namely 'the' and 'a', German also distinguishes between a definite and indefinite article. The German case system (**16–21**A) means that these articles, along with nouns (**28**A) and adjectives (**43–49**A), must be in the appropriate case.

22.2

The definite article 'the' is declined as follows:

	Singular			Plural
	Masculine	Neuter	Feminine	All genders
Nominative	der	das	die	die
Accusative	den	das	die	die
Dative	dem	dem	der	den
Genitive	des	des	der	der

(See **17–21**A for examples of the use of the articles in the various cases)

22.3

The indefinite article 'a' is declined as follows:

	Masculine	Neuter	Feminine
Nominative	ein	ein	eine
Accusative	einen	ein	eine
Dative	einem	einem	einer
Genitive	eines	eines	einer

Although the indefinite article has no plural form, the negative form **kein** 'no', 'not any' does:

Nom **keine**   Acc **keine**   Dat **keinen**   Gen **keiner**

23   *Use of the articles*

German and English use articles in similar ways. Note, however, the following exceptions:

23.1

No article is used in German:

(a) With instruments

> **Er spielt *Gitarre*.**
> He plays the guitar (i.e. any guitar).

(b) With professions, religions and nationalities following the verbs **sein**, **werden** and **bleiben** unless an adjective is inserted:

> **Sie ist *Ingenieurin*.**
> She's an engineer.

> **Er ist *Katholik*.**
> He's a Catholic.

> **Sie ist *Engländerin*.**
> She is English.

> BUT **Er war *ein* guter Arzt.**
> He was a good doctor.

The article is also used if one is referring to a specific person and does not wish to emphasize particularly the person's job:

> **Das ist *die Lehrerin* meines Sohns.**
> That's my son's teacher.

(c) Following **als** in the sense of 'as a':

> **Als Weihnachtsgeschenk hat er mir ein Kleid gekauft.**
> He bought me a dress as a Christmas present/for Christmas.

(d) In certain idiomatic expressions:

> **Wir haben *großen Hunger*.**
> We are very hungry.

> **Gestern war er sehr *guter Laune*.**
> He was in a very good mood yesterday.

> **Wir haben gerade *Besuch*.**
> We have visitors at the moment.

Sie hat *Kopfschmerzen.*
She's got a headache.

Tatsache ist, **daß die Firma große Gewinne erzielt hat.**
It's a fact that the firm has achieved big profits.

Schweren Herzens **ist er nach Hause gegangen.**
He went home with a heavy heart.

(e) Where English uses the indefinite determiners 'some' or 'any':

Wir hatten *Schwierigkeiten.*
We had (some) difficulties.

Haben Sie *Brot?*
Have you got (any) bread?

Hast du *Milch* **gekauft?**
Did you buy (any) milk?

Note, however, that in the negative **kein** is used:

Ich esse *keinen Salat.*
I don't eat salad.

23.2 — Articles are used in German but not in English in the following expressions:

(a) With periods of time and with meals, especially after prepositions:

Es ist *im August/ am Dienstag/ in der Nacht* **passiert.**
It happened in August/on Tuesday/at night.

Der Frühling **ist immer schön.**
Spring is always nice.

Das Abendessen **ist fertig.**
Tea/supper is ready.

Ich werde *vor dem Mittagessen/ nach dem Frühstück* **keine Zeit haben.**
I will not have time before lunch/after breakfast.

(b) Before many abstract nouns denoting specific and familiar concepts, phenomena, movements or interests:

Das Leben **ist hart.**
Life is hard.

Die Zeit **vergeht so schnell.**
Time passes so quickly.

Sie liest gerade ein Buch *über den Faschismus.*
She's reading a book on fascism at the moment.

Ich lebe *für die Musik.*
I live for music.

(c) With infinitives used as nouns:

Das Laufen **ist sein größter Zeitvertreib.**
His favourite pastime is running.

Er hat *das Rauchen* **aufgegeben.**
He's given up smoking.

(d) With the feminine or plural names of countries:

Wir fuhren *in die Türkei.*
We travelled to Turkey.

Die Hauptstadt *der Niederlande.*
The capital of Holland.

With masculine country names the article is optional. It is, however, more common to use it:

Er wohnt *in dem Irak* **(but also in Irak).**
He lives in Iraq.

(e) With parts of the body and clothes:

Er hat sich *am Kopf* **verletzt.**
He's injured his head.

Sie machte *die Augen* **zu.**
She closed her eyes.

Zieh *den Mantel* **aus.**
Take your coat off.

Sie zog ihrem Sohn *das Hemd* **aus.**
She took her son's shirt off him.

Where there is a qualifying adjective, however, the possessive adjective is used, as in English:

Er hob *seinen* **verletzten Arm.**
He raised his injured arm.

(f) When giving an amount or a price:

hundert Kilometer *die Stunde*
a hundred kilometres an hour

sechzehn Mark *das Kilo*
sixteen marks per/a kilo

zehn Mark *das Stück*
ten marks each

(g) With the names of performers or famous people, and with personal names in spoken German:

Der Beckenbauer **war ein begabter Spieler.**
Beckenbauer was a gifted player.

Die Dietrich **war damals unsere beste Schauspielerin.**
Dietrich was our best actress in those days.

Kennst du *den Heinrich?*
Do you know Heinrich?

(h) Before the names of countries, towns, etc. when they are preceded by an adjective:

das heutige **Rußland**
present-day Russia

das schöne **Schottland**
beautiful Scotland

das alte **Freiburg**
old Freiburg

(i) With geographical names for features such as lakes and mountains, as well as with the names of planets:

am **Bodensee**
by/near Lake Constance

östlich *des Genfer Sees*
to the east of Lake Geneva

auf *dem Mars*
on Mars

(j) With the names of streets and buildings:

Fahren Sie *die Beethovenallee* **entlang.**
Drive along Beethoven Avenue.

> **Er ging über *den Potsdamer Platz*.**
> He crossed Potsdam Square.

In addresses, however, the article is omitted:

> **Wir wohnen Bahnhofstraße 57.**
> We live at 57 Bahnhofstraße.

But note that some streets include the article in the name: **An den Fichten 2**.

(k) With certain medical conditions:

> **Er leidet an *einer Lungenentzündung*.**
> He suffers from pneumonia.

(l) In several common phrases:

> **aus dem Bett** 'out of bed'
> **im allgemeinen** 'in general'
> **in der Kirche** 'in church'
> **in der Schule** 'at school'
> **in der Stadt** 'in town'
> **in der Tat** 'in (actual) fact'
> **mit dem Bus, Zug, usw.** 'by bus, train, etc.'
> **mit der Post** 'by post'
> **zur Kirche** 'to church'
> **zur Schule** 'to school'

24 Determiners

Determiners that decline like the definite article will be referred to here as '**der** words', and those which decline like the indefinite article as '**ein** words'.

24.1 *Der* words

(a) **dieser** 'this', **jeder** 'each/every' and **jener** 'that' can be used either as pronouns (see **31.1**A) or determiners.

When the determiners **dieser** and **jener** are used together, **dieser** denotes relative proximity and **jener** relative remoteness:

> ***Dieses* Buch ist interessanter als *jenes*.**
> This book is more interesting than that.

Where this contrast is not important, **dieser** often corresponds to English 'that':

> *Dieses* **Auto würde ich nicht kaufen.**
> I wouldn't buy that car.

Another meaning is former (**jener**) and latter (**dieser**):

> **Karl und Hans arbeiten schon lange hier.** *Dieser* **ist 56 Jahre alt, jener 58.**
> Karl and Hans have worked here a long time. The latter is 56, the former 58.

(b) **welcher**, **mancher**, **solcher** ('which/what', 'many', 'such') are all declined as **der** words:

> **Aus** *welcher* **Stadt kommen Sie?**
> Which/What town are you from?

> *Manche* **Studenten haben finanzielle Probleme.**
> Many students have financial problems.

> **In** *solchen* **Fällen muß man vorsichtig sein.**
> One has to be careful in such cases.

(c) **derjenige** 'that one' is written as one word but both parts decline. It is usually linked to a relative clause (see **10**A):

> **Wir suchen** *diejenigen* **in der Firma,** *die* **Interesse an einer zusätzlichen Qualifikation haben.**
> We are looking for people in the company interested in gaining an additional qualification.

> **Kennst du** *denjenigen,* *der* **gestern den Fritz abgeholt hat?**
> Do you know that man who picked Fritz up yesterday?

(d) **derselbe** 'same' is again declined like two words but written as one:

> **Wir machen immer** *dieselben* **Aufgaben.**
> We are always doing the same jobs.

With a shortened preposition (see **18.3**A, **19.5**A) the two constituent parts are written separately:

> *am selben* **Ort/** *im selben* **Gebäude**
> at the same place/in the same building

24.2

Ein words

(a) **kein**, **irgendein** 'not a/not any', 'any'

The negative **kein** is an **ein** word, as is **irgendein**:

Ich habe *keine* **Lust, ins Kino zu gehen.**
I don't want to go to the cinema.

Wir wollen doch nicht *irgendein* **Auto kaufen.**
We don't want to buy any (old) car.

Note the use of **was für ein** 'what sort of'. The case of **ein** here depends on the phrase's function in the sentence:

Was für *ein* **Mensch war er?**
What sort of a person was he?

In was für *einem* **Büro arbeitet ihr?**
What sort of an office do you work in?

Was für *einen* **Wagen hast du gekauft?**
What sort of car have you bought?

(b) **beide** 'both', **irgendwelche** 'some/any' (the plural of **irgendein**) and **sämtliche** 'all' are used only in the plural.

Sie kennt *beide* **Schwestern.**
She knows both sisters.

Hast du hier *irgendwelche* **Freunde?**
Do you have any friends here?

Sie haben *sämtliche* **Brötchen gekauft.**
They bought all the bread rolls.

For the use of **alle** see **44.3–44.4**A.

(c) The undeclined **solch** is used before **ein** (usually only in fairly formal written style):

Solch einen Film **sieht man nicht jeden Tag.**
It is not every day that one sees a film like that.

Alternatively, **ein** can come first, in which case the declined form **solcher** is used:

Einen solchen Film **sieht man nicht jeden Tag.**

The undeclined **manch** is rarely found in modern German.

25 *Gender*

German has three genders: masculine, feminine and neuter. In most instances grammatical gender is not based on natural gender. Although there are a few rules which can help predict the gender of a noun, the following can only ever serve as guidelines; many exceptions will be found. The safest approach to gender is always to learn each noun with the appropriate definite article (**der**, **die** or **das**).

25.1 Most nouns with the following endings are masculine:

-ant	**der Lieferant** 'distributor'
-ast	**der Palast** 'palace'
-ent	**der Dirigent** 'musical conductor'
-er	**der Sprecher** 'speaker'
-ich	**der Teppich** 'carpet'
-ig	**der König** 'king'
-ing	**der Ring** 'ring'
-ismus	**der Kapitalismus** 'capitalism'
-ist	**der Komponist** 'composer'.
-ling	**der Häftling** 'prisoner'
-or	**der Motor** 'engine'
-us	**der Modus** 'mode'

25.2 The following groups of nouns are mostly masculine:

(a) Days of the week, months, seasons:

> **der Tag** 'day', **der Mittwoch** 'Wednesday', **der November** 'November', **der Frühling** (BUT **das Frühjahr**) 'spring'

(b) Points of the compass and vocabulary relating to weather:

> **der Westen** 'west', **der Nordosten** 'north east', **der Wind** 'wind', **der Nebel** 'fog', **der Schnee** 'snow', **der Regen** 'rain'

(c) Male persons and male animals:

> **der Bruder** 'brother', **der Ingenieur** 'engineer', **der Hund** 'dog', **der Löwe** 'lion'

(d) Makes of car:

> **der Mercedes, der Opel, der VW, der BMW**

(e) Rocks and minerals:

> **der Granit** 'granite', **der Ton** 'clay', **der Diamant** 'diamond'

(f) Alcoholic drinks:

> **der Schnaps, der Wein** 'wine', **der Whisky** (but note **das Bier** 'beer')

25.3 The following endings indicate the noun is feminine:

-age	**die Garage** 'garage'
-anz	**die Allianz** 'alliance'
-ei	**die Druckerei** 'printing works'
-enz	**die Existenz** 'existence'
-ette	**die Diskette** 'disk/diskette'
-heit	**die Gesundheit** 'health'
-ie	**die Melodie** 'melody'
-ik	**die Kritik** 'criticism'
-in	**die Lehrerin** 'teacher'
-ion	**die Fusion** 'merger/fusion'
-keit	**die Schwierigkeit** 'difficulty'
-schaft	**die Freundschaft** 'friendship'
-sis	**die Skepsis** 'scepticism'
-tät	**die Sexualität** 'sexuality'
-ung	**die Forschung** 'research'
-ur	**die Figur** 'figure'

25.4 The following groups of nouns are mostly feminine:

(a) Female persons and animals (but see also **25.5**A for **Mädchen** and **Fräulein**):

die Frau 'woman', **die Mutter** 'mother', **die Katze** 'cat', **die Gans** 'goose'

(b) Most trees and flowers:

die Eiche 'oak', **die Buche** 'beech', **die Tulpe** 'tulip', **die Narzisse** 'narcissus' (BUT **der Ahorn** 'maple')

(c) Nouns derived from measurement or size adjectives:

die Ferne 'distance', **die Länge** 'length', **die Höhe** 'height', **die Stärke** 'strength'

(d) Numerals used as nouns:

die Fünf 'five', **die Hundert** 'hundred', **die Million** 'million', **die Milliarde** 'billion'

(e) Motor-cycles, ships and aeroplanes:

die Harley-Davidson, **die Titanic**, **die Concorde**, **die Boeing**

25.5

Most nouns with the following endings are neuter:

-at	**das Quadrat** 'square'
-chen	**das Mädchen** 'girl'
-ett	**das Lazarett** 'military hospital'
-icht	**das Gewicht** 'weight'
-il	**das Ventil** 'valve/outlet'
-it	**das Dynamit** 'dynamite'
-ium	**das Laboratorium** 'laboratory'
-lein	**das Fräulein** 'young woman/miss'
-ma	**das Schema** 'scheme/plan'
-ment	**das Experiment** 'experiment'
-sal	**das Schicksal** 'fate'
-tel	**das Viertel** 'area of a town/quarter'
-tum	**das Beamtentum** 'civil servants'
-um	**das Datum** 'date'

The vast majority of collective nouns with the prefix **Ge-** are also neuter:

> **das Gebäck** 'cake and biscuits', **das Gepäck** 'luggage', **das Gemüse** 'vegetables'

25.6

The following groups of nouns are neuter:

(a) Young persons and animals:

> **das Baby** 'baby', **das Kind** 'child', **das Küken** 'chick', **das Lamm** 'lamb'

(b) Adjectives, pronouns, conjunctions, prepositions and infinitives used as nouns (see also **28.5**A):

> *Das Grün* **des Meeres.**
> The green of the sea.

> **Gern nehme ich** *das Du* **an.**
> I'm happy for us to call each other 'du'.

> **Ich höre nur** *das Wenn und Aber.*
> All I hear are ifs and buts.

> **Ich habe** *mein Gegenüber* **besucht.**
> I visited my opposite number.

> *Das Laufen* **macht fit.**
> Running gets you fit.

(c) Cafés, restaurants, hotels and cinemas:

das Kempinski, das Kaiser Wilhelm, das Savoy, das Odeon

(d) Names of towns, countries and continents:

das alte Dresden 'old Dresden', das heutige Griechenland 'present-day Greece', das neue Europa 'the new Europe'

(e) Letters of the alphabet:

das ABC, mit kleinem "p" 'with a small "p" ', ein großes Ypsilon 'a capital "y" '

(f) Chemical elements and metals:

das Blei 'lead', das Gold 'gold', das Kupfer 'copper', das Silber 'silver'

(g) Scientific units and measurements:

das Atom 'atom', das Elektron 'electron', das Neutron 'neutron', das Pfund 'pound', das Gramm 'gram'

26 *Compound nouns and acronyms*

26.1

The last part of a compound noun decides the overall gender and number:

der Kupferstich 'copper engraving' is made up of das Kupfer and *der Stich.*
die Studentenkneipe 'student pub' is made up of der Student and *die Kneipe.*
das Kopfsteinpflaster 'cobble stones' is made up of der Kopfstein and *das Pflaster.*
die Busreise 'bus trip' is made up of der Bus and *die Reise.*

26.2

Acronyms take their gender from the principal noun:

der DGB 'Federation of German Trade Unions': der Deutsche Gewerkschafts*bund*
die SPD 'Social Democratic Party': die Sozialdemokratische *Partei* Deutschlands
das BAFöG 'National Law on Support for Education and Training': das Bundesausbildungsförderungs*gesetz*

27 Gender variations

27.1 A few nouns have alternative genders which frequently depend on regional usage:

> in Germany and Austria **das Foto**, **das Radio** and **das Taxi**, but in
> Switzerland **die Foto**, **der Radio** and **der Taxi**
> in Germany and Switzerland **der Keks** 'biscuit', but in Austria **das Keks**

27.2 There are several nouns which are identical in form in the singular but whose gender depends on their meaning. These often have different plural forms:

> **der Band**, plural **die Bände** 'volume/book'
> BUT **das Band**, plural **die Bänder** 'ribbon/tape'
> AND **das Band**, plural **die Bande** 'bonds'
> ALSO **die Band**, plural **die Bands** 'band/pop group'
>
> **der Leiter**, same plural, 'leader'
> BUT **die Leiter**, plural **die Leitern** 'ladder'
>
> **der Pony**, no plural, 'fringe of hair'
> BUT **das Pony**, plural **die Ponys** 'pony'
>
> **der See**, plural **die Seen** 'lake'
> BUT **die See**, no plural, 'sea'

28 Noun declensions

28.1 General rules for noun declension are that:

(a) Feminine nouns do not change their ending in the singular:

> **die Tat** (nom), **die Tat** (acc), **der Tat** (dat), **der Tat** (gen)

(b) Masculine and neuter nouns add -**(e)s** in the genitive singular (see also **28.1e**A):

> **des Tag(e)s**, **des Flughafens**, **des Baums**

(c) All nouns add -**n** in the dative plural if the nominative plural does not already end in -**n** or -**s**:

> **auf den Tischen** 'on the tables;'
> **mit den Katzen** 'with the cats'
> BUT **bei Lehmanns** 'at the Lehmanns''
> **in den Autos** 'in the cars'

(d) The basic, regular pattern of noun declension (sometimes called the 'strong' declension) is thus as follows:

Singular	Masculine	Neuter	Feminine
Nominative	**der Ring**	**das Brot**	**die Frau**
Accusative	**den Ring**	**das Brot**	**die Frau**
Dative	**dem Ring**	**dem Brot**	**der Frau**
Genitive	**des Rings**	**des Brotes**	**der Frau**

Plural			
Nominative	**die Ringe**	**die Brote**	**die Frauen**
Accusative	**die Ringe**	**die Brote**	**die Frauen**
Dative	**den Ringen**	**den Broten**	**den Frauen**
Genitive	**der Ringe**	**der Brote**	**der Frauen**

(e) Nowadays the **-es** genitive ending is usually used only in monosyllabic nouns where pronunciation might otherwise prove difficult (**des Jahres**), but it must be used in nouns or syllables ending in:

> -s (**des Hauses**)
> -sch (**des Tisches**)
> -ß (**des Fußes, des Flusses**)
> -st (**des Dienstes**)
> -z (**des Schmerzes**)

With neuter nouns ending in **-is** the genitive singular is always **-isses** (**des Ergebnisses**).

(f) The use of the dative singular ending **-e** with some masculine and neuter nouns is very old-fashioned and is rarely found except in certain set phrases:

> **nach Hause** 'home'
> **zu Hause** 'at home'
> **im Laufe** 'in the course of'
> **im Grunde genommen** 'basically'
> **in gewissem Maße** 'to a certain degree'

28.2 Weak declension

(a) The term weak denotes masculine nouns which add **-n** or **-en** to the nominative singular form in the accusative, dative and genitive singular, and in the plural. Weak nouns need to be learnt when they are first met (see **28.4**A):

	Singular	Plural
Nominative	**der Mensch**	**die Menschen**
Accusative	**den Menschen**	**die Menschen**
Dative	**dem Menschen**	**den Menschen**
Genitive	**des Menschen**	**der Menschen**

There are relatively few weak nouns; they include mostly nouns denoting living beings:

> **der Affe** 'monkey'
> **der Chirurg** 'surgeon'
> **der Franzose** 'Frenchman'
> **der Junge** 'boy'
> **der Neffe** 'nephew'
> **der Oberst** 'colonel'
> **der Spatz** 'sparrow'

(b) A small number of weak nouns have an **-ns** ending in the genitive singular. The most common are:

> **der Buchstabe** 'letter (of alphabet)'
> **der Friede** 'peace'
> **der Gedanke** 'thought'
> **der Glaube** 'faith'
> **das Herz** 'heart' (but note the accusative singular **das Herz**)
> **der Name** 'name'
> **der Wille** 'will'

28.3 — **Variations**

A fairly small number of nouns feature the normal masculine/neuter genitive singular in -**(e)s** but the weak plural in -**n**. For example:

> **das Bett, des Bett(e)s, die Betten**
> **der Staat, des Staat(e)s, die Staaten**
> **der See, des Sees, die Seen**

28.4 — Like strong verbs (see **33**A) and noun gender (see **27**A), irregularities in noun declension need to be learnt when the noun is first met, since there is no way of knowing just by looking at the noun whether it is of weak or regular declension. The three key elements to learn are a noun's nominative singular, its genitive singular and its nominative plural. These, along with the gender, will usually be given in any good dictionary: e.g. **Tisch, m., -es, -e** indicates that the noun is masculine, that the genitive form is **des Tisches** and that the plural is **die Tische**.

28.5 — **Adjectival declension**

A large number of adjectives can serve as nouns when spelt with an initial capital letter. They always take the appropriate adjective endings following the definite article and the determiners (see **22**A, **24**A, **44**A), the indefinite article (see **22**A, **45**A) or the adjective without any preceding defining word (see **46**A):

Sehen Sie *den* Alt*en* in der Ecke?
Do you see the old man in the corner?

Sie spricht mit einer *der* Krank*en*.
She's talking to one of the (female) patients.

Er wohnt bei *einer* Deutsch*en*.
He lives with a German (woman).

Arbeitslose haben in dieser Stadt wenig Chance.
Unemployed people don't have much of a chance in this town.

Er ist Beamt*er* geworden.
He's become a civil servant.

Infinitives as nouns

The infinitive of almost any verb can be given an initial capital letter and turned into a regular (i.e. strong) neuter noun:

> **das Essen** 'food/meal', **das Lesen** 'reading', **das Rauchen** 'smoking', **das Schwimmen** 'swimming'

29 *Plurals*

There are several different ways to form noun plurals in German. It is very difficult to predict plural endings with complete certainty and therefore, once again, learners are strongly advised to learn the plural form when they first encounter the noun.

There are five clear types of plural ending, some of which are typical of certain genders or suffixes. These are listed below:

Plural in *-n* or *-en*

A very large number of nouns fall into this category, including:
(a) Feminine nouns ending in:

-e	**die Schulen** 'schools'
-ei	**die Metzgereien** 'butchers' shops'
-heit	**die Weisheiten** 'wise sayings'
-in	describing job titles; a second **n** is inserted before the plural ending: **die Ärztinnen** 'doctors'
-keit	**die Schwierigkeiten** 'difficulties'
-schaft	**die Errungenschaften** 'achievements'
-ung	**die Empfindungen** 'feelings'

(b) All nouns ending in:

-ant	die **Diamanten** 'diamonds'
-ent	die **Präsidenten** 'presidents'
-enz	die **Referenzen** 'references'
-ie	die **Batterien** 'batteries'
-ik	die **Kritiken** 'criticisms'
-ion	die **Informationen** 'information'
-ist	die **Sozialisten** 'socialists'
-oge	die **Biologen** 'biologists'
-tät	die **Universitäten** 'universities'

29.3 Plural in *-e* or umlaut + *-e*

(a) The **-e** ending is taken by a large number of masculine and neuter monosyllabic nouns:

> der **Blick**, die **Blicke** 'looks'
> der **Film**, die **Filme** 'films'
> der **Hund**, die **Hunde** 'dogs'
> der **Schuh**, die **Schuhe** 'shoes'
> der **Tag**, die **Tage** 'days'

(b) In many such nouns an umlaut appears on the stressed vowel: **Stühle** 'chairs', **Pläne** 'plans'. These plural forms simply have to be learnt when the noun is first met. The umlaut + **-e** ending is found in a number of feminine nouns too: **Hände** 'hands', **Städte** 'towns/cities', **Würste** 'sausages'.

(c) Nouns ending in:

-är	die **Millionäre** 'millionaires'
-eur	die **Jongleure** 'jugglers'

29.4 No change in the plural

(a) Most masculine nouns in:

-el	die **Deckel** 'lids'
-en	die **Reifen** 'tyres'
-er	die **Koffer** 'suitcases'

(b) Diminutives in:

-chen	die **Häuschen** 'small houses'
-lein	die **Entlein** 'ducklings'

29.5

Plural in umlaut only

The stressed vowel receives an umlaut in the plural without any other change being made:

> die Äpfel 'apples'
> die Brüder 'brothers'
> die Läden 'shops'
> die Töchter 'daughters'

29.6

Plural in *-er* or umlaut + *-er*

(a) The **-er** ending appears mostly in monosyllabic neuter nouns and a few monosyllabic masculine ones:

> das Ei, die Eier 'eggs'
> das Kleid, die Kleider 'dresses'
> das Lied, die Lieder 'songs'
> der Geist, die Geister 'spirits'

(b) Wherever there is a vowel which can take an umlaut, there is an umlaut with the **-er** plural ending:

> das Dach, die Dächer 'roofs'
> der Mann, die Männer 'men'
> der Reichtum, die Reichtümer 'riches'
> der Wald, die Wälder 'forests'

29.7

Plural in *-s*

(a) Nouns taken from English, French and Italian over the past hundred years:

> die Babys
> die Hotels
> die Parks
> die Radios
> die Schecks
> die Shows

(b) Acronyms and words which have been shortened:

> die LKWs 'lorries'
> die Muttis 'mums'
> die PKWs 'cars'

29.8 | **Other miscellaneous plural forms**

(a) Greek and Latin derivations ending in **-os**, **-us** or **-um** usually take **-en** in the plural:

> **das Epos**, **die Epen** 'epics'
> **das Museum**, **die Museen** 'museums'
> **der Mythos**, **die Mythen** 'myths'
> **das Visum**, **die Visen** 'visas'

(b) Certain other nouns derived from Latin retain their Latin plural form:

> **das Tempus**, **die Tempora** 'tenses'
> **das Genus**, **die Genera** 'genuses/genders'

(c) Nouns ending in **-ma** have plural in **-men**:

> **die Firma**, **die Firmen** 'firms'
> **das Thema**, **die Themen** 'topics'

29.9 | **Double plural forms**

A number of nouns which are identical in form in the singular but whose gender depends on the meaning, have different plural forms (see **27.2**A for these).

There are also a few nouns with two meanings whose singular form and gender are identical but which have divergent plural forms:

> **die Bank**, **die Bänke** 'benches' and **die Banken** 'banks'
> **die Mutter**, **die Mütter** 'mothers' and **die Muttern** 'nuts', i.e. for bolts
> **der Rat**, **die Räte** 'councils' and **die Ratschläge** 'pieces of advice'
> **der Stock**, **die Stöcke** 'sticks' and **die Stockwerke** 'storeys'
> **das Wort**, **die Wörter** 'individual words' and **die Worte** 'connected words'

V Pronouns

30 Pronoun reference and forms

30.1

German pronouns preserve the gender and number (singular or plural) of the nouns to which they refer. For example:

> **Der Tisch ist zu klein. >** *Er* **ist zu klein.**
> The table is too small. > It is too small.

> **Die Tür ist auf. >** *Sie* **ist auf.**
> The door is open. > It is open.

> **Das Fenster ist zu. >** *Es* **ist zu.**
> The window is closed. > It is closed.

> **Die Fenster sind zu. >** *Sie* **sind zu.**
> The windows are closed. > They are closed.

However, the case of the pronoun depends on its role in the sentence:

> *Der* **Tisch war teuer. Wir haben** *ihn* **nicht gekauft.** *Er* **war aber schön.**
> The table was expensive. We didn't buy it. But it was nice.

30.2

The personal pronoun system is set out below. Note that there is a formal and a familiar second person mode of address (see **60.1**B), and that the second person formal is identical for the singular and the plural.

(a) The nominative forms are:

	Singular	Plural
First person	**ich** 'I'	**wir** 'we'
Second person (familiar)	**du** 'you'	**ihr** 'you'
Third person	**er, sie, es** 'he, she, it'	**sie** 'they'
Second person (formal)	**Sie** 'you'	**Sie** 'you'

(b) Each pronoun also has an accusative and a dative form:

Singular			Plural		
Nom	Acc	Dat	Nom	Acc	Dat
ich	**mich**	**mir**	**wir**	**uns**	**uns**
du	**dich**	**dir**	**ihr**	**euch**	**euch**
er	**ihn**	**ihm**	**sie**	**sie**	**ihnen**
sie	**sie**	**ihr**	**sie**	**sie**	**ihnen**
es	**es**	**ihm**	**sie**	**sie**	**ihnen**
Sie	**Sie**	**Ihnen**	**Sie**	**Sie**	**Ihnen**

(c) The genitive forms (**meiner, deiner, seiner, ihrer, seiner, Ihrer; unser, euer, ihrer, ihrer, ihrer, Ihrer**) are very rare and are only found with verbs governing the genitive case:

> **Wir gedenken *ihrer*.**
> We commemorate them.

> **Ich bin mir *seiner* sicher.**
> I am sure of him.

The forms **meinetwegen, deinetwegen, seinetwegen, ihretwegen, Ihretwegen; unsertwegen, euretwegen, ihretwegen, ihretwegen, Ihretwegen** mean 'because of me (etc.)/for my (etc.) sake':

> **Sie mußte *meinetwegen* warten.**
> She had to wait on my account/because of me.

30.3 Possessive adjectives (corresponding to 'my', 'your', 'his', 'her', etc.) are closely related to these pronoun forms. Their endings change according to case. Their stems are:

	Singular	Plural
First person	**mein**	**unser**
Second person	**dein**	**euer**
Third person (formal)	**sein**	**ihr**
	ihr	**ihr**
	sein	**ihr**
Second person (formal)	**Ihr**	**Ihr**

All possessive adjectives follow the **ein** declension. See **45**A for the declension of these forms.

> **Das ist *mein* neuer Wagen.**
> This is my new car.

Haben Sie mein*en* neuen Wagen gesehen?
Have you seen my new car?

Wir sind mit mein*em* neuen Wagen gefahren.
We drove in my new car.

When used predicatively (see **43**A), however, the possessive pronoun has two distinct forms. These are **meiner** (masculine nominative) and **meins** (neuter nominative and accusative):

Ist das dein Wagen? Ja, das ist mein*er*.
Is that your car? Yes, that's mine.

Ist das dein*e* Diskette? Ja, das ist mein*e*.
Is that your diskette? Yes, that's mine.

Ist das dein Buch? Ja, das ist mein*s*.
Is that your book? Yes, that's mine.

Hast du mein Buch gesehen? Nein, ich habe dein*s* nicht gesehen.
Have you seen my book? No, I haven't seen yours.

Otherwise the same endings are used as for attributive use (see **43.2**A):

Hast du meinen Wagen gesehen? Nein, ich habe dein*en* nicht gesehen.
Have you seen my car? No, I haven't seen yours.

Hast du meine Diskette gesehen? Nein, ich habe dein*e* nicht gesehen.
Have you seen my diskette? No, I haven't seen yours.

Fahren wir mit deinem Wagen? Ja, mit mein*em*.
Shall we go in your car? Yes, in mine.

Kann ich mit deiner Diskette arbeiten? Nein, nicht mit mein*er*.
Can I work with your diskette? No, not with mine.

(See **10**A for relative pronouns)

30.4

There are two interrogative pronouns: **wer** 'who' and **welcher** 'which'.

(a) **wer** has all four case forms:

Nom	**wer**
Acc	**wen**
Dat	**wem**
Gen	**wessen**

> ***Wer* ist das? *Wen* heiratest du? Mit *wem* hast du gesprochen?**
> Who is that? Who are you marrying? Who did you speak to?

The genitive form **wessen** is rather formal and German speakers tend to avoid it by using an alternative structure:

> ***Wessen* Schuld ist das? > *Wer* ist daran schuld?**
> Whose fault is that? > Who is to blame for it?

> ***Wessen* Auto ist das? > *Wem* gehört das Auto?**
> Whose car is it? > Who does the car belong to?

(b) **welcher** tends not to be used in the genitive:

Nominative	**welcher**
Accusative	**welchen**
Dative	**welchem**

> ***Welcher* Politiker ist das?**
> Which politician is that?

> **An *welchem* Computer arbeitest du?**
> Which computer are you working on?

31 Other forms used as pronouns

Note the following, some of which can also be used as determiners:

(See also **24**A for determiners)

31.1

dieser/diese/dieses is sometimes used in place of **er/sie/es**:

> **Dann hat der Vater angerufen. Und *dieser* sagte,...**
> And then his/her father rang. And he said ...

dieser and **jener** are also used for 'the latter' and 'the former' respectively (see **24.1**A).

31.2

The definite article **der/die/das** is often used in place of personal pronouns, especially in the spoken language:

> ***Die* wohnt drüben.**
> She lives over there.

> ***Den* kenne ich schon lange.**
> I've known him for a long time.

> *Das* wissen wir schon.
> We already know that.

> Ich bin mir *dessen* bewußt.
> I am aware of that.

> Mit *dem* kann man handeln.
> With him one can do business.

31.3 **einer/eine/eins** 'one'. This declines like the predicative **meiner/meine/meins** (see **30.3**A):

> Hast du *einen/ eine/ eins*?
> Have you got one?

Often it is used with a degree of emphasis:

> In der Schweiz spricht man nicht nur *eine* Sprache.
> They don't just speak *one* language in Switzerland.

31.4 **man** 'one', 'people in general', 'they':

> *Man* versteht das schon.
> People understand that.

In the accusative and dative **man** becomes **einen** and **einem** respectively:

> Wenn *man* arbeitslos wird, trifft das *einen* hart.
> If you become unemployed it affects you badly.

31.5 **jemand** 'someone' and **niemand** 'no one' decline as follows:

Nom	**jemand**	**niemand**
Acc	**jemanden**	**niemanden**
Dat	**jemandem**	**niemandem**
Gen	**jemandes**	**niemandes**

In spoken German the accusative and dative are frequently left uninflected, as **jemand** and **niemand**:

> Ich suche *niemanden/ niemand.*
> I'm not looking for anyone.

> Sie spricht gerade *mit jemandem/ mit jemand* am Telefon.
> She's speaking to someone on the phone at the moment.

In relative clauses **jemand** is construed as masculine, i.e. **jemand, der**... 'someone who...' However, in feminist usage, **jemand, die**... is found.

32 *Pronouns used after prepositions*

The correct use of pronouns with prepositions depends on distinguishing between people and things. Where the reference is to an inanimate object or a general state of affairs, the form **da** + preposition is used (see **50.6**A):

Referring to **der Sohn** 'the son':

> **Sein Vater hat einen großen Einfluß *auf ihn* gehabt.**
> His father had a great influence on him.

Referring to **der Plan** 'the plan':

> **Sein Vater hat einen großen Einfluß *darauf* gehabt.**
> His father had a great influence on it.

VI Verbs

Finite verb, infinitive and participle

All verbs have (a) an infinitive form, (b) a present and a past participle, and (c) several finite forms:

(a) The infinitive form is the form found in dictionaries. It is the usual way of referring to the verb as a concept. Thus, **arbeiten** means 'to work' and **sagen** means 'to say'.

(b) The present participle is an adjective derived from the verb. English present participles end in '-ing'. Thus, **eine arbeitende Frau** is 'a working woman' and **ein nichtssagender Brief** is 'a letter that says nothing'.

The past participle is used in forming two of the past tenses (see **33.3**A): the perfect and the pluperfect. Thus, **ich habe gearbeitet** means 'I have worked' and **Was hast du gesagt?** means 'What did you say?' The past participle is also used in the formation of the passive (see **40**A).

(c) The finite forms of a verb (see **5.1**A) carry specific information about:

> person: whether the verb is in the 'I' form or the 'you' form, for example
> number: whether the verb is in the singular or the plural, e.g. whether it is in the 'I' form or the 'we' form
> tense: whether the verb is in the present, past or future.

For example, **studiere** reveals that the verb is first person singular ('I') and present tense ('I study'); and **studiertest** reveals that it is second person (familiar) singular, and past tense ('you studied').

Infinitives and participles do not carry this information. They each have only one fixed form. Where they are used as part of the verb they must be accompanied by a finite form, such as the forms in **ich *habe* gearbeitet und du *hast* auch gearbeitet** 'I have worked and you have worked too'.

33.2

Weak, strong and irregular verbs

There are regular patterns which most verbs follow, though some verbs follow irregular patterns and a special effort must be made to learn these. Many of the most frequently used verbs are not regular. It is useful to distinguish the following types of verb:

(a) Weak verbs (see **33.4**A) are entirely regular and their forms are therefore completely predictable. They always add the standard endings to the verb stem, which never changes. The following are all forms of the weak verb **machen** 'to make/do': **mache, machst, machte, gemacht.**

(b) Strong verbs (see **33.5**A) have a change in the verb stem when forming the simple past tense. The following are forms of **singen** 'to sing'. The forms with the change in the verb stem are past tense: **singe, singst, sang, sangst.**

(c) A small number of verbs combine aspects of the weak and the strong patterns. These are known as 'mixed' verbs (see **33.6**A).

(d) Irregular verbs (see **33.7**A) are typically strong verbs which also change the verb stem in some of the present tense forms. The verb **nehmen** 'to take' has present tense forms based on the stem **nehm-** such as **nehme** and **nehmt**, but it also has **nimmst** and **nimmt** in the present tense.

33.3

The six tenses

All verbs have forms corresponding to the six basic tenses. In the table below, all the finite forms of the verbs are in italics. The examples show one weak verb (**studieren**) and one strong verb (**kommen**):

There are two simple tense forms:

Present	sie *studiert* 'she studies/is studying'
	sie *kommt* 'she comes/is coming'
Simple past	sie *studierte* 'she studied/was studying'
	sie *kam* 'she came/was coming'

and four compound tense forms:

Perfect	sie *hat* studiert 'she has studied/she studied'
	sie *ist* gekommen 'she has come/came'
Pluperfect	sie *hatte* studiert 'she had studied'
	sie *war* gekommen 'she had come'
Future	sie *wird* studieren 'she will study'
	sie *wird* kommen 'she will come'
Future perfect	sie *wird* studiert haben 'she will have studied'
	sie *wird* gekommen sein 'she will have come'

The compound tenses are formed as follows:

> Perfect: a finite form of either **haben** or **sein***, in the present tense, + the past participle of the main verb.
>
> Pluperfect: a finite form of either **haben** or **sein***, in the simple past tense, + the past participle of the main verb.
>
> Future: a finite form of **werden**, in the present tense, + the infinitive of the main verb.
>
> Future perfect: a finite form of **werden**, in the present tense, + the past participle of the main verb, + either **haben** or **sein***.
> * See below (**33.8**A)

33.4   Weak verbs are completely regular and always retain the verb stem. The majority of verbs follow this pattern and any new verbs which enter the language are 'weak', e.g. **privatisieren** 'privatize', **harmonisieren** 'harmonize', **testen** 'test', **interviewen** 'interview'.

(a) In the present tense, the regular endings are added to the stem of the verb. The present tense forms of **machen** 'to do/make' are:

ich mach*e*	wir mach*en*
du mach*st*	ihr mach*t*
er/sie/es mach*t*	sie mach*en*
Sie mach*en*	Sie mach*en*

Where the stem of the verb ends in **-d** or **-t**, an extra **-e** is introduced in some positions to ease pronunciation:

ich arbeite	wir arbeiten
du arbeitest	ihr arbeitet
er/sie/es arbeitet	sie arbeiten
Sie arbeiten	Sie arbeiten

(b) In the simple past, weak verbs add a **-t** and a slightly different set of regular endings to the verb stem. Note that the **ich** form and the **er/sie/es** forms are identical in the simple past:

ich mach*te*	wir mach*ten*
du mach*test*	ihr mach*tet*
er/sie/es mach*te*	sie mach*ten*
Sie mach*ten*	Sie mach*ten*

Where the stem of the verb ends in **-d** or **-t**, an extra **-e** is introduced in all positions to ease pronunciation:

ich arbeit*ete*	wir arbeit*eten*
du arbeit*etest*	ihr arbeit*etet*
er/sie/es arbeit*ete*	sie arbeit*eten*
Sie arbeit*eten*	Sie arbeit*eten*

(c) The perfect and pluperfect tenses of weak verbs are formed with the past participle, and this is formed by adding **ge-** to the beginning of the verb stem, and **-(e)t** to the end. The verbs **arbeiten** 'to work', **machen** 'to make/do' and **testen** 'to test' have the following forms:

Infinitive	Past participle	Perfect tense	Pluperfect tense
arbeiten	*gearbei*tet	ich habe gearbeitet	ich hatte gearbeitet
machen	*gemach*t	ich habe gemacht	ich hatte gemacht
testen	*getest*et	ich habe getestet	ich hatte getestet

The finite verb in these tenses is not always a form of **haben** (see **33.8**A).

Note that verbs ending in **-ieren** and verbs beginning with an inseparable prefix (see **57.2**A) do not add **ge-** in forming the past participle. For example, the verbs **studieren** 'to study', **privatisieren** 'to privatize' and **verreisen** 'to depart' have the following forms:

Infinitive	Past participle	Perfect tense	Pluperfect tense
studieren	studier*t*	ich habe studiert	ich hatte studiert
privatisieren	privatisier*t*	ich habe privatisiert	ich hatte privatisiert
verreisen	verreis*t*	ich bin verreist	ich war verreist

The finite verb in these tenses is not always a form of **haben** (see **33.8**A).

33.5 The main feature of strong verbs is that the form of the verb stem itself undergoes a change in the simple past and often in the past participle too.

(a) In the present tense most strong verbs follow the regular pattern of endings found in weak verbs (see **33.4a**A). For example, the verbs **gehen** 'to go' and **kommen** 'to come' have the following predictable forms:

ich geh*e*	wir geh*en*	ich komm*e*	wir komm*en*
du geh*st*	ihr geh*t*	du komm*st*	ihr komm*t*
er/sie/es geh*t*	sie geh*en*	er/sie/es komm*t*	sie komm*en*
Sie geh*en*	Sie geh*en*	Sie komm*en*	Sie komm*en*

(b) In the simple past strong verbs have a change within the stem of the verb, usually a vowel change, and they add a different set of endings to those found in weak verbs.

The simple past forms of **gehen** and **kommen** are:

ich ging	**wir ging***en*	**ich kam**	**wir kam***en*
du ging*st*	**ihr ging***t*	**du kam***st*	**ihr kam***t*
er/sie/es ging	**sie ging***en*	**er/sie/es kam**	**sie kam***en*
Sie ging*en*	**Sie ging***en*	**Sie kam***en*	**Sie kam***en*

Note that the **ich** form and the **er/sie/es** form are simply the changed verb stem without any ending at all.

The change in the verb stem needs to be learnt for all strong verbs:

Infinitive	Simple past
gehen	**ging**
kommen	**kam**
etc.	

Thus, if we know that the verb **singen** 'to sing' has the simple past **sang**, we can predict the following forms: **ich sang** 'I sang', **du sangst** 'you (familiar) sang', **sie sang** 'she sang', **wir sangen** 'we sang', etc.

(c) The perfect and pluperfect tenses of strong verbs are formed with the past participle, and this is formed by adding **ge-** to the beginning of the verb stem and **-(e)n** to the end. The verbs **gehen** 'to go', **kommen** 'to come' and **singen** 'to sing' have the following forms:

Infinitive	Past participle	Perfect tense	Pluperfect tense
gehen	*ge*gang*en*	**ich bin gegangen**	**ich war gegangen**
kommen	*ge*komm*en*	**ich bin gekommen**	**ich war gekommen**
singen	*ge*sung*en*	**ich habe gesungen**	**ich hatte gesungen**

The finite verb in these tenses is not always a form of **haben** (see **33.8**A).

Note that verbs beginning with an inseparable prefix (see **57.2**A) do not add **ge-** in forming the past participle. For example, the verbs **bekommen** 'to receive' and **vergehen** 'to pass' (of time) have the following forms:

Infinitive	Past participle	Perfect tense	Pluperfect tense
vergehen	**vergang***en*	**es ist vergangen**	**es war vergangen**
bekommen	**bekomm***en*	**ich habe bekommen**	**ich hatte bekommen**

33.6

There are a few so-called 'mixed' verbs which combine features of the weak and the strong patterns by adding the regular endings to a changed vowel stem in the simple past. The most common 'mixed' verbs are:

Infinitive	Simple past stem	
bringen	**brachte**	'to bring'
denken	**dachte**	'to think'
brennen	**brannte**	'to burn'
kennen	**kannte**	'to know' (a person or place)
nennen	**nannte**	'to name/call'
rennen	**rannte**	'to race'
wissen	**wußte**	'to know' (a piece of information)

(a) In the present tense these verbs are entirely regular except for **wissen**, which has an irregular pattern (see **33.7a**A).

(b) In the simple past the regular weak endings are added to the simple past stem.

Thus, present tense forms include **ich bringe, du denkst, es brennt**, etc., and simple past forms include **ich kannte, du nanntest, er rannte**, etc.

(c) The perfect and pluperfect tenses of mixed verbs are formed with the past participle, and this is formed by adding **ge-** to the beginning of the simple past stem and **-t** to the end. The forms are:

Infinitive	Simple past stem	Perfect tense
bringen	**brachte**	**ich habe gebracht**
denken	**dachte**	**ich habe gedacht**
brennen	**brannte**	**ich habe gebrannt**
kennen	**kannte**	**ich habe gekannt**
nennen	**nannte**	**ich habe genannt**
rennen	**rannte**	**ich bin gerannt**
wissen	**wußte**	**ich habe gewußt**

The finite verb in these tenses is not always a form of **haben** (see **33.8**A).

33.7

Irregular verbs fall into several different categories, but they share one basic feature: they have an irregular pattern in the present tense. In addition, most irregular verbs are strong verbs. These are very common verbs and are part of the basic vocabulary of all speakers of German. A special effort needs to be made to learn them.

(a) The verbs **sein** 'to be', **werden** 'to become', **wissen** 'to know', **haben** 'to have' have the following forms:

Structures

Present tense

sein			werden	
bin	sind		werde	werden
bist	seid		wirst	werdet
ist	sind		wird	werden
sind	sind		werden	werden

wissen			haben	
weiß	wissen		habe	haben
weißt	wißt		hast	habt
weiß	wissen		hat	haben
wissen	wissen		haben	haben

Simple past

sein			werden	
war	waren		wurde	wurden
warst	wart		wurdest	wurdet
war	waren		wurde	wurden
waren	waren		wurden	wurden

wissen			haben	
wußte	wußten		hatte	hatten
wußtest	wußtet		hattest	hattet
wußte	wußten		hatte	hatten
wußten	wußten		hatten	hatten

Perfect and pluperfect

ich bin gewesen 'I have been/was'	**ich war gewesen** 'I had been'
ich bin geworden 'I have become/became'	**ich war geworden** 'I had become'
ich habe gehabt 'I have had/had'	**ich hatte gehabt** 'I had had'
ich habe gewußt 'I have known/knew'	**ich hatte gewußt** 'I had known'

(b) All modal verbs are irregular (see **35**A).

(c) A number of common strong verbs (see **33.5**A) have a vowel change in the stem of the verb in the **du** and the **er/sie/es** forms of the present tense. This means that there is an extra feature to learn when studying the principal parts of these verbs (see **33.9**A). In the early stages of learning, the principal parts of each verb must be learnt individually. The following is a guide to some common patterns. Note that the change to the stem in the present tense is always found in the **du** and **er/sie/es** forms only (printed in italic):

Stem vowel changes from **e** to **i**: **geben** 'to give', **nehmen** 'to take', **helfen** 'to help':

gebe	geben	nehme	nehmen	helfe	helfen
gibst	gebt	*nimmst*	nehmt	*hilfst*	helft
gibt	geben	*nimmt*	nehmen	*hilft*	helfen
geben	geben	nehmen	nehmen	helfen	helfen

Other verbs which follow this pattern include: **brechen** 'to break', **essen** 'to eat' (**du ißt, er ißt**), **gelten** 'to be valid' (**es gilt**), **messen** 'to measure', **sprechen** 'to speak', **treten** 'to step/kick' (**er tritt**), **treffen** 'to meet', **vergessen** 'to forget', **werfen** 'to throw'.

Stem vowel changes from **e** to **ie**: **sehen** 'to see', **empfehlen** 'to recommend', **lesen** 'to read':

sehe	sehen	empfehle	empfehlen	lese	lesen
siehst	seht	*empfiehlst*	empfehlt	*liest*	lest
sieht	sehen	*empfiehlt*	empfehlen	*liest*	lesen
sehen	sehen	empfehlen	empfehlen	lesen	lesen

Other verbs which follow this pattern include: **befehlen** 'to order/instruct', **stehlen** 'to steal', **geschehen** 'to happen' (**es geschieht**, 'it happens').

Stem vowel changes by umlaut: **fahren** 'to travel/drive', **schlafen** 'to sleep', **fallen** 'to fall':

fahre	fahren	schlafe	schlafen	falle	fallen
fährst	fahrt	*schläfst*	schlaft	*fällst*	fallt
fährt	fahren	*schläft*	schlafen	*fällt*	fallen
fahren	fahren	schlafen	schlafen	fallen	fallen

Other verbs which follow this pattern include: **halten** 'to stay/halt' (**er hält**), **laden** 'to load' (**er lädt**), **raten** 'to advise' (**du rätst, er rät**), **tragen** 'to carry', **wachsen** 'to grow'.

Note also:

> **stoßen** 'to hit/bump into': **du stößt, er/sie/es stößt**
> **laufen** 'to run/walk': **du läufst, er/sie/es läuft**
> **saufen** 'to drink alcohol': **du säufst, er/sie/es säuft**

33.8

Using *haben* or *sein* with the past participle

The use of **haben** or **sein** as the auxiliary in the perfect and pluperfect is determined mainly by the following factors:

(a) The auxiliary is **haben**:

When the verb is transitive, i.e. takes an accusative object:

> **Sie hat ihn gefragt.**
> She asked him.

When the verb has a transitive sense even though the object is not expressed in the accusative. The verb may take a dative object (see **19.6**A), for example, or be a prepositional verb (see **38**A):

>**Wir haben ihm geholfen.**
>We helped him.

>**Der Fall der Mauer hat zu dieser Entwicklung beigetragen.**
>The fall of the Wall has contributed to this development.

When the verb is intransitive and expresses an ongoing state:

>**Wir haben lange gestanden und gewartet.**
>We (have) stood and waited for a long time.

>**Es hat lange gedauert.**
>It lasted a long time./It took a long time.

>**Es hat geregnet, geschneit und gedonnert.**
>It (has) rained, snowed and thundered.

(b) The auxiliary is **sein** when the verb is used intransitively and:

When the verb is **sein, bleiben, werden**:

>**Es ist sehr warm geblieben.**
>It remained very warm.

When the verb is a verb of motion:

>**Sind Sie nach Köln gefahren oder geflogen?**
>Did you drive or fly to Cologne?

When the verb expresses something that has happened to people that is outside their control rather than something that people have done:

>**Sie ist 1934 geboren, 1992 erkrankt, und 1994 gestorben.**
>She was born in 1934, fell ill in 1992, and died in 1994.

>**Es ist passiert.**
>**Es ist geschehen.**
>**Es ist vorgekommen.**
>It happened.

(c) These guidelines offer a substantial aid to using **haben** and **sein** correctly. Note, however, the following:

>**Es ist mir gelungen.**
>I succeeded (it worked out for me).

but:

> **Es hat geklappt.**
> It worked out.

(**gelingen** is an impersonal verb: see **42.3h**A)

> **Ich bin ihm begegnet.**
> I met him (by chance).

but:

> **Ich habe ihn getroffen.**
> I met him (by chance or design).

There are a small number of verbs which are used with **sein** even though they are transitive verbs. Note especially **loswerden** 'to get rid of' and **durchgehen** 'to go through something':

> **Endlich** *bin* **ich ihn** *losgeworden*!
> At last I have got rid of him!

> **Er** *war* **die ganze Zeitung** *durchgegangen*.
> He had been through the whole newspaper.

Also, **haben** can be used with intransitive verbs of motion when the focus is on the general activity rather than on the specific question of where you went. Usage varies here:

> **Ich** *bin* **heute** *geschwommen*.
> **Ich** *habe* **heute** *geschwommen*.
> I had a swim today.

> **Ich** *bin* **in das kleine Becken** *geschwommen*.
> I swam into the small pool.

> **Ich** *habe* **im kleinen Becken** *geschwommen*.
> I swam in the small pool.

(d) As the previous example shows, some verbs can be used with both **haben** and **sein**, with a change in meaning:

> **Wir** *sind* **nach Köln** *gefahren*.
> We drove (travelled) to Cologne.

> **Sie** *hat* **den BMW** *gefahren*.
> She drove (has driven) the BMW.

> **Ich *bin* nach Oslo *geflogen*.**
> I flew (have flown) to Oslo.

> **Die Versicherungsfirma *hat* ihn nach London zurück*geflogen*.**
> The insurance company flew him back to London.

Some verbs have more than one meaning, and this is reflected in the use of **haben** and **sein**:

> **Ein Unfall *ist* gestern *passiert*.**
> An accident happened yesterday.

> **Wir *haben* den Zoll noch nicht *passiert*.**
> We haven't gone through customs yet.

Any two verbs sharing the same stem (e.g. **kommen** and **bekommen**) follow the same strong or weak pattern. But the use of **haben** or **sein** as auxiliary depends on the meaning:

> **Sie *ist* um halb acht *gekommen*.**
> She came at half past seven.

> **Sie *hat* meinen Brief *bekommen*.**
> She received my letter.

33.9 ## Principal parts of the verb

The principal parts of the verb which need to be learnt are thus:

(1)   the infinitive

(2)   the present tense third person singular (for those verbs which have a change in the stem in the present tense)

(3)   the simple past first/third person singular

(4)   **haben** or **sein** as auxiliary

(5)   the past participle

Most dictionaries list these for strong verbs, together with the Subjunctive II forms (see **39.2**A). For weak verbs, the forms are absolutely predictable:

1	2	3	4	5	
machen	**macht**	**machte**	**hat**	**gemacht**	'to make/do'
reisen	**reist**	**reiste**	**ist**	**gereist**	'to travel'
studieren	**studiert**	**studierte**	**hat**	**studiert**	'to study'

For mixed verbs, the change in the stem must be learnt:

1	2	3	4	5	
bringen	**bringt**	**brachte**	**hat**	**gebracht**	'to bring'
rennen	**rennt**	**rannte**	**ist**	**gerannt**	'to race'

Most attention should be given to strong verbs. Here is a partial list showing some important patterns of vowel change. Where there is no entry in column (2) this means that the present tense is regular.

1	2	3	4	5	
(a > ä > ie > a)					
schlafen	schläft	schlief	hat	geschlafen	'to sleep'
fallen	fällt	fiel	ist	gefallen	'to fall'
(a > ä > i > a)					
fangen	fängt	fing	hat	gefangen	'to catch'
(e > i > a > o)					
sprechen	spricht	sprach	hat	gesprochen	'to speak'
brechen	bricht	brach	hat	gebrochen	'to break'
helfen	hilft	half	hat	geholfen	'to help'
nehmen	nimmt	nahm	hat	genommen	'to take'
(e > i > a > e)					
geben	gibt	gab	hat	gegeben	'to give'
(ie > - > o > o)					
fliegen		flog	ist/hat	geflogen	'to fly'
bieten		bot	hat	geboten	'to offer'
schließen		schloß	hat	geschlossen	'to close'
(ei > - > ie > ie)					
bleiben		blieb	ist	geblieben	'to remain'
schreiben		schrieb	hat	geschrieben	'to write'
(ei > - > i > i)					
greifen		griff.	hat	gegriffen	'to grab'
schneiden		schnitt	hat	geschnitten	'to cut'
(i > - > a > u)					
singen		sang	hat	gesungen	'to sing'
gelingen		gelang	ist	gelungen	'to succeed' (see **36.2c**A)
(i > - > a > o)					
beginnen		begann	hat	begonnen	'to begin'
schwimmen		schwamm	ist/hat	geschwommen	'to swim'

Note especially the following common verbs which do not conform exactly to these patterns and should be learnt individually:

1	2	3	4	5	
sein	ist	war	ist	gewesen	'to be'
werden	wird	wurde	ist	geworden	'to become'
tun		tat	hat	getan	'to make/do'
gehen		ging	ist	gegangen	'to go'

kommen		kam	ist	gekommen	'to come'
laufen	läuft	lief	ist	gelaufen	'to run'
fahren	fährt	fuhr	ist/hat	gefahren	'to travel/drive'
sitzen		saß	hat	gesessen	'to sit'
liegen		lag	hat	gelegen	'to be lying'
stehen		stand	hat	gestanden	'to be standing'
heißen		hieß	hat	geheißen	'to be called'
essen	ißt	aß	hat	gegessen	'to eat'
saufen	säuft	soff	hat	gesoffen	'to drink alcohol'
stoßen	stößt	stieß	hat	gestoßen	'to strike/ bump into'
ziehen		zog	hat/ist	gezogen	'to move/pull'

34 *Use of tenses*

34.1 — German has only one form of the verb in each tense, unlike English. Compare:

> **Er findet es schwer**
> He finds it hard.
> He is finding it hard.
> He does find it hard.
> **Er fand es schwer.**
> He found it hard.
> He was finding it hard.
> He did find it hard.

34.2 — **Present tense**

(a) Describes events or states belonging in the present time:

> **Ich verstehe Ihre Frage nicht.**
> I do not understand your question.

(b) Describes eternal truths and scientific facts:

> **Die Zeit vergeht schnell.**
> Time passes quickly.

> **Öl schwimmt auf Wasser.**
> Oil floats/will float on water.

(c) Describes events in the near or foreseeable future (where the context makes the future reference obvious):

> **Ich finde es morgen.**
> I'll find it tomorrow.

(d) Describes events or states which started in the past but are still going on (note the use of **seit** + dative):

> **Sie ist seit zwei Jahren verlobt.**
> She has been engaged for two years.

34.3 **Future**

As well as expressing future time, the future often conveys a prediction, a statement of intent or desirability, or a supposition:

> **Wir werden gewinnen.**
> We are going to win.

> **Das wird (wohl) die Post sein.**
> That'll be the post.

34.4 **Future perfect**

(a) Expresses a completed action envisaged at a point in the future, often with an element of determination or desirability:

> **Vor meinem vierzigsten Jahr werde ich mein eigenes Haus gebaut haben.**
> Before I am forty I will have built my own house.

(b) Can also express supposition:

> **Er wird in die Kneipe gegangen sein.**
> He'll have gone to the pub (I suppose).

34.5 **Simple past (see also 34.7A)**

(a) Describes completed actions:

> **Sie spielten Tennis und dann fuhren sie in die Stadt.**
> They played tennis and then went into town.

(b) Describes incomplete or continuing actions and states in the past:

> **Er schrieb (gerade) den Brief, als ich anrief.**
> He was (just) writing the letter when I phoned.

(c) Describes actions and states which precede a focal point in the past:

> **Ich lernte ihn 1994 kennen. Er wohnte (schon) seit zwei Jahren in Berlin.**
> I got to know him in 1994. He had been living for two years in Berlin.

(d) Expresses habitual actions in the past:

> **Jeden Samstag machten wir eine Wanderung.**
> Every Saturday we went/used to go/would go for a walk.

34.6 Perfect

(a) Conveys individual or isolated actions in the past:

> **Sie sind nach München geflogen.**
> They flew/have flown to Munich.

(b) Often implies that the action in the past has some continuing relevance to the present situation:

> **Das haben wir erst gestern erfahren.**
> We only just found that out yesterday.

> **Die Wiedervereinigung hat schwere Folgen für die deutsche Wirtschaft gehabt.**
> Reunification has had serious consequences for the German economy.

(c) Can have future reference, referring to an event which will have been completed before another one begins:

> **Nachdem wir den Tisch abgeräumt haben, spülen wir ab/werden wir abspülen.**
> After we have cleared the table we will wash up.

> **Bis morgen habe ich es geschafft.**
> I will have done it by tomorrow.

34.7 Simple past or perfect?

(a) Often there is no distinction in meaning between these two tenses. Thus, **sie spielten Tennis** and **sie haben Tennis gespielt** can convey exactly the same sense.

(b) There is a tendency in northern Germany for the simple past to be the preferred past tense, whereas in southern Germany the perfect is preferred in spoken German.

(c) Where the focus is on the present result of an action, the perfect is used (as it is in English):

> **Die Gäste kamen an.**
> The guests arrived/were arriving.

Die Gäste sind angekommen.
The guests have arrived. (i.e. they are here now!)

Compare:

Sie schrieb gerade den Brief, als ich anrief.
She was (just) writing the letter when I phoned.

and:

Sie hat den Brief gerade geschrieben, als ich anrief.
She had just written the letter when I phoned.

(d) There may also be a tendency for the opening (and closing) statement in a narrative to be in the perfect, with the rest in the simple past:

Wir sind also einkaufen gegangen. Aber im ersten Geschäft hatten sie nur billige Sachen, und im nächsten war alles viel zu teuer. Da gingen wir zu Meyers in der Gartenstraße. . . Wir sind ja halb tot in den Zug gefallen.
So we went shopping. But in the first shop they only had cheap stuff, and in the next everything was much too dear. So we went to Meyers in the Gartenstraße. . . We fell into the train half dead.

34.8 · **Pluperfect**

Expresses an action or event that took place before another began:

Nachdem sie ein Glas Wein bekommen hatten, gingen sie in den Garten.
After they had received a glass of wine they went into the garden.

35 *Modal verbs*

35.1 · **Modal + infinitive**

A modal verb is one that combines with another verb to modify the statement:

Sie kommt morgen.
She is coming tomorrow.

Sie will morgen kommen.
She wants to come tomorrow.

German modal verbs combine with another verb in the infinitive:

Sie kann später kommen.
She can (is able to) come later.

Sie muß später kommen.
She must (has to) come later.

Sie will später kommen.
She wants to (intends to) come later.

Sie darf später kommen.
She can/is permitted to come later.

Sie mag später kommen.
She may (possibly) come later.

Sie soll später kommen.
She is expected to (is supposed to) come later.

Sie möchte später kommen.
She would like to come later.

Note also **lassen** 'have or make sb. do sth.':

Sie läßt ihn warten.
She makes him wait (has him wait).

Most of these verbs can also be used on their own, with an accusative object:

Ich *mag* diesen Herrn.
I like this gentleman.

In this case they are not functioning as modal verbs (see **35.3**A).

35.2   **Tense forms**

The present and simple past forms are as follows. Irregular forms are in italics:

könnnen		müssen		wollen	
Present					
kann	können	*muß*	müssen	*will*	wollen
kannst	könnt	*mußt*	müßt	*willst*	wollt
kann	können	*muß*	müssen	*will*	wollen
können	können	müssen	müssen	wollen	wollen
Past					
konnte	konnten	mußte	mußten	wollte	wollten
konntest	konntet	mußtest	mußtet	wolltest	wolltet
konnte	konnten	mußte	mußten	wollte	wollten
konnten	konnten	mußten	mußten	wollten	wollten
dürfen		mögen		sollen	
Present					
darf	dürfen	*mag*	mögen	*soll*	sollen
darfst	dürft	*magst*	mögt	*sollst*	sollt
darf	dürfen	*mag*	mögen	*soll*	sollen
dürfen	dürfen	mögen	mögen	sollen	sollen

Past

durfte	durften	mochte	mochten	sollte	sollten
durftest	durftet	mochtest	mochtet	solltest	solltet
durfte	durften	mochte	mochten	sollte	sollten
durften	durften	mochten	mochten	sollten	sollten
lassen		möchten			

Present

lasse	lassen	möchte	möchten
läßt	laßt	möchtest	möchtet
läßt	lassen	möchte	möchten
lassen	lassen	möchten	möchten

Past

ließ	ließen	No past tense
ließt	ließt	
ließ	ließen	
ließen	ließen	

35.3 | **Past participle of modal verbs**

(a) The past participle form of these modal verbs is identical to the infinitive, and the auxiliary is **haben**. Note the distinctive pattern:

> **Er *hat* später kommen *wollen.***
> He wanted to come later.

> **Ich *habe* später kommen *sollen.***
> I was supposed to come later.

(See **8.6**A for the word order in subordinate clauses)

(b) However, when used as full verbs in their own right (i.e. with an accusative object, not with another verb), they have a different set of past participles:

gekonnt	gemußt	gewollt	
gedurft	gemocht	gesollt	gelassen

> **Ich kann nicht Französisch.**
> I can't speak French.

> **Ich habe Französisch nicht *gekonnt.***
> I couldn't speak French.

> **Ich mag ihn sehr.**
> I like him a lot.

> **Ich habe ihn sehr *gemocht.***
> I liked him a lot.

> **Ich will das Geld nicht.**
> I don't want the money.

> **Ich habe das Geld nicht** *gewollt.*
> I didn't want the money.

> **Ich lasse den Scheck auf dem Tisch.**
> I'm leaving the cheque on the table.

> **Ich habe den Scheck auf dem Tisch** *gelassen.*
> I (have) left the cheque on the table.

35.4 **Word order of modal verbs**

For the word order used in modal constructions see **5.2e**A and **5.4**A.

35.5 **Omitting the infinitive**

Note the tendency for the infinitive to be omitted when the meaning is obvious from the context:

> **Nächste Woche muß ich nach Köln.**
> Next week I have to go to Cologne.

> **Ich kann ein bißchen Spanisch.**
> I can speak a little Spanish.

35.6 **Meanings of the modal verbs**

The modal verbs have a range of general and special meanings:

(a) The general meanings are:

> **können** 'to be able to/have the ability to'
> **müssen** 'to have to/be obliged to'
> **wollen** 'to intend to/want to'
> **dürfen** 'to be allowed/permitted to'
> **mögen** 'to like to'

> N.B. The use of **mögen** as a modal is actually quite rare in this meaning; other constructions such as **gern(e) machen** are much more common: **Ich gehe gern(e) nach Paris** 'I like going to Paris'.

> **sollen** 'to be expected to/thought to/believed to'

N.B. This verb expresses other people's anticipation or expectation.

lassen 'to allow/cause something to happen or someone to do something'
möchten 'would like to'

N.B. This is actually a Subjunctive II form (see **39.2**A) of **mögen**, and is a common polite alternative to **wollen**.

(b) In addition to their main meanings, the following idiomatic meanings should be noted:

können often covers the meaning of **dürfen**:

> **Kann ich morgen zum Fußballspiel?**
> Can/May I go to the football match tomorrow?

or it can express supposition:

> **Das kann die Antwort sein.**
> That may be the answer.

müssen with a negative (**nicht, kein**) means 'doesn't have to':

> **Das müssen Sie nicht sagen.**
> You don't have to say that.

müssen can express an assumption or a deduction:

> **Er muß schon gegessen haben.**
> He must already have eaten.

> **Er muß schon gegangen sein.**
> He must already have gone.

wollen in a question can express an invitation or suggestion:

> **Wollen wir ins Kino gehen?**
> Let's go to the cinema.

wollen can express the meaning 'claims to':

> **Sie will mich gestern am Strand gesehen haben.**
> She claims to have seen me yesterday on the beach.

dürfen with a negative (**nicht, kein**) means 'must not/not allowed to':

> **Das dürfen Sie nicht sagen – ich darf kein Bier trinken.**
> You mustn't say that – I can't (am not allowed to) drink beer.

mögen more often means 'may' or 'might':

> **Das mag (wohl) wahr sein.**

That may (well) be true.

sollen always expresses the idea of an expectation or belief on the part of someone else. There are various English translations:

> **Er soll hereinkommen!**
> Tell him to come in.

> **Sie soll eine Ferienwohnung in Italien haben.**
> They say she has a holiday flat in Italy.

The simple past, **sollte**, is either a past tense of the main meaning or expresses the idea 'ought to, but doesn't'. In this sense it often occurs with **eigentlich**:

> **Diese neuen Maschinen sollten eigentlich keine Wartung brauchen.**
> These new machines shouldn't really need servicing (but they do).

Another use of **sollte** expresses surprise or reservation:

> **Sollte das wahr sein?**
> Can this be true?

lassen is quite common with reflexive constructions (see **37**A):

> **Ich lasse mich sehen.**
> I let myself be seen.

> **Er läßt sich nicht beraten.**
> He won't take advice.

> **Das läßt sich nicht machen.**
> That can't be done.

> **Ließe sich das machen?**
> Could that be done?

(See **39.3d**A for the Subjunctive II forms of modal verbs)

35.7

muß + negative and *darf* + negative

As noted above (**35.6b**A), these have meanings which are easily confused by English speakers: 'must' is rendered by **müssen**, 'must not' by **nicht dürfen**, while **nicht müssen** means 'does not have to':

> **Sie darf kein Darlehen aufnehmen.**
> She must not/is not allowed to take out a loan.

> **Sie muß kein Darlehen aufnehmen.**
> She doesn't have to take out a loan. (But she can if she wants.)

Note that an alternative to **nicht müssen** is **nicht brauchen zu** + infinitive ('does not need to'):

> Sie *braucht* das Darlehen *nicht* zurückzuzahlen.
> She doesn't need to repay the loan.

36 *Separable and inseparable verbs*

36.1

Verbs with a separable prefix

Separable verbs consist of a verb and a verbal prefix, e.g. **ab*fahren** 'to drive off'. The prefix is typically, but not always, a preposition.

(a) The meaning of a separable verb is often obvious from the meaning of its parts (see **57**A):

> **fahren** 'to drive/travel'
> **ab*fahren** 'to drive off/depart'

but the meaning of many separable verbs is not transparent:

> **fangen** 'to catch'
> **an*fangen** 'to begin'

(b) It is possible to hear when a verb is separable because the stress is always on the separable prefix, i.e. *ab****fahren**, *an****fangen**.

(c) The verbal prefix separates from the rest of the verb in the present tense and the simple past (see **5.5**A):

> **Die Vorstellung** *fängt* **um halb acht** *an.*
> The performance begins at half past seven.

> **Die Vorstellung** *fing* **um halb acht** *an.*
> The performance began at half past seven.

and in infinitive constructions with **zu** (see also **42.3f**A and **8.7**A for word order):

> **Es ist nötig, mit der Vorstellung sofort** *anzufangen.*
> It is necessary to begin the performance straight away.

In the past participle the two parts of the verb are separated by **-ge-** (written as one word):

> **Die Vorstellung hat um halb acht** *angefangen.*
> The performance began at half past seven.

(See also **8.7b**A on word order.)

(d) Common verbal prefixes which are always separable include: **ab-**, **an-**, **auf-**, **aus-**, **ein-**, **fern-**, **mit-**, **nach-**, **vor-**, **weg-**, **zu-**, **zurück-**, **zusammen-** (see **57**A for a list of their meanings):

> **Der Zug ist *abgefahren*.**
> The train has departed.

> ***Rufen* Sie mich bitte *an*.**
> Please ring me.

> **Sie *nimmt* das Konzert auf Kassette *auf*.**
> She is recording the concert on cassette.

> **Vergessen Sie nicht, auch die Benzinkosten *einzukalkulieren*.**
> Don't forget to include the cost of the petrol as well.

> **Ich *sehe* kaum noch *fern*.**
> I hardly watch TV any more.

> ***Machen* Sie *mit*, wenn Sie wollen.**
> Join in if you want.

> **Ich brauche mehr Zeit, um die Details *nachzuschlagen*.**
> I need more time to look up the details.

> **Heute *habe* ich etwas Besonderes *vor*.**
> Today I've got something special planned.

> ***Werfen* Sie die Verpackung bitte nicht *weg*!**
> Please don't throw the packaging away.

> **Die Banken *machen* um zwölf *zu*.**
> The banks close at twelve.

> **Er *kommt* in einer Stunde *zurück*.**
> He is coming back in an hour.

> **Wir haben unser ganzes Geld *zusammengelegt*.**
> We pooled all our money.

Virtually any preposition can become a verbal prefix and will be separable if the literal meaning of the preposition features in the meaning of the verb as a whole. For example, **entgegen** means 'in the opposite direction' and **entgegenkommen** is a separable verb meaning 'to come towards':

> **Sie ist mir *entgegengekommen*.**
> She came towards me.

(e) Some separable verbs obviously began as verb + noun combinations:

> **Die Konferenz *findet* in Buenos Aires *statt*.**
> The conference is taking place in Buenos Aires.

Note also the tendency for some verb + noun combinations to behave like separable verbs in some respects:

> **Der Teppich *fängt* bald *Feuer*.**
> The carpet will catch fire soon.

> **Ich *fahre* jeden Tag *Auto*.**
> I drive (a car) every day.

However, these phrases are always written as two distinct words:

Er fängt Feuer.	**Sie fährt Auto.**
It catches fire	She drives.
Er fing Feuer.	**Sie fuhr Auto.**
It caught fire.	She drove.
Er hat Feuer gefangen.	**Sie ist Auto gefahren.**
It caught fire.	She has been driving/drove.
Er kann Feuer fangen.	**Sie kann Auto fahren.**
It can catch fire.	She can drive/go driving.
Er begann, Feuer zu fangen.	**Sie begann, Auto zu fahren.**
It began to catch fire.	She began to drive.

36.2 Verbs with an inseparable prefix

Some verbal prefixes are always inseparable, i.e. they always form a single word with the verb to which they are attached.

(a) It is possible to hear when a verb is inseparable because the stress is typically on the main verb (not on the prefix), i.e. be*steh*en, ge*nieß*en.

(b) The past participle is without **ge-**, and in infinitive constructions with **zu**, the **zu** comes before the verb:

> **Er *bestand* das Examen.**
> He passed the exam.

> **Er hat das Examen *bestanden*.**
> He passed/has passed the exam.

> **Man kommt nicht weiter, ohne das Examen *zu bestehen*.**
> One doesn't progress any further without passing the exam.

(See **42.3f**A for verb completion by an infinitive clause with **zu**; see also **8.7**A for word order)

(c) The inseparable prefixes are **be-**, **emp-**, **ent-**, **er-**, **ge-**, **miß-**, **ver-**, **zer-**:

beschreiben 'to describe'

>> **Er hat dich sehr genau *beschrieben*.**
>> He described you exactly.

empfinden 'to feel/sense'

>> **Ich habe das als unfair *empfunden*.**
>> I felt that was unfair.

entlasten 'to relieve/lighten the burden'

>> **Ist es möglich, mich ein bißchen *zu entlasten*?**
>> Is it possible to lighten my load a little?

erfüllen 'to fulfil'

>> **Sie haben den Vertrag nicht *erfüllt*.**
>> You have not fulfilled the contract.

genießen 'to enjoy/have the benefit of'

>> **Sie hat die Ferien in Irland *genossen*.**
>> She enjoyed the holidays in Ireland.

mißlingen 'to go wrong'

>> **Es *mißlingt* mir. (Es ist mir *mißlungen*.)**
>> It's going wrong (it went wrong) for me.

verstehen 'to understand'

>> **Ich habe alles ganz gut *verstanden*.**
>> I understood everything very well.

zerschlagen 'to smash (to pieces)'

>> **Der Junge *zerschlug* das Fenster und rannte davon.**
>> The boy broke the window and ran off.

Some verbs have a 'double-prefix', and where the first prefix is inseparable, the verb as a whole is inseparable:

>> **Sie *beanspruchen* Kindergeld.**
>> They are making a claim for child allowance.

> **Er *vernachlässigt* seine Frau.**
> He neglects his wife.

(d) Note however that **mißverstehen** 'misunderstand' is basically inseparable, but has the stress on the prefix and has **zu** inside the infinitive:

> **Sie mißverstehen mich.**
> You misunderstand me.

> **Sie haben mich mißverstanden.**
> You have misunderstood me.

> **Es ist unmöglich, diese Warnung *mißzuverstehen*.**
> It is impossible to misunderstand this warning.

Note that the verb **anerkennen** 'to recognize/acknowledge' is used both as a separable verb and (less commonly) as an inseparable verb:

> **Ich erkenne das als richtig an.**
> **Ich anerkenne das als richtig.**
> I acknowledge that as right.

36.3 Verbs with a variable prefix

(a) A few verbal prefixes can be separable or inseparable: **durch-, über-, um-, unter-, voll-, wider-**.

(b) Where the same verb + prefix combination can be both separable and inseparable, there is a subtle distinction in meaning. Usually, the separable verb retains the literal meaning of the preposition, while the inseparable verb contains an extended or figurative meaning:

um*gehen 'to circulate/go round'

> **Diese Gerüchte *gehen* seit Monaten *um*.**
> These rumours have been going around for months.

umgehen 'to circumvent/avoid'

> **Die neue Straße *umgeht* das Dorf.**
> The new road avoids the village.

> **Diese neue Verkaufsmethode hat das Gesetz *umgangen*.**
> This new sales method has got round the law.

um*schreiben 'to rewrite/change'

> **Es ist jetzt nötig, das Dokument *umzuschreiben*.**
> It is now necessary to rewrite the document.

umschreiben 'to paraphrase'

> **Es ist jetzt nötig, das Dokument kurz *zu umschreiben.***
> It is now necessary to paraphrase the document briefly.

(c) Note how separable verbs often repeat the preposition elsewhere in the sentence or add **hin-** or **her-** to the preposition to give it a clear directional meaning:

durch*schauen 'to look through'

> **Ich habe durch das Fernglas *durchgeschaut.***
> I looked through the binoculars.

durchschauen 'to see through' (not be fooled)

> **Ich habe ihn sofort *durchschaut.***
> I saw through him straight away.

über*fahren 'to travel/drive across'

> **Wir sind nach Frankreich *hinübergefahren.***
> We crossed over into France.

> **Mein Bruder war bereit, mich *hinüberzufahren.***
> My brother was prepared to drive me over there.

überfahren 'to run (someone) over'

> **Wir sind durch Paris gefahren, ohne jemanden *zu überfahren.***
> We drove through Paris without running anyone over.

(d) Other verbs to note include:

Inseparable:

> **übersetzen** 'to translate'
> **überbieten** 'to outbid/go one better than'
> **überfordern** 'to overwork/ask too much of'
> **überschätzen** 'to overestimate'
> **übertreiben** 'to exaggerate'
> **unterbieten** 'to bid less'
> **unterfordern** 'to underwork/ask too little of'
> **unterschätzen** 'to underestimate'
> **untertreiben** 'to understate'
> **umreißen** 'to outline'
> **widersprechen** 'to contradict'
> **widerstehen** 'to resist'

widerstreben 'to oppose/go against'
wiederholen 'to repeat' (this is the only inseparable verb beginning with **wieder-** 'again')

Separable:

um*reißen 'to pull down (buildings)'
unter*bringen 'to accommodate/find a place for'
wider*spiegeln 'to reflect/mirror'
wider*hallen 'to echo' (the latter are the only two separable verbs beginning with **wider-** 'against')

37 *Reflexive verbs*

37.1 These are verbs with a reflexive object, i.e. an object which refers back to the subject of the verb:

> **Ich wasche mich.**
> I wash (myself).

However, not all German reflexives can be translated by 'myself', 'yourself', etc.

37.2 The reflexive pronoun has an accusative and a dative form:

Subject	Reflexive	
	Accusative	Dative
ich	**mich**	**mir**
du	**dich**	**dir**
er/sie/es	**sich**	**sich**
Sie	**sich**	**sich**
wir	**uns**	**uns**
ihr	**euch**	**euch**
sie	**sich**	**sich**
Sie	**sich**	**sich**

37.3 Most verbs which can be used reflexively can also be used as normal transitive verbs. Note the following patterns:

(a) **Er rasiert *sich.***
He shaves (himself).

but also:

Er rasiert *mich.*
He shaves me.

Er rasiert *dich.*
He shaves you.

Er rasiert *ihn.*
He shaves him (i.e. another person).

The basic pattern here is subject + reflexive verb with the reflexive pronoun in the accusative.

(b)   **Sie stellt *sich* das neue Büro vor.**
             She imagines the new office.

but also:

Sie stellt *mir* das neue Büro vor.
She shows the new office to me.

Sie stellt *dir* das neue Büro vor.
She shows the new office to you.

Sie stellt *ihr* das neue Büro vor.
She shows the new office to her.

The basic pattern here is subject + reflexive verb with the reflexive pronoun in the dative + accusative object. **Sich** (dat) **etwas** (acc) **vor*stellen** literally means 'to place sth. in front of oneself.'

(c)   **Sie hat *sich* einen Computer gekauft.**
             She (has) bought (herself) a computer.

but also (see **19.2**A):

Sie hat *mir* einen Computer gekauft.
She (has) bought me a computer.

Sie hat *dir* einen Computer gekauft.
She (has) bought you a computer.

Sie hat *ihnen* einen Computer gekauft.
She (has) bought them a computer.

The basic pattern here is subject + verb + accusative object + reflexive pronoun in the dative which explicitly shows the recipient or beneficiary of the action. The dative pronouns could be left out of these sentences: **Sie hat einen Computer gekauft** 'She (has) bought a computer'.

37.4 The dative reflexive pronoun is used to express washing and cleaning oneself when a part of the body is mentioned:

> **Ich muß *mir* die Hände waschen.**
> I must wash my hands.

37.5 A number of verbs can only be used reflexively, i.e. they always have a reflexive pronoun.

(a) Most reflexive verbs have the reflexive pronoun in the accusative:

sich befinden 'to be situated'

> **Die britische Botschaft befindet sich jetzt in Berlin.**
> The British embassy is now in Berlin.

sich über etw. (acc) freuen 'to be pleased about'

> **Freust du dich über dein Weihnachtsgeschenk?**
> Are you pleased with your Christmas present?

sich auf etw. (acc) freuen 'to look forward to'

> **Freust du dich auf dein Weihnachtsgeschenk?**
> Are you looking forward to your Christmas present?

sich ereignen 'to happen' (this is always used in the third person)

> **In der Nacht hat sich ein Flugzeugunglück ereignet.**
> There was a plane crash in the night.

sich um etw. bewerben 'to apply for sth.'

> **Ich bewerbe mich um die Stelle.**
> I am applying for the job.

sich um etw. oder jmdn. drehen 'to revolve around sth. or sb.'

> **Alles dreht sich um das Geld.**
> Money is at the centre of everything.

sich nach etw. oder jmdm. erkundigen 'to enquire about sth. or sb.'

> **Sie erkundigt sich nach dir.**
> She is asking after you.

sich vor etw. oder jmdm. fürchten 'to be afraid of sth. or sb.'

> **Fürchten Sie sich vor ihm?**
> Are you afraid of him?

sich in jmdn. verlieben 'to fall in love with sb.'

> **Sie hat sich in ihn verliebt.**
> She has fallen in love with him.

sich irren 'to be mistaken'

> **Ich irre mich.**
> I am mistaken.

sich mit jmdm. über etw. (acc) **unterhalten** 'to have a conversation with sb. about sth.'

> **Er hat sich mit mir über das Wetter unterhalten.**
> He talked to me about the weather.

> ALSO **Wir haben uns über das Wetter unterhalten.**
> We talked about the weather.

(b) Verbs with the reflexive pronoun in the dative include:

sich etw. (acc) **ein*bilden** 'to imagine wrongly'

> **Du hast dir diese Krankheit eingebildet.**
> You have imagined this illness.

sich etw. (acc) **überlegen** 'to reflect on sth./think it over'

> **Ich überlege mir dieses Angebot.**
> I am considering this offer.

(c) Note also the impersonal reflexive:

es handelt sich um etw. oder jmdn. 'it concerns sb. or sth./it is a matter of sth.'

> **Es handelt sich hier um ein dringendes Problem.**
> This is an urgent problem.

38 *Prepositional verbs*

38.1

A large number of verbs are linked idiomatically to a particular preposition, i.e. are always used with the same preposition. For example, **glauben an** 'believe in', **warten auf** 'wait for'. Some verbs can be used with more than one preposition, with a change in meaning (e.g. **bestehen auf** 'to insist on', **bestehen aus** 'to consist of'). German prepositional verbs need to be learnt as a unit: verb + preposition + case. Some common prepositional verbs are listed below according to the preposition they take and the case governed by the preposition:

an (+ acc)

> **glauben an** 'to believe in'
> **denken an** 'to think of/about'
> **erinnern an** 'to remind sb. of/about'
> **sich erinnern an** 'to remember'
> **(sich) gewöhnen an** 'to get used to'
>
> **Wir haben an dich gedacht.**
> We were thinking of you.

an (+ dat)

> **liegen an** 'to be because of/be the reason for'
> **teil*nehmen an** 'to participate in'
>
> **Es lag an mir, daß er nicht gekommen ist.**
> It was because of me/my fault that he didn't come.

auf (+ acc)

> **reagieren auf** 'to react to'
> **warten auf** 'to wait for'
> **verzichten auf** 'to go without'
> **an*kommen auf** 'to depend on'
> **sich freuen auf** 'to look forward to'
>
> **Wie haben sie auf die Nachricht reagiert?**
> How did they react to the news?

auf (+ dat)

> **bestehen auf** 'to insist on'
> **beruhen auf** 'to rest on/be built on'
>
> **Sie hat auf ihrem Recht bestanden.**
> She insisted on her rights.

aus (+ dat)

> **bestehen aus** 'to consist of'
>
> **Unser Team besteht aus einer Frau und zwei Männern.**
> Our team consists of one woman and two men.

für (+ acc)

> **sich interessieren für** 'to be interested in'
> **jmdm. danken für** 'to thank sb. for'
>
> **Ich interessiere mich sehr für die Musik der zwanziger Jahre.**
> I am very interested in the music of the twenties.

in (+ acc)

> **sich verlieben in** 'to fall in love with'
>
> **Er hat sich sofort in sie verliebt.**
> He fell in love with her straight away.

mit (+ dat)

> **rechnen mit** 'to reckon with'
> **sprechen mit** 'to talk to/with'
> **beginnen mit** 'to begin (with)'
> **an*fangen mit** 'to begin (with)'
> **auf*hören mit** 'to stop'
> **(sich) beschäftigen mit** 'to occupy oneself with/work on'
> **sich befassen mit** 'to work on'
>
> **Ab Mai müssen Sie mit einem höheren Preis rechnen.**
> From May you have to reckon with a higher price.

nach (+ dat)

> **fragen nach** 'to enquire after/about'
> **sich erkundigen nach** 'to enquire about'
> **riechen nach** 'to smell of'
> **schmecken nach** 'to taste of'
>
> **Meine Frau fragt nach Ihrer Mutter.**
> My wife asks after your mother.

über (+ acc)

> **reden über** 'to talk about'
> **sprechen über** 'to talk about'
> **nach*denken über** 'to think about/reflect on'
> **streiten über** 'to argue about'
> **jmdn. informieren über** 'to inform sb. about'
> **sich freuen über** 'to be pleased about'
>
> **Ich möchte über dieses Problem ein bißchen nachdenken.**
> I would like to think over this problem for a while.

um (+ acc)

> **kämpfen um** 'to fight for'
> **werben um** 'to try to recruit/persuade/win over'
> **sich bewerben um** 'to apply for'
> **jmdn. bitten um** 'to ask sb. for'
> **jmdn. bringen um** 'to deprive sb. of'

Er hat sich um die Stelle in Aachen beworben.
He has applied for the job in Aachen.

von (+ dat)

reden von 'to talk of/about'
sprechen von 'to talk of/about'
träumen von 'to dream of/about'
ab*hängen von 'to depend on'
jmdn. überzeugen von 'to convince sb. of'

Das Picknick hängt natürlich von dem Wetter ab.
The picnic depends on the weather, of course.

vor (+ dat)

jmdn. warnen vor 'to warn sb. about'
jmdn. retten vor 'to save/rescue sb. from'
jmdn. schützen vor 'to protect sb. from'
Angst haben vor 'to be afraid of'

Die Wettervorhersage warnt vor einem Unwetter morgen.
The weather forecast is warning of a storm tomorrow.

zu (+ dat)

gehören zu 'to belong to/be part of'
passen zu 'to go with/match'
etw. (acc) bei*tragen zu 'to contribute to'

Deutschland trägt eine Menge zur Europäischen Union bei.
Germany contributes a lot to the European Union.

38.2

da + preposition

The preposition in prepositional verbs is often found in a form beginning **da-**: **daran, darauf, daraus, dafür, darin, damit, danach, davon, davor, darüber, darum, dazu,** etc.

The preposition is preceded by **da-** or **dar-** (see **50.6**A) when:

(a) the prepositional verb is completed by a clause:

Sie hat mich *davor* gewarnt, *daß die Preise hier höher sind.*
Daß die Preise hier höher sind, *davor* hat sie mich gewarnt.
She warned me that the prices here are higher.

(See **42.3e**A for this construction)

(b) the prepositional verb refers back to the meaning of a previous clause:

Wir brauchen einen Urlaub. **Du hast mich** *davon* **überzeugt.**
We need a holiday. You've convinced me of it.

39 *The subjunctive*

Overview

(a) German has two subjunctive forms of the verb (called Subjunctive I and Subjunctive II) which are used to describe actions or states which might happen or which are reported to have happened.

(b) The subjunctive forms are used in the following contexts:

> Subjunctive I is used most often in reported speech.
> Subjunctive II is used in conditional sentences. It can also substitute for Subjunctive I in reported speech.

Subjunctive II is more frequent, so it will be described first (see **39.2–3**A).

(c) Each subjunctive has a present and a past tense. For example, the third person singular forms of **sein** and **haben** are:

Subjunctive I	Present	**sei**	**habe**
Subjunctive I	Past	**sei gewesen**	**habe gehabt**
Subjunctive II	Present	**wäre**	**hätte**
Subjunctive II	Past	**wäre gewesen**	**hätte gehabt**

In the subjunctive there is only one past tense, i.e. there is no distinction between simple past and perfect (see **34.7**A). There is no future tense and reference to future events is made using the present tense.

(d) The Subjunctive II forms are based on the simple past of the verb. The Subjunctive I forms are based on the infinitive. It is important to realize that Subjunctive II (e.g. **hätte**) is NOT the past tense of Subjunctive I (e.g. **habe**).

(e) In addition, the use of **würde** + infinitive, with the sense 'would do (if)', is widespread (see **39.7**A). **Würde** is actually a Subjunctive II form of **werden**:

> **Ich würde nach Hause gehen und schlafen.**
> I would go home and sleep.

Use of Subjunctive II

(a) The main use of this form of the verb is to express hypothetical or conditional actions or states. Note that the present tense forms can and often do refer to future states and actions:

Es *wäre* schön, wenn wir morgen zusammen fahren könnten.

It *would be* nice if we could travel together tomorrow.

Ich *hätte* morgen mehr Zeit, mit dir zu essen.

I *would have* more time tomorrow to eat with you.

(b) Subjunctive II is also used to soften the directness of a question or a suggestion out of politeness:

Ich *hätte* eine Frage...

I'*d like to* ask a question if I may...

Ich *möchte* noch ein Stück Kuchen.

I *would like* another piece of cake.

39.3 Formation of Subjunctive II

(a) The present tense of the second subjunctive is formed from the simple past by adding **-e** to the simple past **ich/er/sie/es** form. Strong and irregular verbs also add an umlaut where possible:

war > **wäre** 'would be'
hatte > **hätte** 'would have'
ging > **ginge** 'would go'

The second subjunctive forms of most weak verbs are indistinguishable from the normal past tense forms:

machte 'would do'
arbeitete 'would work'
übte 'would practise'

One mixed verb, however, can add an umlaut:

bräuchte 'would need'

(b) The past tense of Subjunctive II is a combination of **wäre** or **hätte** + the past participle (depending on whether the verb takes **sein** or **haben** in the perfect: see **33.8**A):

Infinitive	Subjunctive II	
	Present	Past
sein	**wäre**	**wäre gewesen**
haben	**hätte**	**hätte gehabt**
werden	**würde**	**wäre geworden**
gehen	**ginge**	**wäre gegangen**
geben	**gäbe**	**hätte gegeben**

With a past participle, the meaning is 'would have been', 'would have had', 'would have become', 'would have gone', 'would have given', etc.:

> **Es wäre schön gewesen.**
> It would have been nice.
>
> **Ich hätte mehr Zeit gehabt.**
> I would have had more time.

(c) The forms of **sein** and **haben** are as follows:

Present

wäre	**wären**	**hätte**	**hätten**
wär(e)st	**wär(e)t**	**hättest**	**hättet**
wäre	**wären**	**hätte**	**hätten**
wären	**wären**	**hätten**	**hätten**

English: 'would be (were)/would have'

Past

wäre gewesen (etc.)	**hätte gehabt** (etc.)

English: 'would have been/would have had'

(d) The modal verbs have the following Subjunctive II forms:

können	**könnte**	**hätte... können**
müssen	**müßte**	**hätte... müssen**
wollen	**wollte**	**hätte... wollen**
sollen	**sollte**	**hätte... sollen**
dürfen	**dürfte**	**hätte... dürfen**
mögen	**möchte**	**hätte... mögen**
lassen	**ließe**	**hätte... lassen**

Some of these forms carry special meanings. They are widely used as polite or tactful forms when making requests. Note the following:

könnte 'would be able to'

> **Könnten Sie bitte lauter sprechen?**
> Could you please speak louder?
>
> **Das könnte die Antwort sein.**
> That could be the answer.

müßte 'would have to'

> **Wenn ich keine Reiseschecks hätte, müßte ich jetzt auf die Bank.**
> If I didn't have traveller's cheques I would have to go to the bank now.

> **Das müßte die Antwort sein.**
> That must be (would have to be) the answer.

dürfte 'would be allowed to/is probably'

> **Wenn du älter wärst, dürftest du mit den anderen spielen.**
> If you were older you could play with the others.

> **Das dürfte die Antwort sein.**
> That could well be (probably is) the answer.

sollte 'ought to' (often used with **eigentlich** to suggest that something has not happened which should have happened, or vice versa)

> **Er sollte eigentlich schon hier sein.**
> He really should be here by now (but he isn't).

> **Er sollte eigentlich nicht hier sein.**
> He really shouldn't be here (but he is).

möchte 'would like to'

> **Ich möchte heute im Restaurant zu Mittag essen.**
> I would like to have lunch in a restaurant today.

wollte 'wanted to' (often implying an intention that now looks unlikely to be fulfilled; also often used with **eigentlich** in this sense)

> **Ich wollte eigentlich heute abend ins Kino gehen.**
> I wanted to go to the cinema this evening.

39.4 — ## Use of Subjunctive I

(a) The main use is to characterize a stretch of speech as a report, i.e. not necessarily voicing the speaker's own words or opinions:

> **Er sagte, er *habe* jetzt keine Zeit.**
> He said he had no time right now.

But in fact, both Subjunctive I and Subjunctive II are used for this purpose.

(b) Subjunctive I is also used in expressions with the sense of 'let it be so':

> **Es *lebe* die neue Demokratie!**
> Long live the new democracy!

> **ABC *sei* ein gleichschenkliges Dreieck.**
> Let ABC be an isosceles triangle.

39.5 **Formation of Subjunctive I**

(a) The present tense of Subjunctive I is formed from the infinitive by removing the final -**n** to obtain the **er/sie/es** form:

er sei   **sie habe**   **es gehe**

Subjunctive I is rarely used outside the **er/sie/es** form, and there are usually no clear Subjunctive I forms in other persons of the verb (e.g. in the **wir** or the third person plural **sie** forms). Where Subjunctive I forms are not clearly recognizable, the appropriate Subjunctive II is used instead: **er habe** (Subjunctive I) but **wir hätten** (Subjunctive II) etc.

Indeed, some speakers tend to favour Subjunctive II as the preferred form for much reported speech, so usage varies considerably. Learners should certainly know the Subjunctive I forms but should listen carefully to German speakers to find out whether and to what extent native speakers are using Subjunctive I. The best advice is probably to follow the usage of the native speaker you are talking to.

(b) The past tense of Subjunctive I is a combination of **sei** or **habe** + the past participle (depending on whether the verb takes **sein** or **haben** in the Perfect: see **33.8**A):

sei gewesen   **habe gehabt**   **sei gegangen**

(c) The forms of **sein** and **haben** are as follows:

Present

sei	**seien**	**habe**	**haben**
seiest	**seid**	**habest**	**habet**
sei	**seien**	**habe**	**haben**
seien	**seien**	**haben**	**haben**

Past

sei gewesen (etc.)   **habe gehabt** (etc.)

(d) The Subjunctive I forms of the modal verbs are:

Present: **könne, müsse, wolle, solle, dürfe, möge, lasse:**

> **Sie meinte, sie *wolle* und *könne* diese Rolle im Stück spielen.**
> She said she wanted to and was able to act this part in the play.

Past: **habe** + infinitive of verb + **können, müssen, wollen**, etc.

> **Sie sagte, sie *habe* diese Rolle immer spielen *wollen.***
> She said she had always wanted to act this part.

(See **35.3a**A for the perfect tense forms of modal verbs; and **8.6**A for the word order in subordinate clauses)

39.6 — **Reported speech**

(a) Subjunctive I keeps the tense of the original words which are being reported. German differs from English here. In English, the tense of the reported verb is influenced by the tense of the introductory verb:

Original words	I am the mayor of this town
Report	He *says* he *is* the mayor of this town.
	He *said* he *was* the mayor of this town
Original words	I was (have been) the mayor of this town.
Report	He *says* he *was* the mayor of this town.
	He *said* he *had been* the mayor of this town.

German keeps the tense of the original but shifts the form of the verb into Subjunctive I:

Original words	**Ich bin hier der Bürgermeister.**
Report	**Er *sagt*, er *sei* hier der Bürgermeister.**
	Er *sagte*, er *sei* hier der Bürgermeister.
Original words	**Ich bin hier der Bürgermeister gewesen/war hier der Bürgermeister.**
Report	**Er *sagt*, er *sei* hier der Bürgermeister *gewesen*.**
	Er *sagte*, er *sei* hier der Bürgermeister *gewesen*.

(b) Where German speakers use both Subjunctive I and Subjunctive II for reported speech, the use of the second subjunctive usually implies a greater distance between the speaker and the truth of what is being reported, even an air of doubt and scepticism:

Actual words	**Ich habe keine Zeit.**
Neutral report	**Er *sagte*, er *habe* keine Zeit.**
Report with possible doubt	**Er *sagte*, er *hätte* keine Zeit.**
	He said he didn't have any time.

39.7 — **Using *würde* + infinitive**
Würde + infinitive is a common alternative to Subjunctive II in conditional sentences.
(a) The forms of **würde** are:

würde	**würden**
würdest	**würdet**
würde	**würden**
würden	**würden**

(b) A combination of **würde** + infinitive is quite commonly used instead of a Subjunctive II form and has exactly the same meaning:

> **Ich *ginge* zur Party. = Ich *würde* zur Party *gehen.***
> I would go to the party.

This is especially so for some of the strong verbs which have irregular and unpredictable Subjunctive II forms:

Infinitive	Simple past	Subjunctive II	
helfen	**half**	**hülfe =**	**würde helfen**
stehen	**stand**	**stünde =**	**würde stehen**

The following common Subjunctive II forms are not normally replaced by **würde** + infinitive: the modal verbs, **wäre** 'would be', **hätte** 'would have', **es gäbe** 'there would be' (from **es gibt** 'there is, there are': see also **69.1**B). For other verbs, the Subjunctive II forms are about as common as **würde** + infinitive.

(c) The Subjunctive II forms of weak verbs (e.g. **arbeitete; verdiente**) are indistinguishable from ordinary simple past tenses. In a conditional sentence, at least one of the two verbs (either one) needs to be marked as a conditional and this is done using **würde** + infinitive. For this reason, the **würde** construction is widely used with weak verbs:

> **Wenn ich länger *arbeitete, würde* ich kaum mehr Geld *verdienen.***
> **Wenn ich länger *arbeiten würde, verdiente* ich kaum mehr Geld.**
> If I worked longer I would hardly earn any more money.

As long as one of the two verbs in this kind of 'if... then' construction is clearly marked as conditional, this is enough to show that the whole sentence is a conditional, and the other verb may appear in the (ambiguous) Subjunctive II form. However, the use of **würde** + infinitive in both halves of such a sentence is ungainly and tends to be avoided. Frequently, a modal verb in Subjunctive II is found here:

> **Wenn ich länger *arbeiten würde, könnte* ich kaum mehr Geld *verdienen.***
> If I worked longer I could hardly earn any more money.

(d) The **würde** construction is also widely used with strong verbs, since many German speakers are uncomfortable with the Subjunctive II forms of some verbs:

> **Wenn sie langsamer reden könnte, *verstünde* ich sie besser.**
> **Wenn sie langsamer reden könnte, *würde* ich sie besser *verstehen.***
> If she could talk more slowly I would understand her better.

(e) The **würde** construction is widely used when there are several main verbs in a sequence, some of which may be weak and some of which may be strong:

Wenn er jetzt käme, *würden* **wir Feierabend** *machen,* **ein Bier** *trinken,* **und ins Kino** *gehen.*

If he came now we would knock off work, have a beer, and go to the cinema.

40 The passive

40.1 Active and passive sentences

The subject of a passive construction is not the doer of the action but the object of the action:

Active:

> **Jeden Tag bauen wir zehn neue Häuser.**
> Every day we build ten new houses.

Passive:

> **Jeden Tag werden zehn neue Häuser (von uns) gebaut.**
> Every day ten new houses are built (by us).

In German, only transitive verbs which can have an accusative object (see **18.1**A and **18.8**A) can be used in this kind of passive sentence.

40.2 The passive with *werden*

(a) The most common passive construction uses **werden** as an auxiliary (where English uses the verb 'to be'). The forms of **werden** are given below. Note the special past participle **worden** which is used only for passive constructions:

Present		Simple past	
werde	werden	wurde	wurden
wirst	werdet	wurdest	wurdet
wird	werden	wurde	wurden
werden	werden	wurden	wurden

Perfect: **ist** + past participle + **worden**

> **Es** *ist gemacht worden.*
> It has been done.

Pluperfect: **war** + past participle + **worden**

> **Es** *war gemacht worden.*
> It had been done.

Structures

Future: **wird** + infinitive + **werden**

> **Es** *wird gemacht werden.*
> It will be done.

But see **34.2c**A for the common use of the present tense in obvious contexts:

> **Das** *wird* morgen *gemacht.*
> That will be done tomorrow.

Future Perfect: **wird** + past participle + **worden sein**

> **Es** *wird gemacht worden sein.*
> It will have been done.

(b) German can distinguish between the process of an action and the resulting state once the action has been completed. The **werden** passive focuses on the process:

> **Der Flug** *wurde* (von ihm) gebucht.
> The flight was (being) booked (by him).

> **Der Flug** *ist* (von ihm) gebucht *worden.*
> The flight was/has been booked (by him).

The focus here is on the act of booking the flight.

However, using **sein** + past participle focuses on the resulting state:

> **Der Flug** *ist* gebucht.
> The flight is booked.

The focus here is on the result of the action, the status of the flight. Note that here the past participle is really quite like an adjective. Compare:

> **Der Flug ist teuer.**
> The flight is expensive.

(c) Verbs with a dative or genitive object behave in a special way in the passive. An impersonal subject, **es**, is introduced. Note that **es** is singular (so that **werden** always appears in a singular form), and that **es** disappears when another word occupies first position in the sentence:

Active:

> **Sie haben ihm nicht geglaubt.**
> They didn't believe him.

Passive:

> **Es wurde ihm nicht geglaubt.**
> **Ihm wurde nicht geglaubt.**
> He was not believed.

> **Mir wurde gesagt, daß. . .**
> I was told that. . .

> **Ihr wurde der erste Preis verliehen.**
> She was awarded the first prize.

Verbs taking a genitive object are rare:

> **Wir haben der Opfer gedacht.**
> We commemorated the victims.

> **Es wurde der Opfer gedacht.**
> **Der Opfer wurde gedacht.**
> The victims were commemorated.

40.3 — *von* and *durch*

(a) The person who carries out the action can be expressed in a passive sentence using **von** 'by':

> **Meine Mutter hat den Flug gebucht.**
> My mother (has) booked the flight.

> **Der Flug wurde *von meiner Mutter* gebucht.**
> **Der Flug ist *von meiner Mutter* gebucht worden.**
> The flight was booked (has been booked) by my mother.

(b) **durch** is also used where English uses 'by', but tends to express an action as opposed to an agent:

> **Dieser Entschluß hat alles geändert.**
> This decision (has) changed everything.

> **Durch diesen Entschluß wurde alles geändert.**
> **Durch diesen Entschluß ist alles geändert worden.**
> Everything was (has been) changed by this decision.

(c) Note, however, that **durch** can be used when an action is performed by someone acting on someone else's instructions:

> **Der Tisch wurde *durch die Sekretärin* gebucht.**
> The table was booked by the secretary (i.e. acting for the boss).

Kuwait wurde *durch die alliierten Truppen* zurückerobert.
Kuwait was retaken by the allied troops.

41   Imperatives

41.1

The imperative forms of the verb are used to give direct commands or instructions to someone. The imperative has a formal and a familiar form corresponding to whether the correct form of address is **Sie** or **du** (plural **ihr**). The imperative forms of **sein** and **haben** are:

Sie form	**seien Sie!**	**haben Sie!**
du form of address	**sei!**	**hab!**
ihr form of address	**seid!**	**habt!**

Thus, **Sei ruhig!**, **Seid ruhig!**, and **Seien Sie bitte ruhig!** all mean 'Be quiet!'

41.2

The various imperatives are formed as follows. Note that in written German the exclamation mark is normal usage:

For the **Sie** form, invert subject and verb:

>   **Machen Sie das!**
>   Do that!

For the **ihr** form, use the normal present tense form on its own:

>   **Schlaft gut!**
>   Sleep well!

For the **du** form, take the -**(e)st** ending off the **du** form, present tense:

>   **Mach das!**
>   Do that!

However, note the following points about the imperative **du** form:

(a) Verbs which add an umlaut in the present tense for the **du** form (see **33.7c**A) lose it in the imperative:

>   **Du schläfst**
>   You are sleeping.

>   **Schlaf gut!**
>   Sleep well.

> **Du fährst nicht nach London.**
> You are not going to London.

> **Fahr nicht nach London!**
> Don't go to London!

(b) Verbs which have the vowel change **e > i** in the present tense (see **33.7c**A) retain this change in the imperative:

> **Du gibst es mir.**
> You give it to me.

> **Gib es mir!**
> Give it to me!

> **Du nimmst es nicht.**
> You're not taking it.

> **Nimm es nicht!**
> Don't take it!

(c) An extra syllable (**-e**) may be added to the imperative **du** form, especially when the verb stem ends in **-b**, **-g**, **-d** or **-t**:

> **Sag/sage ihm nichts!**
> Don't tell him anything!

> **Schneide es hier!**
> Cut it here!

> **Arbeite nicht so viel!**
> Don't work so much!

> **Beschreibe es mir!**
> Describe it to me!

Note also that **du** and **ihr** can be used together with an imperative in order to give an emphatic contrast:

> **Mach *du* das!**
> *You* do it!

41.3

Some examples of imperative forms:

Infinitive	du	ihr	Sie
geben	gib	gebt	geben Sie
haben	hab	habt	haben Sie
kommen	komm	kommt	kommen Sie
laufen	lauf	lauft	laufen Sie
machen	mach	macht	machen Sie
nehmen	nimm	nehmt	nehmen Sie
sagen	sag	sagt	sagen Sie
schlafen	schlaf	schlaft	schlafen Sie
schreiben	schreib	schreibt	schreiben Sie
sprechen	sprich	sprecht	sprechen Sie

For other ways of giving instructions see Modal verbs (**35**A); The subjunctive (**39**A); **90.4**B on 'Requesting patience'; and **92**B on 'Asking for something to be done'.

42 Verbs and their completion: the basic sentence patterns

This section describes the basic patterns for constructing simple sentences. These patterns are determined by the verb. The following key explains the notation used:

	KEY
S	Subject (noun or pronoun in the nominative case: see **17**A)
=	The verbs **sein, bleiben, werden**
adj	Adjective
V	Verb
Vp	Prepositional verb
Oa	Noun or pronoun in the accusative case (see **18**A)
Od	Noun or pronoun in the dative case (see **19**A)
Og	Noun or pronoun in the genitive case (see **20**A)
loc	Word or phrase denoting location in time or space
dir	Word or phrase denoting direction
ext	Word or phrase denoting extent in time or space

42.1

It is useful to learn the whole of the basic pattern needed to use a verb properly in order to make a simple statement. Nearly all simple sentences consist of a subject (S) and a verb (V). For some verbs this is all that is needed to produce a simple sentence:

SV

> **Sie schläft.**
> She is sleeping.

Sie ruht.
She is resting.

42.2

Most verbs require some kind of element apart from S and V in order to complete the sense. The verbs **sein, bleiben, werden** equate two things or persons and so each side of the equation is in the subject case, nominative. Or the completion may be an adjective:

S=S

Sie wird *Wirtschaftsprüferin.*
She is going to be a chartered accountant.

Er bleibt *ein guter Freund.*
He remains a good friend.

S=adj

Sie ist *intelligent.*
She is intelligent.

Sie ist ihm *ähnlich.* (see **19.9**A)
She is like him.

42.3

The vast majority of verbs require one or two further elements in order to complete their sense, and these cannot be in the nominative (subject) case if they are nouns or pronouns. The basic patterns are:

(a) Completion with one element

SVOa

Ich kaufe *den Computer.* (See **18.1**A)
I buy the computer.

SVOd

Der Test dient *einem wichtigen Zweck.* (See **19.6**A)
The test serves an important purpose.

SVOg

Dieses Ergebnis bedarf *einer Erklärung.* (See **20.4**A)
This result requires an explanation.

SVpOa

Ich warte *auf den günstigsten Augenblick.* (See **38**A)
I am waiting for the most favourable moment.

SVpOd

> **Ich bestehe *auf meinem Recht.*** (See **38**A)
> I insist on my rights.

SVloc

> **Das Theaterstück beginnt *bald.***
> The play begins soon.

> **Das Theaterstück beginnt *in einer Stunde.***
> The play begins in one hour.

> **Das Theaterstück beginnt *nach dem Konzert.***
> The play begins after the concert.

> **Das Geld liegt *dort.***
> The money is there.

> **Das Geld liegt *auf dem Tisch.***
> The money is on the table.

> **Wir wohnen *dort.***
> We live there.

> **Wir wohnen *in der Stadtmitte.***
> We live in the town centre.

> **Wir wohnen *auf dem Land.***
> We live in the country.

SVdir

> **Wir fahren *dorthin.***
> We're driving there.

> **Wir fahren *in die Stadtmitte.***
> We're driving into the town centre.

> **Wir fahren *aufs Land.***
> We're driving into the country.

SVext

> **Das Theaterstück dauert *lange.***
> The play lasts a long time.

> **Das Theaterstück dauert *den ganzen Abend.***
> The play lasts the whole evening.

Sie ist *(um) einen Kopf kleiner* als ihr Bruder.
She is a head smaller than her brother.

(b) Completion with two elements

SVOaOd/SVOdOa

Sie zeigt *dem neuen Kollegen die Arbeitsmethode.*
She shows the routine to the new colleague.

Sie zeigt *ihm die Arbeitsmethode.*
She shows him the routine.

Sie zeigt *sie ihm.*
She shows it (to) him.
She shows him it.

(See **12**A for noun and pronoun objects)

SVOaOa

Der Brief hat *mich den ganzen Abend* gekostet.
The letter cost me the whole evening.

(See **18.8**A for the use of the accusative)

SVOaOg

Sie beschuldigte *ihn des Mordes.*
She accused him of murder.

(See **20.4**A on verbs taking the genitive)

SVpOaOa

Die Experten schätzen *den Schaden auf eine Million Mark.*
The experts estimate the damage at one million marks.

Die Experten schätzen *ihn auf eine Million Mark.*
The experts estimate it at one million marks.

SVpOaOd

Die Experten warnen *die Regierung vor der Inflationsgefahr.*
The experts warn the government of the danger of inflation.

Die Experten warnen *sie vor der Inflationsgefahr.*
The experts warn them of the danger of inflation.

Die Experten warnen *sie davor, daß Inflationsgefahr besteht.*
The experts warn them that there is a danger of inflation.

Die Experten warnen *sie davor.*
The experts warn them about it.

Die Experten warnen *sie vor diesem Mann.*
The experts warn them about this man.

Die Experten warnen *sie vor ihm.*
The experts warn them about him.

SVOa[=]Oa

Ich nannte *ihn einen Lügner.*
I called him a liar.

SVOa[=]adj

Die Zutaten machen *das Essen interessant.*
The ingredients make the meal interesting.

SVOaloc

Ich habe *meine Brieftasche in der Schublade* **gefunden.**
I found my wallet in the drawer.

Ich habe *sie dort* **gefunden.**
I found it there.

Er hat *die Konferenz für diesen Mittwoch* **anberaumt.**
He has called the conference for this Wednesday.

Er hat *sie für dann* **anberaumt.**
He has called it for then.

SVOadir

Sie legt *das Geld dorthin.*
She puts the money there.

Sie legt *das Geld auf den Tisch.*
She puts the money on(to) the table.

Sie legt *es dorthin.*
She puts it there.

Sie legt *es auf den Tisch.*
She puts it on(to) the table.

Wir haben *die Konferenz auf nächsten Freitag* **verschoben.**
We have postponed the conference till next Friday.

Wir haben *sie auf nächsten Freitag* **verschoben.**
We have postponed it till next Friday.

(c) It is sometimes difficult to be sure which pattern a particular reflexive verb fits. It all depends on whether the reflexive pronoun is seen as an integral part of the verb or as just one of the possible object completions of the verb:

Ich stelle mir *die Zukunft* **vor.** (SVOa)
I imagine the future.

Ich stelle *Ihnen meinen neuen Freund* **vor.** (SVOdOa)
I introduce my new friend to you.

Er stellte sich *der Polizei.* (SVOd)
He gave himself up to the police.

Sie vergewissert sich *der finanziellen Lage.* (SVOg)
She assures herself of the financial situation.

Ich erinnere mich *an letztes Jahr.* (SVpOa)
I remember last year.

Die Reeperbahn befindet sich *in Hamburg.* (SVploc)
The Reeperbahn is in Hamburg.

Ich begebe mich *hinein/ins Theater.* (SVpdir)
I'm going in/(in)to the theatre.

Die neue Siedlung erstreckt sich *bis zum Wald.* (SVext)
The new housing estate stretches to the wood.

(d) Dictionaries and grammars often provide 'shorthand' guides to these completion patterns using general words like **jemand-** (in the appropriate case form) and **etwas.** Where the verb is completed by 'someone or something', the case required can be deduced from the form of **jemand-.** Thus **jemandem oder etwas dienen** 'to serve someone or something' requires any noun or pronoun to be in the dative: **es dient keinem Zweck** 'it serves no purpose'; **ich habe Ihnen gedient** 'I have been of service to you'. Often, the forms **jemanden, jemandem** and **jemandes** are abbreviated (e.g. to **jmdn., jmdm.** and **jmds.**), but they always show the required case ending.

Here is a representative list of the basic patterns:

Subject + verb

schlafen 'to sleep/be sleeping'
intelligent sein 'to be intelligent'
Wirtschaftsprüfer sein 'to be a chartered accountant'

ein guter Freund sein 'to be a good friend'
jmdm. ähnlich sein 'to be like someone'

Subject + verb + one completion

jmdn. kennen 'to know sb.'
jmdm. oder etw. (dat) dienen 'to serve sb./sth.'
jmds oder etw. (gen) bedürfen 'to be in need of sb./sth.'

Subject + prepositional verb + one completion

auf jmdn./etw. (acc) warten 'to wait for sb. or sth.'
auf jmdm. oder etw. (dat) bestehen 'to insist on sb. or sth.'

Subject + verb + two completions

jmdm. etw. (acc) zeigen 'to show someone sth.'
jmdm. einer Sache (gen) beschuldigen 'to accuse sb. of sth.'
jmdn. etw. (acc) nennen 'to call sb. sth.'
jmdn./etw. (acc) interessant machen 'to make sb./sth. interesting'

Subject + prepositional verb + two completions

etw. (acc) auf etw. (acc) schätzen 'to estimate sth. at so much'
jmdn. vor jmdm. oder etw. (dat) warnen 'to warn sb. about sb./sth.'

Subject + verb + location

irgendwo liegen 'to be lying somewhere'
sich irgendwo befinden 'to be situated somewhere'

Subject + verb + direction

irgendwohin gehen 'to go somewhere'
sich irgendwohin begeben 'to go somewhere' (formal: lit. to betake
oneself somewhere)

Subject + verb + object + direction

jmdn./etw. (acc) irgendwohin tun 'to put sb./sth. somewhere'

Subject + verb + object + location

jmdn. oder etw. (acc) irgendwo finden 'to find sb./sth. somewhere'

Subject + verb + extent

einen Augenblick dauern 'to last a moment'
um einen Kopf größer oder kleiner sein 'to be a head taller or shorter'

(e) Completion by a clause

In many of the above patterns the verb can be completed by a clause instead of a noun or pronoun. The subject can also be a clause. For example, instead of noun phrases in the SVOa pattern:

>**Diese Tatsache erklärt seine gute Laune.**
>This fact explains his good mood.

the object completion can be a clause:

>**Diese Tatsache erklärt,** *warum er jetzt den ganzen Tag singt.*
>This fact explains why he sings all day now.

or the subject can be a clause:

>*Daß er bald heiratet,* **erklärt seine gute Laune.**
>The fact that he is getting married soon explains his good mood.

or both can be clauses:

>*Daß er bald heiratet,* **erklärt,** *warum er jetzt den ganzen Tag singt.*
>The fact that he is getting married soon explains why he sings all day now.

Note how prepositional verbs make a clause completion using **da** + preposition (see **38.2**A):

>**Sie hat** *darauf* **bestanden,** *daß sie das Wochenende frei haben müßte.*
>She insisted that she had to have the weekend free.

(f) Completion by an infinitive clause with **zu**

Some verbs can be completed by an infinitive clause with **zu**, either on its own:

>**Ich habe vor,** *in den Ferien Spanisch zu lernen.*
>I intend to learn Spanish in the holidays.

>**Sie beabsichtigt,** *nächstes Jahr nach Japan zu fahren.*
>She intends to go to Japan next year.

or as one of two completions:

>**Er half** *mir, diese Wohnung zu finden.*
>He helped me to find this apartment.

>**Sie ermahnte** *ihn, langsamer zu fahren.*
>She urged him to drive more slowly.

(See also **8.7a**A for word order in infinitive clauses)

(g) Sometimes a 'dummy subject' **es** occupies first position, when the real subject (in italics in the examples below) comes later in the sentence. This pattern is a variation on the standard SV pattern. Compare English 'There is.../There are...':

> **Es fehlt** *ein Hundertmarkschein.* (= *Ein Hundertmarkschein* fehlt.)
> A hundred mark note is missing.
> There is a hundred mark note missing.

> **Es besteht** *die Gefahr,* daß... (= *Die Gefahr* besteht, daß...)
> There is the danger that... (lit. The danger exists that...)

Note that the dummy **es** can also be used with a plural subject:

> **Es kommen bald** *bessere Verkaufszahlen.* (= *Bessere Verkaufszahlen*
> **kommen bald.**)
> Better sales figures are coming soon.

(h) Impersonal verbs with **es** as the subject are best learnt as a unit:

Es gelingt (+ dat) 'to succeed'

> **Es ist mir gelungen, nach Amerika zu kommen.**
> I succeeded in coming to America.

Es handelt sich um (+ acc) 'it concerns/it is about'

> **Es handelt sich um eine ehemalige Angestellte.**
> It concerns a former female employee.

Es geht um (+ acc) 'it concerns/the issue is/what is at issue is'

> **Es geht um die Zukunft Europas.**
> The future of Europe is at issue.

Es stellt sich heraus, daß 'it turns out that'

> **Es stellte sich heraus, daß er gelogen hatte.**
> It turned out that he had been lying.

(i) It is quite common for some completing elements to be omitted when the meaning is obvious from the context. For example:

> **Wie geht es dir?**
> How are things with you?

> **Wie geht es?**
> How are things?

> **Es geht mir gut, danke.**
> **Es geht ganz gut, danke.**
> **Es geht, danke.**
> OK, thanks.

> **Das hat uns kaum überrascht.**
> That hardly surprised us.

> **Das hat kaum überrascht.**
> That was hardly a surprise.

> **Wir haben doch schon Geld an die Kirche gegeben.**
> **Wir haben doch schon an die Kirche gegeben.**
> **Wir haben doch schon gegeben.**
> But we have already given (money) (to the church).

(j) It is often possible to introduce a dative into some of these patterns to express the person involved or interested in the action:

> **Ich kaufe (mir) einen neuen Computer.**
> I buy (myself) a new computer.

(See **19.2**A for the dative and **37.3**A on reflexive verbs)

Note especially the S=adj pattern, usually with **zu**, with the meaning 'too... for me/him etc.'/'as far as I/he, etc., is concerned' (see **19.9**A on the dative):

> **Das ist *mir* (zu) wichtig.**
> That is (too) important for me.

> **Sie ist *mir* zu klug.**
> She is too clever for my liking.

(k) The following unusual completion patterns should be noted:

> **mich friert** 'I am freezing'
> **mir ist kalt** 'I am cold'
> **mir ist warm** 'I am warm'
> **mir ist heiß** 'I am hot'

Er ist warm/kalt is a statement about a person's character, not about temperature, and **Ich bin heiß** means 'I am sexually aroused', and should only be used of animals in polite discourse (**die Hündin ist heiß** 'the bitch is on heat'). Be careful!

VII Adjectives and adverbs

43 Predicative and attributive adjectives

43.1
Adjectives describe nouns. If used predicatively, that is if they are placed after the finite verb (see **5.1**A), very often some form of **sein**, they do not take any endings:

> **Das Buch war ganz *interessant.***
> The book was really interesting.

> **Die Äpfel sind jetzt *reif.***
> The apples are ripe now.

> **Ihre Stimme klingt *fröhlich.***
> Her voice sounds cheerful.

43.2
However, if used attributively, i.e. before the noun they describe, adjectives are declined:

> **Hast du das *neue* Plakat gesehen?**
> Have you seen the new poster?

> **Die *reifen* Äpfel schmecken wirklich gut.**
> The ripe apples taste really nice.

43.3
Attributive adjectives can have a **der**, **ein** or zero declension. All three declensions are regular and involve no more than minor variations in endings. The particular declension used depends on what determiner (if any) precedes the adjective (see **24**A).

44 Der *declension*

44.1

Singular	Masculine	Neuter	Feminine
Nominative	**der groß*e* Hut**	**das klein*e* Dorf**	**die schön*e* Stadt**
Accusative	**den groß*en* Hut**	**das klein*e* Dorf**	**die schön*e* Stadt**

| Dative | dem groß*en* Hut | dem klein*en* Dorf | der schön*en* Stadt |
| Genitive | des groß*en* Hutes | des klein*en* Dorfes | der schön*en* Stadt |

Plural (all genders)

Nominative	die gut*en* Kinder
Accusative	die gut*en* Kinder
Dative	den gut*en* Kindern
Genitive	der gut*en* Kinder

44.2 — These adjective endings are used after **der** words (see **24.1**A):

> *Dieser* groß*e* Mann wohnt bei uns im Gebäude.
> This/That tall man lives in our building.

> Sie arbeiten in *jenem* baufällig*en* Haus.
> They are working in that tumbledown house.

> Er kommt immer mit *vielem* gut*en* Stoff.
> He always comes with a lot of good material.

> Sie beschrieb die wirtschaftlichen Probleme *sämtlicher* europäisch*en* Länder.
> She described the economic problems of all the European countries.

Following **beide**, **irgendwelche** and **solche**, **der**-declension endings are usual but the zero declension (see **46**A) is also found:

> Wir haben *beide* verletzt*en* (or verletzt*e*) Soldaten gesehen.
> We saw both injured soldiers.

> Solche komisch*en* (or komisch*e*) Leute findet man hier öfters.
> You quite often get funny people like that here.

Note the **der**-declension ending after personal pronouns (see **30**A):

> Wir Deutsch*en* wollen unsere D-Mark behalten.
> We Germans want to hold on to our deutschmark.

44.3 — The plural **alle** 'all' is also followed by **der**-declension adjective endings, but note that any following possessive adjectives (e.g. **mein**, **dein**, **sein**, etc.) or demonstrative adjectives (e.g. **dieser**, **jener**) take the same endings as **alle**:

Nominative	all*e* dein*e* gut*en* Freunde 'all your good friends'
	all*e* jen*e* gut*en* Freunde 'all those good friends'
Accusative	all*e* dein*e* gut*en* Freunde

                        all*e* jen*e* gut*en* Freunde
Dative   all*en* dein*en* gut*en* Freunden
                        all*en* jen*en* gut*en* Freunden
Genitive   all*er* dein*er* gut*en* Freunde
                        all*er* jen*er* gut*en* Freunde

Alle diese schönen Sommertage nützen mir nichts, wenn ich die ganze Zeit arbeiten muß.
All these lovely summer days are no good to me if I have to work all the time.

In allen unseren Büros ist es furchtbar kalt.
It's terribly cold in all our offices.

Kennst du *alle jene neuen* Spieler?
Do you know all those new players?

44.4

After **alles** 'everything', the adjective declines like a **der**-declension neuter adjective but usually has an initial capital letter:

Nominative   **alles Gut*e*** 'all the best'
Accusative   **alles Gut*e***
Dative   **alles Gut*em***
Genitive   **alles Gut*en***

Ich wünsche euch alles Gute.
I wish you all the best.

45 Ein *declension*

45.1

Singular	Masculine	Neuter	Feminine
Nominative	ein neu*er* Wagen	ein alt*es* Haus	eine leer*e* Dose
Accusative	einen neu*en* Wagen	ein alt*es* Haus	eine leer*e* Dose
Dative	einem neu*en* Wagen	einem alt*en* Haus	einer leer*en* Dose
Genitive	eines neu*en* Wagens	eines alt*en* Hauses	einer leer*en* Dose

Plural (all genders)

Nominative	keine reich*en* Leute		
Accusative	keine reich*en* Leute		
Dative	keinen reich*en* Leuten		
Genitive	keiner reich*en* Leute		

45.2

The **ein**-declension endings are used after **ein**, **kein** and the possessive adjectives **mein** 'my', **dein** 'your', **sein** 'his', **ihr** 'her/its/their', **unser** 'our', **Ihr** 'your' (polite form), **euer** 'your' (pl. of **dein**):

> **Das Haus braucht ein neu*es* Dach.**
> The house needs a new roof.

> **Ein jung*er* Mann namens Ehlers sucht dich.**
> A young man called Ehlers is looking for you.

> **Er ist mein best*er* Freund.**
> He's my best friend.

> **Wir können unsere schwer*en* Koffer nicht mehr tragen.**
> We cannot carry our heavy bags any longer.

46 *Zero declension*

46.1

Singular	Masculine	Neuter	Feminine
Nominative	**französisch*er* Wein**	**hell*es* Bier**	**frisch*e* Sahne**
Accusative	**französisch*en* Wein**	**hell*es* Bier**	**frisch*e* Sahne**
Dative	**französisch*em* Wein**	**hell*em* Bier**	**frisch*er* Sahne**
Genitive	**französisch*en* Weins**	**hell*en* Biers**	**frisch*er* Sahne**

Plural (all genders)			
Nominative	**reich*e* Leute**		
Accusative	**reich*e* Leute**		
Dative	**reich*en* Leuten**		
Genitive	**reich*er* Leute**		

46.2

The zero-declension endings are used:

(a) When an adjective is not preceded either by an article or by a determiner:

> **Rot*er* Wein gefällt mir am besten.**
> I like red wine best.

> **Ich empfehle Ihnen frisch*es* Obst.**
> I recommend you eat/buy fresh fruit.

> **Ich mag den Geschmack frisch gebacken*en* Brotes.**
> I like the taste of freshly baked bread.

> **Bei schön*em* Wetter gehen wir oft wandern.**
> In nice weather we often go walking.

(b) After **ein paar** 'a few':

> **Ich habe ein paar gut*e* Freunde in Berlin.**
> I have a few good friends in Berlin.

(c) After any numeral other than one:

> **Ich habe sechs alt*e* Weinflaschen gefunden.**
> I've found six old wine bottles.

46.3 Following **etwas** 'something', **viel** 'much', **wenig** 'little', **nichts** 'nothing', and **allerlei** 'all kinds of', the adjective declines like a zero declension neuter adjective and usually begins with a capital letter:

Nominative	**nichts Interessant*es*** 'nothing of interest'
Accusative	**nichts Interessant*es***
Dative	**nichts Interessant*em***
Genitive	**nichts Interessant*en***

The genitive form is rarely found.

> **Ich habe wenig Neu*es* zu berichten.**
> I have little new to report.

> **Wir brauchen etwas Konkreter*es*.**
> We need something more concrete.

> **Er ist mit allerlei Neu*em* nach Hause gekommen.**
> He came home with all sorts of new things.

46.4 After the indefinites **einige** 'some/a few', **etliche** 'several', **folgende** 'following', **manche** 'some', **mehrere** 'several', **viele** 'many' and **wenige** 'few', the adjective also takes zero-declension endings (though **manche** can have a following adjective with a **der** declension ending):

> **Wir haben wenige kalt*e* Tage gehabt.**
> We had few cold days.

> **Einige arm*e* Rentner können sich nicht richtig ernähren.**
> Some poor pensioners are unable to feed themselves properly.

> **Dank vieler gut*er* Ratschläge hat sich unser Geschäft erfolgreich entwickelt.**
> Thanks to much good advice our business has developed successfully.

46.5

When **viel** and **wenig** precede singular, so-called 'uncountable' nouns, or when they are used as adverbs, they are not declined, and the following adjective takes zero-declension endings:

> **Viel gut*er* Wein ist verschwendet worden.**
> A lot of good wine has been wasted.

> **Dieser Sessel ist aus wenig haltbar*em* Stoff gemacht.**
> This armchair is made of not very hard-wearing material.

46.6

Note that a string of adjectives before a noun all have the same endings, whether they take **der-**, **zero-** or **ein-**declension endings:

> **In dem Moment ist ein freundlich*er* alt*er* Polizist vorbeigekommen.**
> At that moment a friendly old policeman came by.

> **Hast du schon die schön*en*, rund*en* spanisch*en* Apfelsinen gegessen?**
> Have you eaten the beautiful, round Spanish oranges yet?

> **Trocken*er* französisch*er* Wein schmeckt mir gar nicht.**
> I don't like dry French wine at all.

In the masculine or neuter dative singular the second element may take the **der**-declension ending **n** rather than the zero-declension **m**:

> **Der Anzug ist aus teurem italienisch*en* Stoff.**
> The suit is made of expensive Italian material.

47   *Other adjective types*

47.1

Invariable *-er* ending

(a) German readily forms adjectives from the names of cities and towns by adding **-er** to the place name. Adjectives thus formed have an initial capital letter and do not decline:

> **Hast du denn das Berlin*er* Stadtschloß schon besucht?**
> Have you been to Berlin Castle yet?

> **Die Basl*er* Fastnacht ist ein echtes Erlebnis.**
> The Basel Carnival is a real experience.

> **Wegen des London*er* Gipfeltreffens ist diese Straße heute gesperrt.**
> This street is closed today because of the London summit.

> **Waren Sie schon im Ulm*er* Dom?**
> Have you ever been to Ulm Cathedral?

(b) Adjectives formed from numerals also end in **-er** and do not decline:

> **In den fünfzig*er* Jahren hatten wir ja wenig Geld.**
> Of course we had little money in the fifties.

47.2 Spelling of certain adjectives

(a) The adjective **hoch** loses its **c** in declined forms:

> **Die Kosten sind zu hoch.**
> The costs are too high.

> BUT **Sie erstiegen den *hohen* Fernsehturm.**
> They climbed the high television tower.

> **In den *hohen* Bergen ist es immer viel kühler.**
> Up in the (high) mountains it's always a lot cooler.

(b) The **e** preceding the final **-l, -n** and **-r** is lost in declined forms:

> **Die Firma ist nicht mehr rentabel.**
> The firm/business is no longer viable.
> BUT **die *unrentable* Firma**

> **Er erzählt *ungeheure* Lügen.**
> He tells outrageous lies.

> **Das war ein *miserables* Spiel.**
> That was a rotten game.

> **Der Mann in der *dunklen* Jacke.**
> The man in the dark jacket.

> **Infolge des *sauren* Regens sind hier viele Bäume gestorben.**
> Many trees have died here as a result of acid rain.

Note also **Basler** from **Basel** in **47.1a**A above.

47.3 Non-declinable adjectives

Certain adjectives do not take case endings. There are three main categories here:

(a) Adjectives used exclusively in spoken German, such as **klasse**, **prima**, **super**, all of which have similar meanings:

> **Der ist ein *prima* Typ.**
> He's a smashing/really nice person.

> **Wir hatten eine *super* Zeit bei euch.**
> We had a great time at your place.

(b) The colour adjectives **beige, lila, orange, rosa**:

> **Sie trug ein *rosa* Kleid.**
> She wore a pink dress.

> **Sie liebt die *lila* Hose.**
> She loves the purple trousers.

> **Er hat ein *orange* Hemd** (BUT **ein orangefarben*es* Hemd**).
> He's got an orange shirt.

(c) **ganz** and **halb** when used before place names without a preceding article or determiner:

> ***Ganz* Deutschland war in Trümmern.**
> The whole of Germany was in ruins.

> **In *ganz* Frankreich finden morgen Wahlen statt.**
> There are elections tomorrow in the whole of France.

> **Durch *halb* Europa sind wir gereist.**
> We've travelled halfway round Europe.

47.4 Adjectives with prepositions

Adjectives are often used in combination with specific prepositions which ought to be learnt along with the adjective. A few examples of this widespread phenomenon are:

> **bereit zu** (+ dat) 'ready for'
> **eifersüchtig auf** (+ acc) 'jealous of'
> **gleichgültig gegenüber** (+ dat) 'indifferent towards'
> **reich an** (+ dat) 'rich in'
> **typisch für** (+ acc) 'typical of'
> **verwandt mit** (+ dat) 'related to'

> **Er ist *eifersüchtig auf* seinen Bruder.**
> He is jealous of his brother.

> **Das ist ja *typisch für* diese Leute.**
> That's typical of those people.

> **Antje ist, glaube ich, *mit* dem Bernd *verwandt*.**
> Antje is related to Bernd, I think.

47.5
The negative prefix *un-*

The German prefix **un-** can correspond to a variety of English negative prefixes:

> **undiszipliniert** 'undisciplined'
> **unhöflich** 'discourteous/impolite'
> **unmöglich** 'impossible'
> **unverständlich** 'incomprehensible'

48 *Comparison of adjectives*

48.1

The majority of the simple adjectives in **43–47**A can be used to compare one thing or person with another. German comparatives (the form of the adjective used to compare things or persons with each other) and superlatives (the form used to denote the greatest intensity of a quality) are formed by appending **-er** and **-est/-st** respectively to the basic adjective and then adding the appropriate adjective endings:

> **Ich lese ein interessant*eres* Buch als dieses.**
> I'm reading a more interesting book than that.

> **Das muß wohl das interessant*este* Buch in der ganzen Bibliothek sein.**
> That must be the most interesting book in the whole library.

> **Die breit*ere* Straße bringt ja nur noch mehr Verkehr.**
> The wider road will only bring more traffic.

> **Wir landeten auf der breit*esten* Landebahn.**
> We landed on the widest runway.

48.2

Most common adjectives of one syllable add an umlaut to **a**, **o** or **u** in the comparative or superlative. These include:

> **alt** 'old'
> **dumm** 'stupid'
> **grob** 'coarse/rough'
> **hart** 'hard/harsh'
> **kalt** 'cold'
> **klug** 'clever'
> **krank** 'ill'
> **kurz** 'short'
> **lang** 'long'
> **scharf** 'sharp'
> **schwach** 'weak'
> **schwarz** 'black'

stark 'strong'
warm 'warm'

Das ist ja eine viel *längere* Straße als unsere.
That's a much longer street than ours.

Wir möchten in einem *wärmeren* Klima leben.
We'd like to live in a warmer climate.

Die *jüngste* Tochter ist schon verheiratet.
The youngest daughter is already married.

48.3 The superlative with **-est** is usually employed with adjectives whose simple or basic form ends in **-d, -s, -sch, -ß, -t, -tz, -x** or **-z**:

Warum habe ich das härt*este* Bett?
Why have I got the hardest bed?

Sie hat das blass*este* Gesicht, das ich je gesehen habe.
She's got the palest face I've ever seen.

Damals hatten wir immer die wild*esten* Partys.
We always had the wildest parties in those days.

48.4 Common irregular comparative and superlative forms include:

groß 'big'	**größer** 'bigger'	**das größte** 'the biggest'	**am größten** 'biggest'
gut 'good'	**besser** 'better'	**das beste** 'the best'	**am besten** 'best'
hoch 'high'	**höher** 'higher'	**das höchste** 'the highest'	**am höchsten** 'highest'
nah 'near'	**näher** 'nearer'	**das nächste** 'the nearest'	**am nächsten** 'nearest'
viel 'much'	**mehr** 'more'	**das meiste** 'the most'	**am meisten** 'most'
wenig 'little'	**weniger** 'less/fewer'	**das wenigste** 'the least'	**am wenigsten** 'least/fewest'
	minder 'less'	**das mindeste** 'the least'	

Note that the alternative comparative forms of **wenig** are indeclinable:

Ich habe *weniger* Chancen im Leben gehabt als mein Bruder.
I've had fewer opportunities in life than my brother.

minder is only used in formal written German and serves to qualify an adjective:

> **Unsere Gruppe war nicht *minder* benachteiligt als eure.**
> Our group was no less disadvantaged than yours.

48.5

Adjectives used predicatively (see **43**A) do not decline. In the superlative, the predicative form is **am** + superlative ending in **-en**. For example, **am schnellsten** 'the quickest', **am besten** 'the best', etc.:

> **Dieses Haus ist *am schönsten*.**
> This house is the nicest.

> **Das erste Mädchen war *am klügsten*.**
> The first girl was the cleverest.

48.6

(a) English 'than' and 'as' in comparisons are expressed by **als** and **so... wie** respectively. The following noun, pronoun or adjective agrees in case with the thing or person being compared:

> **Sie ist *älter als ich*.**
> She's older than I am.

> **Eure Wohnung ist *größer als unsre*.**
> Your flat is bigger than ours.

> **Die Webers sind nicht *so reich wie die Müllers*.**
> The Webers are not as rich as the Müllers.

> **Birgit ist fast *so groß wie Maria*.**
> Birgit is almost as tall as Maria.

The comparison can be reinforced by **genauso** or **ebenso**:

> **Dieser Film ist *genauso langweilig wie* der von letzter Woche.**
> This film is just as boring as last week's.

> **In Italien im Sommer ist es *ebenso heiß wie* in Griechenland.**
> Italy is just as hot in summer as Greece.

Comparatives can also be reinforced by the use of a preceding **noch** or **viel**, and superlatives by the use of **aller-** or **bei weitem**:

> **Dieser Anzug ist *noch billiger*.**
> This suit is even cheaper.

> **Diese Aufgabe ist *viel langweiliger*.**
> This task is much more boring.

Sie ist zur Zeit die *allerschnellste* Radfahrerin der Welt.
She is currently the fastest cyclist in the world.

Das ist *bei weitem* seine beste Leistung.
That is by far his best performance.

(b) In the superlative, English 'of' is expressed by **von** or the genitive case:

Unser Kaninchen war *das schönste von* allen.
Our rabbit was the prettiest of them all.

Das ist ja *das schwierigste* uns*r*er viel*en* Probleme.
That is certainly the most difficult of our many problems.

(c) When used in the comparative, attributive adjectives can express the sense of 'fairly' or 'quite':

Sie haben eine *kleinere* Summe verlangt.
They demanded a fairly small sum (of money).

(d) 'more and more' in a comparative phrase is conveyed by German **immer** and the predicative comparative adjective:

Die Situation wird *immer ernster.*
The situation is getting more and more serious.

Die Nächte werden *immer kälter.*
The nights are getting more and more cold/colder and colder.

(e) English 'the more... the more' is expressed in German by **je** + **-er...**, **um so -er** or **desto -er**:

Je *schneller* du es machst, *um so früher* kriegst du das Geld.
The quicker you do it, the sooner you get the money.

Je *länger* wir die Antwort hinausschieben, *desto schwieriger* wird es für sie sein.
The longer we delay answering, the more difficult it will be for them.

49 *Extended adjectival phrases*

Also known as 'extended participial phrases', adjectival phrases consist of a participle used as an attributive adjective (see **43**A) placed before the noun it describes. The participle can either be present or past:

> *Dieses von Siemens entwickelte Verfahren* **ist sehr bedeutend.**
> This process developed by Siemens (lit. This by Siemens developed process) is very significant.

> *Die das Streikrecht verteidigenden Arbeiter* **suchen die Unterstützung ihres Abgeordneten.**
> The workers who are defending the right to strike (lit. The the right to strike defending workers) are seeking the support of their MP.

> *Die sich* **auch in Großbritannien schnell** *entwickelnde ökologische Bewegung* **übt einen großen Einfluß auf die Wähler aus.**
> The ecology movement which is also growing quickly in Great Britain (lit. The also in Great Britain quickly developing ecological movement) has a great influence on voters.

As the last two examples show, the adjectival phrase may be extended by objects, adverbs and reflexive pronouns, with the result that article and noun are separated by several other elements. Note that English uses a phrase or subordinate clause placed after the noun to render these German phrases.

N.B. These extended adjectival phrases are generally not used in spoken German but occur frequently in newspapers, magazines, legal and other official documents.

50 Adverbs

50.1

Adverbs qualify verbs and tell us how, why, at what time or in what place the action of the verb was performed. There are several categories of adverb, including ones of:

(a) time (e.g. **endlich** 'finally', **noch einmal** 'once again', **unterdessen** 'meanwhile')

(b) degree (e.g. **fast** 'almost', **genug** 'enough', **teilweise** 'partly')

(c) manner (e.g. **gründlich** 'thoroughly', **schnell** 'quickly', **umsonst** 'in vain')

(d) place (e.g. **draußen** 'outside', **drüben** 'over there', **oben** 'up/upstairs')

Some separable prefixes (**los-**, **weg-**, **zurück-**, etc., but see also **36.1**A) are adverbs too.

50.2

The simple, i.e. uninflected, form of the adjective can usually be used as an adverb:

> **Sie haben die Arbeit** *gut* **gemacht.**
> You've done the job well.

> **Der Zug ist** *pünktlich* **angekommen.**
> The train arrived on time.

50.3 — There are, in addition, a number of characteristic adverbial endings which are added to the simple adjective. The most common are: **-e**, **-erweise**, **-lang**, **-lich**, **-s**, **-wärts**, **-weise**:

> **Wie lang*e* wohnen Sie schon in Bonn?**
> How long have you lived in Bonn?

> **Glücklich*erweise* ist nichts passiert.**
> Fortunately nothing happened.

> **Sie haben stunden*lang* darüber diskutiert.**
> They spent hours discussing it.

> **Das hast du aber sicher*lich* schon gemacht, oder?**
> But you've surely done that already, haven't you?

> **Wir treffen uns meisten*s* abend*s*/vormittag*s*/montag*s*.** (N.B. small letters because they are adverbs)
> We usually meet in the evenings/mornings/on Mondays.

> **Er fuhr rück*wärts* in die Garage.**
> He reversed (the car) into the garage.

> **In der 9. Klasse lernt man Französisch, wahl*weise* auch Russisch.**
> You study French in Year 9 and you can also take Russian as an option.

50.4 — **hin** and **her** are added to several prepositions as a prefix (e.g. **hinüber**, **herbei**, **hingegen**, **herauf**) and to a small number of adverbs of place as a suffix (e.g. **dorthin**, **hierher**). They indicate motion to (**her**) or motion away from (**hin**) the speaker:

> **Kommen Sie *herein*.**
> Come in.

> **Wir gingen die Treppe *hinauf*.**
> We went up the stairs.

> **Gehen Sie hier die Straße *hinunter*.**
> Go down this street.

> **Sie liefen *dorthin*.**
> They ran there.

> **Komm *hierher*!**
> Come here!

Notice also the hybrid form **gehen Sie 'raus!** 'get out!'

Often **hin** and **her** simply serve to reinforce the meaning of the preposition:

Structures

Sie rannte *aus* dem Haus *hinaus*.
She ran out of the house.

Wir liefen *um* den Sportplatz *herum*.
We ran around the sports ground.

50.5 (a) Interrogatives, or question words, represent another type of adverb. Some are formed with the suffix **hin** or **her**:

> **wann** 'when?'
> **warum** 'why?'
> **was** 'what?'
> **wer** 'who?'
> **wie** 'how?'
> **wo** 'where?'
> **woher** 'where from?'
> **wohin** 'where to?'

(b) Several interrogatives consist of **wo** + preposition. Note that if the preposition begins with a vowel, **r** is inserted:

> **wodurch** 'by/through what?'
> **wohin** 'where to?'
> **womit** 'with what?'
> **wo*r*aus** 'out of what?'
> **wo*r*in** 'what in?'
> **worüber** 'what about?'
> **wovon** 'about what?'

> ***Wohin* fahrt ihr morgen?**
> Where are you going tomorrow?

> ***Wovon* handelt das Buch?**
> What's the book about?

> ***Worüber* haben Sie sich unterhalten?**
> What did you talk about?

50.6 For each of the interrogatives in **50.5b**A there is a corresponding adverb:

> **dadurch** 'through it/that'
> **danach** 'after it/that'
> **daraus** 'out of it/that'
> **davor** 'before/in front of it', etc.

dahin 'to there' and **daher** 'from there' (also 'therefore') are the corresponding forms for **wohin** and **woher** respectively.

Note also **darum** 'for this reason'.

> **Ich bin *danach* sofort nach Hause gegangen.**
> I went straight home after that.

> **Siehst du das rote Auto *davor*?**
> Can you see the red car in front of it?

> ***Daher* habt ihr keine Alternative. Ihr müßt mitkommen.**
> You therefore have no choice. You must come with us.

For the order of adverbials in a sentence or clause see **11A**.

51   *Comparison of adverbs*

51.1   The comparative of adverbs is essentially the same as that of adjectives:

> **schnell** 'quickly/fast', **schneller** 'more quickly/faster'
> **gut** 'well', **besser** 'better'
> **effizient** 'efficiently', **effizienter** 'more efficiently'

51.2   As with adjectives, 'than' in a comparison is expressed by **als**:

> **Horst behauptet, er habe seine Hausaufgaben *besser als* alle anderen gemacht.**
> Horst claims he did his homework better than all the others.

51.3   The superlative form of the adverb is the same as that of the predicative adjective:

> **Sie läuft *am schnellsten*.**
> She runs the fastest.

> **In unserer Familie spricht mein Vater Englisch *am besten*.**
> My father is the best English speaker in our family.

51.4   The superlative of adverbs can also be formed in other ways:

(a) Through the use of **äußerst**, **höchst** or **möglichst**:

> **Er hat die Sache *äußerst* schnell erledigt.**
> He dealt with the matter extremely quickly.

> **Die Studenten haben *höchst* leichtsinnig reagiert.**
> The students reacted in a most thoughtless manner.

> Teilen Sie uns bitte *möglichst bald* mit, ob Sie unsere Kampagne unterstützen werden.
> Please let us know as soon as possible whether you will support our campaign.

(b) An alternative to **am schnellsten, am besten**, etc. is the use of **aufs schnellste, aufs beste**, etc.:

> Wir haben ihm per Brief *aufs wärmste* gratuliert.
> We sent him a letter with our warmest congratulations.

> Die Konferenz war *aufs beste* organisiert.
> The conference was extremely well organized.

The sense here is 'could not be warmer/better'.

51.5 There are a small number of irregular comparative and superlative adverbial forms:

bald 'soon'	**eher/früher** 'sooner'	**am ehesten/am frühesten** 'soonest'
gern 'gladly/keenly'	**lieber** 'more gladly/rather'	**am liebsten** 'most gladly/most of all'
nah 'closely'	**näher** 'more closely'	**am nächsten** 'most closely/closest'
oft 'often'	**öfter** 'more often'	**am öftesten** (or **am häufigsten**) 'most often'
viel 'much'	**mehr** 'more'	**am meisten** 'most'

Note the adverbial superlative forms in **-ens**, the most common of which are:

> **bestens** 'very well'
> **höchstens** 'at the most'
> **meistens** 'mostly'
> **mindestens** 'at least'
> **nächstens** 'shortly'
> **schnellstens** 'as quickly as possible'
> **strengstens** 'strictly'
> **wärmstens** 'most warmly'
> **wenigstens** 'at least'

> In der U-Bahn ist das Rauchen *strengstens* verboten.
> Smoking in the underground is strictly forbidden.

> Der Aufsatz wird *höchstens* vier Seiten lang sein.
> The essay will be four sides long at most.

Mein Kollege in Bochum hat Sie *wärmstens* empfohlen.
My colleague in Bochum has given you the warmest of
recommendations.

VIII Word structure and word formation

52 Principles of word formation

52.1 — This section describes the main ways in which complex words are formed by combining vocabulary elements. For example: **Um+welt+freund+lich+keit** 'environmental friendliness' is composed of **Umwelt** 'environment' + **Freundlichkeit** 'friendliness'. Each of these in turn is built up as follows:

> **um** 'around' + **Welt** 'world' > **Umwelt** 'environment'
> **Freund** 'friend' + **-lich** > **freundlich** 'friendly' + **-keit** > **Freundlichkeit** 'friendliness'

The patterns of word formation are listed in this section simply according to whether they involve elements added to the beginning of a word (prefixes), to the end of a word (suffixes) or some other process.

52.2 — It is important to realize that you cannot generalize from most of these patterns to predict other words. This is as true of English as it is of German. Note the following three pairs of words:

> **tief > Tiefe; schön > Schönheit; schnell > Schnelligkeit**
> deep > depth; beautiful > beauty; fast > speed

Learning English involves knowing that the noun formed from the adjective 'steep' is not 'stepth'. Similarly, learning German involves knowing that the word for 'speed' is not **Schnelle**.

52.3 — The irregularity of these patterns makes them largely unpredictable for someone in the early stages of learning the language. It is advisable not to coin words you have not met before on the basis of one of these patterns. But a knowledge of them will prove very useful in recognizing the meaning of words encountered for the first time and is therefore important in building vocabulary.

52.4 Some word formations have acquired specialized meanings. Thus, **die Höhle** (derived from **hohl** 'hollow') ought to mean 'hollowness' but actually means 'cave', and **hitzefrei** might mean 'free from heat' but actually means 'on official holiday from school because of extremely hot weather'.

52.5 The umlaut is sometimes involved in the process of word formation in German, but it is not always possible to predict when it will be present.

The most important patterns are listed below.

53 *Forming verbs*

53.1 **Without a prefix**
All the verbs in this section are weak (see **33.4**A).

(a) **-ieren** can form verbs from nouns:

> **die Analyse** 'analysis' > **analysieren** 'to analyse'
> **die Kontrolle** 'check/control' > **kontrollieren** 'to check/control'
> **das Telefon** 'telephone' > **telefonieren** 'to speak on the phone'

(b) **-en** can be added to a noun to form a verb, sometimes following a pattern which begins with an adjective:

> **warm** 'warm' > **die Wärme** 'warmth' > **wärmen** 'to warm'
> **stark** 'strong' > **die Stärke** 'strength' > **stärken** 'to strengthen'
> **die Farbe** 'colour' > **färben** 'to colour'

(c) Many verbs recently imported from English add **-en** to the English word:

> **boxen** 'to box', **checken** 'to check/make sure'

(See **36**A on separable and inseparable prefixes, and see **57**A on the meaning of verbal prefixes)

54 *Forming nouns*

(See also **58.1**A on formal nominal style)

54.1 **Using prefixes**
Common prefixes include:

Fehl- 'false/wrong/mistaken'

der **Fehlstart** 'false start', die **Fehleinschätzung** 'mistaken estimate', **die Fehlprognose** 'false prognosis'

Grund- 'basic/essential'

die **Grundregel** 'basic (ground) rule', **das Grundprinzip** 'basic principle', die **Grundhaltung** 'basic attitude', die **Grundschule** 'primary (elementary) school'

Haupt- 'main'

das **Hauptargument** 'main argument', die **Hauptsache** 'main thing', **das Hauptfach** 'main subject of study'

Miß- 'wrong' (like English 'mis-')

der **Mißerfolg** 'failure/fiasco', der **Mißbrauch** 'abuse/improper use', **das Mißverständnis** 'misunderstanding'

Neben- 'secondary/incidental'

das **Nebenargument** 'secondary argument', **das Nebenfach** 'subsidiary subject of study', die **Nebenwirkung** 'side effect'

Nicht- 'non-'

der **Nichtraucher** 'non-smoker', der **Nichtschwimmer** 'non-swimmer', **der/die Nichtversicherte** 'non-insured person'

Riesen- 'enormous'

der **Riesenerfolg** 'huge success', das **Riesenproblem** 'huge problem', die **Riesensumme** 'huge amount (of money)'

Schein- 'illusory/not real'

das **Scheinargument** 'bogus argument', der **Scheinerfolg** 'illusory success', die **Scheinehe** 'fictitious marriage'

Scheiß- (colloquial, potentially offensive) expresses contempt and dislike

das **Scheißargument** 'rotten/poor argument', die **Scheißehe** 'awful marriage'

Teil- 'part/partial'

der **Teilerfolg** 'partial success', die **Teilzeitarbeit** 'part-time work'

Un- gives a negative

der Unsinn 'nonsense', das Unglück 'unhappiness'. Some of the words it forms have unusual nuances: das Ungewitter 'thunder storm', der Unmensch 'inhumane person/monster', die Unmenge 'huge quantity'

Ur- 'original/ancient'

die Urquelle 'original source', der Urgroßvater 'great-grandfather'

54.2 Meaning and gender of compound nouns

(a) The final element in a compound determines the meaning and gender of the whole (see 26.1A):

die Maschine 'machine'
das Büro 'office'
die Büro*maschine* is a particular kind of machine: an 'office machine'
der Büromaschinen*hersteller* is a particular kind of Hersteller 'manufacturer': a 'manufacturer of office machines'

(b) A 'linking' letter, (e)s or (e)n, is sometimes found between the main elements of the compound word:

Büromaschinenhersteller 'manufacturer of office machines'
Geschwindigkeitsgrenze 'speed limit'

(c) German can be more precise than English in the meanings which are combined. In English, a 'film-maker' may have made many films, or one. In German, the plural of der Film is die Filme and we have either der Filmmacher (one particular film) or der Filmemacher (more than one).

54.3 Using suffixes

(See also 25.1A; 25.3A; 25.5A)

Common suffixes are shown below. Note that all nouns formed by adding the same suffix have the same gender. Where an umlaut can be added as part of this process, this is added only where there is a vowel which can take an umlaut (a, o, u, au).

-chen/-lein (with umlaut on the stressed vowel) form neuter nouns denoting diminutives:

das Häuschen 'little house'

-heit/-keit/-igkeit form feminine nouns from adjectives and other nouns, usually denoting an abstract concept:

die Kindheit 'childhood', die Sicherheit 'safety/security', die Klugheit 'cleverness', die Eitelkeit 'vanity', die Geschwindigkeit 'speed', die Minderheit 'minority', die Möglichkeit 'possibility'

Structures

-e (with umlaut on the stressed vowel) forms feminine nouns from adjectives, denoting an abstract quality:

> **die Tiefe** 'depth', **die Größe** 'size', **die Schärfe** 'sharpness'

-e forms feminine nouns from some verbs, denoting a concrete event:

> **die Durchsage** 'announcement', **die Anfrage** 'enquiry'

-ei forms feminine nouns, denoting collections of things:

> **die Datei** 'data bank', **die Kartei** 'card index'

-er forms masuline nouns denoting a person (or thing) who performs the action described in a verb:

> **der Verteidiger** 'defender', **der Fahrer** 'driver', **der Computer** 'computer'

-erei forms feminine nouns denoting a repeated and/or annoying action:

> **die Angeberei** 'idle boasting', **die Schweinerei** 'dirty trick/awful mess'

-ik forms feminine nouns, usually denoting academic disciplines:

> **die Informatik** 'information technology', **die Statistik** 'statistics', **die Mathematik** 'mathematics' BUT oceans have the gender **der: der Atlantik, der Pazifik**

-in forms feminine nouns identifying a person as female:

> **die Verteidigerin** 'defender/defence counsel', **die Professorin** 'professor', **die Amerikanerin** 'American woman'

-ling forms masculine nouns denoting a person:

> **der Säugling** '(suckling) infant', **der Feigling** 'coward'

-nis forms mostly neuter nouns:

> **das Hindernis** 'obstacle' BUT **die Finsternis** 'darkness'

-schaft forms feminine abstract nouns:

> **die Brüderschaft** 'brotherhood', **die Mutterschaft** 'motherhood'

-tum forms mainly neuter nouns denoting an abstract category or a collective group:

> **das Wachstum** 'growth', **das Bürgertum** 'middle classes', **das Altertum** 'antiquity' BUT **der Reichtum** 'wealth'

-ung forms feminine nouns from verbs, and denotes either a process or the result of a process:

> **die Behandlung** 'treatment', **die Betreuung** 'supervision', **die Bestrafung** 'punishment', **die Bohrung** 'drilling/hole', **die Verfilmung** 'filming/filmed version of a book' BUT **die Wohnung** 'flat/apartment', **die Sitzung** 'session (of a meeting)'.

-wesen forms neuter nouns denoting a system or organism:

> **das Bankwesen** 'banking (system)', **das Verkehrswesen** 'transport (system)', **das Lebewesen** 'living organism'

Adjectival nouns with the gender **das** denote a general or abstract quality:

> **das Mögliche** 'what is possible', **das Gemeinte** 'what was intended', **das Vergangene** 'what is past', **das Aktuelle** 'what is topical'

(See **25–27**A for rules on the gender of compound nouns.)

54.4

Forming nouns from the principal parts of verbs

There are four patterns for forming nouns from verbs:

(a) From the infinitive, with the gender **das**, usually denoting the act of performing the activity described by the verb:

> **das Warten** 'waiting'
> **das Reden** 'talking'
> **das Trinken** 'drinking'

Any infinitive can be turned into a noun in this way. Occasionally, the noun formed in this way can have an additional meaning. For example, **das Schreiben** can mean both '(act of) writing' and 'written document'.

(b) From the present participle, usually denoting the person or thing performing the action:

> **der, die Studierende** 'student'
> **der, die Mitsingende** 'the person singing along'
> **der, die Nichtshabende** 'person who has nothing'
> **der, die Umziehende** 'person who is moving house'

(c) From the past participle. The past participle of transitive verbs usually has a passive sense:

> **der, die Angeklagte** 'the accused' (**jmdn. an*klagen** 'to accuse sb.')
> **das Vereinbarte** that which has been agreed (**etw. vereinbaren** 'to agree on sth.')

The past participle of intransitive verbs simply denotes an action which happened in the past:

> **der, die Umgezogene** 'person who (has) moved house' (**um*ziehen** 'to move house')

(d) Using the vowel changes in the strong verb pattern to form masculine nouns. The principal parts involved are the present tense stem, the simple past stem and the past participle (see **33.9**A):

beginnen	i – a – o	'to begin'	**der Beginn**	'beginning'
springen	i – a – u	'to jump'	**der Sprung**	'jump'
greifen	ei – i – i	'to grab'	**der Griff**	'handle'
schneiden	ei – i – i	'to cut'	**der Schnitt**	'cut'
sitzen	i – a – e	'to be sitting'	**der Sitz**	'seat'
stehen	e – a – a	'to stand'	**der Stand**	'stand'
stoßen	o – ie – o	'to push'	**der Stoß**	'push/collision'

Some nouns are formed using an additional vowel change:

brechen	i – a – o	'to break'	**der Bruch**	'break/fracture'
fliegen	ie – o – o	'to fly'	**der Flug**	'flight'
ziehen	ie – o – o	'to pull'	**der Zug**	'train/draught'
schließen	ie – o – o	'to close/to conclude'	**der Schluß**	'conclusion/ending'

55 *Forming adjectives*

55.1 Using suffixes

(a) The following form adjectives from nouns:

-bar '-able/-ible'

> **machbar** 'doable/viable', **erreichbar** 'reachable/attainable', **sichtbar** 'visible'

-haft 'like'

> **lehrerhaft** 'schoolmasterly', **meisterhaft** 'masterful'

-isch (sometimes with umlaut)

> **kindisch** 'childish', **exemplarisch** 'exemplary', **spöttisch** 'mocking'

-lich (sometimes with umlaut)

> **kindlich** 'childlike', **freundlich** 'friendly', **vertraglich** 'contractual', (BUT **verträglich** 'agreeable, digestible') **täglich** 'daily', **wöchentlich** 'weekly', **monatlich** 'monthly', **jährlich** 'yearly', **zweijährlich** 'biennial'.

-en/-ern (sometimes with umlaut)

> **golden** 'golden', **eisern** 'made of iron', **hölzern** 'wooden'

-ig (sometimes with umlaut)

> **eisig** 'icy', **brüchig** 'fragile', **dreistündig** 'lasting three hours', **zweitägig** 'lasting two days', **dreiwöchig** 'lasting three weeks', **viermonatig** 'lasting four months', **sechsjährig** 'lasting six years'

-mäßig 'pertaining to'

> **gefühlsmäßig** 'emotional', **planmäßig** 'according to (the) plan', **geschäftsmäßig** 'businesslike'

-freundlich 'friendly towards/good for'

> **umweltfreundlich** 'environmentally friendly', **kinderfreundlich** 'good for children', **familienfreundlich** 'good for the family'

-feindlich 'hostile towards/bad for'

> **umweltfeindlich** 'bad for the environment', **kinderfeindlich** 'anti-children/not catering for children', **familienfeindlich** 'hostile to the family'

-nah 'close to'

> **bürgernah** 'close to ordinary people', **praxisnah** 'applied' (rather than theoretical)

-fern 'distant from'

> **bürgerfern** 'remote from ordinary people', **praxisfern** 'not very practically orientated/theoretical'

-reich 'rich in/high in'

> **kinderreich** 'having many children', **ideenreich** 'with lots of ideas', **phosphatreich** 'high in phosphates'

-arm 'poor in/low in'

> **kinderarm** 'with not many children', **phosphatarm** 'low in phosphates'

-los 'without'

> **kinderlos** 'childless', **ideenlos** 'without ideas', **rücksichtslos** 'thoughtless/inconsiderate'

-frei 'free from'

> **phosphatfrei** 'phosphate-free', **koffeinfrei** 'caffeine-free', **ideologiefrei** 'free from ideology'

(b) The present participle and the past participle of all verbs can be used adjectivally. Here are some examples:

Past participle

> **geeignet** 'suitable', **gefragt** 'popular (often asked for)', **gelernt** 'trained/qualified', **erfahren** 'experienced'

Present participle

> **führend** 'leading', **fragend** 'questioning', **stehend** 'standing', **durchgehend** 'continuous/non-stop'

55.2 Using prefixes

There are many prefixes which alter or intensify the meaning of an adjective, including **un-** 'not'; **ur-** 'original/very old'; and several which intensify the meaning, such as **hoch-** 'very' and **höchst-, riesen-, super-** 'extremely':

> *un*interessant 'uninteresting' (see **47.5**A)
> *ur*alt 'ancient'
> *hoch*interessant 'extremely interesting'
> *höchst*wahrscheinlich 'most probably'
> *riesen*groß 'enormous'
> *super*fit 'super fit'

56 *Forming adverbs*

56.1

Most adjectives can be used as adverbs without a change in their form (see **50.2**A). For patterns forming distinct adverbs, see **50.3**A.

56.2

Where an adjective form exists alongside an adverbial form ending in **-erweise**, the adverb is almost always a sentence adverb, i.e. it relates to the sentence as a whole rather than to a specific word:

> **Das hat er *glücklicherweise* nicht erfahren.**
> Fortunately, he didn't find that out.

56.3

Note that the adverbial form ending in **-weise** is occasionally used adjectivally, with the full range of adjective endings (see **44–46**A):

> **Das stimmt *teilweise*.**
> That is partly true.

> **Ist das nicht ein *teilweiser* Widerspruch?**
> Isn't that a partial contradiction?

> **Das ist eine *teilweise* Erklärung.**
> That is a partial explanation.

57 *The meaning of verbal prefixes*

57.1

Prefixes which are always separable (see **36.1**A)
ab- 'away/off/finish off'

> **ab*fahren** 'to depart'
> **etw. ab*schließen** 'to finish off/conclude'
> **jmdn./etw. ab*tun** 'to discard/dismiss/put aside'

an- 'on, onto/a little bit'

> **jmdn./etw. an*schauen** 'to look at sb./sth.'
> **ein Gerät an*machen** 'to switch on an appliance'
> **jmdn./etw. an*brennen** 'to burn slightly, singe sb./sth.'

auf- 'up/open'

> **etw. auf*hängen** 'to hang sth. up'
> **etw. auf*wärmen** 'to warm sth. up'
> **etw. auf*machen** 'to open'

aus- 'off/out (of), from'

> **ein Gerät aus*machen** 'to switch off an appliance'
> **jmdn./etw. aus*machen** 'to make sb./sth. out (see clearly)'

ein- 'in, into/get used to'

> **ein*schränken** 'to constrain/limit (contain within a limit)'
> **sich ein*arbeiten** 'to get used to the work'

entgegen- 'towards/in the opposite direction'

> **jmdm. entgegen*kommen** 'come towards sb./be accommodating'

fern- 'distant'

> **fern*sehen** 'to watch TV'
> **fern*bleiben** 'to stay away'

hinzu- 'in addition'

> **etw. hinzu*schreiben** 'to add sth. (in writing)'
> **etw. hinzu*sagen** 'to say sth. in addition'

mit- 'as well'

> **mit*machen** 'to join in'
> **mit*singen** 'to sing along'

nach- 'after/follow, imitate, repeat'

> **etw. nach*schlagen** 'to look sth. up'
> **jmdm. etw. nach*machen** 'to imitate/copy sb.'
> **jmdm. nach*singen** 'to sing what sb. else has just sung'

vor- 'before, in front of/show how to'

> **etw. vor*zeigen** 'to show, present sth.'
> **jmdm. etw. vor*werfen** 'to accuse sb. of sth.' (lit. 'to throw sth. in front of sb.')
> **jmdm. etw. vor*machen** 'to show sb. how to do sth.'

weg- 'away'

> **weg*fahren** 'to drive off'
> **weg*bleiben** 'to stay away'

wieder- 'again' (see **36.3d**A)

> **jmdn. wieder*sehen** 'to see someone again'
> **wieder*kehren** 'to return'

zu- 'to, towards/closed'

> **zu*schauen** 'to watch (as a spectator)'
> **jmdm. etw. zu*flüstern** 'to whisper sth. to sb.'
> **etw. zu*machen** 'to close/shut'

zurück- 'back/return'

> **zurück*blättern** 'to flick back through the pages'

zusammen- 'together/collapse'

etw. **zusammen*tun** 'to pool, put sth. together'
zusammen*brechen 'to collapse' (lit. 'break together')
jmdn. **zusammen*hauen** 'to beat sb. up'

57.2

Prefixes which are always inseparable (see 36.2A)

be- and **be-... -ig-** (sometimes with umlaut) produce verbs with an accusative object from nouns and adjectives:

der Nachteil 'disadvantage' > **jmdn. benachteiligen** 'to disadvantage sb.'
die Vollmacht 'power of authority' > **jmdn. bevollmächtigen** 'to give sb. power of authority'
die Schranke 'barrier' > **jmdn./etw. beschränken** 'to restrict sb./sth.'
rein 'clean' > **etw. bereinigen** 'to clear sth. up (misunderstanding etc.)/put straight'

be- also forms verbs with an accusative object which can be used instead of a verb + preposition sequence:

auf eine Frage antworten > **eine Frage beantworten** 'to answer a question'

ent- often suggests removing something (cf. English 'dis-', 'de-'):

jmdn. entmutigen 'to discourage/make sb. feel dispirited'
entkommen 'to escape'

er- produces verbs with an accusative object, and suggests going through to the final consequence of an action:

jmdn. ermutigen 'to encourage/cheer up sb.'
eine Lohnerhöhung erstreiken 'to get a wage increase by striking'
jmdn. erschießen 'to shoot a person dead'

miß- 'wrong'

mißhandeln 'to maltreat'
mißverstehen 'to misunderstand'

ver- (sometimes ending in **-ern**) can form verbs from nouns and adjectives with a variety of meanings, usually denoting some kind of process:

der Stein 'stone' > **versteinern** 'turn to stone/ossify'
die Ursache 'cause' > **verursachen** 'to cause'
tief 'deep' > **vertiefen** 'to deepen'
groß 'large' > **größer** 'larger' > **vergrößern** 'to enlarge'

ver- sometimes marks the process as a negative one:

> **jmdn. verleiten** 'to lead sb. astray'
> **verkommen** 'to go to ruin'
> **etw. verlernen** 'to forget sth. you have learned'

sich ver- 'make a mistake'

> **sich versprechen** 'to make a slip of the tongue'
> **sich verirren** 'to stray/get lost'
> **sich vertun** 'to make an error'

zer- 'into small pieces'

> **etw. zertreten** 'to break sth. by standing on it'
> **etw. zerlegen** 'to disassemble carefully/analyse sth.'

57.3 — **Prefixes which can be separable or inseparable** (see 36.3A)
durch- 'through'

> **jmdn./etw. durchschauen** 'to see through/not be fooled by sb. or sth.'
> **durch etw. durch*schauen** 'to look through sth.'

hinter- 'behind' (nearly always inseparable verbs)

> **etw. irgendwo hinterlegen** 'to deposit sth. somewhere for safe keeping'

über- 'over, across/too much/do again'

> **etw. oder jmdn. über*setzen** 'to ferry sb. or sth. across'
> **etw. übersetzen** 'to translate sth.'
> **etw. oder jmdn. überschätzen** 'to overestimate sb. or sth.'
> **etw. überarbeiten** 'to rework sth.'

um- 'around/change'

> **(her-)um*gehen** 'to walk round'
> **jmdn./etw. umgehen** 'to evade sth. or sb.'
> **etw. um*schreiben** 'to rewrite sth.'
> **etw. umschreiben** 'to paraphrase sth.'

unter- 'under, underneath/too low'

> **jmdn./etw. irgendwo unter*bringen** 'to put sb. up/provide
> accommodation for sb./find a place for sth.'
> **etw. unternehmen** 'to undertake sth.'
> **etw. unterschreiben** 'to sign a document'
> **jmdn./etw. unterschätzen** 'to underestimate sb. or sth.'

There are also a number of inseparable verbs beginning with **unter-** which now have only a remote connection to the meaning 'under', e.g. **unterrichten** 'to teach/instruct', **unterbrechen** 'to interrupt'.

voll- 'complete/full'

> **voll*tanken** 'to fill up with petrol'
> etw. **vollbringen** 'to succeed in doing sth./accomplish sth.'

wider- 'against'

> **jmdm./etw. widersprechen** 'to contradict sb. or sth.'

There are only two separable verbs beginning with **wider-**:

> etw. **wider*spiegeln** 'to reflect/mirror sth.'
> **wider*hallen** 'to echo'.

IX Style and orthography

58 Formal and informal style

The following features should be noted because they are characteristic of formal (or informal) style:

58.1

Formal nominal style

(a) A particular feature of modern German is the use of a noun + verb construction in which the noun is derived from a verb (see **54**A). For example, **die Buchung** 'booking' is derived from the verb **buchen** 'to book'. The phrase 'to make a booking' is, in German, **eine Buchung vor*nehmen**. Note that the verb in this kind of construction (here **vor*nehmen**) simply has the meaning 'to carry out the action expressed in the noun'. This is a feature commonly found in formal written German, but it can also be used in spoken German, where it sounds extremely formal.

(b) Sometimes a compound noun is found as part of this formal style:

> **Er hatte keine Zeit,** *den Flug* zu *buchen.*
> He had no time to book the flight.

> **Er hatte keine Zeit,** *die Flugbuchung vorzunehmen.*
> He had no time to make the flight reservation.

(c) The preference in this formal kind of style for nouns over other word classes sometimes produces a chain of nouns with, for example, the second noun in the genitive. Compare:

> **Das Austauschprogramm fördert die deutsch–amerikanischen Beziehungen.**
> The exchange programme furthers German–American relations.

> **Das Austauschprogramm dient der Förderung der deutsch–amerikanischen Beziehungen.**
> (lit.) The exchange programme serves the furtherance of German–American relations.

(See **19.6**A for verbs with a dative object)

(d) The verb most commonly found in this kind of formal construction is **treffen**:

> **etw./sich auf etw.** (= acc) **vor*bereiten**
> to prepare sth. or oneself for sth.

> **Vorbereitung(en) für etwas treffen**
> to make preparation(s) for sth.

> **eine Auslese/eine Auswahl treffen** (from **etw. aus etw. aus*lesen** and **etw. aus etw. aus*wählen**)
> to make a selection

However, not all such phrases can be traced back to a verb:

> **eine Maßnahme treffen**
> to introduce a measure, to take action

> **Vorkehrungen treffen**
> to take precautions

58.2 **Informal style and verb forms**
(See also **60.1**A on using **du** and **Sie**)

(a) In informal (colloquial) speech, it is quite common for the endings to be dropped from the verb stem in the first person, present tense:

> **Ich mache es gleich.** > **Ich *mach* es gleich.**
> I'll do it straight away.

> **Ich habe es schon getan.** > **Ich *hab* es schon getan.**
> I have already done it.

It is also quite common in this kind of everyday style of speech to run sounds together, e.g. **Ich hab's schon getan.**

(b) Imperatives in the **du** form can also be made to sound even more informal by dropping the final **-e** from the verb where there is one (see **41.2c**A):

> **Sag's niemandem!**
> Don't tell anyone!

(c) Casual articulation of **du** and **Sie** following the forms of the verb are sometimes a sign that the speaker is being informal or familiar:

> **Hast du gebucht?** > ***Haste* gebucht?** (spoken German only)
> Have you booked?

> **Haben Sie Geschwister?** > **Haben** *Se* **Geschwister?**
> Do you have any brothers and sisters?

In the latter example, a speaker who has previously been using **Sie** could be signalling that he or she finds using **Sie** a bit too formal and would be happier using **du**.

58.3   Informal responses

In informal conversation it is quite common to omit the object of the verb or some other completion when responding to what the other person has just said, where the context makes the meaning obvious. This leads to sentences in which the finite verb appears to be in first position (compare **5.1–5.2**A):

> **Kennst du den Harald?** > **Nein, kenn ich nicht.**
> Do you know Harald? > No, don't know him.

> **Hast du den Wein schon kaltgestellt?** > **Hab ich schon heute morgen gemacht.**
> Have you cooled the wine? > Did it this morning.

> **Kannst du morgen bei mir vorbeikommen?** > **(Nein,) geht (leider) nicht.**
> Can you come round tomorrow? > (No,) (unfortunately I) can't.

> **Mir ist kalt, und dir?** > **Mir auch.**
> I am cold, and you? > Me too.

> **Die Musik stört die ganze Nachbarschaft.** > **Uns nicht.**
> The music is disturbing the entire neighbourhood. > Not us.

58.4   Verb-final position in informal style

In subordinate clauses, verbal elements which should appear at the end of the clause in careful, formal speech (see **8.1–8.2**A) are often brought forward in everyday informal speech:

> **Ich war nicht da, weil ich ein paar Stunden aufräumen** *mußte* **nach der Party.**
> I wasn't there because I had to tidy up for a few hours after the party.

Often this is a result of the speaker trying to make it easier for the listener to pick up the whole verb complex without having to wait until the end of a long clause. But note that even in the last example, where the finite verb has moved forward in the sentence, it is still not the 'second idea' (see **5.1**A).

59 *Spelling and punctuation*

A major revision of spelling and punctuation is currently being discussed in the German-speaking countries of Europe. Sections **59.1**–**59.5**A give an outline of current usage, while section **59.6**A gives an outline of the main proposed changes which may be introduced in the near future.

59.1

Capital letter or small letter?

(a) Generally, a word begins with a capital letter when it is:

- the first word in the sentence, except at the beginning of a letter (see **60.7b**B)
- a noun of any kind, including adjectival nouns, e.g. **der Versicherte** 'the person insured', **das Baden** 'bathing', **die Sieben** 'the number seven'
- any form of the formal second person **Sie** (and in letters, any form of the familiar **du** and **ihr**: see **60.1**A)
- an adjective which is part of a title, e.g. **die Europäische Union** 'the European Union', **Friedrich der Große** 'Frederick the Great'; or if the phrase has acquired a specialized meaning, e.g. **die Erste Hilfe** 'first aid', **das Schwarze Brett** 'noticeboard' (which does not have to be black at all)
- an adjective derived from a place name, e.g. **das Münchner Hofbräuhaus** 'the Munich Hofbräuhaus'

(b) All other words in a sentence begin with a small letter, including adjectives denoting nationalities, e.g. **die europäischen Regierungen** 'the European governments'.

(c) Note, however, the following cases concerning the use of adjectives:

- the adjective has a capital letter if it has the gender **das** and has a general reference, e.g. **das Wichtigste** 'the most important thing', **das Gute an der Sache** 'the good thing about the matter'
- the adjective also has a capital letter if it has a specialized meaning as a noun, but the same adjective will be written with a small letter if it has a particular reference and if the noun to which it refers can be deduced from the context:

> **Dann kam *der Alte* und sagte...**
> Then the old man (OR someone's father) came and said...

> **Der neue Wagen gefällt mir nicht so gut wie *der alte*.**
> I don't like the new car as much as the old one.

An exception to this rule, however, is **der einzelne** 'the individual'.

(d) Note also the following instances where words which look like nouns are written with a small letter. This is because they are seen as part of an adverbial, or some other kind, of construction:

> **heute** *nachmittag,* **heute** *abend,* **morgen** *vormittag*
> this afternoon, this evening, tomorrow morning

> *abends* **und** *nachmittags*
> in the evenings and afternoons

> **in** *bezug* **auf**
> concerning/with reference to

> **im** *großen* **und** *ganzen*
> on the whole

> **im** *allgemeinen*
> in general

> **im** *voraus*
> in advance

> **ein** *bißchen*
> a (little) bit

The spelling of the separable verbs **rad*fahren** 'to cycle' and **ski*fahren** 'to ski' is inconsistent, but both retain the capitalized noun, where it is separated from the verb:

> **Ich fahre gern** *Ski.*
> I like skiing.

> **Sie fährt jeden Tag** *Rad.*
> She cycles every day.

Note that **Schlittschuh laufen** 'to skate' is almost always written as noun + verb, while both **ski*laufen** and **Ski laufen** are found for 'to ski' (see **59.4**A).

(e) Capital letter or small letter with a change in meaning

Note the following, where the same word form occurs either with a capital letter or with a small letter, but the two are not interchangeable:

● 	 **ein paar** means 'several/a few', **ein Paar** means 'a pair'
● 	 **deutsch sprechen; Deutsch sprechen**

With a capital letter, **Deutsch** refers to the German language as a whole, and has the same sense as **das Deutsche**:

> **Er spricht kaum Deutsch.**
> He can hardly speak German.

> **Du sprichst gut (gutes) Deutsch.**
> You speak good German.

> **Das Buch wurde aus dem Englischen ins Deutsche übersetzt.**
> The book was translated into German from the English.

deutsch is written with a small letter when it functions as an adverb, adding an important detail to a sentence. Often it can be replaced by the phrase **auf deutsch** when referring to the language in which a conversation is held:

> **Ich fühle mich (gar nicht) deutsch.**
> I (don't) feel German (at all).

> **Sie denkt deutsch.**
> She thinks like a German (in a German way).

> **Sie denkt auf deutsch.**
> She thinks in German.

> **Wir können uns (auf) deutsch unterhalten.**
> We can talk in German.

> **Ich habe mit ihr (auf) deutsch, nicht (auf) englisch gesprochen.**
> I talked German, not English with her.

As the last example shows, the same principle applies to any adjective denoting nationality

● **hundert, tausend; Hundert, Tausend**

These are written with a small letter and are undeclined when used as a standard numeral (like **zwanzig, dreißig**, etc.):

> **nach hundert Kilometern**
> after a hundred kilometres

> **nach zweihundert Kilometern**
> after two hundred kilometres

> **nach vielen hundert Kilometern**
> after many hundred kilometres

They are written with a capital letter, and are plural nouns, when used as nouns of quantity in contexts such as:

> **mit Tausenden von Mitgliedern**
> with thousands of members

mit Zehntausenden von Mitgliedern
with tens of thousands of members

mit mehreren Tausenden von Mitgliedern
with several thousands of members

Splitting up words

When dividing up a word at the end of a line, the hyphen is generally placed before the consonant which begins the next syllable:

in-teressant
Va-ter

However, single vowels at the beginning or end of a word, and the component parts of complex words are never separated off in this way:

*a*tonal
atonal

Ruh*e*
peace and quiet

ver-einigt
unified

aus-atmen
breathe out

Sequences of two consonants are split down the middle:

Mit-te
middle

Mil-lion
million

But **st** is not split in simple words:

Fen-ster
window

Gang-ster
gangster

Prefixes and other meaningful parts of a word are preserved intact:

Aus-tausch
exchange

> **Diens-tag**
> Tuesday

The sequence **ck** is rewritten as **kk** for the purpose of splitting:

> **drük-ken (drücken)**
> to press

ß can be split either as **-ß** or as **s-s**:

> **So-ße, Sos-se**
> sauce

Where a sequence of three identical consonants has been compressed into two during word formation, the split word reinstates the third consonant. For example, **still** 'quiet' + **legen** 'to lay' = **stillegen** 'to close down (a factory)'. When split at the end of a line, the separable verb **stillegen** is written **still-legen**.

59.3
ss or *ß*?

ss is written between vowels when the preceding vowel is short, e.g. **Flüsse** [flüse] 'rivers'. **ß** is written in all other contexts:

- at the end of a word or a component part of a word, regardless of the length of any preceding vowel: **Haß** [has] 'hatred', **haßerfüllt** [haserfült] 'full of hatred', **Maß** [ma:s] 'measure', **Maßnahme** [ma:sna:me] 'step/measure', **Mißerfolg** [miserfolk] 'failure'
- before a consonant: **mißt** 'measures', **läßt** 'lets'
- between vowels where the preceding vowel is long: **Füße** [fü:se] 'feet'

Thus the forms of the modal verb **müssen** are spelt as follows: **ich muß, du mußt, er muß; Sie müssen; wir müssen, ihr müßt, sie müssen; Sie müssen.**

Note that **ß** is not used in Switzerland, and is never used when writing capitals. Writing **ß** where **ss** is the correct form is a mistake; but writing **ss** where **ß** is the correct form is not unacceptable.

59.4
One word or two?

(a) Note the following inconsistencies:

wieviel?	**soviel**
how much?	so much
wie viele?	**so viele**
how many?	so many
irgendwer	**irgendwelcher**
someone	some

irgend jemand
someone

irgend etwas
something

jedes Mal and **jedesmal** 'every time' are both possible and are interchangeable.

(b) Sometimes writing one word or two depends on a difference in meaning:

so lange
for such a long time

solange
as long as (conjunction: see **8.3**A)

so bald
so soon

sobald
as soon as (conjunction: see **8.3**A)

wo möglich
if possible

womöglich
perhaps/possibly

wie weit
how far (away)

wieweit
to what extent

sitzen bleiben
to remain seated

sitzen*bleiben
to stay back a year in school/repeat the year

59.5 **Use of commas, colons and apostrophes**

(a) The main use of the comma in German is to mark clause boundaries. In this case it is obligatory:

Ich glaube nicht, daß sie kommt.
I don't think that she'll come.

Daß sie gekommen ist, hat mich überrascht.
That she came surprised me.

Commas divide clauses joined by **und** or **oder** when the two clauses do not share the same subject word:

> **Mein Bruder studiert Maschinenbau, und Martin will Pilot werden.**
> My brother is studying mechanical engineering and Martin wants to be a pilot.
> **Mein Bruder studiert Maschinenbau und will Pilot werden.**
> My brother is studying mechanical engineering and wants to be a pilot.

(b) The main use of the colon is to introduce direct speech:

> **Er sagte sofort: 'Ich bezahle das.'**
> Straight away he said, 'I'll pay for that.'

(c) The apostrophe is used to show omitted letters:

> **Ich versteh's nicht.**
> I don't understand it.

but it is not supposed to be used (as it is in English) to indicate possession:

> **Georgs Wohnung**
> Georg's flat

(d) When writing numbers, a gap is left between units of a thousand (where English has a comma), and a comma is used to show decimal values (where English has a point):

> **1 000 (eintausend)**
> 1,000 (one thousand)
>
> **1,5 (eins komma fünf)**
> 1.5 (one point five)
>
> **DM 1 234,56 (eintausendzweihundertvierunddreißig Mark sechsundfünfzig)**
> 1,234 Marks 56 Pfennigs

When writing large numbers, a point is sometimes used:

> **17.450.263**
> 17,450,263

Proposed reforms

— 59.6 —

This section draws on published proposals for reforming German spelling and punctuation (e.g. in **Sprachreport (Extraausgabe)** December 1994, Institut für deutsche Sprache, ISSN 0178-664 X). The proposed spelling reforms are intended to remove the major inconsistencies and make the spelling conventions more predictable for learners. The main principle underlying these proposed reforms is the so-called **Stammprinzip**, i.e. that spelling should wherever possible preserve the relationship between words that are regarded as belonging to the same root or stem. For example, the spelling of **plazieren** 'to place' is to be changed to **platzieren** to show that it belongs to the same word family as **der Platz** 'place'. The remainder of this section gives further details of the proposed reforms, with current practice shown on the left-hand side of the page, and the proposed reform on the right, i.e.:

Present convention   Proposed reform

(a) The following examples illustrate the logic of the **Stammprinzip**:

Platz > plazieren	**Platz > platzieren**
packen > Paket	**packen > Packet**
Nummer > numerieren	**Nummer > nummerieren**
Zigarre > Zigarette	**Zigarre > Zigarrette**
Schnauze > schneuzen	**Schnauze > schnäuzen**

(b) Splitting words at the end of a line (cf. **59.2**A):

Proposed changes affect the splitting of **st**, **ck** and initial vowel:

Mu-ster	**Mus-ter**
Zuk-ker	**Zuc-ker**
Ofen	**O-fen**

There will also be greater flexibilty in splitting 'foreign words' – a thorny problem for many Germans:

Si-gnal	**Si-gnal** or **Sig-nal**
Päd-agogik	**Päd-agogik** or **Pä-dagogik**

(c) Where three identical consonants come together as a result of word formation, all three will be written (cf. **59.2**A):

still + legen > stillegen	**stilllegen**
Schiff + Farht > Schiffahrt	**Schifffahrt**
Fluß + Sand > Flußsand	**Flusssand**

Similarly, where an **h** has been omitted before **-heit**, it will be restored:

roh + -heit > Roheit	**Rohheit**

(d) **ß** will be written only after a long vowel or a diphthong. On all other occasions, **ss** will be written (cf. **59.3**A):

daß	**dass**
Fluß, Flüsse	**Fluss, Flüsse**
hassen, Haß	**hassen, Hass**
ich muß, er muß, ihr müßt	**ich muss, er muss, ihr müsst**
Maß, Fuß, Straße	**Maß, Fuß, Straße**
draußen, beißen	**draußen, beißen**

(e) One word or two?

Most separable verbs with a noun or adverbial element are to be written as two separate words (like **Auto fahren**, cf. **59.1d**A):

staub*saugen	**Staub saugen**
rad*fahren	**Rad fahren**

Where an adjective or a verb is the separable part of a separable verb, these will usually be written as two words. In some instances, there will be only one form to cover two distinct senses of a word:

sitzen*bleiben	**sitzen bleiben** (cf. **59.4b**A)
übrig*bleiben	**übrig bleiben**

Other inconsistencies to be eliminated include (cf. **59.4a**A):

irgend jemand	**irgendjemand** (like **irgendwer**)
irgend etwas	**irgendetwas** (like **irgendwer**)
soviel	**so viel** (like **so viele**)
wieviel	**wie viel** (like **wie viele**)

(f) Capital letter or small letter?

Nouns in fixed phrases, especially when preceded by a preposition, will be written with a capital letter (cf. **59.1d**A):

im großen und ganzen	**im Großen und Ganzen**
im allgemeinen	**im Allgemeinen**
in bezug auf	**in Bezug auf**

In fixed phrases consisting of adjective and noun, the adjective will normally have a small letter unless the phrase denotes a specific individual institution or phenomenon (cf. **59.1a**A):

das Schwarze Brett	**das schwarze Brett**
die Erste Hilfe	**die erste Hilfe**
der Deutsche Bundestag	**der Deutsche Bundestag**

Nouns used adverbially in time expressions are to have a capital letter (cf. **59.1d**A):

heute abend	**heute Abend**

But nouns used in fixed constructions with the verbs **sein**, **werden** and **bleiben** will continue to be written with a small letter:

schuld sein	**schuld sein**

(g) Wherever practicable, the letter combinations **ph**, **th**, **rh**, **gh** are to be replaced by **f**, **t**, **r** and **g** respectively. Alternative spellings will be allowed in many cases:

Orthographie	**Orthographie** or **Ortografie**
Alphabet	**Alphabet** or **Alfabet**
Thunfisch	**Tunfisch**
Panther	**Panter**
Apotheke	**Apotheke** or **Apoteke**
Rhythmus	**Rhythmus** or **Rytmus**
Joghurt	**Joghurt** or **Jogurt**

Other 'Germanized' spellings include:

Kommuniqué	**Kommuniqué** or **Kommunikee**
Ketchup	**Ketchup** or **Ketschup**

(h) The formal second person form **Sie** will continue to have a capital letter, but all the forms of the informal **du** and **ihr** will have a small letter, even in letters (cf. **59.1a**A, **60.1**A)

(i) The use of the comma to divide off clauses which are joined by the co-ordinating conjunction **und** or **oder** will be relaxed. Commas will be optional here.

Functions

X Social contact

Greeting

The following are the most common expressions for 'to greet' in German:

> **jmdn. grüßen** 'to greet sb.'
> **viele Grüße/einen schönen Gruß (an jmdn.)** 'many/best wishes (to sb.)'
> **jmdm. einen schönen Gruß sagen** 'to give/send sb. (one's) best wishes'
> **jmdm. Grüße bestellen** 'to give/send regards to sb.'
> **jmdm. Wünsche aus*richten** 'to convey (good) wishes to sb.'
> **jmdn. jmdm. empfehlen** 'to convey sb.'s respects to sb.' (formal)
> **sich jmdm. empfehlen** 'to send one's regards to sb.' (formal)
> **jmd. läßt jmdn. grüßen** 'sb. sends his/her regards'
> **jmdn. von jmdm. grüßen** 'to pass on sb.'s good wishes'

Using *du, ihr* and *Sie*

For greeting, and indeed any interaction with Germans, it is very important that English-speaking learners of German become familiar with the following guidelines on the use of the familiar pronouns **du** (with its plural **ihr**) and the polite or distant **Sie**. Failure to use the correct form can cause offence.

(a) Use of **du** and **ihr**

Du/ihr is used when addressing:

- relatives and close friends
- children up to about the age of 14 or 15
- fellow pupils and students
- colleagues in manual or blue-collar jobs
- animals, objects and God

(b) Use of **Sie**

Sie is used in all other circumstances of which the following should be particularly noted:

● with adults who are strangers
● with colleagues in non-blue-collar jobs (often even after years of working together)
● by teachers when addressing pupils in the senior classes of secondary school
● for all student–lecturer communication in higher education

(c) When to start using **du**

Du is usually associated with first-name terms, but first names are, for example, used with **Sie** in the senior classes of secondary school. The point in a relationship at which the **du** form becomes appropriate is very difficult to define. Native English speakers are advised to follow the lead of Germans on this matter. It is normal for the older/more senior person to offer the **du** form to the younger/junior person. If ever in doubt, use **Sie**. The verbs corresponding to the pronouns **du** and **Sie** are **jmdn. duzen** and **jmdn. siezen** respectively:

> **Wollen wir uns duzen?**
> Shall we use the **du** form?

(d) Spelling of **du/ihr** and **Sie**

In letters **du/ihr** and the related possessive adjectives, i.e. **dein**, etc. and **euer**, etc. (see **30.3**A), are written with capital letters:

> **Ich danke *Dir* für *Deinen* langen Brief.**
> Thank you for your long letter.

> **Was habt *Ihr* im Sommer vor?**
> What do you have planned for the summer?

Otherwise they are always written with a small letter.

In all contexts the various forms of **Sie** and the possessive adjective **Ihr** are written with a capital letter:

> **Wann fahren *Sie* in die Stadt?**
> When are you going to town?

> **Wie geht es *Ihnen/Ihrem* Mann?**
> How are you?/How is your husband?

60.2 Initial greeting

(a) In spoken German a simple **Hallo!** is very common, especially amongst friends, colleagues and young people (see also **90.1**B). **Grüß dich!** 'greetings' is also frequently heard.

(b) **Guten Tag** 'Good day' is the standard greeting for a stranger or informal acquaintance and can be used throughout the day. In the morning **Guten Morgen** might be used, while in the evening **Guten Abend** is likely to be preferred (see **18.7**A for this use of the accusative). These forms might be reinforced by **schön**:

> **Schön(en) guten Morgen!**
> A very good morning to you!

(c) In southern Germany and Austria **Grüß Gott!** is frequently employed, as is **Servus!** (lit. 'your servant'), which can also mean 'cheerio' (see also **62.1**B on saying goodbye). In Switzerland and the very south of Germany **Grüß Sie!** and **Grüzi!** are standard greetings when talking to people with whom one is not on first name terms.

60.3 Conveying greetings

(a) If passing on personal greetings via a friend to a third person, either in speech or writing, one of the following would be appropriate:

> *Sag* ihm *einen schönen Gruß* von mir.
> Give him my best wishes.

> *Einen schönen Gruß an* deine Schwester.
> Give your sister my best wishes.

> *Grüß* deinen Vater (von mir)!
> Say hello to your father (for me).

> *Grüß mir* deine Mutter!
> Say hello to your mother for me.

(See **19.2**A for this dative usage)

> *Bestell* Raimund viele *Grüße* von mir.
> Give Raimund my best regards.

The above can also be used in the **Sie** form for less informal occasions:

> Bitte *grüßen Sie* Ihre Kollegin (vielmals) von mir!
> Please send your colleague my (very) best regards.

> *Viele Grüße an* Ihren Mann.
> Kind regards to your husband.

In very formal usage the following might occur:

> Bitte *richten Sie* ihm meine besten *Wünsche aus.*
> Please convey my best wishes to him.

Meine Empfehlungen an Ihre Frau. (formal)
My regards to your wife.

Bitte *empfehlen Sie mich* Ihrer Frau. (formal)
Please convey my regards to your wife.

This last example is also a little old-fashioned.

(See **12.3**A for word order with noun and pronoun objects)

(b) If passing on someone else's greetings, use the following:

Manfred *läßt grüßen/läßt* euch *schön grüßen.*
Manfred sends his regards/sends you his best regards.

Ich soll dich von Katrin *grüßen./Ich soll Grüße* von Katrin *bestellen.*
Katrin says to send you her best wishes.

(See **35.1**A for the use of these modal verbs)

60.4   Responding to greetings

The greetings in **60.2**B can simply be returned in the same form. One of the following would be an appropriate response to **60.3a**B:

Ja, (das) mach ich (gern).
Yes, I'll (gladly/certainly) do that.

Auf jeden Fall.
Certainly/I certainly will.

Ja!/Jawohl!/Ja, (aber) natürlich/selbstverständlich.
Of course (I will).

Gerne.
Gladly.

(Ganz) bestimmt./Ja, (ganz) sicher.
I (most) certainly will.

Na klar./Aber sicher.
Sure, of course.

60.5   Enquiring about well being

(a) To ask someone how they are, use:

Wie geht's?/Wie geht es Ihnen?/Wie geht's dir?
How are you?

This structure requires the dative of the person when mentioned and the subject of the verb is always **es**. Responses could include:

> **Danke, gut/es geht.**
> Thanks, I'm well/I'm OK.

> **Es geht mir/uns sehr gut/bestens.**
> I am/we are very well/extremely well.

> **Wir sind alle ganz gesund/wohlauf.**
> We are all very well/in good health.

Note that **wohlauf** is now considered a little old-fashioned.

> **Na ja, es geht!**
> Oh, all right.

> **Danke, einigermaßen.**
> Not so bad, thanks.

Alternatively, if things are not so good:

> **Mir geht's schlecht.**
> I'm not well/I'm ill.

> **Es geht (mir) nicht so gut/gar nicht gut.**
> I'm not too well/not at all well.

(b) To return the question, use:

> **Und (wie geht es) dir/euch/Ihnen?**
> And how are you/what about you?

(c) When asking about a third person, use:

> **Und wie geht es Ihrem Mann?**
> **Und wie geht es Ihrem Gatten?** (formal)
> And how is your husband?

> **Und was macht (die) Petra?**
> And how's Petra?

> **Und was machen die Kinder?**
> And how are the children (doing)?

(See **19.7**A and **42.3h**A for the use of impersonal verbs)

60.6

Welcoming

> **(jmdm.) willkommen sein** 'to be welcome'
> **jmdn. willkommen heißen** 'to welcome sb.'
> **jmdn. begrüßen** 'to greet sb.'
> **jmdm. ein Willkommen bereiten** 'to give sb. a welcome'
> **jmdn. auf*nehmen/empfangen** 'to receive sb.'

(a) The standard welcome is **Willkommen!** but there are a number of variations:

> **Seien Sie/Sei/Seid herzlich willkommen.**
> A warm welcome to you.

> **Ein herzliches Willkommen!**
> Welcome indeed!

> **Herzlich willkommen (in Berlin/im Hotel 'Rostock')!**
> Welcome (to Berlin/the Hotel 'Rostock')!

> **Sie sind uns** (= dat) **jederzeit willkommen.**
> You are always welcome here.

(See **19.9**A for the use of the dative; see also **96**B on invitations)

(b) Following the initial welcome one of the following may be used:

> **Bitte, kommen Sie herein!**
> Please, do come in.

(See **50.4**A for the use of **herein**)

> **Haben Sie eine gute Reise gehabt?**
> Did you have a good journey?

> **Wie war die Fahrt?**
> How was the journey?

(c) A more formal welcome might be expressed:

> **Im Namen der Stadt Mainz möchte ich Sie herzlich *willkommen heißen*.**
> I would like to offer you a warm welcome on behalf of the city of Mainz.

(See **28.2**A for the declension of **Name** and weak nouns in general)

(d) Other ways of expressing welcoming include:

> **Ein großes Kaminfeuer *begrüßte ihn* bei seiner Ankunft.**
> A large fire welcomed him on his arrival.

Ein Glas Wein stand *zu ihrer Begrüßung* **auf dem Tisch.**
There was a glass of wine on the table to greet her.

Man hat mir dort *ein herzliches Willkommen bereitet.* (formal)
I was given a very warm welcome there.

Wir *wurden* **dort sehr freundlich** *empfangen.*
We were received there in a most friendly manner.

Man *hat* **ihn sehr** *freundlich aufgenommen.*
He was received/accommodated in a most friendly manner.

Die Gelegenheit, die Entscheidungen des Finanzrates zu überprüfen, *ist uns* (= dat) *sehr willkommen.*
We very much welcome the opportunity to review the finance committee's decisions.

60.7 Beginning a letter

(a) Formal letters

If the name of the addressee is known, use:

Sehr geehrter Herr Rösler/Sehr geehrte Frau Simon
Dear Mr Rösler/Dear Mrs/Ms Simon

Note that 'Ms' is conveyed by **Frau** which is now also the usual rendering of 'Miss', with **Fräulein** considered a relic of more sexist days.

(For the pronunciation of **geehrter** see **4.4**A)

If the person you are writing to has a title, it will follow **Herr** or **Frau**:

Sehr geehrter Herr Professor Wegener/Sehr geehrte Frau Dr. Matthäus
Dear Professor Wegener/Dear Dr Matthäus

If the person's name is not known, use:

Sehr geehrte Damen und Herren
Dear Sir/Madam

Sehr geehrte Herren 'Dear Sirs' is only used if it is known that the addressees are exclusively male.

(b) Informal letters

The normal form of address here is:

Lieber Paul/Liebe Heidi
Dear Paul/Dear Heidi

If addressing two people it is usual to repeat the 'Dear':

Lieber Paul, lieber Harald/Liebe Elke und lieber Paul
Dear Paul and Harald/Dear Elke and Paul

To address a whole family, simply write:

Liebe Familie Huber
Dear Huber family

If the addressees are close friends or relatives, **Ihr Lieben** 'Dear All' could be used.

A comma will usually follow all these openings and the letter proper will begin with a small letter (unless the first word is a noun). It is accepted practice not to begin a letter with **ich**.

60.8 Postcard greetings

The following formulations might be used either to begin or end a postcard message:

Einen schönen Gruß aus München (von/schickt dir, Harald).
Best wishes from Munich (from Harald).

Grüße/Herzliche Grüße/Liebe Grüße aus dem Schwarzwald.
Greetings/warmest greetings/good wishes from the Black Forest.

60.9 Compliments

A compliments slip (**-r Empfehlungszettel**) will normally bear the words:

mit den besten Empfehlungen
with (the) compliments

This will be followed by the person's title, e.g. **vom Direktor** 'of the Director'. Some business cards (**-e Visitenkarte**) will have the same wording.

61 Making introductions

Introductions can be expressed as follows:

> **sich vor*stellen** 'to introduce oneself'
> **jmdn. jmdm. vor*stellen** 'to introduce sb. to sb.'
> **jmdn. kennen*lernen** 'to be introduced to/get to know sb.'
> **jmdn. mit jmdm. bekannt machen** 'to introduce sb. to sb.'
> **mit jmdm. bekannt sein** 'to know/be acquainted with sb.'
> **jmds. Bekanntschaft machen** 'to make sb.'s acquaintance' (formal)
> **das ist/sind...** 'this is/here are...'
> **jmdn. kennen** 'to know sb.'
> **sich (= acc) kennen** 'to know each other'
> **heißen** 'to be called'
> **jmdm. begegnen** 'to meet sb.'

61.1 Making initial contact

(a) To attract someone's attention say:

> **Entschuldigung!/Verzeihung!**
> Excuse me./I'm sorry. (See also **68.1**B on 'Apologizing and seeking forgiveness'.)

> *Entschuldigen Sie*, **bitte, wo ist hier der Bahnhof?**
> Excuse me, can you tell me where the station is?

(b) To attract someone's attention or to hail someone from afar, **Hallo!** might be used. Alternatively, if the aim is to attract attention urgently or to warn someone, the following would be more appropriate:

> **Vorsicht, passen Sie doch auf!**
> (Be careful), watch out!

> **Heh!/Heh, du! Paß mal auf!** (informal)
> Hey/hey you. Listen.

Depending on the tone of voice, the second of these may sound rude or mildly threatening.

> **Vorsicht!/Achtung!**
> Look out!/Watch it!

He, du da! 'Oi, you!' is distinctly rude.

61.2 Reacting when spoken to

(a) Appropriate responses to the above include:

> **Bitte?**
> I'm sorry?

Ja, (bitte)?
Yes (what is it)?

Ja, was gibt's?
Yes, what's the matter?

(b) More informally and abruptly one could say:

Na, was denn?
Well, what is it?

Formal introductions

(a) When introducing oneself, say:

Darf ich mich vor*stellen?
May I introduce myself?

It is quite common for people to introduce themselves in formal and business situations by their surname only: **Guten Tag, Meier** 'Hello, my name's Meier'.

(b) In responding to a formal introduction, say **angenehm** (lit. 'pleasant') or:

(Es) freut mich (, Sie kennenzulernen).
I'm pleased to meet you.

(See **42.3g**A for impersonal verbs with the dummy subject **es**)

Remember that in Germany it is customary to shake hands with people each time one meets them, not just when being introduced to them for the first time.

(c) When introducing two people to each other, it is considered good form first to tell a woman a man's name or a more senior person a younger person's name. Expressions for introductions include:

Darf ich (Ihnen) Herrn Arnold *vor*stellen*?
May I introduce Mr Arnold (to you)?

(See **28.2**A for the declension of **Herr**)

Ich möchte (Ihnen) Frau Pühmeyer *vor*stellen.*
I'd like to introduce Mrs Pühmeyer (to you).

Darf ich (Sie) *bekannt machen*? Frau Pühmeyer, das ist Herr Arnold.
May I introduce you? Mrs Pühmeyer, this is Mr Arnold.

Frau Pühmeyer, *darf ich* Sie mit Herrn Arnold *bekannt machen*?
Mrs Pühmeyer, may I introduce you to Mr Arnold?

(See also **61.6b**B on 'Making acquaintances'.)

The following are used on less formal occasions:

> **Frau Weingarten,** *kennen Sie* **Herrn Zeisig?**
> Mrs Weingarten, do you know Mr Zeisig?

> **Herr Doktor Gutmann,** *kennen Sie schon* **Manfred Seeler?**
> Dr Gutmann, do you know Manfred Seeler?

> *Das sind* **Herr und Frau Neumann.**
> This is Mr and Mrs Neumann.

> *Kennen Sie sich* **schon?**
> Do you already know each other?

61.4 Official introductions

(a) In dealing with officialdom, either in person or by letter, there are a few variations on the above:

> **(Wie ist Ihr) Vorname/Familienname/Nachname/Mädchenname?**
> (What is your) first name/surname/maiden name?

> **Wie heißen Sie mit Vornamen und (mit) Familiennamen/Nachnamen?**
> What is your first name and your surname?

> **Sind Sie Herr Schwarz?**
> Are you Mr Schwarz? (Answer: **Ja, das bin ich**, 'Yes I am')

(See also **73.2**B on 'Supplying personal details')

(b) On forms and other documents the following may be found in connection with a woman's married name:

> **Angelika Hauptmann geb. (geborene) Freud**
> Angelika Hauptmann, née Freud

61.5 Informal introductions

(a) Introducing oneself

The verb **heißen** can be used in all contexts to ask a person's name and to supply one's own:

> **Wie heißen Sie/heißt du?**
> What is your name?

> **Wer sind Sie/bist du?**
> Who are you?

> **Guten Tag, ich heiße/mein Name ist Bruno (Wegener).**
> Hello, my name is Bruno (Wegener).

Among young people, in particular, **Hallo** followed by a first name often serves as an introduction:

> **Hallo, Uli,** *ich bin* **(die) Marlies/(der) Wolfgang**
> Hello, Uli, I'm Marlies/Wolfgang

(See **23.2g**A for the use of the definite article in German)

(b) Introducing someone else. Expressions here include many mentioned under **61.3c**B, but in the **du** or **ihr** forms of the verb:

> **Peter,** *kennst du* **(die) Gabi/(den) Hubert?**
> Peter, do you know Gabi/Hubert?

> *Das hier ist* **(der) Frank/mein Mann.**
> This is Frank/my husband.

> **Hans,** *du kennst* **doch** *sicher* **den Rudi?**
> Hans, you know Rudi, don't you?

> **Sabine,** *du kennst* **doch** *schon* **die Antje?**
> Sabine you already know Antje, don't you?

> *Kennst du* **meinen Bruder Stephan?**
> Do you know my brother Stephan?

> *Er heißt* **Stephan, aber alle** *nennen ihn* **Steff.**
> He's called Stephan but everyone calls him Steff.

> *Das ist* **meine Cousine.** *Sie heißt* **Karin.**
> That's my cousin. She's called Karin.

> *Ihr kennt euch* **ja schon, oder?**
> You already know each other, don't you?

61.6 Making acquaintances

(a) The verb **kennen*lernen** can be used in almost all contexts:

> *Ich habe* **sie schon vor Jahren** *kennengelernt.*
> I met them (several) years ago.

> **Sie hatten** *sich* **in London** *kennengelernt.*
> They had met in London.

(b) The word **bekannt** can be used to express existing acquaintance or, with **machen**, the act of introducing someone else:

> **Sie *sind* schon lange *miteinander bekannt*.**
> They have known each other for a long time.

(See **34.2d**A for this use of the present tense)

> **Ich werde ihn mit meinem Vetter *bekannt machen*.**
> I'll introduce him to my cousin.

(c) A rather more formal way to express acquaintance is with the noun **Bekanntschaft**:

> **Wo haben Sie seine *Bekanntschaft gemacht*?**
> Where did you make his acquaintance?

(d) Alternatively, the less formal **begegnen** can be used:

> **Wir sind ihm zum ersten Mal in München begegnet.**
> We first met him in Munich.

61.7 ## Introductions on the telephone

> **jmdn. sprechen** 'to speak to sb.'
> **mit jmdm. sprechen** 'to speak to sb.'
> **jmdn. melden** 'to announce (a caller)'
> **mit jmdm. verbunden sein** 'to be connected/through to sb.'
> **jmdn. (mit jmdm.) verbinden** 'to put sb. through (to sb.)'

(a) When answering the telephone a simple **Hallo!** or **Ja, bitte?** 'Yes, how can I help you?' will suffice. To identify oneself, it is usual to give one's surname or, less commonly, both first name and surname. Children may also give both first name and surname:

> **Erschens/Neumann/Heinz Meyer**
> Hello, Erschens/Neumann/Heinz Meyer (speaking).

Alternatively, one of the following could be used:

> **Ich bin's, der Manfred (Schulz).**
> It's me, Manfred (Schulz).

> **Hallo, hier ist Horst (Kaiser).**
> Hello, Horst (Kaiser) speaking.

> **Hier (ist) Birgit.**
> Birgit (speaking).

In a family the following might be used:

> **Familie Meyer**
> Hello, the Meyers/the Meyer household

Another way of announcing the family name, or of answering someone's telephone for them, is:

> **Hier bei Bauer.**
> The Bauers' (home).

(Note that on letters **bei Bauer** means 'c/o the Bauers'.)

If the caller has asked to speak to you personally, say:

> **Am Apparat./Ja, bitte?**
> Speaking (how can I help?)

To speak to someone else, say:

> ***Kann ich* bitte (den) Günther *sprechen*?**
> Can I speak to Günther, please?

(See **23.2g**A for the use of the definite article here)

(b) To find out who is on the line, ask:

> **Mit wem spreche ich, bitte?**
> Who am I speaking to, please?

> **Wer spricht?/Wer ist am Apparat, bitte?**
> Who's calling?/Who is it, please?

> **Sabine, bist du es?** (informal)
> Is that you Sabine?

A possible response upon discovering who is calling might be:

> **Ach, du bist es!**
> Oh, it's you!

A firm will identify itself as follows:

> **Hier Firma Hahn.**
> This is the firm of Hahn & Co.

> **Hahn und Co., guten Morgen.**
> Good morning, Hahn & Co.

An individual may identify himself or herself:

> **Hahn und Co., hier Schneider.**
> This is Hahn & Co., Mr/Ms Schneider speaking.

(c) When calling a switchboard or some other contact person, the following will be useful:

> **Ich möchte bitte Apparat 671 (sechs sieben eins).**
> Can you give me extension 671, please?

> **Mit wem bin ich verbunden?**
> Who am I through to?/Who am I speaking to?

(See **30.4a**A for the full declension of **wer**)

> **Verbinden Sie mich bitte mit der Personalabteilung.**
> Please put me through to Personnel.

> **Kann ich bitte den Personalleiter sprechen?**
> Can I speak to the Head of Personnel, please?

> **Kann ich bitte mit Herrn Maibaum sprechen?**
> Can I speak to Mr Maibaum, please?

(d) A telephonist or secretary is likely to ask:

> **Wen soll/darf ich melden, bitte?**
> Who shall I say is calling, please?

Or a caller may be asked to wait briefly:

> **Einen Augenblick, ich verbinde (Sie).**
> Just a moment, I'll put you through.

(e) When calling a company's answering machine, the following type of message may be heard:

> **Hier ist der automatische Anrufbeantworter, Firma Carl Dan Pedinghaus.**
> You are through to the answering machine of the firm Carl Dan Pedinghaus.

A more typical message for a domestic answering machine might be:

> **Guten Tag, Sie haben den Anschluß von Anke Weber gewählt.**
> Hello, you have dialled Anke Weber's number.

Since many people prefer not to put their name on the tape, the following is becoming more typical:

Es ist im Moment niemand da. Bitte hinterlassen Sie Ihre Nachricht, Ihren Namen und Ihre Rufnummer nach dem Signal und wir rufen sobald wie möglich zurück.

There is nobody here to take your call at present. Please leave your message, name and number after the beep and we'll get back to you as soon as we can.

(f) To indicate a wrong number say:

Es tut mir leid, Sie sind falsch verbunden.
I'm sorry, you've got the wrong number.

61.8

When entering a room or someone's office, it would usually be appropriate to say one of the following:

Kann ich/Darf ich (rein*kommen)?
Can/may I (come in)?

Störe ich?
Am I disturbing you?

Sind Sie frei?
Are you free?

Hast du einen Moment Zeit für mich?
Do you have a moment?

61.9

Inviting someone in

(a) When responding positively to a knock on the door, say:

Herein!/Ja!/Ja, bitte!
Come in!

(b) More generally:

Kommen Sie (bitte) (rein).
(Please) come (in).

Sie können ruhig rein*kommen.
Do come in.

(See **50.4**A for the use of **hin** and **her**. See also **80.7**B on 'The speaker's perspective')

(c) To invite a person to sit down, say:

Setzen Sie sich doch./Setz dich doch.
Have a seat.

Bitte, nehmen Sie doch Platz.
Please do sit down.

Möchten/Wollen Sie sich nicht setzen?
Wouldn't you like to sit down?

(d) A more general welcome (see also **60.6**B on 'Welcoming') could include:

Fühlen Sie sich wie zuhause.
Please make yourself at home.

Machen Sie es sich bequem.
Make yourself comfortable.

When offering refreshment, say:

Bedienen Sie sich, bitte.
Please help yourself.

61.10 — ## Exchanging personal details
(See also **73.2**B on 'Supplying personal details')

> **kommen/stammen aus** (+ dat) 'to come from'

(a) To swap addresses and numbers, say:

Wie ist Ihre/deine Adresse/Telefonnummer?
What is your address/telephone number?

(b) To discover a person's place of origin, ask:

Wo bist du geboren?
Where were you born?

Woher kommen Sie/kommst du?
Where are you from?

Woher stammen Sie/stammst du?
Where do you come from (originally)?

The verb **stammen** has a slightly formal ring to it.

Possible responses are:

Ich komme aus Schottland/aus den USA/aus dem Libanon/aus der Türkei.
I'm from Scotland/the USA/the Lebanon/Turkey.

Wir stammen aus Düsseldorf.
We come from Düsseldorf (originally).

> **Ich bin Engländer(in).**
> I'm English.

(See **23.1**A for the omission of the indefinite article)

> **Ich bin in Paris geboren.**
> I was born in Paris.

(c) If discussing families, the following will be useful (see also **74.9**B on 'Family relationships'):

> **Haben Sie/Hast du Geschwister?**
> Do you have any brothers or sisters?

> **Ich habe zwei Schwestern aber keinen Bruder.**
> I have two sisters but no brother.

> **Wir sind zu dritt/zu viert/zu fünft in der Familie.**
> There are three/four/five of us in our family.

A family of four, five, etc. is **eine vierköpfige/fünfköpfige Familie.**

(d) Typical questions and answers when meeting a foreigner include:

> **Waren Sie/warst du schon einmal in Deutschland/im Ausland?**
> Have you been to Germany/abroad before?

> **Nein, ich bin zum ersten Mal hier.**
> No, it's my first time here.

> **Sind Sie/Bist du zum ersten Mal in der Schweiz?**
> Is this your first visit to Switzerland?

> **Nein, ich bin öfters hier.**
> No, I often come here.

(e) If talking about foreign languages, note the following:

> **Sprechen Sie Deutsch?**
> Do you speak German?

> **Können Sie auch Französisch?**
> Do you speak French too?

(See **35.5**A for the omission of the infinitive with modal verbs)

> **Ich spreche nur sehr wenig Deutsch.**
> I speak very little German.

Formal letter openings

(See also **60.7a**B on formal letters; **60.7b**B on informal letter openings; and **67.3**B on 'Thanking in a formal letter')

> **bezugnehmend auf** (+ acc) 'with reference to'
> **mit Bezug auf** (+ acc) 'with reference to'
> **sich beziehen auf** (+ acc) 'to refer to'
> **auf etw.** (= acc) **aufmerksam machen** 'to draw attention to sth.'
> **auf etw.** (= acc) **hin*weisen** 'to indicate/point sth. out'
> **aufgrund** (+ gen) 'on the basis/strength of'
> **in Beantwortung** (+ gen) 'in reply to'
> **gemäß** (+ dat) 'further to'

Referring back to previous correspondence can be expressed by any of the following:

> *bezugnehmend auf/mit Bezug auf* **Ihr Schreiben/Ihre Anfrage vom 10. Januar...** (+ verb)
> with reference to your letter/enquiry of 10 January...

> *Ich beziehe mich auf* **Ihren/meinen Brief vom 23. September.**
> I refer to your/my letter of 23 September.

(See **42.3c**A for reflexive verb completion)

> **Wir möchten** *auf* **unser Schreiben vom 16. Februar** *aufmerksam machen/hin*weisen.*
> We would like to draw your attention to our letter of 16 February.

> *aufgrund* **Ihres Schreibens vom 1. Juni...** (+ verb)
> on the basis of your letter of 1 June...

> *in Beantwortung* **Ihres freundlichen Schreibens...** (+ verb)
> in reply to your (kind) letter...

Alternatively, if the previous contact was by telephone:

> *gemäß* **unserem Telefonat...** (+ verb) (formal)
> further to our telephone conversation...

> *gemäß* **unserer telefonischen Abmachung...** (+ verb) (formal)
> as we agreed on the telephone...

> *wie* **heute am Telefon** *besprochen...*
> as discussed today on the telephone...

62   *Taking leave*

Saying goodbye

> **sich** (= acc) **verabschieden von** (+ dat) 'to take one's leave from'

(a) 'Goodbye' can be expressed by **(Auf) Wiedersehen!** (except on the telephone: see **62.1d**B). Very late in the evening **Gute Nacht** 'Good night' is preferred.

In spoken German one of the following is more likely to be heard:

> **Tschüs!/Tschüß!/Tschau!**
> Bye./See you.

In southern Germany you will often hear **Servus!** (which can also mean 'hello': see also **60.2c**B) and **Ade!** (pronounced 'Ah-day', with the stress on the second syllable).

Other options include:

> **Bis später/dann.**
> See you later.

> **Bis bald/demnächst.**
> See you soon.

> **Bis morgen/Mittwoch/nächstes Jahr/irgendwann mal.**
> See you tomorrow/on Wednesday/next year/some time.

(See **18.2**A for **bis** and other prepositions taking the accusative)

(b) Preparing to leave can require a number of preliminary phrases such as:

> **Wir müssen jetzt wirklich gehen.**
> We really must be going now.

> **Es wird langsam Zeit, daß wir nach Hause gehen.**
> It's about time we were going home.

> **Es wird Zeit für uns.**
> It's time for us to go.

Or, very formally:

> **Ich darf mich verabschieden.**
> I'll say goodbye, then.

Much more informally one might say:

> **Du, ich muß weg/gehen.**
> I've got to go.

(See **35.5**A for the omission of the infinitive with modal verbs)

(c) Asking someone to call again can be conveyed by:

> **Bitte schauen Sie in acht bis zehn Tagen wieder vorbei.**
> Please call back in 8–10 days' time.

> **Sie wissen, Sie sind hier jederzeit herzlich willkommen.**
> You know you are very welcome here any time.

Or, more informally:

> **Komm doch mal wieder vorbei.**
> Call in again sometime.

> **Laß dich mal wieder (bei uns) sehen.**
> Come and see us again some time.

(See **35.6b**A for this use of **lassen**)

(d) On the telephone the standard 'goodbye' is **(Auf) Wiederhören!** or, more informally, **Tschüß** 'bye'. Other options are:

> **Danke für den/Ihren/deinen Anruf.**
> Thanks for calling.

> **Ruf doch mal wieder an.**
> Call again some time.

Note that **Auf Wiederhören** is also used on the radio.

Wishes for the journey

(a) Wishing someone a pleasant trip:

> **Gute Reise!/Gute Fahrt!/Gute Heimfahrt!**
> Hope you have a good journey (home).

> **Fahren Sie bitte vorsichtig.**
> Drive carefully.

> **Kommen Sie/Komm gut nach Hause!/Kommen Sie/Komm gut an!**
> (Have a) safe journey.

(b) Checking everything has been taken:

> **Haben Sie alles mit/dabei?**
> Have you got everything?

> **Hoffentlich habe ich nichts vergessen/liegenlassen/dagelassen.**
> I hope I haven't forgotten anything/left anything behind.

(c) Asking to confirm safe arrival:

> **Bitte ruf uns an, wenn du zu Hause bist.**
> Please give us a ring when you get home.

62.3 Finishing a formal letter

> **sich (bei jmdm.) bedanken** 'to thank (sb.)'
> **jmdm. dankbar sein** 'to be grateful to sb.'
> **in Erwartung** (+ gen) 'in the expectation of'
> **hoffen auf etw.** (= acc) 'to hope for sth.'
> **sich** (= acc) **freuen auf** (+ acc) 'to look forward to'
> **etw.** (= dat) **entgegen*sehen** 'to look forward to sth.'
> **jmdm. weiter*helfen** 'to help sb.'
> **jmdm. dienen** 'to be of service to sb.'
> **bei etw.** (= dat) **bei*liegen** 'to be enclosed with sth.'
> **etw.** (= dat) **bei*legen** 'to enclose sth. with/attach sth. to'
> **den Empfang bestätigen** 'to confirm receipt'
> **mit freundlichen Grüßen/Empfehlungen** 'yours sincerely/with kind regards'
> **i. A.** (= **im Auftrag**)/**i. V.** (= **in Vertretung**) 'pp.'

(a) Thanking in advance:

> **Vielen Dank im voraus.**
> Thank you very much in advance.

> **Ich bedanke mich/Wir danken Ihnen im voraus.**
> Thank you/we thank you in advance.

(See also **67.2a**B on expressing formal thanks)

(b) Closing the letter

If the writer wishes to encourage a response, one of the following may be appropriate:

> *Für* eine baldige Antwort *wäre ich* (Ihnen) sehr *dankbar.*
> I would be grateful (to you) for an early reply.

(See **39.2**A on the use of the subjunctive.)

> *In Erwartung* einer baldigen Antwort *verbleibe ich...*
> In the expectation of a prompt reply I remain, yours...

A firm is likely to write:

Wir hoffen auf baldige Antwort.
We hope for a prompt reply.

Wir freuen uns auf Ihre baldige Antwort.
We look forward to (receiving) your prompt reply.

(See **42.3a**A and **42.3c**A for the above two verb completion patterns)

Wir sehen Ihrer baldigen/umgehenden Antwort gern *entgegen.*
We look forward to your prompt/immediate reply.

Wir sehen Ihrer Stellungnahme/Ihrem diesbezüglichen Schreiben gern *entgegen.*
We look forward to (hearing) your view/(receiving) your letter on this matter.

Wir sehen Ihrer werten Bestellung gern *entgegen.*
We look forward to receiving your valued order.

If the letter has provided information, **weiter*helfen** (lit. 'to help further') may well be used, as well as, less commonly nowadays, the verb **dienen** (lit. 'to serve'):

Wir hoffen, *Ihnen* damit *weitergeholfen zu haben.*
We hope this will have helped you.

Wir hoffen, Ihnen hiermit *gedient zu haben.*
We hope to have been of help to you.

Ich hoffe, Ihnen damit wenigstens etwas *dienen zu können.*
I hope this has been of at least some help to you.

(See **19.6**A for verbs taking the dative; see **42.3f**A for verb completion by infinitive clause with **zu**; see also **8.7**A for word order)

(c) Enclosures

If something is enclosed with the letter, **bei*legen** or **bei*liegen** (followed by the dative) are likely to be used:

Einen adressierten Rückumschlag *haben* wir diesem Brief *beigelegt.*
We enclose an addressed envelope with this letter.

Ein internationaler Antwortschein *liegt diesem Brief bei.*
An international reply coupon is enclosed with this letter.

(See **42.3a–42.3b**A for verb completion with the dative, and verb completion with the accusative and dative)

Anbei erhalten Sie mein Manuskript.
My manuscript is enclosed.

At the end of the letter, following the signature, the word **Anlage(n)** or the abbreviation
Anl. denotes 'enclosures' ('Enc.'). This may be accompanied in the body of the letter by:

In der Anlage finden Sie eine Kopie des Briefes.
A copy of the letter is enclosed.

A request such as the following will be made if receipt has to be acknowledged:

Bitte bestätigen Sie den Empfang des Paketes.
Please acknowledge receipt of the parcel.

(d) Signing off

The standard closure to a business or formal letter is:

Mit (vielen) freundlichen Grüßen
Yours sincerely/faithfully

Less common is:

Mit freundlichen/(den) besten Empfehlungen
With kind/best regards

Less formal, but still not informal endings would be:

Mit bestem Gruß/mit (den) besten Grüßen. . .
With best wishes. . .

Es grüßt Sie herzlich. . .
Very best wishes. . .

(See **42.3g**A for the use of the dummy subject **es**)

Note that **Hochachtungsvoll** 'Yours faithfully', is now considered rather old-fashioned.

Finally, if the letter is signed on behalf of someone, the abbreviations **i. A. (im Auftrag)**
or **i. V. (in Vertretung)** will be found; these are the equivalents of English 'pp.'

62.4

Finishing an informal letter
(See also **60.7b**B for opening an informal letter)

> **Schluß machen/schließen** 'to close/finish'
> **sich melden** 'to get in touch/write'
> **von sich** (= dat) **hören lassen** 'to get in touch' (lit. 'to let sb. hear about oneself')

(a) Preparing to sign off:

> **Ich muß jetzt *Schluß machen/schließen*.**
> I must close now.

> ***Das wär's* dann für heute.**
> That's enough for today then.

(See **39.2**A for the use of the subjunctive)

(b) Requests to keep in touch:

> **Bis bald.**
> See you soon.

> **Schreib bald.**
> Write soon.

> **Schreib mal wieder.**
> (Do) write again.

> **Melde dich bald.**
> Get in touch soon.

> **Laß bitte bald was von dir hören.**
> Get in touch soon/write soon.

(See **35.6a**A for the modal verb **lassen**)

(c) Signing off (see also **60.8**B on 'Postcard greetings'):

> **Alles Liebe/Alles Gute**
> All the best

> **Viele liebe Grüße, dein/deine. . .**
> Very best wishes. . .

63 *Eating and drinking*

These can involve any of the following expressions:

> **Hunger/Durst haben** 'to be hungry/thirsty'
> **etw.** (= acc) **möchten** 'to want sth. (to eat)'
> **zum Essen ein*laden** 'to invite sb. to have sth. to eat'
> **eine Runde aus*geben/spendieren** 'to buy a round'
> **essen gehen** 'to go (for sth.) to eat'
> **wollen wir** (+ infinitive)... 'shall we...'
> **gehen wir** (+ infinitive)... 'let's go to...'

63.1

Expressing hunger and thirst

(a) Personal wishes:

> **Ich habe (keinen) Hunger/Durst.** (informal)
> I am (not) hungry/thirsty.

> *Ich trinke* **ein Glas Rotwein, bitte.**
> I'll have a glass of red wine, please.

> *Er möchte* **ein Glas Weißwein.**
> He would like a glass of white wine.

(See **21.2**A for the use of apposition)

(b) Proposing/inviting:

> *Darf ich* **Sie zum Essen** *ein*laden?*
> May I invite you to eat/have something to eat with me?

> **Was darf ich dir (an*)bieten?**
> What can I offer you?

> *Möchten Sie* **etwas essen/trinken?**
> Would you like something to eat/drink?

> *Was möchtest du* **essen?**
> What would you like to eat?

> *Wollen wir* **was trinken?**
> Shall we have something to drink?

> **Sie** *gibt* **heute** *einen aus.*
> She's buying everyone a drink today.

> **Sie haben uns ein Bier/eine Runde** *ausgegeben.*
> They bought us a beer/a round of drinks.

> **Ich** *möchte* **euch ein Eis/eine Runde** *spendieren.*
> I'd like to buy you an ice cream/buy you all an ice cream.

(See **19.2**A for the use of the dative here)

> ***Gehen wir* einen *trinken.*** (informal)
> Let's go and have a drink.

> ***Gehen wir* heute abend *essen*?**
> Shall we go (out) for something to eat this evening?

> **Komm, *ich lade* dich zum Kaffee *ein*.**
> Come on, I'll buy you a coffee.

In addition a waiter might ask:

> **Was darf ich Ihnen bringen?**
> What can I bring you?

> **Und zum Trinken?**
> And what would you like to drink?

> **Trinken Sie noch ein Bier?**
> Would you like another beer?

> **Haben Sie sonst noch einen Wunsch?**
> Can I get you anything else?

63.2 Finding somewhere to sit in a café/restaurant

(a) In certain restaurants a waiter or a cloakroom attendant may offer to take a guest's coat:

> **Darf ich Ihnen den Mantel ab*nehmen?**
> May I take your coat?

(b) Asking about availability:

> **Haben Sie einen Tisch frei?**
> Do you have a spare table?

> **Haben Sie einen Tisch für zwei?**
> Do you have a table for two?

> **Haben Sie einen Hochstuhl für unsere kleine Tochter?**
> Do you have a high-chair for our young daughter?

> **Ich *habe* schon *reserviert*.**
> I've (already) booked.

> **Wir *haben einen Tisch* für vier Personen für Keller *reserviert*.**
> We ordered a table for four in the name of Keller.

(c) Asking if something is occupied:

> **Ist dieser Tisch/Stuhl/Platz noch frei?**
> Is this table/chair/seat free?

> **Ist hier noch frei?**
> Is this (chair/table) free?

> **Ist hier noch Platz?**
> Is there room/space here?

(d) Discussing location:

> **Gibt es hier eine (Nicht)Raucherecke?**
> Is there a (no) smoking section here?

> **Haben Sie einen Tisch am Fenster/auf der Terrasse?**
> Do you have a table by the window/on the terrace?

> **Ich möchte drinnen/draußen/in der Ecke sitzen.**
> I'd like to sit inside/outside/in the corner.

63.3 Ordering food and drink

> **etw. wählen/bestellen** 'to choose/order sth.'
> **etw. empfehlen** 'to recommend sth.'
> **etw. nehmen/probieren** 'to have/try sth.'
> **jmdm. etw. bringen/reichen** 'to bring/pass sb. sth.'

(a) Getting the menu:

> **Die (Speise)Karte bitte!**
> (I'd like) the menu, please.

> **Die Weinliste bitte!**
> (Bring us) the wine list, please.

> **Ich hätte gern die Getränkekarte.**
> I'd like the drinks list.

(See **39.2**A for this subjunctive form)

It should be noted, however, that wine is usually ordered after food has been chosen. To place an order tell the waiter:

> **Wir möchten (gern) bestellen.**
> We'd like to order.

Or, if more time is required:

> **Wir haben noch nicht gewählt.**
> We haven't chosen yet.

(b) Consulting the waiter

The waiter or waitress will probably ask:

> **Haben Sie schon gewählt?**
> Have you decided what you want?

> **Was darf es sein?/Was möchten Sie?**
> What is it to be?/What would you like?

If help is needed choosing, say:

> **Was empfehlen Sie?**
> What do you recommend?

This is likely to elicit a response such as:

> **Ich empfehle Ihnen das Brathähnchen.**
> I would recommend the roast chicken.

(See **42.3b**A on verb completion)

Other questions one is likely to want to ask are:

> **Was ist denn Eisbein?**
> What is 'Eisbein'?

Or, more formally:

> **Können Sie erklären, was ein Eisbein ist?**
> Can you explain what 'Eisbein' is?

> **Sauerkraut – was ist das?**
> What is 'Sauerkraut'?

> **Haben Sie ein Schinkenbrot, bitte?**
> Do you have a(n open) ham sandwich?

> **Was für Suppen haben Sie?**
> What soups do you have?

(See **24.2a**A for the determiner **was für ein**)

> **Welche Eissorten haben Sie?**
> What ice cream flavours do you have?

To check on a dish's ingredients, ask:

> ***Sind* in dieser Torte Nüsse?**
> Are there any nuts in this gateau/flan?

> ***Enthält* dieser Obstsalat Kiwi?**
> Is there kiwi in this fruit salad?

(c) Ordering

It should be noted that in German restaurants it is not uncommon to order all courses in one go at the start of the meal:

> **Ich nehme Menü drei./Ich nehme das Menü zu 35 Mark.**
> I'll have menu number 3/the 35 mark menu.

> **Als Hauptgericht/Vorspeise/möchten wir...**
> For our main course/starters we would like...

> **Zum Nachtisch/Als Nachspeise nehmen wir Eis.**
> For sweet we'll have ice cream.

If more of something is required, say:

> **Ich möchte noch etwas Reis/Salat.**
> I'd like some more rice/salad.

To tell the person serving how much is wanted, say:

> **Ich nehme eine kleine Portion Kartoffeln/eine große.**
> I'll have a small helping of potatoes/a large helping.

(See **21.2**A for the use of apposition)

> **Danke, das reicht.**
> Thank you, that's enough.

> **Bitte nicht so viel.**
> Not so much, please.

A waiter may ask:

> **Haben Sie noch einen Wunsch?**
> Would you like anything else?

> **(Darf es) sonst noch etwas (sein)?**
> (Would you like) anything else?

When the wine is about to be served, the waiter will probably ask:

> **Möchten Sie den Wein probieren?**
> Would you like to try the wine first?

Note that **Danke** as a response to this question would mean 'no, thank you'.

When the food arrives a group will be asked:

> **Wer bekommt die Zwiebelsuppe?**
> Who is having the onion soup?

A possible response would be:

> **Ja, die bekomme ich.**
> Yes, that's me/for me.

If condiments are wanted, ask:

> **Können Sie uns bitte Salz/Pfeffer/Senf/Zucker bringen/geben?**
> Could you please bring/pass us (some) salt/pepper/
> mustard/sugar?

This request can be rendered more formal by substituting **reichen** for **bringen** or **geben**. If buying a snack from an **Imbißstube** (café or snack-bar), the following would be a more appropriate way to order:

> **Einmal/Zweimal Bratwurst mit Pommes frites, bitte.**
> (Fried) sausage with chips once/twice, please.

63.4   **Dealing with problems**

> **es fehlt** (+ noun) 'there's a... missing'
> **etw. brauchen** 'to need sth.'
> **etw. aus*wechseln** 'to change/replace sth.'
> **etw. um*tauschen** 'to swap/change sth.'

(a) If the order is delayed the waiter/waitress might be asked:

> **Müssen wir noch lange warten?**
> Will we have to wait much longer?

> **Warum dauert es denn so lange?**
> Why is it taking so long?

> **Ich habe schon vor einer halben Stunde bestellt.**
> I ordered half an hour ago.

A placatory waiter will probably reply:

Ihre Suppe kommt sofort/gleich.
Your soup will be here very shortly/in just a moment.

(b) If, when it finally arrives, the order is incorrect or there is something else wrong with it, one of the following might be appropriate:

Das habe ich aber nicht bestellt.
That's not what I ordered.

Das Essen ist ja kalt.
The food is cold.

Das Schnitzel ist nicht durch.
The schnitzel is not done/cooked properly.

(c) On the other hand, more utensils may be required or something dirty may need replacing:

Es fehlt ein Löffel.
There's a spoon missing.

(See **42.3g**A for this use of the dummy subject **es**. See also **70**B on talking about absence)

Wir brauchen noch ein Glas, bitte.
We need another glass, please.

Bringen Sie mir bitte einen anderen Teller!
Bring me another (i.e. a different) plate, please.

Mein Glas ist nicht sauber. Könnten Sie es bitte auswechseln?
My glass isn't clean. Could you change it, please?

(See **39.3d**A for the subjunctive of modal verbs)

(d) Alternatively, reference may need to be made to the menu again:

Bitte bringen Sie mir nochmal die Speisekarte.
Could I see the menu again, please.

(e) If the bill is not what was expected, say:

Ich glaube, die Rechnung stimmt nicht.
I think the bill is wrong.

Könnten Sie bitte gerade noch einmal die Rechnung durch*gehen/prüfen.
Could you just go through/check the bill again, please.

(See also **94.1**B for putting someone right)

63.5

Paying the bill

(a) To attract the waiter's attention at the end of the meal, call:

> **(Wir möchten) zahlen bitte!/Die Rechnung bitte!**
> We would like to pay, please!/The bill, please!

> **Könnten Sie uns bitte die Rechnung bringen!**
> Could you bring us the bill, please!

(b) If there are two or more at the table, the waiter/waitress is likely to ask:

> **(Geht das) zusammen oder getrennt?**
> Is the bill for everyone or is it to be paid separately?

To identify what you have to pay for, say:

> **Ich bezahle den Salatteller und zwei Bier.**
> I'm paying for the salad and two beers.

If feeling flush, you might then offer:

> **Zusammen./Ich bezahle.**
> All together./I'll pay.

(c) Leaving a tip

To find out if service is extra, ask:

> **Ist die Bedienung/der Service inbegriffen?**
> Is service included (in the price)?

The waiter will say what the bill comes to:

> **Das macht 37 Mark 50.**
> That's/comes to DM 37.50.

The normal method of tipping is to pay a slightly larger amount and round the bill up. For example, if the bill comes to DM 37.50:

> **40 Mark. Stimmt so.**
> DM 40. It's OK as it is.

> **Das stimmt so./Danke, das stimmt.**
> That's OK as it is./Thanks, that's fine (as it is).

63.6 **Talking about food and drink**

> **etw. kochen** 'to cook sth.'
> **zum Frühstück/Mittagessen essen** 'to have for breakfast/lunch'
> **etw. gern essen** 'to like eating sth.'
> **etw. (= nom) schmeckt jmdm.** 'sb. likes sth.'

(a) Talking about eating habits:

> **Ich koche immer selbst.**
> I do all my own cooking.

> **Wer kocht bei euch?**
> Who does the cooking in your house?

> **Was ißt du zum Frühstück/zu Mittag/zu Abend?**
> What do you eat for breakfast/lunch/tea?

> **Zum Mittagessen/Mittags esse ich immer etwas Warmes.**
> I always have something warm for lunch.

(See **46.3**A for the use of **etwas**)

> **Zum Abendessen/Abends essen wir Suppe mit Brot und Käse oder Fleisch.**
> For tea/in the evenings we have soup with bread and cheese or meat.

(b) Talking about general likes and dislikes (see also **104**B on likes and dislikes):

> **Was ist dein Lieblingsessen?**
> What is your favourite food?

> **Ich *esse gern* Nudeln.**
> I like (eating) nudels.

> **Ich *trinke gern* Mineralwasser.**
> I like (drinking) mineral water.

> **Wir *trinken keinen* Alkohol.**
> We don't drink alcohol./We are teetotal.

> **Salzkartoffeln *mag ich* nicht.** (informal)
> I don't like boiled potatoes.

> **Ich *esse lieber* Kartoffelsalat.**
> I prefer potato salad.

(See **51.5**A for irregular comparative adverbs. See also **105**B on 'Indicating preferences')

Rosenkohl *esse* **ich sehr** *gern.*
I really like Brussels sprouts.

(c) Talking about reactions to food and drink

Enquiring about specific likes and dislikes usually involves the verb **schmecken** which literally means 'to taste' but has the implication 'to taste good':

Wie *schmeckt* **dir der Apfelkuchen?**
How do you like the apple cake?

(See **19.7**A for impersonal verbs. See also **115**B on 'Enjoyment and pleasure')

Hat es geschmeckt?
Did you like it?

Es war sehr gut/ausgezeichnet/zu salzig/leider nicht so gut.
It was very good/excellent/too salty/not so good, I'm afraid.

To express a food's particular quality one might say:

Das Essen ist zu kalt/heiß.
The food is too cold/hot (in temperature).

Das ist zu scharf/süß/sauer.
That is too hot (i.e. in flavour)/sweet/sour.

To find out if someone has tried a particular item, ask:

Hast du den Kuchen schon versucht/probiert?
Have you tried the cake yet?

(d) Making plans to eat and drink

If offering to prepare food and drink, one might say (see also **96.2**B on 'Making an offer'):

Soll ich Kaffee/etwas zu essen machen?
Should I make some coffee/something to eat?

Was sollen wir kochen?
What shall we cook/make?

To find out when food will be ready, ask:

Wie lange dauert es noch?
How much longer will it take?

Wann ist das Essen fertig?
When will the meal be ready?

Wann gibt es Essen?
At what time are we eating?

(See **34.2c**A for this use of the present tense)

64   *Giving and receiving compliments*

British learners should note that many Germans do not appreciate the implications of understatement and are likely to interpret it as lack of interest. On the other hand, American learners should be aware that the majority of Germans view overstatement with some suspicion.

64.1   Complimenting

> **jmdm. ein Kompliment machen** 'to pay sb. a compliment'
> **etw. (= nom) gefällt jmdm.** 'sb. likes sth.'

(a) To pay a compliment is **ein Kompliment/Komplimente machen**. It takes the dative of the person being complimented (see **19.1–19.2**A):

> **Er hat ihr *ein* großes *Kompliment gemacht.***
> He paid her a great compliment.
>
> **Wenn Sie das sagen, *ist das* wahrhaftig *ein Kompliment*/heißt das schon etwas.**
> That's quite a compliment.

A compliment 'on something' is **wegen** (+ gen).

Many of the following expressions can be applied to different subjects. The subsections are intended to be illustrative only.

(b) On clothes:

> **Der Rock ist sehr hübsch/super/toll/schick.**
> The skirt is very pretty/great/brilliant/elegant.
>
> **Er steht dir gut.**
> It suits you.
>
> **Dein Kleid gefällt mir sehr.**
> I really like your dress.
>
> **Ich finde den Anzug sehr elegant.**
> I think the suit is very elegant.

(c) On a house/flat:

Es ist wirklich gemütlich bei euch.
Your flat/house is really comfortable/cosy.

Ich finde eure neue Wohnung sehr schön.
I think your new flat is really beautiful.

Das hast du (aber) gut/prima gemacht.
You've done that well/really well.

(d) On a performance:

Wie gut du das kannst!
You are really good at that!

Spielt die gut!
She certainly plays well.

(See **31.2**A for the emphatic (and often colloquial) use of **der**, **die**, **das** as personal pronouns)

(Das war) eine Glanzleistung!
That was a superb performance!

Bravo!
Bravo/well done!

(e) On use of language:

Sie sprechen aber sehr gut Deutsch.
You speak German very well.

Sie sprechen ja schon fast fließend.
You are almost fluent already.

(f) On cooking:

Mein Lob/Kompliment dem Koch/der Köchin.
My compliments to the chef (used both in restaurants and humorously amongst friends and relatives).

(g) General expressions of delight/approval (see also **104**B on likes and dislikes; **112**B on satisfaction and dissatisfaction; **109**B on expressing agreement):

(Oh/Ei) wie schön!
(Oh) how lovely!

Mensch ist das *schön*!
That really is nice/beautiful.

Das ist ja großartig/phantastisch/ausgezeichnet/klasse/fein!
That is really great/fantastic/excellent/tremendous/superb!

Alle Achtung!
Good for you/him/her, etc.

Responding to compliments

(a) The simplest response will usually be **Danke!** 'thank you', but depending on the type of compliment one of the following may be more appropriate:

Das freut mich.
I'm pleased (i.e. that you like it).

Das ist sehr freundlich/nett von Ihnen/dir.
That's very kind/nice of you.

Gleichfalls.
You do too./Yours does too./The same to you. (i.e. the meaning depends on context)

(b) As in English, a token question may be offered in response to a compliment:

Das Kleid ist schön. – Ja, gefällt's dir?
The dress is beautiful. – Do you like it?

Ja, nicht?
Yes, it is isn't it?

(c) An explanation of the origin of something may be given:

Das habe ich vom Karstadt./Das habe ich schon lange.
I got it at Karstadt./I've had it a long time.

65 *Expressing commiseration*

To express sympathy or empathy any of the following might be used:

> **jmd. tut jmdm. leid** 'sb. feels sorry for sb.'
> **Pech haben** 'to be unlucky'
> **Mitleid für etw./mit jmdm. haben** 'to have sympathy for sth./with sb.'
> **mit jmdm. mit*fühlen** 'to sympathize with sb.'
> **Verständnis für etw. haben** 'to show understanding for sth.'
> **jmdm. Verständnis entgegen*bringen** 'to show sb. understanding'
> **jmdm. etw. nach*fühlen/nach*empfinden** 'to understand sb.'s feelings'
> **sich in jmds. Lage (hinein*)versetzen** 'to put oneself in sb.'s position'

65.1

Sympathizing

(See also **111**B on 'Expressing happiness, fear and sadness')

(a) To express sorrow at something, use:

> **Es tut mir (wirklich) leid.**
> I'm (really) sorry.

(See also **68.1a–68.1b**B on 'Apologizing and seeking forgiveness')

(b) But with people use:

> **Er/Sie tut mir leid.**
> I feel sorry for him/her.

> **Die Kinder tun mir leid.**
> I feel sorry for the children.

Alternatively, 'poor' might be placed before the person or after **du/Sie**:

> **Der arme Willi!/Die arme Frau!**
> Poor Willi!/The poor woman!

(See **23.2g**A for the use of the definite article in German)

> **Du Arme(r)!/Sie Arme(r)!**
> Poor you.

(See **28.5**A on adjectival nouns)

(c) There is a wide range of possible exclamations which convey sympathy. The most common are:

> **Schade!**
> What a pity!

> **Das ist (aber) schlimm/schrecklich/schade!**
> That's bad/terrible/a pity.

Pech (gehabt)! (informal)
Bad luck!

So ein Pech!/Was für ein Pech!
What bad luck.

Du bist ein echter Pechvogel!
You really are unlucky/a walking disaster area.

(d) To express sympathy with someone's situation, Germans might use one of the following: **Mitleid** 'pity/compassion' and the adjectives **mitleidvoll/ mitleidig** 'compassionate/pitying/sympathetic', or **Mitgefühl** 'sympathy' and the verb **mit*fühlen** 'to feel for somebody/sympathize with someone':

Ich kann *mit dir mit*fühlen.*
I can sympathize with you.

Ich habe großes *Mitleid mit* ihr.
I have a lot of sympathy with her.

(See **46.1–46.2a**A for the use of the zero declension)

Er hat sein *Mitgefühl ausgesprochen.*
He expressed his sympathies.

Frau Debus hat viel *Mitgefühl für* meine Sorgen *gezeigt.*
Mrs Debus showed a lot of sympathy for my concerns.

(e) Understanding for someone or something is expressed by means of **Verständnis**:

Sie müssen *Verständnis für* seine Probleme *haben.*
You must show some understanding for his problems.

Wir müssen ihnen *Verständnis entgegen*bringen.* (formal)
We must show them some understanding.

(f) Limits to sympathy can be expressed by:

Ich *kann* Ihnen das *nach*fühlen/ nach*empfinden,* aber ich kann ja nichts dafür.
I can understand your feelings but there's nothing I can do about it.

(See **35.5**A for the omission of the infinitive with modal verbs)

Erwarte kein *Mitleid von* ihm.
Don't expect any pity from him.

(g) To persuade someone to see something from another point of view, use:

Versuche doch einmal, *dich* in meine schwierige Lage zu *versetzen*.
Do try to see it from my point of view./Try to appreciate what a difficult
position I am in.

Consoling

> **jmdn. trösten** 'to console sb.'
> **sich trösten** 'to console oneself'
> **jmdn. über etw. (= acc) hinweg*trösten** 'to help sb. over sth.'
> **jmdm. Trost zu*sprechen/bringen** 'to console sb.'

(a) To console a person immediately after he or she has accidentally damaged
something, say:

> **Es macht nichts./Es ist schon OK.**
> It's doesn't matter./It's OK.
>
> **Es ist doch (gar) nicht so schlimm.**
> It's not (at all) so bad.

(b) To encourage somone who is feeling 'down', one might say:

> **Kopf hoch!**
> (Come on) cheer up!

(c) The words **Trost**, **trösten** and **tröstlich** are the normal means of expressing
consolation.

To express the act of consoling someone, use:

> **Der Pfarrer hat ein paar *tröstende* Worte gesagt.**
> The priest/minister said a few words of comfort.
>
> **Mein Bruder hat mich *über die Krise hinweggetröstet*.**
> My brother helped me over (lit. 'consoled me over') the crisis.
>
> **Er hat der Frau *Trost zugesprochen/gebracht*.**
> He consoled/comforted her.

The means of consolation following **trösten** is expressed by **mit**:

> **Er *tröstet sich mit* dem Gedanken an das Geld.**
> He's consoling himself by thinking about the money.

(See **38.1**A for prepositional verbs)

Feeling comforted or consoled by something is expressed by means of **Trost** or
tröstlich:

> *Es ist ein Trost/ tröstlich zu wissen, daß du immer da bist.*
> It's a comfort/comforting to know you are always there.

(See **42.3e**A for verb completion by a clause)

> *Ein Trost, daß jetzt alles vorbei ist.*
> It's a relief that everything is now over.

> **Das Kind ist *unser einziger Trost.***
> The child is our only comfort.

> ***Zum Trost* kann ich Ihnen sagen, daß wir zur Zeit ähnliche Probleme haben.**
> It may comfort you to know that we are currently having similar problems.

Fairly common ironic expressions are:

> **Das ist *ein* schwacher/schöner/schlechter *Trost.***
> That's some comfort (i.e. not much comfort).

> **Das ist ja sehr *tröstlich*!**
> Some comfort that is.

Trösten Sie sich! or **tröste dich!** are used in an ironic sense when telling a person who has a problem about someone else's similar difficulty – in the sense of 'console yourself with the thought that you are not the only one'.

65.3 | ## Bereavement

> **an etw. (= dat) Anteil nehmen** 'to feel sorry about sth.'
> **Beileid aus*drücken/aus*sprechen** 'to express sympathy'
> **zutiefst erschüttert sein** 'to be deeply shocked'
> **Mitgefühl entgegen*nehmen** 'to accept sympathy'
> **mit jmdm. (mit*)fühlen** 'to feel for sb.'
> **(jmds.) Leid teilen** 'to share (sb.'s) sorrow'
> **entschlafen/hin*scheiden** 'to pass away/die'
> **um jmdn. trauern** 'to mourn sb.'

(a) Sympathies to someone, either personally or in writing, could be conveyed by one of the following:

> ***Mein* herzliches/aufrichtiges *Beileid zum Tode* deiner Schwester.**
> My deepest/sincere condolences on the death of your sister.

> **Wir sind in Gedanken bei euch.**
> You are in our thoughts.

Rather more formally one might write:

> **Wir** *nehmen Anteil am Tode* **Ihres Mannes.**
> We are/feel deeply sorry about the death of your husband.

> **Wir möchten Ihnen unser aufrichtiges** *Beileid ausdrücken/aussprechen.*
> We would like to express our sincere condolences.

> *Zutiefst erschüttert* **hörten wir vom Tode Ihrer Frau.**
> We were deeply shocked to hear of the death of your wife.

(See also **111.3j**B on 'grief and mourning'; and **111.3k**B and **114.6**B on 'expressing shock')

Most formally of all:

> **Bitte** *nehmen Sie* **mein tiefempfundenes** *Mitgefühl zu* **Ihrem schweren Verlust** *entgegen.*
> Please accept my deeply felt sympathy at your terrible loss.

(b) On a card one might write:

> **Mit tiefstem Beileid.**
> With deepest sympathy.

(See **46.1**A for the zero declension.)

> **Wir fühlen mit Ihnen.**
> We feel for you.

> **Wir teilen Ihr Leid.**
> We share your sorrow.

(See also **111.3j**B on 'grief and mourning'.)

(c) An obituary notice in the paper might employ the highly formal and literary verbs **entschlafen** and **hin*scheiden**:

> **Gestern** *entschlief* **nach langem Leiden mein lieber Gatte, Rudolf Engel. In tiefer/stiller Trauer, Katharina Engel.**
> My dearly beloved husband, Rudolf Engel, passed away yesterday following a long illness. Sadly missed by Katharina Engel.

> **Am Freitag** *schied* **nach kurzer Krankheit meine liebe Frau, Mechthild Sammer,** *hin. In stiller Trauer,* **Alois Sammer.**
> My dearly beloved wife, Mechthild Sammer, died on Friday following a short illness. Sadly missed by Alois Sammer.

Wir *trauern um* unseren verstorbenen Bruder, Harald Meier.
We mourn the loss of our recently departed brother, Harald Meier.

(See **38.1**A for prepositional verbs)

(d) Another typical newspaper notice is:

Wir bedanken uns für alle *Beileidsbeweise*.
Thank you for all expressions of condolence.

(e) The reason for someone's absence or for the cancellation of an event may be given as:

***Wegen eines Trauerfalls* in der Familie muß die heutige Veranstaltung leider aus*fallen.**
Owing to a family bereavement today's event has had to be cancelled.

(f) See **67.1–67.3**B on 'Thanking' for acknowledging commiseration.

66 *Expressing good wishes*

The following cover a wide range of reasons for wishing someone well:

> **jmdm. etw. wünschen** 'to wish sb. sth.'
> **viel Glück/Spaß** 'good luck/have a good time'
> **viel Erfolg/Vergnügen** 'every success/hope you enjoy yourself'
> **viel Freude** 'much joy/happiness'
> **alles Gute** 'all the best'
> **gute Besserung** 'get well soon'
> **Gesundheit!** 'bless you!'
> **sich (= dat) etw. schmecken lassen** 'to enjoy food'
> **guten Appetit!** 'enjoy your meal'
> **zum Wohl!** 'cheers!'

Almost all the greetings and expressions of good wishes that follow are assumed to be preceded by **Ich wünsche Ihnen/dir...** 'I wish you...' and as a result expressions are in the accusative case. Inclusion of the verb is more typical of fairly formal style, as in the third example of **66.8a**B.

66.1 — General wishes

(a) The following may be used when wishing someone well for a forthcoming activity or event:

> **Viel Glück!**
> Good luck!

> **Viel Spaß (beim Autorennen)!**
> Hope you have fun/a good time (at the motor racing).

(See also **115.3**B on 'Enjoying things')

> **Viel Vergnügen!**
> Hope you enjoy it.

(b) In spoken German between friends and at the end of informal letters, good wishes may be conveyed by:

> **Mach's gut!/Ich wünsche dir was.**
> (I wish you) all the best.

Mit den besten Wünschen, however, can only be used in letters.

(c) At work colleagues might wish each other **Mahlzeit!** 'bon appetit' at lunch time (see also **66.5**B on food and drink). You should say the same (or **Guten Appetit!**) when passing people who are eating. After work it is normal to say **(Schönen) Feierabend!** 'Have a nice evening/Enjoy your evening off'. On Fridays **Schönes Wochenende!** 'Have a nice weekend', is more likely to be used.

(d) To return good wishes simply say **Gleichfalls** or **Ihnen/dir auch** 'To you too'.

(See **67.1–67.3**B for thanking people for their good wishes)

(e) To wish someone joy of something:

> **Ich wünsche dir viel Freude an dem Auto.**
> I hope you enjoy the car./I wish you much pleasure with the car.

66.2 For good health

(a) To wish someone a speedy recovery from illness, say or write:

> **Gute Besserung!**
> Get well soon.

> **Werde schnell wieder gesund.**
> Get well/better soon.

> **Ich hoffe, du bist bald wieder gesund.**
> I hope you're better soon.

Slightly more formally one might write:

Alles Gute/Beste Wünsche für eine baldige Genesung.
All the best/best wishes for a speedy recovery.

(See **44.4**A for the adjective declension after **alles**)

(b) If someone sneezes, say **Gesundheit!** 'Bless you!' (lit. 'good health').

66.3 For an examination

The normal way of expressing good luck is:

Viel Glück bei **der Prüfung.**
Good luck in the exam.

Alles Gute zum **Examen.**
All the best for the examination.

A more formal variant is:

Viel Erfolg bei **der bevorstehenden Prüfung.**
(I wish you) every success in the forthcoming exam.

66.4 For a new home

Alles Gute **im neuen Heim.**
All the best in your new home.

Viel Glück **in eurem neuen Haus.**
Good luck in your new house.

66.5 With food and drink

(a) The standard thing to say before starting a meal is **Guten Appetit!** 'bon appetit/I hope you enjoy your meal'. This is used a great deal in Germany. The normal response would be **Danke/(Danke,) gleichfalls** 'Thanks/(Thanks,) you too'.

Another option is:

Lassen Sie es sich schmecken./Laß es dir (gut) schmecken.
I hope you enjoy it.

(See **35.6b**A for the use of **lassen**)

(b) If offering a toast, choose one of the following:

Prost! (informal)
Cheers!

Prosit!/Zum Wohl!
Cheers!/Good health!

> **Auf Ihr Wohl!** (formal)
> To your good health!

If responding to a toast, simply reply in kind: **(Ja,) zum Wohl!**

When toasting a particular occasion or activity use **auf**:

> **Auf ein gutes Neues Jahr.**
> Here's to a Happy New Year.

(See also **66.8d**B on New Year celebrations)

> **Auf gute Zusammenarbeit.**
> Here's to a fruitful collaboration.

Generally speaking, a guest should not start drinking until the host or hostess has offered a toast. Clinking of glasses is by no means universal but it is rather more common in Germany than in Britain or the USA.

66.6

At night

(a) To wish someone good night, you could say:

> **Schlafen Sie gut!**
> Sleep well.

> **Ich hoffe, Sie haben eine ruhige Nacht.**
> I hope you have a peaceful night.

Or simply, **Gute Nacht!** 'Good night'.

(b) To a child one might say:

> **Schlaf gut.**
> Sleep well.

> **Träume süß!**
> Sweet dreams.

Dropping the final **-e** from the imperative form is a sign of greater informality (see **58.2b**A).

66.7

Congratulating

> **jmdn. zu etw.** (= dat) **beglückwünschen** 'to congratulate sb. on sth.'
> **herzliche Glückwünsche zu etw.** (= dat) 'many congratulations on sth.'
> **jmdm. zu etw. gratulieren** 'to congratulate sb. on sth.'
> **jmdm. etw. zu etw. wünschen** 'to wish sb. sth. on the occasion of sth.'

(a) Congratulations are usually expressed by the verb **beglückwünschen** 'to congratulate' or the phrase **herzliche Glückwünsche** 'many congratulations':

> *Herzliche Glückwünsche zu* **eurem Erfolg.**
> Many congratulations on your success.

(b) Congratulations on a new job or a promotion:

> *Herzlichen Glückwunsch zur* **neuen Stelle.**
> Congratulations on the new job.

> **Ich** *beglückwünsche* **Sie** *zur* **Beförderung.**
> I congratulate you on your promotion.

(See **38.1**A for prepositional verbs)

(c) Congratulations on a birth:

> **Wir** *gratulieren* **(Ihnen)** *zum* **neuen Baby/***zur* **Geburt Ihres ersten Kindes.**
> We send our congratulations on the arrival of the new baby/the birth of your first child.

(See **19.6** for verbs that take the dative)

(d) Congratulations on examination success:

> **Ich** *gratuliere zur* **bestandenen Prüfung.**
> Congratulations on passing your exam.

(e) An official wedding announcement in the newspaper is also a form of congratulation:

> **Wir** *geben* **die Vermählung unseres Sohnes** *bekannt.*
> We have pleasure in announcing the marriage of our son.

(f) In Catholic families the First Communion is an important event on which children are congratulated, particularly by godparents:

> *Zu* **deiner Erstkommunion** *wünscht* **dir** *alles Gute* **und** *Gottes Segen,* **dein Taufpate.**
> All the best and God's blessing to you on the occasion of your First Communion, your godfather.

Similarly, children are congratulated by their sponsors on their Confirmation (the Catholic **Firmung** or Protestant **Konfirmation**):

> *Zu* **deiner Firmung, Hans,** *wünscht* **dir** *alles Gute* **dein Firmpate/deine Firmpatin.**

All the best to you Hans for your Confirmation, your sponsor.

(g) See **67.1–67.3**B on thanking for responding to good wishes.

Celebrations

(a) Along with **herzlichen Glückwunsch zu...** (see **66.7a–66.7b**B on 'Congratulating'), **alles Gute zu...** is the most common means of wishing someone well on a personal celebration, such as a birthday or anniversary:

> *Alles Gute zum* **(60.) Geburtstag.**
> Best wishes on/All the best for your (60th) birthday.

> *Alles Gute zum* **Namenstag.**
> Best wishes on your name day/Saint's day.

> *Zu* **eurer Hochzeit wünsche ich (euch)** *alles Gute/viel Glück.*
> I wish you all the best/good luck on your wedding day.

A more formal greeting for this last example, such as might appear on a card, would be:

> **Dem glücklichen Paar** *viel Freude* **am Hochzeitstag und für das Leben zu zweit.**
> Much joy to the happy couple on their wedding day and in their (future) life together.

(b) Good wishes for public holidays of any kind can be conveyed by:

> **Schöne Feiertage!/Schönen Feiertag!**
> Enjoy the/Have a good holiday.

Note that holidays spent away from home would normally elicit the wish **Schönen Urlaub!** 'Have a good holiday', while for longer holidays away from, say, school, you could wish someone **Schöne Ferien!**

(c) At Christmas one of the following would be appropriate either in spoken or written German:

> **Frohe/Fröhliche Weihnachten!**
> Merry/Happy Christmas.

> **Gesegnete Weihnachten!** (formal, literary)
> Happy (lit. blessed) Christmas.

> **Frohes Weihnachtsfest!/Frohes Fest!**
> Merry Christmas.

(d) At New Year the most idiomatic greeting is **Guten Rutsch (ins neue Jahr)!** meaning literally 'have a good slide into the New Year'. Other possibilities are:

> **Ein Glückliches Neues Jahr!/(Ein) Gutes Neues Jahr!**
> Happy New Year.

> **Frohes/Glückliches Neujahr!**
> Happy New Year.

> **(Frohe Weihnachte) und die besten Wünsche zum Neuen Jahr!**
> (Merry Christmas) and best wishes for the New Year.

> **Alles Gute zum Neuen Jahr!**
> All the best for the New Year.

The following could be used as a toast:

> **Prost Neujahr!**
> Here's to the New Year.

(e) Easter greetings are usually conveyed by:

> **Frohe Ostern!/Ein frohes Osterfest!**
> Happy Easter.

(See **46.1**A for the zero declension of adjectives)

67 *Giving and receiving thanks, expressing appreciation*

There are many ways in which thanks and appreciation can be expressed:

---

vielen/herzlichen Dank für etw. (= acc) 'many thanks for sth.'
jmdm. für etw. (= acc) **danken** 'to thank sb. for sth.'
sich bei jmdm. für etw. (= acc) **bedanken** 'to thank sb. for sth.'
jmdm. (zu Dank) verpflichtet sein 'to be indebted to sb.'
jmdm. Dankbarkeit zeigen 'to show sb. gratitude'
Verdienst/Leistung an*erkennen 'to recognize sb.'s merit/performance'
etw. zu schätzen/würdigen wissen 'to value/appreciate sth.'
es ist das Verdienst von (+ dat) 'it is thanks to'
etw. dankend erhalten 'to be grateful for (receiving) sth.'
etw. dankend bestätigen 'to acknowledge receipt gratefully'
jmdm. einen Dienst erweisen 'to do sb. a service'
etw. dankend an*nehmen 'to take/accept gratefully'

67.1 **Thanking someone informally**

(a) Simple thanks can be expressed by **Danke**. More emphatically, say:

> **Danke sehr./Vielen Dank./Herzlichen Dank.**
> Thank you very much./Many thanks./Sincere thanks.

Alternatively the verb **danken** may be used:

> **Wir *danken* euch sehr.**
> Thank you very much.

(See **19.6**A for verbs that take the dative)

In very informal usage some people might say **tausend Dank** 'thanks a million'.

(b) To thank someone for something use **für**:

> ***Danke* sehr *für* die Einladung.**
> Thank you very much for the invitation.

But to thank someone for *having done* something, a clause with **daß** is required (see **8.1–8.2**A):

> ***Vielen Dank (dafür), daß* Sie das Auto repariert haben.**
> Many thanks for mending the car.

(c) Other ways to thank people informally include:

> **Danke, das war doch wirklich nicht nötig.**
> Thanks, but it really wasn't necessary.

> **Es war sehr nett/freundlich von dir, uns einzuladen.**
> It was very nice/kind of you to invite us.

(See **42.3f**A for verb completion by infinitive clauses with **zu**; see also **8.7**A for word order)

> **Wir wissen nicht, *wie wir* euch *danken können*.**
> We don't know how we can thank you.

> **(Es/das ist) nett, daß Sie an mich gedacht haben.**
> (It is) nice of you to think of me.

(See **38.1**A for prepositional verbs)

> **Das ist/Ich finde das sehr lieb/freundlich (von Ihnen).**
> That is/I think that is very nice/kind (of you).

And, slightly more formally:

> **Das ist sehr liebenswürdig von Ihnen.**
> That is very kind of you.

(d) Thanks to deity or to providence (often with no religious connotation) can be expressed as follows:

> **Gott sei Dank!**
> Thank God/heavens.

(See **39.5**A for this subjunctive form)

> ***Zum Glück*** **ist nichts passiert.**
> Fortunately nothing happened.

— 67.2 — **Thanking and expressing appreciation formally**

(a) The verb **sich** (= acc) **bedanken** is frequently used, particularly in written communications (see also **67.3**B on 'Thanking in a formal letter'):

> **Wir möchten *uns* bei Ihnen *bedanken*.**
> We would like to thank/express our thanks to you.

> ***Ich bedanke mich* herzlich/recht herzlich *für* Ihre Hilfe.**
> Thank you very much/most sincerely for your help.

This expression would also be used in front of an audience; note the use of **bei** before the person being thanked:

> **Wir möchten *uns bei Ihnen* für Ihre Unterstützung *bedanken*.**
> We would like to thank you for your support.

(b) A very formal but quite common expression is **(zu Dank) verpflichtet sein**:

> ***Ich bin* Ihnen *zu Dank verpflichtet*.**
> I am indebted to you./I owe you a debt of gratitude.

> ***Wir sind* Ihnen sehr *verpflichtet*.**
> We are indebted to you/very grateful.

(c) On official occasions and when awards are to be made, e.g. in the work situation, the following may be said:

> **Darf ich *mich* auch im Namen des Geschäftsführers für Ihr Engagement**
> ***bedanken*.**
> Allow me to thank you on behalf of the manager as well for your commitment.

Note that **Engagement** is pronounced as in French.

(See **28.2b**A for the declension of **Name** and other weak nouns)

> **Wir möchten Ihnen unsere *Dankbarkeit zeigen.***
> We should like to show you our gratitude.

(See **12.3**A for the order of noun and pronoun objects)

> **Wir *schätzen* ihren Beitrag sehr.**
> We value her contribution highly.

> ***In Anerkennung* Ihrer großen Leistungen bei uns in der Firma möchten wir Ihnen diese Uhr schenken.**
> We would like to present you with this clock in recognition of your great achievements in the firm.

(See **5.2a**A for the position of the verb here)

> **Wir möchten Ihr *Verdienst*/Ihre *Leistung* auf folgende Weise *an*erkennen.***
> We would like to recognize your contribution/performance in the following way.

> **Alle Kollegen *wissen* sein Verdienst *zu schätzen.***
> All his colleagues value his contribution.

> **Die Firma *weiß* Ihre Arbeit *zu würdigen.***
> The firm greatly appreciates your work.

> ***Es ist das Verdienst* der indischen Regierung, daß die Pest so schnell unter Kontrolle gebracht wurde.**
> It is thanks to the Indian government that the (spread of the) plague was controlled so quickly.

> **Sie haben uns einen großen *Dienst erwiesen.***
> You have done us a great service.

(d) A notice of thanks in the newspaper might take the following form:

> ***Herzlichen Dank* allen, die uns zu unserer Hochzeit so reichlich mit Geschenken und Glückwünschen erfreut haben.**
> Sincere thanks to all those who sent so many delightful gifts and good wishes on the occasion of our wedding.

67.3 Thanking in a formal letter

Thanks in a letter usually refer back to a previous communication (see also **61.11**B on 'Formal letter openings'):

(a) Letters:

> **Wir *danken* Ihnen *für* Ihr Schreiben vom 24. August.**
> Thank you for your letter of 24 August.
>
> **Wir *bestätigen dankend* den Eingang Ihres Briefs.**
> We acknowledge with thanks the receipt of your letter.
>
> **Wir *haben* Ihren Brief *dankend erhalten*.**
> We are grateful for your letter.

(b) Enquiries:

> **Wir *bedanken uns für* Ihre Anfrage vom 11. April.**
> Thank you for your enquiry of 11 April.

(c) Orders:

> ***Besten Dank*/Wir *danken bestens für* Ihre Bestellung.**
> Many thanks for your order.
>
> **Hiermit möchte ich *mich für* die Zusendung der Materialien *bedanken*.**
> I would (hereby) like to thank you for sending the materials.

This can be rendered more informally by adding **recht herzlich**:

> **Hiermit möchte ich *mich recht herzlich für* die Zusendung der Materialien *bedanken*.**
> I would like to thank you very much for sending the materials.
>
> **Wir *bestätigen dankend* den Erhalt/Empfang Ihrer werten Bestellung.**
> (formal)
> We gratefully acknowledge receipt of your valued order.

(d) Offers/quotes:

> **Ich *danke für* die Übermittlung Ihres Angebots vom 3. Januar.**
> Thank you for forwarding/sending your offer dated 3 January.

67.4 **Acknowledging thanks**

(a) Germans are far more likely than the British to acknowledge explicitly someone's expression of thanks. **Bitte** 'Don't mention it/You're welcome' is rarely omitted in response to **Danke**. Slightly more forcefully you might use **Bitte schön!**, **Bitte sehr!** or **Aber bitte!**

(b) Other possible responses are:

> **Nichts zu danken!**
> Don't mention it.

Keine Ursache!
Not at all./Think nothing of it. (lit. no cause)

Gern geschehen!
You're welcome.

Das ist doch nicht der Rede wert./Das ist doch selbstverständlich.
Don't mention it. (lit. That's hardly worth mentioning)

(See **20.3**A for the use of the genitive with certain adjectives)

Schon gut!
That's all right

Note that **schon gut!** is also used in response to a suggestion or a complaint in the sense of 'yes, all right'.

(c) To say an action was performed gratefully, use **dankend** or **mit Dank**:

Sie *nahm* das Buch *mit Dank/dankend an*.
She took the book with gratitude/gratefully.

67.5 — **Declining help and offers**

(a) To turn down an offer of material help of some sort, say:

Das darf/kann ich nicht (von Ihnen) an*nehmen.
I am not allowed/cannot accept that (from you).

This might be followed by:

Trotzdem vielen Dank.
Thanks all the same.

(b) When telling someone not to meddle (declining help when it has not been requested, as it were), say:

Das geht Sie gar nichts an.
That's none of your business.

This rather rude formulation can be rendered less harsh by adapting it slightly:

Entschuldigen Sie, aber das geht Sie wirklich nichts an!
Excuse me, but that really isn't any of your business.

Alternatively, use the fairly neutral:

Das betrifft Sie doch nicht.
That doesn't concern you.

Another, less forceful expression is:

> **Entschuldigen Sie, aber überlassen Sie das bitte mir.**
> Please leave that to me, if you don't mind.

On the other hand, to be more abrupt and peremptory one could use:

> **Halten Sie sich da (ganz) raus.**
> Keep (well) out of it.

(c) Note that a simple **Danke** in response to an offer of some sort will mean 'No, thank you'. In order to accept the offer, say either **Ja, bitte** 'Yes, please' or **Ja, gerne** 'Yes, gladly/Yes, I would'.

68 Expressing apologies and regret

The most common expressions include:

> **jmdm. leid tun** 'to be sorry'
> **sich** (= acc) **bei jmdm. entschuldigen** 'to apologize to sb.'
> **etw. mit etw.** (= dat) **entschuldigen** 'to excuse sth. with sth.'
> **sich bei jmdm. entschuldigen lassen** 'to send one's apologies to sb.'
> **jmdn. bei jmdm. entschuldigen** 'to convey sb.'s apologies to sb.'
> **sich** (= dat)/**jmdm. verzeihen** 'to forgive oneself/sb.'
> **jmdn. um Verzeihung bitten** 'to ask sb. for forgiveness/apologize'
> **jmdm. etw. vergeben** 'to forgive sb. sth.'

68.1 Apologizing and seeking forgiveness

(a) To say sorry for a slight mishap or some minor misdemeanour, a simple **Verzeihung!** or **Entschuldigung!** 'sorry' will suffice:

> **Entschuldigung, falsch verbunden.**
> I'm sorry I've got the wrong number. (on the telephone)

> **Verzeihung, ich habe mich verwählt.**
> I'm sorry I've dialled the wrong number.

Tut mir leid, short for **es tut mir leid** (see **68.1b**B), is also used in this sense. In German border regions with France, in particular, the form **Pardon!** (pronounced as in French) may well be heard, while in informal spoken German **Sorry!** is now frequently heard, although it tends to be a lot more superficial than in English and it should not be used for a genuine apology.

(b) The expression **leid tun** is very commonly used to convey apologies and regret, often with an adverb for reinforcement. Note that the verb is always used impersonally (see **19.7**A for impersonal verbs):

> ***Es tut mir* furchtbar/aufrichtig *leid,* daß ich das Buch schon wieder vergessen habe.**
> I am terribly/sincerely sorry for having forgotten the book again.

> ***Es tut uns* sehr/wirklich *leid,* daß ihr nicht mitkommen könnt.**
> We are very/really sorry that you can't come with us.

(See also **113.3**B on 'Disappointment')

(c) A slightly stronger request for forgiveness than the one-word expressions in **68.1a**B is conveyed by the verb **entschuldigen** 'to excuse/forgive' and its reflexive variant:

> ***Entschuldige,* ich hab's nicht gewußt.**
> I'm sorry, I didn't know.

> ***Entschuldigen Sie,* bitte.**
> Please excuse (me).

> ***Entschuldigen Sie* bitte, *daß* ich zu spät gekommen bin.**
> I am sorry I came too late.

> ***Er entschuldigte sich für* die zusätzliche Arbeit.**
> He apologized for the extra work.

In combination with a direct object this is the verb normally used to request forgiveness for something:

> ***Entschuldigen Sie* bitte meine Verspätung.** (formal)
> Please forgive my late arrival.

In formal style:

> **Meine Abwesenheit *bitte ich zu entschuldigen.*** (very formal)
> Please excuse my absence.

With **mit** the excuse can be offered too:

> **Die Studenten *entschuldigten* ihre schlechten Noten *mit* Geldsorgen.**
> The students gave financial worries as the reason for their bad marks.

Entschuldigung and **zu** can also be employed to explain a reason or excuse:

> ***Zu* seiner *Entschuldigung* sagte er, daß er kein Geld gehabt habe.**
> To excuse himself/In his defence he said he didn't have any money.

Note also the expression:

> **Er** *wußte* **keine** *Entschuldigung vorzubringen.*
> He was unable to produce an excuse.

(See **36.1c**A for the use of **zu** with separable verbs)

(d) Certain constructions with **entschuldigen** are used to convey someone else's apologies for absence (note the use of **bei** + dat with the reason or event):

> **Sie mußte gestern den Kollegen** *bei dem Treffen entschuldigen.*
> She had to present her colleague's excuses (for absence) to the meeting yesterday.

> **Können Sie mich bitte** *bei dem Direktor entschuldigen***?**
> Can you send my apologies (for absence) to the Director?

In combination with the modal verb **lassen** (see **35.6b**A), **sich entschuldigen** is also used to pass on apologies for absence:

> **Meine Frau** *läßt sich entschuldigen.* **Sie muß heute arbeiten.**
> My wife sends her apologies. She has to work today.

Entschuldigen is further used to excuse someone from an activity, e.g. in school:

> **Ich möchte meinen Sohn Hans** *für* **morgen** *entschuldigen.*
> I would like to have my son Hans excused for tomorrow.

A more formal way of offering an excuse for someone's absence is:

> **Ich möchte meine Tochter** *wegen* **ihres Fehlens** *entschuldigen.*
> I would like to excuse my daughter for being absent.

(e) Another verb used to seek forgiveness is **verzeihen** 'to pardon/forgive':

> *Verzeihen Sie, daß* **ich so spät an*rufe.**
> I'm sorry for ringing so late.

> *Verzeih* **die Störung.** (informal)
> I'm sorry for disturbing.

(See **58.2b**A for the informal dropping of the **-e** in imperatives.)

Note that **verzeihen** takes a dative object of the person (see **19.1**A):

> **Sie hat** *ihm* **endlich** *verziehen.*
> She finally forgave him.

> **Es sei** *dir* **noch einmal** *verziehen***!**
> You're forgiven!/We'll forgive you one more time! (ironical)

(See **39.4**A for the use of Subjunctive I)

> **Wir können es *uns* nicht *verzeihen, daß* wir ihm nicht geholfen haben.**
> We cannot forgive ourselves for not helping him.

A much more formal and emphatic request for forgiveness is expressed by **um Verzeihung bitten**:

> **Er *bat* sie (vielmals) *um Verzeihung.***
> He apologized to her (profusely).

(See **38.1**A for the use of prepositional verbs)

(f)　The verb **vergeben** is less commonly used. It too takes a dative of the person:

> **Sie hat *ihm* seine Rücksichtslosigkeit *vergeben.***
> She has forgiven him his thoughtlessness.

The verb is also used in the religious sense of forgiveness:

> **Vergib uns unsere Sünden.**
> Forgive us our sins.

(See **19.2**A for this use of the dative; and **12.3**A for the order of noun and pronoun objects)

68.2

Expressing regret
(See also **71**B for expressing availability and **72**B for non-availability)

> **etw. bedauern** 'to regret sth.'
> **zu (jmds.) Bedauern** 'to (sb.'s) regret'
> **bedauerlicherweise** 'regrettably'
> **um Verständnis bitten** 'to ask for understanding'
> **Verständnis für etw. haben** 'to show understanding for sth.'

(a)　The majority of expressions of regret in formal letters involve the verb **bedauern** or the corresponding verbal noun:

> **Wir *bedauern*, nicht früher geantwortet zu haben.**
> We regret not having replied sooner.

> **Wir *bedauern*, Ihnen mitteilen zu müssen, daß diese Veröffentlichung immer noch nicht lieferbar ist.**
> We regret to inform you that this publication is still not available.

(See **42.3f**A for verb completion by infinitive clause with **zu**; and **8.7**A on word order)

Zu unserem großen *Bedauern* müssen Sie mit einer Verzögerung von ca. 10 Wochen rechnen.
Much to our regret you can expect (lit. you must reckon on) a delay of about 10 weeks.

(b) The adverb **bedauerlicherweise** is also frequently found in formal style:

Bedauerlicherweise ist das nun nicht mehr möglich.
Unfortunately that is now no longer possible.

(c) Regret may also involve asking for someone's understanding:

Wir *bitten um* Ihr *Verständnis,* aber die gewünschte Broschüre ist zur Zeit vergriffen.
We would ask for your understanding as the brochure you require is currently out of print.

Bitte *haben Sie Verständnis für* unsere schwierige Lage.
Please show some understanding/sympathy for our difficult position.

(d) In all styles regret can be conveyed by **leider**:

Leider kann ich heute nicht ins Kino.
Unfortunately I can't come to the cinema today.

Ihr Brief ist hier *leider* zu spät eingetroffen.
Your letter unfortunately arrived here too late.

68.3 — ## Accepting an apology

(a) To acknowledge a person's apology, a simple **bitte!** 'that's OK' will often suffice. It can be reinforced as **bitte bitte!** 'that's perfectly all right'.

(b) There are a number of other possible responses for informal usage:

Ist schon gut/OK.
It's all right/OK.

(Das) macht doch nichts.
That's no problem.

Das ist doch nicht so schlimm/tragisch.
That's not so bad/tragic.

Mach dir nichts daraus.
Don't worry about it.

Keine Sorge./Mach dir keine Sorgen.
No problem./Don't worry about it.

> **(Das) spielt keine Rolle.**
> That is of no importance.

(c) Less informal are:

> **Das kann ja (jedem) passieren.**
> These things happen./It could happen to anyone.

(See **19.6**A for the use of the dative)

> **Das ist nicht Ihre Schuld.**
> That's not your fault.

> **Es ist nicht der Rede wert.**
> It's not worth mentioning./Don't even mention it.

(See **20.3**A for other adjectives which require the genitive)

> **Das ist vergeben und vergessen.**
> That's all over and done with.

(d) To indicate a conciliatory mood one might use:

> **Vergessen wir das!**
> Let's just forget about it.

> **Schon vergessen!**
> I've already forgotten (about) it.

XI *Giving and seeking factual information*

69 *Talking and enquiring about existence*

Presence

> **sein** 'to be'
> **da sein** 'to be present/there'
> **-s Dasein** 'presence'
> **existieren** 'to exist'
> **bestehen** 'to exist'
> **anwesend sein** 'to be present'
> **dabei sein** 'to be involved'
> **zur Stelle sein** 'to be on the spot'
> **-e Gegenwart** 'presence'
> **es gibt** 'there is/there are'

(a) Being around/about

sein and **existieren** are the obvious verbs to indicate presence. **Sein** is usually complemented by an adverb:

> **Er *ist da.***
> He is here.

> **Herr Meier *ist hier.***
> Mr Meier is here.

> **Wer *ist da*? Ich bin's.**
> Who is there? It's me.

> **Von der Urgroßmutter *existiert* noch ein Foto aus ihrer Kindheit.**
> There is a photo of great-grandmother (in existence) from her childhood.

When talking about somebody's presence, use **-s Dasein**:

> **Sein *Dasein* gab ihr Trost.**
> His presence comforted her/consoled her.

(b) Being present (for a specific purpose):

> **Zur Abstimmung im Bundestag *müssen* mindestens zwei Drittel der Abgeordneten *anwesend sein.***
> At least two thirds of the MPs/delegates must be present for the vote in (the German) Parliament.
> ***Ist* hier an Bord ein Arzt *anwesend?***
> Is there a doctor on board?
> **Bei einem Unfall *ist* nicht immergleich ein Fachmann *zur Stelle.***
> In an accident there is not always an expert available/on the spot straight away.
> **Die Verlosung muß *in (der) Gegenwart* eines Juristen vollzogen werden.**
> The draw must be conducted in the presence of a lawyer.

The idiomatic way to express occurrence is **es gibt** 'there is/there are'. **Es gibt** is followed by the accusative form of the person/thing or the persons/things that exist:

> **Wo *gibt es* hier seltene Pflanzen *zu sehen?***
> Where can one/we see some rare plants?

> **In der Wüste *gibt es* nur wenige Oasen.**
> There are only a few oases in the desert.

(c) Being involved

dabei sein 'to be present/involved':

> **Viele Veteranen *waren dabei*, als die letzten russischen Soldaten aus Berlin abzogen.**
> Many veterans were present when the last Russian soldiers moved out of Berlin.

> **Wenn Fußball gespielt wird, *ist* er immer *dabei*.**
> If there is football being played he is always there/involved.

(See **8**A for word order)

69.2

Occurrence

> **es gibt** 'there is/there are'
> **vor*kommen/passieren** 'to occur'
> **-s Vorkommen von** 'presence/occurrence/deposit of'
> **-r Bestand** 'stock/supply'
> **-e Gegebenheit** 'condition'
> **gegenwärtige Lage** 'present/current situation'

(a) When talking about occurrence in certain places or at certain times:

> **Es *gibt* über 90 Millionen deutsche Muttersprachler auf der Welt.**
> There are more than 90 million native speakers of German in the world.

> **Damals, in den 20er Jahren, *gab es* schon viele Autos.**
> At that time, in the twenties, there were already many cars.

(**es** stays with the verb, see **5.1–5.2A**)

> **Am Anfang des Krieges *gab es* noch kein Penizillin in den deutschen Krankenhäusern.**
> At the beginning of the war there was no penicillin in German hospitals.

(b) Things that can/cannot happen:

> **Es *kann* natürlich gelegentlich *vorkommen*, daß die Spuren verwischt sind.**
> Obviously it can happen on occasions that the traces have been covered up.

> **Es *ist* noch nie *passiert*, daß eine Datei unwiderruflich verlorenging.**
> It has never happened that a file was irretrievably lost.

> **Es *kommt* sehr oft *vor*, daß die Kinder alleine zu Hause gelassen werden.**
> It very often happens that the children are left at home on their own.

> **Das *hat es doch* noch nie *gegeben*!**
> That has never happened before!

(c) Natural resources:

> **Das *Vorkommen von* Bodenschätzen bedeutet, daß dieses Gebiet besonders umstritten ist.**
> The presence of natural deposits means that this area is particularly disputed.

> **Die Abbildung stellt das Erdöl*vorkommen* in diesem Kontinent dar.**
> The illustration shows the location of oil/where oil is to be found on this continent.

> **Der Baum*bestand* im Schwarzwald ist stark dezimiert.**
> The stock of trees in the Black Forest has been drastically reduced.

(d) Given conditions:

> **Die Wege richten sich nach den *natürlichen Gegebenheiten* des Geländes.**
> The paths follow the natural features of the land.

Bei der *gegenwärtigen* **Wirtschafts***lage* **ist eine Investition nicht angebracht.**
In the current economic climate investment is not appropriate.

69.3 ## Locating things and people

> **sich** (= acc) **befinden** 'to be located'
> **zu finden sein** 'can be found'
> **-r Fundort(e)** 'place where sth. was found'
> **es gibt** 'there is/there are'

Die Spielwarenabteilung *befindet sich* **in der dritten Etage.**
The toy department is on the third floor.

(See **37**A for reflexive verbs)

Der Reporter *befindet sich* **in einem Krisengebiet.**
The reporter is in an area of crisis.

Das Automobilwerk *befindet sich* **im Industriegebiet.**
The car factory is situated on an industrial estate/in an industrial area.

Die Seitenangabe *ist* **im Sachregister** *zu finden.*
The page number can be found in the subject index.

Der *Fundort* **des Homo Sapiens ist auf der Karte gekennzeichnet.**
The place where Homo sapiens was found is indicated on the map.

In diesem Stadtteil *gibt es* **keine chemische Reinigung.**
There isn't a dry cleaners in this part of town.

69.4 ## For events taking place

> **ab*halten** 'to hold'
> **statt*finden** 'to take place'

Die Veranstaltung *findet* **in der Messehalle** *statt.*
The event takes place at the exhibition centre.

Der Ärztekongreß soll wieder in Davos *abgehalten werden.*
The medical conference is to be held in Davos again.

69.5

For accompanying someone to a place or on an instrument

> **jmdn. an** (+ dat) **begleiten** 'to accompany sb. on (an instrument)'
> **jmdn. zu** (+ dat) **begleiten** 'to accompany sb. to (a place)'
> **-e Begleitung** 'company'
> **mit jmdm. an etw.** (= acc)/**zu etw./jmdm. gehen** 'to go to sth./sb. with sb.'

Er *begleitete* sie *am* Klavier/zum Arzt.
He accompanied her at the piano/to the doctor's.

Er war *in Begleitung* eines berühmten Tennisspielers.
He was in the company of/He was accompanied by a famous
tennis-player.

Ich *gehe mit dir* zum Arzt/an den Flughafen.
I'll go with you to the doctor's/to the airport.

70 *Talking and enquiring about absence and non-existence*

70.1

Negation of existence and occurrence

Absence and non-existence are conveyed by means of **nicht** or **kein** with expressions
of existence.

The structures are analogous to the ones described in **69.1–69.4**B:

> **nicht da sein** 'not to be there'
> **weg sein** 'to be away/gone'
> **abwesend sein** 'to be absent'
> **-e Abwesenheit** 'absence'
> **nicht/kein... besteht** 'does not exist'
> **es gibt nicht/kein** 'there is/are no'

Der Geschäftsführer *ist* heute leider *nicht da.*
The manager is unfortunately not here today.

Der Schüler *war* wegen einer schweren Erkrankung vom Unterricht
abwesend.
The pupil missed classes owing to a serious illness.

Der Verkauf wurde *in seiner Abwesenheit* beschlossen.
The sale was agreed in his absence/while he was away.

> **Es *besteht* in diesem Fall *keinerlei* Ansteckungsgefahr.**
> In this case there is no danger of contagion whatsoever.

(See **42.3g**A for the use of the dummy subject **es**)

> **Im Vereinigten Königreich *gibt es keine* Tollwut.**
> There is no rabies in the United Kingdom.

> **Es *gibt keine* Dinosaurier *mehr* auf der Erde: Sie sind ausgestorben.**
> There are no more dinosaurs on earth; they are extinct.

(See **70.4**B for things that have ceased to exist)

70.2 **Being missed and missing something**

(a) Being missed

> **fehlen** 'to be missing, lacking/to be absent'
> **jmdn./etw. vermissen** 'to miss sb./sth.'

> **Hier *fehlt* ein Messer/eine Seite.**
> There is a knife/a page missing here.

> **Wir *vermissen* unsren treuen Hund.**
> We miss our faithful dog.

fehlen with the dative of disdavantage (see **19.3**A; see also **19.7**A for the use of impersonal **es**). The person who is lacking/missing something is in the dative form, whereas the person/item that is missing is in the nominative:

> **Er *fehlt ihr*.**
> She misses him.

> **Mir *fehlen* noch 50 DM.**
> I am still 50 Marks short.

(b) Missing an event

> **fehlen** 'to be absent'
> **etw. verpassen/versäumen** 'to miss something'

> **Wegen seiner Mittelohrentzündung mußte er in der Schule häufig *fehlen*.**
> Because of an infection of the middle ear he was frequently absent from school.

> Ich *habe* den Film/das Spiel *verpaßt.*
> I missed the film/the play.

70.3 **Lack and shortage**

Lack and shortage can be rendered by **mangeln an** (+ dat) and **-r Mangel** 'lack/dearth'.
'Not/hardly enough' is expressed by **nicht/kaum genug**.

> **jmdm.** (= dat) **mangelt es an** (+ dat) 'to be lacking sth.'
> **knapp an etw.** (= dat) **sein** 'to be short of sth.'

Here again, the person in need is in the dative but this time the item he or she is missing is also in the dative following **an**.

> *Es mangelte ihr an* nichts; trotzdem war sie unzufrieden.
> She wanted for nothing, but she was still dissatisfied.

> In diesem Betrieb *mangelt es an* ausgebildeten Arbeitskräften.
> In this firm there is a lack of trained workers.

(See **42.3h**A for the use of impersonal verbs such as **mangeln**)

> Es *herrscht (ein) Mangel an* Studenten in den Naturwissenschaften.
> There is a shortage of students in the natural sciences.

> Er hatte *kaum* Geld.
> He did not have much money.

> Sie hatte *kaum* Freunde.
> She did not have many friends.

> Wir sind *knapp an* Milch und Zucker und sollten mal einkaufen gehen.
> We have hardly any milk and sugar and should go shopping.

Note the idiomatic expression:

> Wir sind *knapp bei* Kasse.
> We are short of money.

70.4 **Having ceased to exist**

(a) Having disappeared without a trace

The adverbs and prefixes **ab** and **weg** are often used to indicate that something has been done away with, put off or has gone/disappeared. **Ab** has the same function as the prefix 'de-' or 'dis-' in English, **weg** the same as 'away' or 'off'.

> **ab sein** 'to be off'
> **weg sein** 'to be gone'
> **verschwinden** 'to disappear'

Der Knopf an meiner Anzugsjacke *ist ab*.
The button on the jacket of my suit has come off/is missing.

Mein Geldbeutel *ist weg*.
My purse is gone/has disappeared.

Das Flugzeug *verschwand* in den Wolken.
The plane disappeared in(to) the clouds.

Note that **verschwinden in** (+ dat) is 'to disappear *into*'.

(b) Being dismantled, demolished

> **abgebaut** 'dismantled'
> **abgerissen** 'demolished'
> **abgetragen** 'mined'

Die unrentablen Fabriken *wurden abgebaut*.
The unprofitable factories were dismantled.

Das alte Theater *ist* jetzt *abgerissen*.
The old theatre has been demolished.

In manchen Gebieten wird die Braunkohle immer noch über Tage *abgetragen*.
In some areas (brown) coal is still mined above ground.

(c) Having been abolished or eradicated

> **abgeschafft** 'abolished'
> **ausgerottet** 'eradicated, exterminated/extinct'
> **gestrichen** 'cancelled/abolished'

Die Todesstrafe ist in Deutschland seit 1949 *abgeschafft*.
The death penalty has been abolished in Germany since 1949.

Die Pest ist in Europa *ausgerottet*.
The plague has been eradicated in Europe.

Der religiöse Feiertag *soll gestrichen werden*.
The religious holiday is to be abolished.

(d) For people and things that have gone away

> **weg*fahren** 'to leave/go away'
> **weg*ziehen aus/nach** 'to move away from/to'
> **weg*laufen** 'to run away'
> **jmdn./etw. verlassen** 'to leave sb./sth. (behind)'

> **Die Zigeuner sind schon *weggefahren*.**
> The gypsies have already moved away.

> **Meine Nachbarn *sind* nach Berlin *weggezogen*.**
> My neighbours have moved (away) to Berlin.

> **Der alten Frau *ist* die Katze *weggelaufen*.**
> The cat has run away from the old woman.

(See **19.3**A on the dative of disadvantage)

> **Sie *will* ihre Familie *verlassen* und auswandern.**
> She wants to leave her family and emigrate.

(e) For things that are out-dated and therefore obsolete

> **veraltet** 'obsolete/out-of-date'
> **altmodisch** 'old-fashioned'

> **Dieses PC Handbuch ist *veraltet*.**
> This PC manual is out-of-date.

> **Diesen *altmodischen* Anzug kannst du aber nicht auf der Hochzeit tragen.**
> You can't possibly wear this old-fashioned suit at the wedding.

(f) For things that have been destroyed

The prefix **zer-** before a past participle indicates something has been completely destroyed.

(See **36.2**A for inseparable prefixes and **57.2**A for the meaning of verbal prefixes)

> **zerschlagen** 'shattered'
> **zerstört** 'destroyed'
> **zertrümmert** 'reduced to ruins'

> **Ihre Hoffnung hatte sich *zerschlagen*.**
> Her hopes were shattered.

> **Die alte Wasserleitung ist total *zerstört*.**
> The old water pipe is completely destroyed.

> **Die alte Wallfahrtskirche ist leider *zertrümmert*.**
> The old pilgrimage church is unfortunately in ruins.

(g)   For things that are consumed or exhausted

(See **72.2b**B below for consumables no longer available)

---

aufgebraucht/verbraucht 'used up'
alle/aus 'run out/used up' (informal)
erschöpft 'exhausted'

> **Das Papier für das FAXgerät ist *aufgebraucht*.**
> The paper for the FAX machine has run out.

> **Die Milch ist *alle*.** (informal)
> The milk is finished.

> **Die Mineralvorkommen in diesem Boden *sind erschöpft*.**
> The mineral deposits in this ground are exhausted.

(h)   For items free from or low in something

The following suffixes indicate lack or absence (see **55.1**A on adjective formation):

-los 'without'
-frei 'free from/of'
-leer 'empty of'
-arm/-reduziert 'low/poor in'

> **partei*los*** 'without party affiliation'
> **bargeld*los* telephonieren** 'to telephone without using cash'
> **arbeits*los*** 'unemployed'
> **beschwerde*frei*** 'free from any ailment'
> **koffein*frei*** 'caffeine-free'
> **inhalts*leer*** 'without content' (of an idea, etc. 'vacuous/superficial')
> **menschen*leere* Straßen** 'deserted streets'
> **fett*arme* Kost** 'low-fat food'
> **kalorien*arm*/kalorien*reduziert*** 'low/reduced in calories'
> **nikotin*arm* im Rauch** 'low nicotine' (for cigarettes, etc.)

(i)   Doing without/choosing not to

auf etw. (= acc) **verzichten** 'to do without sth.'

> **Der Preisträger hat *auf den* Geldbetrag *verzichtet*.**
> The prize-winner chose not to accept/forewent the money.

> **In ihrem sechsbändigen Wörterbuch *verzichten* die Verfasser dar*auf*, Normen zu setzen.**
> In their six-volume dictionary the authors choose not to lay down norms.

(See **38.2**A for clause links with **darauf**, etc.)

(j)   Absence of speech/comment/action

schweigen 'to be silent'

> **Die Presse *schwieg* zu dieser peinlichen Situation.**
> The press was silent/did not comment on this embarrassing situation.

> **Die Waffen *schwiegen*.**
> The weapons/arms fell/were silent.

70.5 Cancelled or failing to happen

etw. (= acc) **ab*sagen** 'to cancel sth.'
etw. (= nom) **fällt aus** 'sth. is cancelled'
etw. (= acc) **ein*stellen** 'to discontinue sth.'
etw. (= nom) **bleibt aus** 'sth. fails to happen'

> **Das Konzert mußte leider *abgesagt werden/ausfallen*.**
> Unfortunately, the concert had to be cancelled.

> **Der Straßenbahnverkehr ist jetzt *eingestellt*.**
> There are no more trams in use now.

> **Der Erfolg *blieb* leider *aus*.**
> Unfortunately, success did not come.

For more expressions of absence see also **72**B on non-availability and **113.3**B on disappointment.

71 *Expressing and enquiring about availability*

It is not always possible to draw a clear line between presence and availability, thus all expressions listed for presence (see **69.1**B) can also be used for availability. The items in this section imply that something is present elsewhere and that the speaker or subject wants to get hold of it.

71.1 Making or having something available

(a) For making something available to someone, use **jmdm. etw. leihen** 'to let sb. have (the use of) sth.' in informal contexts:

> **Ich *leihe Ihnen* gern meinen Wagen.**
> I'll be happy to let you have the use of my car.

Note that in colloquial usage **borgen** can be used here instead of **leihen**:

> **Ich *borge Ihnen* gern meinen Wagen.** (colloquial)
> I'll be happy to let you have the use of my car.

(See also **71.6**B for borrowing)

(b) More formally one of the following can be used:

> **jmdm. etw. zur Verfügung stellen** 'to make sth. available to sb.'
> **jmdm. steht etw.** (= nom) **zur Verfügung** 'sth. is available to sb.'
> **über etw.** (= acc) **verfügen** 'to have something at one's disposal'
> **jmdm. etw. aus*händigen** 'to hand over/issue sth. to sb.'

Verfügung also means 'permission' or 'authority'; **jmdm. etw. zur Verfügung stellen** means 'to make something available to somebody/put something at someone's disposal'.

> **Ich *stelle Ihnen* meinen Wagen gern *zur Verfügung*.**
> You can have my car willingly (lit. I'll gladly make my car available to you).

(See **12**A for the word order of noun and pronoun)

> **Die Gemälde wurden freundlicherweise von der Tate Gallery in London *zur Verfügung gestellt*.**
> The paintings were kindly made available by the Tate Gallery in London.

> **Mein Wagen *steht Ihnen* jederzeit *zur Verfügung*.**
> You can use my car any time.

> Als Dolmetscher muß man *über* einen großen Wortschatz *verfügen.*
> As an interpreter one must have a large vocabulary at one's disposal.

A more official and formal way of expressing the handing over of something is **jmdm. etw. aus*händigen:**

> Ich *händige Ihnen* die Schlüssel zu Ihrem neuen Wagen *aus,* sobald wir Ihren Scheck haben.
> I shall issue the keys to your new car as soon as we have (received) your cheque.

71.2 For items in stock

> **auf Lager haben** 'to have in stock/store'
> **auf Vorrat kaufen/an*schaffen** 'to stock up'
> **vorrätig sein/haben** 'to be/have in stock'
> **-r Bestand an** (+ dat) 'the stock of'

> Wir haben/Es sind zur Zeit alle Campingartikel *auf Lager.*
> We have all camping accessories/All camping accessories are in stock.

> Bevor der Kaffee teurer wird, sollte man genügend *auf Vorrat kaufen.*
> One ought to stock up on coffee before it gets more expensive.

> *Haben* Sie auch Übergrößen *vorrätig?*
> Do you also have outsizes in stock?

> Der *Bestand an* Nahrungsmitteln muß nachgefüllt werden.
> Food stocks must be replenished.

71.3 Being within reach or at hand

> **etw. zur Hand haben** 'to have sth. to hand'
> **vorhanden sein** 'to be at hand/available'
> **parat haben** 'to have ready'

> *Haben* Sie zufällig sein Adreßbuch *zur Hand?*
> Do you by any chance have his address book to hand/handy?

> *Ist* in diesem Gebäude ein Speicher *vorhanden?*
> Is there an attic (for storing things) available in this building?

> *Haben* Sie einen Feuerlöscher *parat?*
> Do you have a fire extinguisher at the ready?

71.4

Reaching for or getting something

> **bekommen** 'to get'
> **an etw. (heran*)kommen** 'to get hold of sth.' (often implying that sth. is hard to get)
> **etw. erreichen** 'to reach sth./manage sth.'

Was muß ich tun, um in Deutsch eine bessere Note zu *bekommen*?
What do I have to do (in order) to get a better grade in German?

Es ist sehr schwierig, *an* diese seltenen Münzen *heranzukommen*.
It is very difficult to get hold of these rare coins.

Wie *kommst* du denn *an* so einen Job, braucht man da Beziehungen?
How do you get a job like that, do you need contacts?

Ich habe *es erreicht*, daß wir mehr Wohngeld bekommen.
I've managed to get us more housing benefit.

71.5

To express availability through purchase

> **kaufen** 'to buy'
> **bekommen** 'to get'
> **erhalten** 'to receive'
> **erhältlich** 'available'
> **etw. von/bei jmdm. bestellen** 'to order sth. from sb.'
> **etw. über jmdn. beziehen** 'to purchase sth. from sb.'
> **zu haben sein** (colloquial) 'to be had'
> **es gibt... (zu kaufen)** 'can be (bought)'

Das Vorlesungsverzeichnis *ist* in der Universitätsbuchhandlung *erhältlich*.
The list of lectures (and seminars, etc.) is available in the university bookshop.

Tabakwaren und Zeitschriften sowie Briefmarken *bekommen* Sie am Kiosk.
Tobacco, magazines and stamps are available at the kiosk.

(See **5.2b**A on word order)

Dieses Produkt kann nur *beim* Fachhandel *bestellt* werden.
This product can only be ordered from a specialist shop.

Alternative Heilmittel kann man *über* eine Reihe von Apotheken *beziehen*.
Alternative remedies can be purchased from a number of pharmacies.

Plastiktüten *sind* an der Kasse *zu haben.*
Plastic bags are to be had at the checkout.

The idiomatic expression **es gibt zu** (+ infinitive) expresses the presence of things e.g. 'to be bought/seen', etc.

Wo *gibt es* Briefmarken *zu kaufen*?
Where can you buy stamps?

71.6 Availability through borrowing, rental

sich (= dat) etw. leihen/borgen 'to borrow sth.'
jmdm. etw. (aus*)leihen 'to lend sth. to sb.'
mieten 'to rent'
vermieten 'to let'

Wir können *euch* leider nicht so viel (Geld) *leihen.*
Unfortunately, we can't lend you so much (money).

Möchtest du *dir* mein Rad *leihen/borgen*?
Would you like to borrow my bike?

In Deutschland *werden* die meisten Wohnungen *gemietet.*
In Germany most flats are rented.

71.7 Establishing if something is free to be used or if someone is free to do something

frei sein 'to be free'
frei haben 'to be free/off duty'
Zeit haben 'to have time'

Der Fensterplatz *ist frei.*
The seat/place at the window is free.

Wann *hast* du abends wieder einmal *frei*?
When are you free again in the evening?/When do you next have an evening off?

Hast du heute *Zeit,* um mir das Regal zu reparieren?
Do you have time today to repair the bookshelf for me?

71.8

To indicate for how long an item is fit for consumption, **haltbar** and **zum baldigen Verbrauch bestimmt** are used.

> **Dieses Milchprodukt** *ist zwei Tage haltbar.*
> This dairy product has a shelf life of two days.

> **Ein Fertiggericht ist** *zum baldigen Verbrauch bestimmt.*
> A ready-to-eat/pre-cooked dish is intended for immediate consumption/should be eaten immediately.

72 *Talking about non-availability*

72.1

Non-availability can be expressed by the negation of the structures used in **71.1–71.3**B.

> **jmdm. etw. nicht zur Verfügung stellen** 'not to make sth. available to sb.'
> **jmdm. steht etw. nicht zur Verfügung** 'sth. is not available to sb.'
> **nicht auf Lager haben** 'not to have in stock/store'
> **etw. nicht vorrätig haben** 'not to have sth. in stock'
> **nicht vorrätig sein** 'not to be in stock'
> **etw. nicht zur Hand haben** 'not to have sth. to hand'
> **etw. nicht/kein etw. da haben** 'not to have sth. here'
> **jmdm. kommt etw. abhanden** 'sb. loses sth.'

> **Ich kann Ihnen den Parkplatz** *nicht mehr zur Verfügung stellen.* (formal)
> I can no longer let you have the parking space.

Less formally, this could be expressed:

> **Sie** *können* **meinen Parkplatz** *nicht* **mehr** *benutzen.*
> You can no longer use my parking space.

> **Wir haben im Moment** *keine* **neuen Fahrpläne** *vorrätig.*
> At the moment we haven't got any new timetables in stock.

> **Ich hatte** *keinen* **Atlas** *zur Hand.*
> I didn't have an atlas to hand.

> **Wir** *haben* **heute** *kein* **Bargeld** *da.*
> We have no cash (here) today.

> **Die Urkunde** *ist mir* **irgendwie** *abhanden gekommen.*
> I have somehow lost the certificate.

(See **19.3**A for the dative of disadvantage)

72.2
Being out or having run out of sth.

(a) If a person is out of something, the prefix **aus-** is usually used in conjunction with the past participle.

(See **40.2b**A for the passive with **sein**)

> **ausgebucht** 'booked up'
> **ausgegeben** 'spent'
> **ausgetrunken** 'drunk up/empty'
> **ausverkauft** 'sold out'
> **aus*laufen** 'to run out/be discontinued'

> **Er** *hat* sein ganzes Taschengeld im Buchladen *ausgegeben.*
> He spent all his pocket money in the bookshop.

> **Die Flasche Weinbrandt** *war* völlig *ausgetrunken.*
> The bottle of brandy was completely empty.

> **Das Modell** *läuft* im Herbst *aus.*
> The model will be discontinued in the autumn.

For further examples using past participles, including **ausgerottet**, see **70.4**B on non-existence.

For further past participles with **aus-**, refer to your dictionary.

(b) With consumables that are finished

> **auf*brauchen** 'to use up'
> **alle** 'gone/finished'
> **leer** 'empty'

> **Die Kartoffeln** *sind*/der Kaffee *ist alle.* (informal)
> We've no more potatoes. We've run out of coffee.

> **Die Kartoffeln** *sind*/der Kaffee *ist* aufgebraucht.
> The potatoes have/the coffee has all been used up.

> **Der Einbrecher** *fand* die Kassen *leer.*
> The intruder found the tills empty.

(See **42.3b**A on sentence patterns and **70.4g**B for more examples of things consumed)

72.3

Indicating something is temporarily unavailable

(a) For occupied/booked seats or engaged lines:

> **Die Toilette/das Telefon ist** *besetzt.*
> The toilet/telephone is engaged.

> **Die Flüge** *sind* **alle** *ausgebucht.*
> The flights are all booked (up).

(b) If an item cannot be bought for some reason

(See also **71.2**B for things in stock)

> **nicht zu kaufen/nicht käuflich** 'not for sale'
> **unverkäuflich** 'not for sale'
> **ausverkauft** 'sold out'
> **vergriffen** 'out of print'

> **Das Ausstellungsstück ist leider** *nicht käuflich/nicht zu kaufen.*
> Sorry, the display item/exhibit is not for sale.

> **Diese Warenprobe ist ein** *unverkäufliches* **Muster.**
> This sample is not for sale.

> **Die Sonderangebote** *sind* **seit gestern alle** *ausverkauft.*
> All the special offers have been sold out since yesterday.

(See **34.2d**A for the use of **seit** with the present tense)

> **Man sollte rechtzeitig auf den Markt gehen, bevor alles** *ausverkauft ist.*
> One should go to the market early, before everything is sold out.

> **Dieser Titel** *ist* **schon längst** *vergriffen.*
> This book has been out of print for a long time.

72.4

Saying that someone is not available for a caller

(a) Indicating a person is engaged in something

> **mit etw. beschäftigt sein** 'to be busy with'
> **anderweitig beschäftigt sein** 'to be busy with sth. else'
> **unterwegs sein** 'to be out/en route (elsewhere)'
> **keine Zeit haben** 'to have no time'
> **alle Hände voll zu tun haben** 'to be busy'
> **verhindert sein** 'to be unable to make it'
> **gerade** 'at the moment'

Er ist *mit dem* Abwasch *beschäftigt* und kann nicht zur Tür kommen.
He is busy with the washing up and cannot come to the door.

Sie konnte sich nicht um den Gast kümmern. Sie war *anderweitig beschäftigt.*
She couldn't look after the guest. She was busy with something else.

Der Klempner ist *noch unterwegs,* er wird Sie später zurückrufen.
The plumber is still out, he'll call you back later.

Ich *habe* jetzt leider *keine Zeit,* um mich mit Ihnen zu unterhalten.
I am sorry, I have no time to chat with you.

Mein Mann *telefoniert gerade/spricht gerade* mit einer Kundin.
My husband is on the phone/is talking to a (female) customer at the moment.

(See also **76.4c**B for indicating that someone is in the process of doing something)

(b) Indicating a person is already 'attached'

---

nicht zu haben sein 'not to be had/not available' (colloquial, often jokingly)
(schon) vergeben sein 'to be (already) spoken for'

Diese junge Dame *ist nicht zu haben,* sie ist verlobt.
This young lady is not 'available', she is engaged.

Und die andere *ist* auch schon *vergeben.*
And the other one is also (already) spoken for.

---

73 *Identifying and seeking identification*

73.1

Means of identification

In Germany everybody has to carry some form of identification.
(**-r Personalausweis/-e Kennkarte** 'identity card' or, alternatively, **r-Reisepaß/Paß** 'passport'.) An ID card is needed, e.g. to open a bank account, to prove your age or to gain admittance.

Darf ich bitte Ihren *Ausweis/*Ihre *Leserkarte* sehen?
May I see your ID card/your reader's card, please?

Kannst du *dich ausweisen*?
Can you prove your identity?

The card carries information, **Angaben zur Person** 'personal particulars' on the subjects in the following sections.

73.2

Supplying personal details

(a) Names

On official forms the following items are listed:

> **-r Name** 'name'
> **Familienname/Nachname** 'surname'
> **Vorname** 'first name/Christian name'
> **Geburtsname/Mädchenname** 'name at birth/maiden name' (usually abbreviated **geb.** for **geborene** 'neé')
> **Künstlername** 'pseudonym/nom de plume'

The following questions would be asked by officials and could sound rather brusque unless they are softened with **denn**:

(See **117.1cB** for the use of modal particles):

> **Wie *heißen Sie denn*?**
> What is your name, please?
>
> **Wie *heißen Sie mit* Nach*namen*?**
> What is your surname?
>
> **Ich *heiße*...**
> My name is...
>
> ***Wie ist* Ihr Mädchen*name*?**
> What is your maiden name?
>
> **Müller.**
> Müller.
>
> ***Haben Sie* einen Künstler*namen*?**
> Do you have a pseudonym?
>
> **Mein Künstlername ist...**
> My pseudonym is...

Checking the spelling of names, etc.:

> ***Wie schreibt* man das?**
> How do you spell that?

> **Bitte *buchstabieren* Sie Ihren Nachnamen.** (formal)
> Please spell your surname.

(See **118.3**B for the spelling alphabet)

(b) Place and date of birth

On official forms:

> **-r Geburtsort** 'place of birth'
> **-s Geburtsdatum** 'date of birth'

The convention for writing dates is date, month, year:

26.09.95 for 26 September 1995.

Asking directly:

> ***Wo sind* Sie *geboren*?**
> Where were you born?

> ***Wann sind* Sie *geboren*?**
> When were you born?

> ***Wann haben* Sie *Geburtstag*?**
> When is your birthday?

(c) Nationality

On forms:

Nationality (**-e Nationalität/-e Staatsangehörigkeit**) on an official document is indicated by an (undeclined) adjective:

> **deutsch** 'German'
> **britisch** 'British'
> **türkisch** 'Turkish'

Asking directly:

> ***Welche Staatsangehörigkeit haben* Sie?**
> What nationality are you?

The answer in spoken German could be either with the undeclined adjective, or with a noun (see **28.5**A on adjectival nouns).

> **Ich bin *Deutsche/Deutscher*.**
> I am German (female/male).

Ich bin *Brite/Amerikaner/Australier.*
I am British/American/Australian.

Kommen Sie *aus einem Land* **in der Europäischen Union/Gemeinschaft?**
Do you come from a country in the European Union/Community?

(d) Special characteristics

On forms:

> **-e Größe** 'height' (in metres, e.g. 1,63m = 5'4")
> **-e Augenfarbe** 'colour of eyes'
> **-s Geschlecht** 'sex'

Not included in passports but used for identification:

> **-r Fingerabdruck** 'fingerprint'
> **genetische Merkmale** 'genetic marks/birth marks'

Asking directly:

> *Wie groß* **bist du?**
> How tall are you?

> *Was für eine Farbe* **haben seine Augen?**
> What colour are his eyes?

(See **24.2a**A for **was für ein**)

> **War der Autofahrer** *männlich* **oder** *weiblich/***ein Mann oder eine Frau?**
> Was the driver male or female/a man or a woman?

(e) Further details in documents

> **-s Ausstellungsdatum/-r Tag der Ausstellung** 'date of issue'
> **gültig bis** 'valid until'

Asking directly:

> *Wie lange* **ist Ihr Paß noch** *gültig?*
> How long is your passport valid for?

(f) Residence

People resident in Germany have to register with the local registration office (**-s Einwohnermeldeamt**). Registration is compulsory (**-e Meldepflicht**; see **86.2**B for **-pflicht**).

A registration form contains the following sections:

> **-r Wohnort** 'place (town) of residence'
> **-r Wohnsitz** 'residence'
> **wohnhaft in** 'resident in'

A passport would only carry the name of the town of residence, whereas the ID card would have the full address:

> **-e gegenwärtige Adresse** 'current address'
> **polizeilich gemeldet in...** 'registered with the police in...' (for people on limited visas)

Asking directly:

> **Wo wohnen Sie?**
> Where do you live?

> **Wo ist Ihr Hauptwohnsitz?**
> Where is your main residence?

73.3 People can be referred to by means of personal pronouns (see **30.2**A and **32**A) and can be identified through a relative clause (see **10**A). In pointing to someone, **der/die/das** (see **31.2**A) or **dieser/diese/dieses** (**24.1a**A) might be used.

> Ist das *der Mann, der* hier gestern ein neues Konto eröffnet hat?
> Is that the man who opened a new account here yesterday?

> *Diese junge Dame* war gestern schon einmal hier.
> This young lady was here yesterday.

(See **74**B for how to describe people)

74 *Describing people*

74.1 ## Descriptions in general

> **beschreiben** 'to describe'
> **-e Beschreibung** 'description'
> **-e Personenbeschreibung** 'description of a person'

> Bitte *beschreiben* Sie mir diese Person.
> Please describe this person.

74.2
Introducing a description

(a) A description can be introduced by referring to someone's features or characteristics, **-e Eigenschaft(en)**:

> **Dieser Mensch hat ganz** *besondere Eigenschaften.*
> This person has very special characteristics/features.

(b) Recognizing people by their characteristics is expressed by **erkennen** 'to recognize' and **-s Kennzeichen (-)** 'characteristic':

> **Den Bademeister** *erkennt man an* **seiner weißen Uniform.**
> The swimming-pool attendant/life-guard can be recognized by his white uniform.

(See **77.2**B for **man**)

74.3
Physical appearance and looks

(a) General appearance

(See **110.1b**B for looking well and **110.8a**B for looking unwell)

> **aus*sehen** 'to look'
> **-s Aussehen** 'looks'
> **-s Äußere** (adjectival noun) 'outward appearance'
> **aus*sehen wie** 'to look like'
> **jmdm. ähnlich sehen** 'to resemble sb.'

> **Das Fotomodell** *sieht* **in diesem Anzug sehr elegant** *aus.*
> The (photo) model looks very elegant in this outfit.

> *Dem Äußeren nach* **zu urteilen, muß sie eine recht ordentliche Person sein.**
> To judge by her outward appearance she must be a very orderly/tidy person.

> **Sie achtet sehr auf ihr** *Äußeres.*
> She takes care of her outward appearance.

(b) Comparing with others

> **Dein Freund** *sieht aus wie* **ein Westernheld.**
> Your friend looks like a hero in a Western.

(See **8.7b**A for word order)

> **Mit den buschigen Augenbrauen** *ähnelt* **er stark** *seinem* **Großvater.**
> With his bushy eyebrows he strongly resembles his grandfather.

(c) For adjectives of physical appearance refer to a dictionary. The following is a short selection of common descriptive terms:

> **körperlich** 'physical'
> **durchschnittlich** 'average'
> **körperlich stark** 'physically strong'
> **schwach** 'weak'
> **behindert** 'handicapped, disabled'
> **unreif** 'immature'
> **groß** 'tall'

> **Er ist über 1,86m *groß*.**
> He is over 1.86m tall.

(See **75.3**B on 'Size and parameter')

74.4 **Character**

(a) General terms

> **-r Charakter** 'character'
> **charakterlich** 'of character/personal'
> **-e Eigenschaft** 'property/characteristic'

> **Diese Führungskraft hat *wichtige charakterliche Stärken/Schwächen*.**
> This executive has important personal strengths/weaknesses.

(b) Positive traits of character

> **erfahren** 'experienced'
> **jmdm. sympathisch sein** 'to be likeable to sb.'
> **mitfühlend** 'sympathetic'
> **eigenartig** 'peculiar/idiosyncratic'

> **Der Verunglückte war ein *erfahrener* Skiläufer.**
> The casualty was an experienced skier.

> **Die neue Lehrerin ist mir besonders *sympathisch*.**
> I think the new teacher is especially likeable/particularly nice.

> **Als Krankenschwester darf man nicht zu *mitfühlend* sein.**
> As a nurse one mustn't be too sympathetic.

Was hältst du von seinem *eigenartigen* Führungsstil?
What do you think about his peculiar/idiosyncratic style of
management?

(c) Habits and tendencies

> **eine Veranlagung/einen Hang zu etw. haben** 'to have a disposition/tendency towards
> sth.'
> **veranlagt sein (zu etw.)** 'to have a talent/gift (for sth.)/be good at sth.'
> **einen Hang zu etw. haben** 'to have a tendency towards sth.'
> **zu etw. neigen** 'to tend towards'
> **etw. zu tun pflegen** 'to have a habit of doing sth.'
> **pflegte** 'used to'

The nouns **Veranlagung** and **Hang** tend to be used in particularly formal contexts.
Einen Hang zu etw. haben suggests a state of mind:

> **Er *hat* noch diesen *Hang zur* Abhängigkeit von seiner Mutter.**
> He still has this tendency to be dependent on his mother.

eine Veranlagung (zu etw.) haben suggests a physiological condition:

> **Ich *habe eine* nervöse *Veranlagung*.**
> I have a nervous disposition.

> **Die Familie *hat eine* erbliche *Veranlagung*.**
> The family has a hereditary condition.

> **Sie *hat eine* gewisse *Veranlagung zur* Fettsucht.**
> She has a certain tendency to obesity.

The following are used in less formal contexts:

> **Schon als sie klein war, konnte man sehen, daß sie *sportlich veranlagt war*.**
> When she was only little one could already see that she had a gift for
> sports.

> **Er *neigt zum* Alkohol/*zur* Verschwendung.**
> He likes to drink/spend. (i.e. he is a drunkard/wastes money)

> **Er machte sonntags *gewöhnlich* einen langen Spaziergang.**
> **Er *pflegte* sonntags einen langen Spaziergang zu machen.** (slightly formal)
> He had a habit of taking/He used to take a long walk on Sundays.

74.5
Capabilities and talents

(a) Capabilities and skills

(See **101.1a**B for the difference between **kennen** and **wissen**. For **können** see **35.6** on modal verbs)

> **sich** (= acc) **mit etw. aus*kennen** 'to know one's way with sth.'
> **-e Fähigkeit/-e Fertigkeit** 'capability/skill'
> **eine Sprache (sprechen) können** 'to be able (to speak) a language'
> **-s Talent** 'talent'
> **-e Begabung** 'gift'
> **für etw. talentiert/begabt sein** 'to be talented/gifted for sth.'
> **-s Vermögen** 'ability'
> **ein Instrument spielen** 'to play an instrument'

Expressing familiarity with something involves the use of **kennen** in some form:

> ***Kennst** du **dich** mit diesen Anweisungen **aus**?*
> Are you familiar with these instructions?

Being capable:

> **Ein Schreiner muß über gute Hand*fertigkeiten* verfügen.**
> A carpenter must have good manual skills.

(See **87.4**B on the difference between **Fertigkeit** and **Fähigkeit**)

Speaking a language:

> ***Könnt** ihr *Französisch*/Arabisch/Spanisch?*
> Can you speak French/Arabic/Spanish?

Playing an instrument or sports:

> **Meine Nachbarin *spielt Geige*.**
> My neighbour plays the violin.

(See **23.1a**A for omission of the article)

> ***Spielt** dein Bruder *Squash*?*
> Does your brother play squash?

(b) Talents

Talents or gifts are referred to as **-s Talent/-e Begabung**:

> **Sie ist ein großes *Talent*.**
> She is a great talent.

Der Musikstipendiat *hat eine seltene Begabung* **für Komposition.**
The music scholar has a rare gift for composition.

Die hoch*begabten*/**weniger begabten Schüler werden in einem besonderen Programm gefördert.**
The highly gifted/less gifted pupils are encouraged/promoted/
taught in a special programme of study.

Er hat ein stark ausgebildetes Analyse*vermögen.*
He has a very thoroughly developed analytical ability.

74.6 — Making an impression on others

einen guten/schlechten Eindruck auf jmdn. machen 'to make a good/bad impression on sb.'
einen Eindruck bei jmdm. hinterlassen 'to leave an impression with sb.'
jmdn. beeindrucken 'to impress sb.'
beeindruckt sein 'to be impressed'
jmdm. etw. an*sehen 'to tell sth. from sb.('s face)'
scheinen/wirken 'to seem/make an impression'

Man *sieht* **es** *ihr* **(an den Augen)** *an,* **daß sie völlig übermüdet ist.**
One can tell (from her eyes) that she is completely overtired.

Der alte Herr *scheint* **heute besonders** *gut aufgelegt zu sein.*
The old gentleman seems to be in a particularly good mood today.

Der Nachrichtensprecher *wirkt* **heute abend** *etwas niedergeschlagen.*
The newsreader seems somewhat depressed this evening.

Wir *waren von* **dem tadellosen Benehmen der Kinder stark** *beeindruckt.*
We were very impressed by the immaculate behaviour of the children.

74.7 — Talking about professions

von Beruf 'by profession'
tätig sein als 'to be working as'
angestellt sein als 'to be employed as'
im Beamtenverhältnis stehen 'to be a (permanent) civil servant'
im Angestelltenverhältnis stehen 'to be a salaried employee'

Mein Vater *ist Lehrer.*
My father is a teacher.

(See **23.1b**A for omission of the article)

> **Sie ist** *von Beruf* **Floristin.**
> She is a florist by profession.

> **Bisher** *war* **sie** *als* **Vorarbeiterin in einem Betrieb** *tätig.*
> Until now she was working as a supervisor in a firm.

> **Möchten Sie nicht lieber** *als* **Vollzeitkraft** *angestellt* **sein?**
> Wouldn't you rather be employed full-time?

74.8 **Social relationships**

(See also **61.3**–**61.5**B on introductions, etc.)

(a) 'To be familiar with' someone or 'knowing' someone is rendered by **jmdn. kennen.**

> **jmdn. kennen** 'to know sb.'
> **jmdn. kennen*lernen** 'to get to know sb.'

> *Kennst* **du den Kandidaten der neuen Partei?**
> Do you know the candidate of the new (political) party?

> **Wir** *kennen uns* **schon seit zwanzig Jahren.**
> We've known each other for twenty years.

> **Wie habt** *ihr euch* **eigentlich** *kennengelernt?* **Beim Tennisspielen.**
> How did you meet/get to know each other? Playing tennis.

(b) Friends and acquaintances

Only close friends are called **-r Freund/-e Freundin.**

Possessive adjectives are very significant here, especially when talking about the other sex, e.g. **mein Freund** 'my boyfriend'.

If a male teenager says **meine Freundin**, he is implying his (one and only) 'girlfriend'.

(See **30.3**A and **45.2**A for possessive adjectives)

> **-r Freund** 'friend'
> **mit jmdm. befreundet sein** 'to be friends with sb.'
> **-r/-e Bekannte** (adjectival noun) 'acquaintance/casual friend'

> **Die beiden waren gut** *miteinander befreundet.*
> They were good friends (with each other).

(See **28.5**A for adjectival nouns)

> **Das sind *gute Bekannte* aus der Studienzeit.**
> They are good friends from university/college days.

(c) People are often described in their professional relationships to others:

> **-r Kollege/-e Kollegin** 'colleague'
> **-r Arbeitskollege** 'colleague at work'
> **-r Mitarbeiter/-e Mitarbeiterin** 'colleague/collaborator'
> **-r/-e Vorgesetzte** 'superior' (adjectival noun)

> **Mein *Mitarbeiter* und ich betreuen zusammen das neue Projekt.**
> My colleague and I are looking after the new project together.

(d) Contemporaries

> **-r Schul-/Klassenkamerad** 'school friend/classmate'
> **-r Schulfreund** '(close) schoolfriend'
> **ein Schüler aus meinem Jahrgang** 'pupil from my year (at school)'
> **-r Studienkollege/-r Kommilitone** 'fellow student'

> **Zum 25. Jahrestag seines Examens waren fast alle früheren**
> ***Studienkollegen* gekommen.**
> Almost all his former fellow students had come to the 25th anniversary
> of his exams.

74.9 — Family relationships

General terms

> **-e Familie** 'family'
> **-r/-e Verwandte** 'related person' (adjectival noun)
> **mit jmdm. verwandt sein** 'to be related to sb.'
> **ein enger/entfernter Verwandter** 'a close/a distant relative'
> **-r/-e Angehörige** 'relative' (adjectival noun)

> **Wir sind miteinander *verwandt*.**
> We are related to each other.

In formal circumstances, e.g. funerals, **-r /-e Angehörige** (short for **-r /-e Familienangehörige**) is used.

(a) Immediate family

Parents and spouses

-e **Eltern** (plural) 'parents'
-r **Vater/-e Mutter** 'father/mother'
-r **(Ehe)mann/-e (Ehe)frau** 'husband/wife'

> **Seine *Eltern* sind schon ziemlich alt.**
> His parents are quite old.

Children

-s **Kind** 'child'
-r **Sohn/-e Tochter** 'son/daughter'

> **Unsre Söhne studieren schon.**
> Our sons are already at university/college.

Brothers and sisters

-r **Bruder/-e Schwester** 'brother/sister'
-e **Geschwister** (plural) 'brothers and sisters/siblings'

> **Der jüngste *Bruder* war erst sechs, als die Eltern nach Köln zogen.**
> The youngest brother was only six when the parents moved to Cologne.
>
> **Sie war die Älteste *von drei Geschwistern*.**
> She was the eldest of three brothers and sisters.

Grandparents and grandchildren

die **Großeltern** 'grandparents'
-r **Großvater/-e Großmutter** 'grandfather/grandmother'
-r **Enkel/-e Enkelin** 'grandson/granddaughter'
-e **Enkel** (plural) 'grandchildren'

> **Viele *Großeltern* sehen ihre Enkel nur selten.**
> Many grandparents see their grandchildren only rarely.

Cousins

-r **Cousin** (French pronunciation) '(male) cousin'
-e **Cousine** '(female) cousin'

> **Gestern kam die *Cousine* von meinem Vater zu uns zum Kaffee.**
> Yesterday my father's (female) cousin had coffee with us.

(b) Once removed

For family relationships that are once removed by a generation , the prefix **Groß-** 'grand' is used:

> **-r Großonkel/-e Großtante** 'great uncle/aunt'
> **-r Großneffe/-e Großnichte** 'great nephew/niece'
> **zweiten Grades** 'once removed'
> **eine Cousine zweiten Grades** 'a cousin once removed' (formal)

> **Tante Margret ist sehr stolz auf ihre *Großnichte*.**
> Aunt Margret is very proud of her great niece.

(c) In-laws

> **-r Schwiegersohn** 'son-in-law'
> **-e Schwiegermutter** 'mother-in-law'
> **angeheiratet** 'related by marriage'
> **ein angeheirateter Vetter** 'a cousin by marriage'

The prefix **Schwieger-** is used for all 'in-laws', except **-r Schwager/-e Schwägerin** brother-in-law/sister-in-law:

> **Mit seinem *Schwager* kommt Thomas besonders gut aus.**
> Thomas gets on especially well with his brother-in-law.

(d) Second marriages

Stief- as a prefix works just like 'step-' in English:

> **-r Stiefsohn/-e Stieftochter** 'step-son/daughter'
> **mein Sohn aus erster Ehe** 'my son from my first marriage'
> **-e Halbschwester/-r Halbbruder** 'half-sister/brother'

> **Ihre Tochter *aus erster Ehe* kann schon auf die kleine Halbschwester aufpassen.**
> Her daughter from her first marriage can already look after her new half sister.

(e) Foster and adoptive arrangements

> **Pflege-** 'foster'
> **Adoptiv-** 'adoptive'
> **jmdn. adoptieren** 'to adopt sb.'
> **-e Pflegeeltern** 'foster-parents'
> **-s Adoptivkind/angenommene Kind** 'adoptive child'

> **Es wird immer schwieriger, gesunde Babies zu *adoptieren*.**
> It is getting harder and harder to adopt healthy babies.

(f) Family status

> **ledig** 'single'
> **sich (= acc) mit jmdm. verloben** 'to get engaged to sb.'
> **jmdn. heiraten** 'to get married to sb.'
> **verheiratet** 'married'
> **geschieden** 'divorced'
> **von jmdm. getrennt sein/leben** 'to be separated from sb.'
> **verwitwet** 'widowed'

> **Sie *hat sich* am 21. Juni mit Hans Richter *verlobt*.**
> She got engaged to Hans Richter on June 21.

Husbands, wives or partners are occasionally referred to as **meine bessere Hälfte** (lit. 'my better half').

74.10 Dating and meeting each other casually

> **mit jmdm. gehen** 'to go out with sb.' (young people's colloquial speech)
> **(mit jmdm.) flirten** 'to flirt (with sb.)'
> **ein (enges) Verhältnis mit jmdm. haben** 'to have a (close/amorous) relationship with sb.'

> ***Geht* der Paul eigentlich immer noch *mit* der Dicken aus der zehnten Klasse?**
> Is Paul still going out with/dating the fat girl from the tenth form?

Arranging to meet someone

> **sich (= acc) mit jmdm. treffen** 'to meet (with) sb.'
> **sich (= acc) mit jmdm. (zu etw.) verabreden** 'to make a date with sb. (for sth.)'

> **Ich *habe mich mit* ihr an der Bar *getroffen*.**
> I met her at the bar.

> **Wir *hatten uns zum* Abendessen *verabredet*.**
> We had arranged to meet for supper.

Meeting someone by chance

> **jmdn. (zufällig) treffen/jmdm. begegnen** 'to meet sb. by chance'

Ich *habe sie zufällig* in der Stadt *getroffen.*/Ich bin ihr zufällig in der Stadt begegnet.
I bumped into her in town.

Weißt du, wer *mir* neulich auf dem Markt *begegnet ist*? Der Andreas.
Do you know who I bumped into the other day at the market? Andrew.

75 *Describing objects*

75.1 Definitions

In order to ask for a definition of an object, use **Was versteht man unter** (+ dat)...? 'What is meant/understood by...?'.

Definitions are given in the following form:

Ein Dreieck *ist* **eine von drei Geraden begrenzte geometrische Figur.**
A triangle is a geometrical shape bordered by three straight lines.

(See **49**A for extended adjectival phrases)

75.2 Shape

(a) A 'line' (**-e Linie**) can be decribed as **krumm/gerade** 'crooked/straight' or **direkt** 'direct'.

(See **80.3**B on 'Describing distances')

(b) Geometrical forms are **-e Gestalt/-e Form**

Kreise, Quadrate und Dreiecke sind *geometrische Formen.*
Circles, squares and triangles are geometric forms.

(c) An 'object/body' (**-r Körper**) could be described as **fest/weich** 'solid/soft'.

75.3 Size and parameter

(a) Basic terms

-e Größe 'size'
Größe can be both 'size' and 'parameter' (e.g. time/force)
kleine Größen are 'small sizes' (e.g. clothes)

Hier haben wir es mit *meßbaren Größen* **zu tun.**
We are dealing here with measurable amounts.

'Height' for people is also given using **groß**, even if the person is in fact small:

>Er *ist* 1,75m *groß.*
>He is 1.75m tall.

>Bei ihrer Geburt *war* Ulrike *nur 42cm groß.*
>At her birth Ulrike measured only 42cm.

(b) Measurements in German-speaking countries are metric. Refer to any large cookbook or DIY book for conversion tables (-e **Umrechnungstabelle**). Remember that commas instead of full stops are used to divide decimals.

(See **59.5d**A for the use of punctuation in decimals)

In Geometry, measurements are given as:

>A *sei* **4cm**, B *sei* **7cm**.
>A is/Let A be 4cm and B 7cm.

(**cm** is pronounced **Zentimeter**.)

(See **39.5**A and **39.4b**A on the subjunctive)

Sizes are often compared to those of common fruits and the like, e.g. **erbsengroß/haselnußgroß** 'pea-/hazelnut size'.

>Die Hagelkörner waren fast *erbsengroß.*
>The hailstones were almost as big as peas.

(c) Dimension

'dimension' is rendered as -s **Ausmaß(e)/-e Dimension (en)**.

Area (-e **Fläche**) is measured in **Quadratzentimeter** (= cm^2)/**Quadratmeter** (= m^2)/**Quadratkilometer** (= km^2) 'square centimetre/metre/kilometre'.

>Meine Wohnung *hat 60 Quadratmeter./ist 60 Quadratmeter groß.*
>My flat is 60 square metres (in area).

In order to describe, for example, an indoor pool, say:

>Das Schwimmbecken hat olympische Maße/Ausmaße: Es ist 50m *lang* und 10m *breit.*/Es ist 50 *mal* 10m groß. (m = Meter)
>The pool is olympic size: it is 50m long and 10m wide. It is 50 metres by 10.

To cover an area, **sich erstrecken/aus*dehnen über** 'to stretch/extend' is used.

(See also **80.4d**B 'For covering an area' and **75.2b**B for **mal**.)

>Das Industriegelände *erstreckt sich über* 25 Hektar.
>The industrial site extends over 25 hectares.

Volume is measured in **-r Kubikzentimeter** (= cm³)/**-r Kubikmeter** (= m³), etc., 'cubic centimetre/cubic metre', etc.

To describe a three-dimensional object, use **lang/breit/hoch** 'long/wide/high':

> **Der Tisch ist 1,40m *lang*, 70cm *breit* und 74cm *hoch*.**
> The table is 1.40m long, 70cm wide and 74cm high.

To describe the depth of something (e.g. cupboards, wardrobes, drawers, etc.), use **tief**:

> **Die Schublade ist 50cm *breit*, 10cm *hoch* und 60cm *tief*.**
> The drawer is 50cm wide, 10cm high and 60cm deep.

Corresponding nouns (see **53.1b**A and **54.3**A for word formation) are
-e Länge/-e Breite/-e Höhe/-e Tiefe 'length/breadth/height/depth'.

> **Der Münchner Fernsehturm hat *eine Höhe von* 290 Metern.**
> The television tower in Munich has a height of 290m.

(See **47.1a**A for adjectives derived from place names)

In order to describe something that is 'x' cm wide by 'y' cm long, **mal** or **auf** ('times') is used.

> **Diese Holzplatte ist *zwei mal drei* Meter lang und zwei cm dick.**
> This wooden board is two metres wide, three metres long and two centimetres thick.

> **Ich brauche eine Tischdecke von 2,40 *auf* 1,70m.**
> I need a tablecloth measuring 2.40m by 1.70m.

(d) Fitting and matching

> **passen** 'to fit/suit/match'
> **etw. paßt zu etw.** 'sth. goes with sth./matches sth.'
> **etw. paßt jmdm.** 'sth. suits/fits sb.'
> **jmdm. stehen** 'to suit'
> **etw. steht jmdm.** 'sth. suits sb./looks nice on sb.'

> **Dieser Schrank *paßt* genau in die Ecke.**
> This cupboard fits exactly into the corner.

> **Diese Gardinen *passen* im Farbton *genau zum* Teppich.**
> The colour of the curtains matches the carpet perfectly.

> **Diese Hose *paßt* aber gar *nicht* zu der Bluse, die du anhast.**
> These trousers don't go at all with the blouse you are wearing.

Deine Frisur *paßt zu dir.*
Your hairstyle suits you.

Die grüne Farbe von dem Kleid *steht dir gut.*
The green colour of your dress really suits you.

(e) Alterations

(For more expressions on alterations, see **76.8a**B)

> **ändern** 'to alter'
> **-e Änderung** 'alteration'

Das Möbelstück *muß geändert werden*; es ist zu hoch/niedrig, etc.
The piece of furniture must be altered, it is too high/low, etc.

In order to be more specific, comparative adjectives are used in verbs with a **ver-** prefix.

(See **57.2**A for the meaning of verbal prefixes)

> **verändern** 'to change'
> **vergrößern** 'to enlarge'
> **verkleinern** 'to reduce' (in size)
> **verlängern** 'to lengthen'
> **verkürzen** 'to shorten'
> **verdoppeln** 'to double'
> **verdreifachen** (etc.) 'to treble' (etc.)

Soll ich das Foto von dir *vergrößern* **lassen?**
Shall I have your photograph enlarged?

Sein Einkommen *hat sich* **in den letzten drei Jahren** *verdoppelt.*
His income has doubled in the last three years.

More informally, you can use **machen** with a comparative:

> **kleiner/gerader/fester/weicher machen** 'to make smaller/straighter/
> stronger/softer'

Kannst du mir schnell das Kleid *kürzer machen*?
Could you quickly shorten my dress?

(f) Expressing strength/power

> **stark** 'strong'
> **-e Stärke** 'strength' (expecially in a compound noun)
> **-e Pferdestärke (PS)** 'horsepower'
> **-e Lautstärke** 'volume'

> **Er ist schon fast *so stark* wie sein großer Bruder.**
> He is already almost as strong as his big brother.

> **Könnten Sie bitte die *Lautstärke* reduzieren?**
> Could you reduce the volume, please?

(g) Expressing weight

'Weight' is rendered as **-s Gewicht** and 'to weigh' as **wiegen** or, more precisely but less frequently, as **wägen**, and is measured in **-s Gramm/Kilogramm**, etc. **-r Zentner** 'hundredweight' and **-e Tonne** ('ton') are also commonly used.

> **-s Gewicht** 'weight'
> **wiegen** 'to weigh'
> **Übergewicht haben** 'to be overwieght'
> **schwer** 'heavy'
> **leicht** 'light'

> **Der Ringkämpfer *wiegt über zwei Zentner*.**
> The wrestler weighs more than two hundredweight.

> **Die Stewardessen sollen *weder Über- noch Untergewicht haben*.**
> Stewardesses are supposed to be neither under- nor overweight.

In order to ask about weight, use **wie schwer/was wiegt**:

> ***Wie schwer* ist dein Koffer?**
> How heavy is your suitcase?

> **Was *hat* das Baby bei der Geburt *gewogen*?**
> How much did the baby weigh at birth?

(See also **110.4cB** on gaining and losing weight)

75.4 | **Describing a state**

(a) General terms

> **-r Zustand** 'condition'
> **fest** 'solid'
> **flüssig** 'liquid'
> **gasförmig** 'gaseous'
> **verdampfen** 'to evaporate'
> **kochen** 'to boil'
> **gefrieren** 'to freeze'

Die neue Brücke ist noch im Planungs*zustand*.
The new bridge is still at the planning stage.

Das Fleisch ist noch in gefrorenem/rohem *Zustand*.
The meat is still in a frozen/raw state.

Die Wohnung ist in einem *Zustand*!
The flat is in a (right) state!

Chemicals are referred to as being **fest/flüssig/gasförmig**, etc. or in **festem/flüssigem/gasförmigem Zustand** 'in a solid/liquid/gaseous form'.

(b) Changing state

Bei einer bestimmten Temperatur *wird* dieses Metall *flüssig*.
This metal becomes liquid at a certain temperature.

Wasser kocht bei 100° C (= Celsius) und *verdampft*.
Water boils at 100° C and evaporates.

Bei 0° C *gefriert* das Wasser.
Water freezes at 0° C.

Temperatures are measured in (**-s**) **Grad Celsius**.

(See also **110.8e**B on running a temperature)

Quantity

(See **31.3**A for the use of **ein** to denote the number one; and **46.4–46.5**A for countables and uncountables)

(a) 'Amount' is rendered as:

> **-e Menge** 'amount'
> **-e Anzahl/-e Zahl** 'number'
> **mengenmäßig** 'by amount'
> **zahlenmäßig** 'by number'
> **quantitativ** 'quantitatively'
> **-e Unmenge von** 'tremendous number/hundreds of'
> **unzählig viele** 'countless many'
> **zahllose** 'innumerable'

> **Die Soldaten waren dem Feind *zahlenmäßig unterlegen*.**
> The soldiers were outnumbered by the enemy.

For quantities that are better not counted or seem too large to be counted, use **-e Unmenge von/unzählig viele/zahllose** 'innumerable':

> **Sie hat wieder einmal *eine Unmenge Geld* ausgegeben.**
> She has spent an awful lot of money again.

> **In dem Teich waren *unzählig viele Fische* und Kaulquappen.**
> There were innumerable fish and tadpoles in the pond.

(b) Unlike in English, there is no 'of' between units of packaging and the description of contents, e.g. **-e Flasche/-e Tasse/-r Kasten** 'bottle/cup/(large) box':

> **ein Becher Milch/eine Schachtel Pralinen/eine Portion Pommes frites**
> a carton of milk/a box of chocolates/a portion of chips

(c) Consumption

> **Eine starke Glühbirne *verbraucht* 100 Watt (Energie) in der Stunde.**
> A bright light-bulb uses 100 Watts in an hour.

Fuel consumption is calculated in litres of petrol (needed) per 100 km:

> **Mein alter Audi *verbraucht* 10 Liter *auf* 100 km.**
> My old Audi uses 10 litres per 100 km.

75.6 **Fractions**

All fractions other than **-e Hälfte** 'half' are neuter (the suffix **-tel** is short for **-s Teil** 'part'):

> **Möchtest du *die Hälfte* von meiner Pizza?**
> Would you like half of my pizza?

(See **23.2f**A for the use of the article here)

> *Ein Sechstel* des Waldes soll gefällt werden.
> A sixth of the wood is to be felled.

> In der Schweiz lebt *ein Viertel* der Gesamtbevölkerung vom Tourismus.
> In Switzerland a quarter of the population lives from tourism.

75.7 Patterns

A pattern (**-s Muster/-r Schnitt/-s Schnittmuster**) can be either **regelmäßig** 'regular' or **unregelmäßig** 'irregular'.

This is a short list of common patterns:

> **(quer-/längs-)gestreift** '(horizontally/vertically) striped'
> **gepunktet/geblümt** 'dotted/flowered'
> **(rot/blau) karriert/schraffiert** '(red/blue) chequed/hatched'

> Der *quergestreifte* Schlips mit dem geblümten Hemd sieht unmöglich aus.
> The horizontally striped tie looks impossible with the flowered shirt.

> Auf diesem Ausdruck läßt sich der *schraffierte* Hintergrund gut erkennen.
> On this print-out the hatched background is clearly visible.

75.8 Referring to quality

(a) High quality (**-e Qualität**) can be indicated by the following adjectives:

> **perfekt** 'perfect'
> **best-** 'best' (+ another adjective)
> **höchst-** 'highest' (+ another adjective)
> **empfohlen** 'recommended'

> Unter diesen Umständen ist das die *bestmögliche* Lösung.
> Under the circumstances this is the best possible solution.

> Welches Pferd ist denn das *höchstdotierte*?
> Which horse has won the most prize money?

Other expressions of high quality are:

> **1A** 'first class/A1'
> **von erster Klasse sein/erstklassig sein** 'to be of top quality'
> **Qualität haben** 'to be of high quality'
> **von erster Güte sein** 'to be of top quality'
> **von einer guten/besonderen Qualität sein** 'to be of good/special quality'

Dieser Wein *hat* wirklich *Qualität.*
This wine is of really high quality.

Der reinrassige Hund *ist von erster Güte.*
The pedigree dog is top quality.

Dieser Stoff *ist von einer besonders guten*/von einer besonderen *Qualität.*
This material is of particularly high quality.

(b) High quality is also implied by **Marken-** 'brand', where products are labelled with **-s Markenzeichen** 'mark of quality':

-s **Markenzeichen** 'mark of quality'
-e **Markenbutter** 'best butter'
-r **Markenname** 'brandname'
-r **Markenartikel** 'proprietary article'
-e **Hausmarke** 'own brand'
-e **Qualitätsmarke** 'mark of quality'

(c) Lists of contents and ingredients often feature **enthalten** or **beinhalten**:

enthalten/beinhalten 'to contain'
-r **Inhalt** 'contents'
-r **Bestandteil** 'constituent'
-e **Zutaten** (plural) 'ingredients'
aus etw. sein 'to be (made) of sth.'
aus etw. bestehen 'to consist of sth.'

Das Produkt *enthält* einen künstlichen Farbstoff.
The product contains artificial colouring.

Für den Kuchen brauchen Sie die *folgenden Zutaten.*
For the cake you will need the following ingredients.

In order to explain what things are made of, **aus** is used:

Der Fallschirm ist *aus* Seide.
The parachute is made from silk.

Dieses Produkt ist *aus* Rohstoffen/wiederverwertetem Glas.
This product is made from raw materials/recycled glass.

Wasser *besteht aus* Wasserstoff und Sauerstoff.
Water consists of hydrogen and oxygen.

(d) In order to describe what something tastes/smells of or looks like, **nach** is used.

Die Suppe riecht/schmeckt *nach* **Spülwasser.**
The soup smells of/tastes of dishwater.

Es sieht *nach* **Regen aus.**
It looks like rain.

(e) Price/cost are described as:

> **preiswert** 'inexpensive' (lit. 'worthy of its price')
> **billig** 'cheap'
> **teuer** 'expensive'
> **das macht** 'that makes/adds up to' (refering to total cost)
> **zusammen** 'together/total'
> **Bedienung/Mehrwertsteuer inbegriffen** 'service/VAT included'

Nein, diese Reise ist mir *viel zu teuer*/**ist viel zu teuer für mich.**
No, this journey is much too expensive for me.

Mit Mehrwertsteuer *macht das* **14,95.**
That is 14.95, including VAT.

(f) Standards and levels

> **-r Standard** 'standard'
> **-s Niveau** 'level'
> **-s Bildungsniveau** 'standard/level of education'
> **ein Niveau erreichen** 'to reach a level'
> **-r Wasserspiegel/Wasserpegel** 'water table'

Meeting requirements or being up to standard is rendered by **Ansprüchen**
(= dat) **genügen/gerecht werden/entsprechen**:

Der Service *entspricht* **nicht** *den Ansprüchen* **unserer Kunden.**
The service does not come up to the standard demanded by our
customers.

(See **112**B for satisfaction)

Being almost up to standard is rendered by **so gut wie/fast/beinahe (fertig)** 'as good
as/almost/nearly (ready)'.

76 *Describing actions and processes*

76.1

Basic words for actions and processes

(a) Doing things

> **tun/machen** 'to do'

There are two essential verbs to convey 'doing': **tun** and **machen**.

As translations for 'to do' they are interchangeable as long as they are not used with a direct object.

tun, however, may be slightly more elevated style:

> **Was soll ich *tun/machen*, damit das Kind schläft?**
> What can I do to make the child sleep?

machen with a direct object is often translated idiomatically:

> **Jetzt *mache* ich erst mal *Pause*.**
> First of all I'll take a break.

> **Könntest du heute *das Essen machen*? Ich habe keine Zeit.**
> Could you prepare the meal today? I haven't got time.

> **Wenn du deine *Hausaufgaben gemacht hast*, kannst du Fußball spielen.**
> When you've done your homework you can play football.

tun with a direct object has similarly idiomatic meanings:

> **Sie wollte ihm *etwas Gutes tun*.**
> She wanted to do something nice/good for him.

> **Er hatte doch *nichts Böses getan*.**
> He had not done anything bad/evil.

(b) For processes occurring naturally or of their own accord, use the verb **gehen** and its derivatives:

> **gehen** 'to go (on)'
> **-r Vorgang (ë)** 'process'
> **-r Rückgang** 'decline/fall'

For ongoing processes:

> **Was *geht* hier *vor*?**
> What's going on here?

Die Produktion von Chlorophyll ist ein *natürlicher Vorgang* **unter Einfluß von Sonnenlicht.**
The production of chlorophyll is a natural process under the influence of sunlight.

Ein *Rückgang* **der Bevölkerungszahl ist zu befürchten.**
A fall in the population is feared.

(c) Saying that things, usually machines and mechanisms, are running/working

gehen 'to go/work'
laufen 'to run'
funktionieren 'to function'

Es *geht.*
It works./It's OK.

Die Uhr *geht.*
The clock/watch is working.

Testen Sie, ob die elektronische Waage *geht.*
Check if the electronic scales are working.

Es *geht* **nicht ohne elektrischen Strom.**
It doesn't work without current.

Der VW Käfer *läuft und läuft und läuft.*
The VW beetle just keeps on running and running (and running).

Können Sie mir sagen, wie dieser Drucker *funktioniert?*
Could you tell me how this printer works?

(d) Production processes

-s Verfahren 'process/method/technique'
-e Verarbeitung 'processing'
-e Textverarbeitung 'word processing'
-e Datenverarbeitung 'data processing'

Die Medikamente werden nach dem neuesten *Verfahren* **hergestellt.**
The medication is produced using the latest techniques.

(e) Referring to courses of events

> **laufen** 'to run'
> **-r Ablauf (ë)** 'course'
> **-r Ablauf der Ereignisse** 'the course of events'
> **-r Handlungsablauf** 'action/development of the plot'
> **im Verlauf der Zeit/des Tages** 'in the course of time/the day'
> **im Verlauf der Verhandlungen/der Krankheit** 'in the course of the negotiations/the illness'

Ablauf as opposed to **Verlauf** is possibly more predictable in running its course:

> **Der *Versuchsablauf* war genau festgeschrieben und konnte nicht geändert werden.**
> The way the experiment was to be conducted was laid down precisely and could not be altered.
> **Beschreiben Sie den *Tagesablauf* eines Bäckers.**
> Describe a typical day in the life of a baker.

(f) Expressing procedures

> **-s Verfahren** 'process/procedure/proceedings'
> **-s Vorgehen** 'action'
> **-r Durchgang** 'round' (also in a competition)
> **-r Wahlgang** 'round' (in an election)
> **-s Bewerbungsverfahren** 'application procedure'
> **-s Gerichtsverfahren** 'legal proceedings'

> **Im zweiten Durchgang war er Sieger.**
> He won in the second round/phase/stage.

> **Der Bundespräsident wurde im dritten Wahlgang gewählt.**
> The (German) President was elected in the third round/phase/ballot.

(See **40**A for the use of the passive)

(g) To refer to unplanned events that merely 'happen', use **geschehen** or **passieren**. The two verbs are interchangeable in meaning. **passieren**, however, sometimes has a negative connotation:

> **Was ist denn *geschehen/passiert*?**
> What has happened?

> **Ein Wunder ist *geschehen*./Es ist ein Wunder *geschehen*.**
> A miracle has occurred.

> **Ein Unfall ist *passiert*./Es ist ein Unfall *passiert*.**
> An accident has happened.

The structure starting with the impersonal **es** is more idiomatic.

(See **42.3g**A for the dummy subject **es**)

76.2 Describing the process of something

(a) Ongoing processes can be described by using nouns formed from infinitives.

(See **54.4a**A for word formation and **25**A and **28.6**A on noun genders)

> **-s Begreifen** 'understanding'
> **-s Schneiden** 'cutting'
> **-s Kaufen** 'purchasing'

(b) For the finished process, nouns formed from other parts of the verb, particularly past participles (see **54.4c–d**A) are sometimes used:

> **-r Begriff** 'concept'
> **-r Schnitt** 'cut'
> **-r Kauf** 'purchase'

76.3 Starting a process

(a) General expressions for starting a process

> **an*fangen** 'to begin'
> **mit etw. an*fangen** 'to begin with sth.'
> **-r Anfang** 'the beginning'
> **los*gehen** 'to start/get under way'
> **aus*gehen von** 'to start from/take as a point of departure'
> **-r Ausgangspunkt** 'point of departure'

> *Am Anfang* war das Wort.
> In the beginning was the Word.

> **Wir *fangen mit* den Vorbereitungen *an*.**
> We are starting with the preparations.

(See **36.1**A for separable verbs)

> **Vielleicht solltest du in deiner Beziehung einen neuen *Anfang machen*.**
> Maybe you should make a fresh start in your relationship.

> **Jetzt *geht* das Gewitter richtig *los*.**
> Now the thunderstorm is really getting under way.

For starting a race:

> **Achtung, fertig, *los*!**
> On your marks, get set, go!

For starting from a false assumption:

> **Sie *gehen von* den falschen Vorraussetzungen *aus*.**
> You are starting from the wrong assumptions.

(b) For starting an engine or machine

| **an*machen/an*stellen** 'to turn/switch on' |

> **Kannst du mir sagen, wie man den Staubsauger *anmacht*?**
> Can you tell me how to turn on the vacuum-cleaner?

> **Ich *habe* die Spülmaschine schon *angestellt*.**
> I have already turned the dishwasher on.

76.4 — ## Continuation of a process

(a) The continuation of a process is often indicated by the separable prefixes **weiter-** or **fort-**. These can also be used as adverbs.

Encouraging or ordering someone to carry on doing something:

> **(Machen Sie) Weiter!/Weiter so!**
> Carry on!/go on!

Asking someone (politely) to carry on:

> **Bitte *lesen* Sie *weiter*!**
> Please carry on reading!

Asking someone formally:

> **Bitte *fahren* Sie in Ihrem Vortrag *fort*.**
> Please continue with your lecture.

Continuing one's education:

> **Man sollte sich ständig *weiterbilden/fortbilden*.**
> One should never stop furthering one's education.

(b) Carrying on an activity can be further emphasized by inserting **immer**:

> **Er spielte *immer weiter.***
> He played on and on.

> **Gehen Sie *immer geradeaus.***
> Carry on straight ahead.

(See **48**A for comparison of adjectives. See also **76.10aB** on 'Repeating actions and processes' for further uses of **immer** and **wieder**)

(c) To indicate that someone is in the process of doing something, use **gerade** 'just' or **gerade dabei sein, etw. zu tun** 'being in the process of doing something':

> **Die Aufnahmen *laufen gerade.***
> The recording is in progress.

> **Er ist *gerade dabei,* den Vertrag zu unterzeichnen.**
> He is just signing the contract now.

(See **87**A for infinitive clauses and **36.2**A for inseparable verbs)

(d) To refer to something done on a regular basis in order to continue a project, use the adverb **stetig** 'continuously':

> **Die Wissenschaftlerin sammelte ihre Daten stetig.**
> The scientist collected her data continuously.

— **76.5** —   **Next step in a process**

(a) The next step in a process is introduced by the adverbs **anschließend**, **dann** or the verb **folgen**.

---

erst 'first'
anschließend 'afterwards/following'
dann 'then/after that'
jmdm./etw. (= dat) **folgen** 'to follow sb./sth.'
auf etw. (= acc) **folgen** 'to follow sth.'

> ***Anschließend* an den Vortrag möchten wir Sie um Diskussionsbeiträge bitten.**
> Following the lecture we would like to ask you for your contributions to the discussion.

dann counts as the first idea and is followed by a verb. However, to ensure good style it should be used as infrequently as possible. It simply links a list of actions:

> ***Erst* frühstücke ich, *dann* putze ich meine Zähne, *dann*...**
> First I have breakfast, then I clean my teeth, then...

> *Auf* sieben magere Jahre *folgen* sieben fette.
> Seven lean years are followed by seven plentiful years.

(b) Taking turns is expressed by **an der Reihe sein/an die Reihe kommen** and **sich** (= acc) **ab*wechseln**

> **Du** *bist* noch nicht *an der Reihe.*
> It's not your turn yet.

(See **38.1**A for prepositional verbs with the dative)

> **Jetzt** *bin* ich aber *dran*!
> Now it's my turn!

> **Der nächste Spieler** *kommt an die Reihe.*
> The next player has his/her turn.

> **Wir** *wechseln uns beim* Fahren *ab*: du fährst bis Hamburg, dann fahre ich.
> We'll take turns with the driving: you drive to Hamburg and then I'll drive.

(c) Giving turns is expressed by **an die Reihe/dran*nehmen** or by **auf*rufen**:

> **Schwester, Sie können jetzt den nächsten Patienten** *drannehmen/aufrufen.*
> Nurse, you can now take/call up the next patient.

(See **38.1**A for prepositional verbs with the accusative)

76.6 **Simultaneity**

If several processes occur concurrently, the following expressions can be used:

(a) In doing something, something else happens:

bei/dabei 'in doing so'

> *Beim* Messen/*Dabei* muß man darauf achten, daß das Gerät nicht beschädigt wird.
> When taking measurements/In doing so one has to be careful not to damage the instrument.

> **Versuchen Sie, die Flüssigkeit in die Flasche zu füllen,** *ohne dabei* etwas zu verschütten.
> Try to put the liquid into the bottle without spilling any.

(b) Achieving something by doing something else:

indem 'while/by doing so'

(See **8.3**A for subordinating conjunctions)

Butter wird gemacht, *indem* **man die Sahne so lange schlägt, bis sie dick ist.**
Butter is made by beating the cream until it is thick.

Du kannst ihm eine Freude bereiten, *indem* **du ihn mal im Altersheim besuchst.**
You can cheer him up by visiting him in the old people's home.

(c) Under certain (weather/mood, etc.) conditions:

bei (+ dat) 'with/in/during'

Bei gutem Wetter **können wir an dem Zaun weiterarbeiten.**
Weather permitting, we can continue working on the fence.

Das kann ich *beim besten Willen* **nicht verantworten.**
With the best will in the world I cannot accept the responsibility for this.

Er ist *bei Nacht und Nebel* **gegen einen Baum gefahren.**
He crashed into a tree at night and in fog/in the dead of night.

(See also **69.2d**B for given conditions)

76.7 Expressing speed

(a) Speed in general is **-e Geschwindigkeit**:

Geschwindigkeit **ist die zurückgelegte Strecke pro Zeit.**
Speed is the distance covered in a certain time.

Eine *Geschwindigkeitsbegrenzung* **von 130km/h sollte eingeführt werden.**
A speed limit of 130km/h should be introduced.

(b) Doing something as quickly as possible

Verarbeiten Sie das Fleisch, *so schnell es geht.*
Process the meat as quickly as possible.

Das Gebäude muß *so schnell wie möglich* **gedeckt werden.**
The building must be roofed as quickly as possible.

(c) Immediacy

sofort 'straight away'

Bitte fahren Sie *sofort* **in die Ulmenstraße. Da ist ein Unfall.**
Please drive to Elm Street straight away. There's been an accident there.

so bald wie möglich 'as soon as possible'

> **Bitte antworten Sie** *so bald wie möglich.*
> Please answer as soon as possible.

(d) Slowness

---

langsam 'slow'
mit Verzögerung 'with delay/time-lag'
zögernd/zögerlich 'hesitant/hesitating'

> **Seine Genesung von der Grippe macht nur** *langsam(e)* **Fortschritte.**
> His recovery from the flu is only very slow (lit. is only making slow progress).

> **Er antwortete nur** *zögernd/zögerlich.*
> He answered only hesitantly.

76.8 Denoting alterations and radical change

(a) Alterations can be described by using the prefix **ver-** in combination with a comparative adjective, e.g. **besser, schöner.**

(See **36.2**A and **57.2**A for word formation and **75.3e** B for alterations)

---

verbessern 'to improve'
-e Verbesserung 'improvement'
verschönern 'to beautify'
-e Verschönerung 'improvement/beautification'
vergrößern 'to enlarge'
-e Vergrößerung 'enlargement'
verkleinern 'to reduce' (in size)
-e Verkleinerung 'diminution/reduction'
verlängern 'to extend/to lengthen'
-e Verlängerung 'extension' (in time, etc.)
ändern 'to alter'
-e Änderung 'alteration'

These verbs of alteration can either be used reflexively or else they can take an object.

(See **37**A for reflexive verbs)

> **Ihre Deutschkenntnisse** *haben sich/*Das Wetter *hat sich verschlechtert.*
> Her German/The weather has deteriorated.

> **Ich** *habe mich* **in Mathematik** *verbessert.*
> I have improved in maths.

In manchen Autobetrieben hat man die Betriebschaft *vergrößert*.
The workforce has been increased in some car factories.

Die Schneiderin muß meinen Rock *ändern*. Er soll *verlängert werden*.
The dressmaker must alter my skirt. It is to be lengthened.

(b) (Radical) change

> **-e Veränderung** 'change/alteration'
> **-r (Um)sturz** 'radical/sudden change'
> **um*schlagen** 'to change'

Die Revolution hatte eine totale *Veränderung* der Gesellschaftsstruktur zur Folge.
The revolution resulted in a total change in the social structure.

Vom Wetter*sturz* bekommen viele Leute Kopfschmerzen.
Many people get a headache from a sudden change in the weather.

Als die Polizei dazukam, *schlug* die Stimmung plötzlich *um*.
When the police arrived the mood suddenly changed.

(c) Turning into something else (gradual or sudden change so that a transformation results), is rendered by **zu etw. werden**:

Der Rhein *wurde* um ca. 250 n. Chr. *zur* Grenze des Römischen Reiches.
In about 250 AD the Rhine became the boundary of the Roman empire.

Das Wasser *wurde zu* Wein.
Water turned to wine.

Selbst kleine Kinder können *zu* kleinen Teufeln *werden*.
Even small children can turn into little devils.

76.9 Denoting the end of a process

> **-s Ende** 'end'
> **enden** 'to end' (intransitive)
> **beenden** 'to end' (transitive)
> **aus*gehen** 'to end/come out'
> **-r Ausgang** 'outcome'

Das Ende des Kriegs ist noch nicht abzusehen.
There is no end to the war in sight.

Der Ausgang des Versuches war anders als erwartet.
The outcome of the experiment was different from what had been expected.

Das *wird* **böse** *ausgehen.*
That will end badly.

Wie *ist* **die Wahl** *ausgegangen?*
What was the result of the election?

(a) Breaking off/interrupting processes or relations

ab*brechen 'to break off'
unterbrechen 'to interrupt'
stören 'to disturb'

Die diplomatischen Beziehungen *wurden abgebrochen.*
Diplomatic relations were broken off.

Wir *unterbrechen* **die Sendung mit einer Sondermeldung.**
We interrupt this programme with a news flash.

(b) Turning off machines, etc.

ab*stellen/aus*machen 'to turn off'

Bitte bei Brandgefahr den Motor *abstellen.*
Please switch off the engine when there is a danger of fire.

Hast **du das Radio/das Bügeleisen** *ausgemacht?*
Have you turned off the radio/the iron?

(c) Bringing a process to an end

ab*schließen 'to bring to an end/finish'
etw. beenden 'to end sth.'
-r Abschluß 'end/finish'

Die Bergungsarbeiten *sind* **vorläufig** *abgeschlossen.*
The rescue operations have been brought to an end for the time being.

Der Bewerber hat ein *abgeschlossenes* **Hochschulstudium.**
The applicant has a degree (lit. finished university studies).

Er *mußte* **seine Beamtenlaufbahn vorzeitig** *beenden.*
He had to end his career as a civil servant prematurely.

Refer to a dictionary for compounds with **Abschluß-**.

(d) Stopping a process by intervention

an*halten 'to stop'

> **Der Polizist *hält* den Verkehr *an*, indem er den rechten Arm hebt.**
> The policeman stops the traffic by lifting his right arm.

(e) Hindering a process

> **behindern** 'to hinder/impede'
> **jmdn (bei etw.) auf*halten** 'to hold up sb. (doing sth.)'
> **jmdn./etw. von etw. ab*halten** 'to keep sb./sth. from doing sth.'

> **Das rücksichtslos geparkte Wohnmobil *behindert* den Verkehr.**
> The inconsiderately parked caravan is impeding/interfering with the traffic.

(See **49**A on extended adjectival phrases)

> **Dieses ständige Fragen *hält* mich beim Arbeiten *auf*.**
> This constant questioning prevents me getting on with my work.

> **Wir konnten ihn nur mit Mühe *vom* Springen *abhalten*.**
> We could only just (lit. with difficulty) prevent him from jumping.

(f) Stopping of its own accord is conveyed by **stehen*bleiben** or **auf*hören**. Note that both are intransitive and that **stehen*bleiben** takes **sein** as its auxiliary:

> **Das Rad *ist stehengeblieben*.**
> The wheel has stopped (turning).

> **Der Regen *hörte* gegen 14.30 *auf*.**
> The rain stopped at about 2.30 pm.

(g) Stopping work for good: retirement

> **-r Ruhestand** 'retirement'
> **in den (Vor-)ruhestand versetzt werden** 'to be given (early) retirement'
> **in den (Vor-)ruhestand treten** 'to retire (early)'
> **pensioniert werden** 'to retire (on a pension)'
> **Rentner/-in werden** 'to become a pensioner'

> **Er *geht in den Ruhestand*.**
> He is retiring.

Sie wurde *in den Vorruhestand versetzt.*
She was given early retirement.

Viele Lehrer möchten vorzeitig *in den Ruhestand treten.*
Many teachers would like early retirement.

Sein Großvater *wurde* **mit 65** *pensioniert.*
His grandfather retired at 65.

Ab Januar *wird* **Frau Debus** *Rentnerin.*
From January Mrs Debus will be an old age pensioner.

(See **23.1b**A for omission of the article)

76.10 **Repeating actions and processes**

> **wiederholen** 'to repeat'
> **immer wieder** 'again and again'
> **noch einmal** 'once again'
> **-e Zugabe** 'encore'
> **-r Refrain** 'chorus'

(a) Doing things again

Bitte *wiederholen* **Sie das Ganze langsam und deutlich.**
Please repeat the whole thing slowly and clearly.

Der Kleine wollte *immer wieder* **Karussell fahren.**
The little boy wanted to go on the roundabout/merry-go-round again and again.

Spielen Sie den dritten Satz *noch einmal* **bitte.**
Please play the third movement (once) again.

(b) Asking for an encore (e.g. at a concert)

Zugabe, **Zugabe!**
Encore!

(c) Repeating verses, e.g. of songs

-r Refrain 'chorus' (of a song, etc.)

Der Refrain **des Kirchenliedes ist ein fröhliches Halleluja.**
The chorus of the hymn is a cheerful Hallelujah.

(See **82**B for cause and effect of actions and processes)

77 *Avoiding describing the agent of processes and actions*

(See **76**B for actions and processes)

77.1 In descriptions of processes the agent of the action need not necessarily be mentioned.

For this, the passive is usually used.

(See **40.2b**A for the distinction between the process of an action and the resulting state)

For the use of **von** and **durch** to express agents of an action, see **40.3**A.

In addition to the passive there are several other ways of not mentioning the agent:

77.2 The agent of the action can be replaced by **man**.

(See also **31.4**A on personal pronouns)

English uses the passive or 'can be':

> **Man hat mir den Mantel *verspritzt*.**
> My coat *has been splashed*.

> **Man *erkennt* die richtige Anwendung am Erfolg der Behandlung.**
> The correct application *can be seen* by the success of the treatment.

Feminists insist on replacing **man** with **frau**, or at least writing **man/frau**.

> **Jetzt kann *man/frau* wieder an dieser Küste baden.**
> Bathing is now possible again at this beach.

77.3 For the workings of nature and sensory perceptions constructions with **es** can be used.

(See **42.3g**A for the dummy subject **es**)

> **Es regnet.**
> It is raining.

> **An der Bergstraße *blüht es* ganz herrlich.**
> On the Bergstraße the blossom is quite beautiful.

> **Hier *riecht es* so gut nach Kölnisch Wasser.**
> There is such a lovely scent of Eau de Cologne here.

77.4 — Indicating that something can be done, is expressed by:

(a) **läßt sich** (plus infinitive).

> **Ein deutlicher Unterschied *ließ sich feststellen*.**
> A distinct difference could be noticed/was noticeable.

> **Das *läßt sich* am besten damit *erklären*, daß das Wasser vorne eingedrungen war.**
> That can best be explained by the fact that the water had entered from the front.

> **Mit dem Betrieb von Windkraft *läßt sich* viel Geld *verdienen*.**
> A lot of money can be made from the operation of wind energy.

(b) the suffix **-bar** of the adjective (see **55.1a**A for word formation with -**bar**):

> **Das Verlängerungsteil ist *abnehmbar*.**
> The extension can be taken off/is removable/detachable.

77.5 — If it is either possible or necessary for something to be done, **ist zu** (+ infinitive) 'can be/must be' (+ past participle) is used:

> **Die Mauer *war* vom Innern des Forums aus *zu sehen*.**
> The wall could be seen/was visible from the inside of the forum.

> **Die Korrespondenzen *sind* bis spätestens Freitag *zu erledigen*.**
> The post/letters have to be dealt with by Friday at the latest.

The exact English translation has to be inferred from the context and the use of adverbs or modal particles (see **117.1c**B for modal particles):

> **Die Handlung ist *wohl* zu rechtfertigen.**
> The action is *probably* to be justified./The action probably can be justified.

> **Ihre Entscheidung ist *unbedingt* zu rechtfertigen.**
> Her decision is *definitely* justified.

77.6 — If neither the agent nor the object of the action is to be named, **es wird** (singular) together with the past participle is used. Here the focus is entirely on the action or process itself. Compare the impersonal use of the passive (see **40.2c**A).

> **Gegenüber dem Bahnhof *wird* jetzt *gebaut*.**
> There is building going on across from the station.

> **In der Kneipe an der Ecke *wird* jeden Freitag *getanzt*.**
> There is dancing every Friday at the pub on the corner.

Vor dem Fest *mußte gekocht* **und** *gebacken werden.*
Before the festival we had to cook and bake.

78 *Describing origins and provenance*

(See **75.8c**B for describing what things are made of and **82.2**B on 'Cause' for further vocabulary relating to origins)

78.1
Geographical origin

Geographical origin can be rendered by **kommen aus, her*kommen aus/von** or its related noun **-e Herkunft**.

(a) Asking where something is from

> **Die** *Herkunft* **dieser Antiquität läßt sich nicht mehr feststellen.**
> The place of origin/provenance of this antique can no longer be ascertained.

> **Man kann nicht mehr feststellen,** *woher* **diese Vasen** *kommen.*
> We can no longer be sure where the vases came from.

> **Die Äpfel** *kommen aus* **Südafrika.**
> The apples come from South Africa.

(b) Asking about someone's place of origin

> *Woher kommen* **Sie?**
> Where do you come from?

(The question usually implies: 'What is your country/town, etc. of origin?', unless there is reference to a specific place or time.)

> **Woher kommen Sie** *gerade*?
> Where have you (just) come from?

(c) Places where something started

-r Ausgangspunkt (e) 'starting point'

> **Marseille war** *Ausgangspunkt* **einer berühmten Entdeckungsreise.**
> Marseille was the starting point of a famous voyage of discovery.

(d) Direction something/someone is coming from

aus Richtung 'from the direction of'

> **Der Zug *aus Richtung* Darmstadt hat heute zehn Minuten Verspätung.**
> The train from Darmstadt is ten minutes late today.

(e) Things that originally came from or were situated elsewhere

ursprünglich 'originally'

> **Das Sprachinstitut befand sich *ursprünglich* in einer alten Villa.**
> The language institute was originally housed in an old villa.

(f) Tracing the origin back to somewhere can be expressed by a number of verbs with the prefix **zurück-**

> **zurück*verfolgen** 'to trace back to'
> **zurück*gehen auf** 'to go/date back to'

> **Der Grundplan für diese Kapelle läßt sich bis ins achte Jahrhundert *zurückverfolgen*.**
> The basic plan for this chapel can be traced back to the eighth century.

> **Diese Tradition *geht auf* heidnische Bräuche *zurück*.**
> This tradition dates back to heathen customs.

78.2 Chronological origin
-e Entstehung/entstehen

It is difficult to find a single translation for this verb. Possible translations include 'arise/come about/originate/be created'. **die Entstehung der Erde** could therefore translate as: 'the origin/creation/of the earth/world'.

> **Der Keil *ist* in der Steinzeit *entstanden*.**
> The arrow-head originated in the Stone Age.

> **Die *Entstehung* der Arten ist nach wie vor nicht ganz geklärt.**
> The origin of the species has still not been completely clarified/explained.

78.3 Origin by profession, social status and family
Profession and social status are often described as **von Hause aus**. It often implies an enduring trait in someone's character:

> **Der Bundespräsident ist *von Hause aus* Jurist.**
> The (German) President is a lawyer (by profession).

> **Sie *stammt aus* einer Medizinerfamilie.**
> She is from a medical family.

78.4

Origin by birth and descent

(a) **Von Geburt, von Geburt her/aus** 'by birth'

> **Er ist *von Geburt (aus/her)* Schweizer./Er ist *gebürtiger* Schweizer.**
> He is Swiss by birth.

A more formal way of alluding to birth or origin is by **seiner** (etc.) **Herkunft nach**:

> **Sie ist *ihrer Herkunft nach* Weißrussin.**
> She is of Belorussian descent.

(See **23.1b**A for omission of the article)

(b) Genetic origin is referred to as

> **-r Ursprung/-e Abstammung** 'origin'
> **von etw.** (= dat) **ab*stammen** 'to be descended from'

> **Der Titel des Werkes heißt: 'Der Mensch von seinen *Ursprüngen* bis zur Gegenwart.'**
> The title of this work is: 'Man from his origins to the present day.'

> ***Stammt* der Mensch vom Affen *ab*?**
> Is man/Are human beings descended from the apes?

(See **28.2**A for the declension of **-r Affe**)

(c) Descent is recorded in the family tree (**-r Stammbaum**) or a book that contains all official registrations, e.g. birth, marriage, death certificates of a family (**-s Stammbuch der Familie**).

(d) Ancestry

Specific ancestors are referred to as follows:

> **-e Urgroßeltern** 'the great-grandparents'
> **-r Urahn (en)/-e Urahne (n)** 'ancestor'
> **-r Vorfahr (en)** '(non-specific) ancestor'

> **Die *Vorfahren* des Präsidenten kamen ursprünglich aus dem Süden.**
> The President's ancestors originally came from the South.

(See **28.2**A on weak noun declension for **-r Vorfahr** and **-r Präsident**)

78.5 **Foundation**

> **Die NATO *wurde* 1949 von zwölf Staaten *gegründet*.**
> NATO was founded in 1949 by twelve states.

> **Hamburg und Bremen *sind* durch Kaiser Karl den Großen**
> ***entstanden./gegründet worden.***
> Hamburg and Bremen were founded by Charlemagne.

78.6 **Origin of action**

Initiatives and actions starting in a certain place or with a certain person are rendered by **von. . . aus**.

von (somewhere) **aus**

> **Die Phönizier *gründeten vom* Libanon *aus* Kolonien im westlichen**
> **Mittelmeer.**
> Starting from the Lebanon the Phoenicians founded colonies in the western Mediterranean.

> ***Von* diesem Büro *aus leitet* er das ganze Unternehmen.**
> He manages the entire enterprise from this office.

aus*gehen von

> **Die Initiative *ging von* einem Angestellten *aus*.**
> The initiative came from an employee.

(See **28.5**A for adjectival nouns)

78.7 **Inheriting**

> **etw. von jmdm. erben** 'to inherit sth. from sb.'
> **-s Erbe/die Erbschaft** 'inheritance/heritage'
> **-r Erbe** 'heir'

> **Er hat den Sekretär von seinem Onkel *geerbt*.**
> He inherited the bureau from his uncle.

> **Er hatte das väterliche *Erbe angetreten*, mußte aber hohe**
> **Erbschaftssteuern zahlen.**
> He had come into his father's inheritance, but had to pay high inheritance tax/death duty.

> **Er war der rechtmäßige/mutmaßliche *Erbe* des Verstorbenen.**
> He was the rightful/presumptive heir of the deceased.

Passing things on

> **jmdm. etw. vermachen** 'to bequeath/to leave sth. to sb.'
> **-s Vermächtnis** 'legacy'
> **hinterlassen** 'to leave behind' (after death)
> **-s Geschenk (e)** 'present/gift'
> **überliefern** 'to pass on/down'

> **Das Schriftstück *war ihr vermacht worden.***
> The document had been bequeathed to her.

(See **40.2a**A for the passive)

> **Er *hinterließ* seinen Enkeln ein großes Vermächtnis.**
> He left a large legacy for his grandchildren.

(See **12.1**A for word order of noun objects)

> **Der Ring war ein *Geschenk* zum zehnten Hochzeitstag.**
> The ring was a gift for (her) tenth wedding anniversary.

> **Das Märchen *wurde* den Brüdern Grimm mündlich *überliefert.***
> The fairy-tale was passed (down) to the brothers Grimm orally.

Authorship

> **stammen von** 'to stem/come from'
> **jmdm. etw. zu*schreiben** 'to attribute sth. to sb.'
> **-r Urheber(-)** 'author/creator/originator'
> **-s Urheberrecht (e)/-s Copyright** 'copyright'

(a) Attributing something to an author

> **Dieser Aphorismus *stammt von* Lichtenberg.**
> This aphorism comes from (Georg Christoph) Lichtenberg.

> **Das Gedicht *wird* dem schottischen Dichter Burns *zugeschrieben.***
> The poem is attributed to the Scottish poet Burns.

(b) Referring to an author as the originator and owner of copyright

> **Der *Urheber* besitzt das *Copyright.***
> The author owns the copyright.

> **Das *Urheberrecht* liegt beim Verlag.**
> Copyright is with the publisher.

XII *Putting events into a wider context*

79 *Giving reasons and purpose*

79.1
Giving reasons and explaining why in general terms

(a) For giving reasons and explaining why, the conjunctions **denn**, **weil** and **da** are used. They are essentially interchangeable.

Note that **denn** is a co-ordinating conjunction (see **6.1**A), whereas **weil** and **da** are subordinating conjunctions (see **8.2–8.3**A).

> **denn** 'for/because/since'
> **weil** 'because'
> **da** 'since/because'

> **Ich habe es gemacht, *denn* es war notwendig.**
> I did it because it was necessary.

> **Ich habe es gemacht, *weil* er es wollte.**
> I did it because he wanted it.

> **Wir haben es geschrieben, *da* es geschrieben werden mußte.**
> We wrote it because it had to be written.

> ***Weil/Da* es gesagt werden muß, sage ich es.**
> Since it has to be said I'll say it.

(See **8**A for subordinate clauses)

(b) The prepositions **wegen** and **aufgrund** are used to apportion blame or responsibility. Both take the genitive:

> ***Wegen des* schlechten Wetters mußten die Ausgrabungsarbeiten unterbrochen werden.**
> The excavations had to be interrupted because of bad weather.

> **Aufgrund eines** Todesfalles in der Familie bleibt das Geschäft heute geschlossen.
>
> The shop remains closed today because of a death in the family.

79.2 ## Giving detailed reasons

(a) Explaining and emphasizing that there was a good reason

> **deshalb** 'for that reason/therefore/that's why'
> **daher/deswegen** 'therefore/that's why'
> **also** 'so/therefore'
> **nämlich** 'namely/you see'
> **infolgedessen** 'consequently'
> **demzufolge** 'accordingly'

> **Ich habe es nur *deshalb* gemacht, weil es notwendig war.**
> The only reason I did it was because it was necessary.

> **Es ist *deshalb* mißlungen, weil wir nicht das richtige Werkzeug hatten.**
> It went wrong because we didn't have the right tool.

> **Gestern kam ich nicht zum Ausdrucken, *deshalb* muß ich es heute machen.**
> Yesterday I didn't get round to printing, therefore I must do it today.

> **Er mußte dringend weg. *Deshalb/Also* müßt ihr auf seine Kinder aufpassen.**
> He had to go away urgently. That's why you have to look after his children.

> **Es war notwendig, *daher/deswegen* habe ich das Antibiotikum genommen.**
> It was necessary, that's why I took the antibiotic.

nämlich also expresses reason, but it is not usually translated. It adds the flavour of 'you see':

> **Du solltest ihm bei der Auswahl der Vorhangstoffe helfen. Er ist *nämlich* farbenblind.**
> You should help him with the selection of curtain materials. He is colour-blind, you see.

(See **117.1cB** for the modal particle **nämlich**)

(b) Something was done in order to make something else possible

> **damit** 'so that'
> **um... zu** 'in order to'

damit is often used with **können**:

> **Er empfiehlt ihr, ein neues Computerprogramm zu kaufen,** *damit* **sie ihre Abrechnung schneller machen** *kann.*
> He advises her to buy a new computer program so that she can do her accounts more quickly.

(See **8.2**A for word order in subordinate clauses)

If the subject of both main and dependent clause is identical, **um zu** is preferred to **damit**. Unlike in English, the **um** cannot be omitted. **um zu** is followed by an infinitive at the end of the clause.

(See **8.7**A for infinitive clauses)

> **Arbeitet man,** *um zu* **leben, oder lebt man,** *um zu* **arbeiten?**
> Does one work in order to live, or (does one) live in order to work?

> **Was soll man bei einer Bruchlandung tun,** *um* **einen möglichen Brand** *zu* **überleben?**
> What should one do during a crash landing (in order) to survive a (possible) fire?

Note:

> **Es ist** *zu* **schön, um wahr zu sein.**
> It is too good to be true.

If there is another **zu** in the previous clause, **um zu** usually means 'too... to be...'

(See also **82.1c**B for this use of **zu**)

79.3

To ask about reasons

> **warum?** 'why?'
> **wieso?** 'why?/how come?'
> **weshalb?** 'why?'
> **wozu?** 'to what purpose?/what... for?/why?'

> *Warum* **hast du so einen großen Mund?**
> Why do you have such a large mouth?

> **Damit ich dich besser fressen kann.**
> The better to eat you with.

> *Wieso* **willst du nicht mitspielen?**
> How come you don't want to play with us?

(**wieso**, particularly the short question **Wieso nicht** 'why not' sometimes sounds impatient and challenging.)

> *Weshalb* **fahren Sie denn immer an den gleichen Ferienort?**
> Why do you always go to the same holiday resort?

weshalb is less commonly used.

> *Wozu* **bist du denn in die Stadt gefahren?**
> Why (lit. To what purpose) did you go into town then?

> *Wozu* **soll das gut sein?**
> What is the point of it?/What is it in aid of?

79.4

Naming the reason

> **-r Grund (ë)** 'reason'
> **etw. mit etw. begründen** 'to justify/give reason'
> **-e Begründung** 'reason/justification'
> **-r Grund** and derivatives are used to give a straightforward reason for doing
> something

> **Er hatte sie geheiratet** *aus dem einfachen Grunde,* **daß sie gute**
> **Beziehungen in der Wirtschaft hatte.**
> He had married her for the simple reason that she had good
> contacts/was well connected in the business world.

(See **58.4**A for the position of the past participle **geheiratet** here)

> **Er wollte sein Vorgehen da***mit begründen,* **daß er seinen Konkurrenten**
> **beseitigen mußte.**
> He tried/wanted to justify his action by claiming he had to get rid of his
> competitor.

> *Mit welcher Begründung* **wollen Sie eigentlich diese Straße absperren?**
> What is your justification in wanting/On what grounds do you want to
> block off this road?

Explaining an action

> -e Erklärung 'explanation'
> erklären 'to explain' (giving reasons)
> unerklärlich 'inexplicable'
> sagen 'to say'
> erläutern 'to explain' (how)

> Ich *bin* ihm eine *Erklärung schuldig.*
> I owe him an explanation.

(See **12.3**A for the order of noun and pronoun)

> **Das Presseamt möchte eine *Erklärung abgeben.***
> The press office would like to make/release a statement.

> **Das Loch in der Wasserleitung *erklärt*, warum wir schon so lange diese Geräusche gehört haben.**
> The hole in the water pipe explains why we have been hearing these noises for such a long time.

(See **9**A for word order in indirect questions)

> **Es ist mir völlig *unerklärlich*, wieso es hier keine Steckdosen gibt.**
> I really can't see/It's a mystery to me why there are no (wall) sockets here.

> **Er hat mir genau *erläutert*, wie man Genmanipulationen an Tomaten durchführt.**
> He explained (to me) exactly how gene manipulations on tomatoes are carried out.

sagen can cover the meaning of both **erklären** and **erläutern** in everyday conversation.

> **Sag mir doch, warum du schon wieder zu spät kommst.**
> Tell me why you are late again.

Justifying an action

> rechtfertigen 'to justify'
> es ist (völlig) gerechtfertigt 'it is (quite) justifiable'
> es ist vertretbar 'it is tenable/defensible/justifiable'
> es ist zu verantworten 'it can be justified'
> etw. vor jmdm. verantworten 'to answer to sb. for sth.'

> Sie *brauchen* diese Handlung *nur* vor Gott und Ihrem Gewissen *zu rechtfertigen.*
>
> You need to justify this action only before God and your conscience.

> Es ist nicht *zu verantworten,* daß wir einen großen Teil des Etats für die Wartung der alten Geräte ausgeben.
>
> We cannot justify spending a large part of.the budget on the maintenance of the old equipment.

(See also **79.4**B on **begründen mit**)

> Wenn den Kindern etwas passiert, müssen *wir* das *vor ihren Eltern verantworten.*
>
> If something happens to the children we will have to answer to their parents (for it).

79.7 | Taking on responsibility

> **etw. verantworten** 'to answer for sth.'
> **sich** (= acc) **verantworten** 'to defend oneself/defend a course of action'
> **verantwortlich sein** 'to be responsible'
> **-e Verantwortung übernehmen** 'to take over/on responsibility'
> **-e Führung/-s Amt übernehmen** 'to take on the leadership/office'

> Der Projektleiter *ist* für die Durchführung des gesamten Projekts allein *verantwortlich.*
>
> The project leader is in sole charge of the entire project.

> Dafür *mußt* du *dich* vor der Standesorganisation *verantworten.*
>
> You must defend/justify yourself (for this) before the professional association.

79.8 | Explaining the purpose (what for)

> **-r Zweck/-r Sinn** 'purpose'
> **-s Mittel zum Zweck** 'means to an end'
> **mit dem Zweck** 'with the purpose'

> Der *Zweck* heiligt die Mittel.
>
> The end justifies the means.

> Das *ist nicht der Zweck* der Übung.
>
> This is not the point of the exercise.

> **Dieser Koffer *erfüllt* seinen *Zweck.***
> This (suit)case serves its purpose.

Refer to a dictionary for further expressions with **zweck-**, e.g. **zweckmäßig** or **zweckgebunden** (**zweckgebundene Gelder** 'ear-marked money'), etc.

> **Der *Sinn* dieser Übung *ist, daß* Sie den Zusammenhang zwischen den Wörtern verstehen.**
> The point of this exercise is that you understand the connection/relationship between the words.

79.9 — Explaining a particular use

dienen zu 'to serve as sth.'
benutzen 'to use'
nützlich sein 'to be useful'
jmdn./etw. zu etw. brauchen 'to need sb./sth. for sth.'
etw. zu etw. gebrauchen 'to use sth. for sth.'

> **Die Zinsen von seinem Sparkonto *dienen zu* seinem Altersunterhalt.**
> The interest from his savings account serves as his old age pension.

> **Diese Allzwecktücher können Sie auch *zum* Fensterputzen *benutzen*.**
> You can also use these all-purpose cloths for window cleaning.

(See **5.2b**A on word order)

> **Ich *brauche* schnell etwas *zum Schreiben*.**
> I need something to write with quickly.

79.10 — Explaining intention

-e Absicht 'intention'
absichtlich 'intentionally'
extra 'deliberately'
beabsichtigen, etw. zu tun 'to intend to do sth.'
etw. vor*haben 'to plan/intend to do sth.'
etw. tun wollen 'to want/intend to do sth.'

> **Dies geschah ausschließlich *mit der Absicht*, daß er hinausgeekelt werden sollte.**
> This happened solely so that that he would be hounded out.

> **Er hat sie *absichtlich* übersehen.**
> He overlooked her intentionally/deliberately.

extra could be used instead of **absichtlich**, but it is informal:

> **Das hast du *extra* gemacht.**
> You did that deliberately.

> **Wir *wollten* nur Strom *sparen*.**
> We only wanted to save electricity.

79.11

Explaining that something happened unintentionally/by mistake

> **-s Versehen** 'oversight'
> **aus Versehen/versehentlich** 'by mistake'
> **nicht absichtlich** 'not intentionally'
> **nicht extra** 'not deliberately'
> **etw. übersehen** 'to overlook sth.'
> **jmdm. ist ein Fehler unterlaufen** 'sb. has made a mistake'

> **Ich habe diese Datei *aus Versehen* gelöscht.**
> I deleted this file by mistake/unintentionally.

> **Er hat *versehentlich* den falschen Mantel mitgenommen.**
> He took the wrong coat with him by mistake.

(See **36**A for inseparable verbs)

80 *Providing spatial context*

80.1

Asking 'where?'

(See **7**A, **9**A and **50.5**A on interrogatives; **69**B and **71**B on existence and availability)

(a) For simply asking 'where?'

> **wo?** 'where'

> ***Wo* habe ich diese Datei gespeichert?**
> Where have I saved this file?

(b) To be more specific, a preposition could be followed by **welch-** (and the appropriate ending).

(See **24.1b**A for the declension of **welcher**)

auf welchem? 'on which?'
in welcher? 'in which?'
in welches? 'into which?'
hinter welchem? 'behind which?'

Auf welchem **Friedhof liegt Beethoven begraben?**
In which cemetery is Beethoven buried?

In welcher **Mappe liegt der Bericht?**
Which folder is the report in?

80.2 Expressing 'here' and 'there'

hier 'here'
da 'there' (sth. fairly close)
dort 'there' (sth. further away)

N.B. **da sein** is also used to denote presence (see **69.1**B).

To pinpoint a place, use:

an dieser Stelle 'at this spot'
an diesem Ort 'at this place'
an diesem Punkt 'at this point'

An dieser Stelle **stand einmal eine Kapelle.**
There used to be a chapel on this spot.

80.3 Describing distances

(a) Distances from 'A' to 'B' are conveyed by **von** (+ dat) **bis zu** (+ dat):

Von **meinem Haus** *bis zum* **Marktplatz sind es ungefähr drei km.**
From my house to the market square it is about three km.

(b) Describing distance from a certain point

Wie *weit* **ist es von Frankfurt bis Berlin** *Luftlinie***?**
How far is it as the crow flies from Frankfurt to Berlin?

(c) Describing distance between two points

Zwischen **Erde und Mond** *liegen* **etwa 390.000 km Entfernung.**
There is a distance of about 243,000 miles between the earth and the
moon.

Wie *weit* ist Potsdam von Berlin *entfernt*?
How far is it from Berlin to Potsdam?

80.4

Covering distances and areas

(a) In order to express distance covered between two towns or countries, use **von** (+ dat) **nach** (+ dat):

> **Wie lange braucht man mit dem Auto *von Heidelberg nach Dresden*?**
> How long is it by car from Heidelberg to Dresden?

(b) For distances between specific places (from 'X' to 'Y'), use **von** (+ dat) **(bis) zu** (+ dat):

> ***Vom Bahnhof bis zum Hotel* sind es nur wenige Minuten.**
> It only takes a few minutes from the station to the hotel.

(c) A formal way to express 'to cover a distance' is **eine Strecke zurück*legen**:

> **Diese Strecke *kann* man kaum zu Fuß *zurücklegen*.**
> It is virtually impossible to cover this distance on foot.

(d) For covering an area

> **sich** (= acc) **erstrecken über** 'to extend over'
> **sich** (= acc) **aus*dehnen über** 'to stretch across'
> **über etw.** (= acc) **ausbreiten** 'to spread (over)'
> **bedecken** 'to cover'
> **flächendeckend** 'covering the entire area'
> **ab*decken** 'to cover'

> **Das Naturschutzgebiet *erstreckt sich über* mehrere tausend Quadratkilometer/*dehnt sich über* mehrere tausend Quadratkilometer *aus*.**
> The nature reserve extends over several thousand square kilometers.

> **Die Tollwut hat *sich* bis jetzt noch *nicht* weiter *ausbreiten können*.**
> Rabies hasn't so far been able to spread any further.

> **Das Staubecken *bedeckt* eine große Fläche, die früher Weideland war.**
> The reservoir covers a large area that used to be grazing land.

> **Über das Satellitennetz können die Nachrichten *flächendeckend* ausgestrahlt werden.**
> The news can be broadcast across the entire area via the satellite network.

ab*decken can be used to describe something abstract rather than physical:

> **Diese Theorie *deckt* aber nicht alle möglichen Fälle *ab*.**
> However, this theory doesn't cover all possible cases.

Direction

(a) To indicate coming 'from' somewhere, **aus Richtung** 'from (the direction)' is used, while 'in the direction of' is rendered by **in Richtung**:

> **Der Heißluftballon wird *aus Richtung Süden/ aus Richtung Bayern* über den Berg fahren.**
> The hot-air balloon will travel from the south/from the direction of Bavaria across the mountain.

> **Fahren Sie *in Richtung Messegelände*.**
> Drive in the direction of the exhibition centre.

(b) Being able to see something from somewhere is conveyed by **von** (+ dat) **aus zu sehen sein**:

> **Die Alpen *sind vom* Südschwarzwald *aus zu sehen*.**
> The Alps can be seen from the southern Black Forest.

(c) To carry on in the same direction, use **(immer) geradeaus** 'keep straight on':

> **Fahren Sie *immer geradeaus* bis zum Arbeiterdenkmal.**
> Keep driving straight on as far as the workers' memorial.

(d) To emphasize movement, use **her-**.

(See **50.4**A, **80.7**B and **81.5f**B for further uses of **her-**)

For going around a place, **um** (+ acc) **herum** is used:

> **Die Sportler müssen eine Ehrenrunde *um den* ganzen Sportplatz *herum* drehen.**
> The athletes must run a lap of honour around the entire stadium/sports field.

For coming out of a place, **aus** (+ dat) **heraus** or **hinter** (+ dat) **hervor** are used:

> **Er kam *hinter dem* Vorhang *hervor*.**
> He came out from behind the curtain.

> **Die Maus kroch *aus dem* Loch *heraus/ hervor*.**
> The mouse crept out of the hole.

80.6

Following and preceding someone/something

(a) In order to express that someone is following someone else, **jmdm. folgen** 'to follow sb.' or the prefixes **nach-** or **hinterher-** before verbs of movement are used. The person being followed is in the dative:

> **Ist es Ihnen auch unangenehm, wenn *Ihnen* nachts jemand *nachgeht*?**
> Do you also find it unpleasant when someone follows you at night?

> **Er war *ihr* wochenlang *hinterhergerannt*.**
> He had been running after her for weeks.

These expressions can also be used in an abstract sense:

> **Diese Sache müssen Sie *weiterverfolgen*./Dieser Sache müssen Sie *nachgehen*.**
> You must follow up this matter.

(b) **voraus-** denotes going ahead of or preceding someone:

> **Da ich mich nicht in der Stadt auskannte, bat ich einen Taxifahrer, *mir vorauszufahren*.**
> Since I didn't know my way about town I asked a taxi-driver to drive ahead of me.

> **Die Nachricht wird *ihr* schon *vorausgeeilt* sein.**
> The news will have gone before her/preceded her.

80.7

The speaker's perspective

The prefixes **her-** and **hin-** indicate the speaker's perspective.

her*kommen is used to refer to someone coming towards the speaker, while **hin*gehen** refers to someone going away from the speaker towards someone or something else.

(See also **50.4A** for adverbs such as **hierher** and **dorthin**)

(a) Towards the speaker

> **Komm jetzt bitte (zu mir) *herunter*!**
> Please come down (to me) now.

> **Woher kommt denn dieser Wein?**
> Where does this wine come from?

(See **117.1cB** for the modal particle **denn**)

(b) Away from the speaker

> **Ich gehe jetzt *zur* Nachbarin *hinüber*.**
> I'm just going over to my neighbour.

> **Wo hast du das Buch hingelegt, das ich dir geliehen habe?**
> Where did you put the book that I lent you?

(c) Both directions

> **Geh jetzt hinauf und hol mir die schmutzige Wäsche herunter.**
> Go upstairs now and bring me down the dirty washing.

(See **41**A for imperatives)

Spatial sequences

80.8

(a) Actions which happen in spatial sequence can be expressed with **erst** 'first' and **dann** 'then':

> **Erst kommt man an dem neuen Supermarkt vorbei, dann stößt man auf das Freizeitzentrum.**
> First you pass the new supermaket, then you come to the leisure centre.

(b) Systematic sequence is often referred to by **-e Reihe**

> **-e Reihe** 'row'
> **-e Reihenfolge** 'sequence'
> **der Reihe nach** 'one after the other'

> **Die Namen der Gewinner sind in alphabetischer Reihenfolge aufgeführt.**
> The names of the winners are listed in alphabetical order.

> **Ich gehe jetzt die Teilnehmerliste der Reihe nach durch.**
> I am going through the list of participants, one after the other.

(See also **76.5b**B for taking turns)

(c) To imply that something is right next to something without a gap in between, use **anschließend an** (+ acc) 'adjacent to':

> **Anschließend an den Versorgungsraum finden wir die Empfangsräume der römischen Villa.**
> Next to the supplies room we find the reception rooms of the Roman villa.

(See **81.13b**B for temporal uses of **anschließend**)

81 *Providing temporal context*

Now

(a) The present moment in time is expressed by:

> **im Moment/im Augenblick/momentan** 'at the moment'
> **gerade** 'at the moment/just now/just then'
> **jetzt/nun** 'now'
> **bis jetzt/bisher** 'until now/hitherto'
> **gegenwärtig** 'currently/at present'
> **zur Zeit** 'at present'
> **heute** 'today'
> **dieses Jahr** 'this year'
> **dieses Jahrzehnt** 'this decade'

> **Wir haben *momentan* sehr viel zu tun.**
> We are very busy *at the moment*.

> **Wo seid ihr *gerade*?**
> Where are you at the moment/just now?

(See **81.2**B on another use of **gerade**)

> **Jetzt/Nun geht es aufwärts mit der Wirtschaft.**
> The economy is picking up now.

(b) 'Until now' is rendered by **bis jetzt/bisher**:

> **Bis jetzt gibt es keine Cholera in dem Lager.**
> Until now there has been no cholera in the camp.

(See **81.7**B below for ways to express 'not yet', and **34.2d**A for this use of the present tense)

(c) More general terms for 'currently/at present' are **gegenwärtig/zur Zeit** (abbreviated to **z.Zt.**): as an adjective, **gegenwärtig** occurs in expressions such as **-e gegenwärtige Finanzlage** 'the current financial situation':

> **Der Bundeskanzler befindet sich *zur Zeit* in Washington.**
> The Federal Chancellor is currently in Washington.

81.2 **A few moments ago**

gerade/eben/soeben used with either the simple past or the perfect (see **34.5–34.6**A for tenses) implies that something has just happened:

> **Tut mir leid, der Chef ist *gerade* aus dem Haus gegangen.**
> Sorry, the boss has just left the building.

> ***Eben* waren sie noch da; jetzt sind sie weg.**
> They were here a minute ago, now they've gone.

vorhin lies a little bit further back in time; it refers to the same afternoon, morning, etc. but other events may have happened in the meantime.

> ***Vorhin* habe ich noch daran gedacht; dann kam mir ein Anruf dazwischen.**
> I remembered it a little earlier, then a phone call intervened.

81.3 **Recently**

(a) For referring to recent events without specifically giving a date, the following can be used:

> **vor kurzem** 'a short time ago/the other day' (implying days, rather than minutes or hours ago)
> **kürzlich/neulich** 'recently'

> ***Neulich* stand in der Zeitung, daß sich Peter verlobt hat.**
> It was in the paper recently that Peter has got engaged.

(b) In order to refer to a specific point in the recent past, the following can be used:

> **letzten/vorigen Montag/Mittwoch** 'last Monday/Wednesday'
> **letzte/vorige Woche** 'last week'
> **vorletzten Dienstag** '(the) Tuesday before last'

81.4 **At a specified time in the past**

(a) For a non-specific time in the past

> **vor x Jahren** 'x years ago/before'

> **Sie hatten *vor* zehn Jahren in einem Chor gesungen.**
> They had sung in a choir ten years *ago*.

(b) For a specific time in the past

> **Dienstag vor einer Woche** 'a week ago last Tuesday'
> **letzten Freitagabend** 'last Friday evening'
> **in der Nacht zum Donnerstag** 'on Wednesday night'

(Note here that Germans refer to a night preceding rather than following a day.)

heute nacht, if mentioned in the morning, however, refers to the previous night:

> **Wie hast du *heute nacht* geschlafen?**
> How did you sleep last night?

81.5 **Events in the distant past**

> **damals** 'at the time'
> **einst** 'once'
> **damalig** (adj) 'then'
> **einstig** (adj) 'former' (formal)
> **früher** (adj) 'former/earlier'
> **früher** (adv) 'in the old days'
> **einmal** 'once'
> **es war einmal** 'once upon a time'
> **eines Tages** 'one day'
> **irgendwann** 'at some (unknown) time'
> **als ich klein war** 'when I was little'
> **es ist lange her** 'it has been a long time'
> **alt** 'old'
> **jung** 'recent/young'

(a) When talking about events in the distant past, **damals** 'then' and **einst** 'one day/once' are used:

> ***Damals* gab es noch kein elektrisches Licht.**
> Then/In those days there was no electric light.

> **Der *damalige* Bürgermeister von Berlin war W. Brandt.**
> The mayor of Berlin at that time was W. Brandt.

> **Die Baracken dienten *einst* zur Unterbringung von Flüchtlingen.**
> The huts once served as accommodation for refugees.

> **Die *einstigen* Beziehungen zu den osteuropäischen Staaten waren durch den eisernen Vorhang abgebrochen worden.**
> The Iron Curtain had put an end to earlier relations with Eastern European states.

Note that **einstig** tends to be more formal than **früher** (used as an adjective).

(See **43**A for adjectives and **50**A for adverbs)

(b) Older people use **früher** 'in the old days/then' to refer to their own past:

> *Früher* war der Main oft zugefroren, und wir konnten darauf Schlittschuh laufen.
> The (river) Main used to get frozen over and we were able to ice skate on it.

(c) For a single occurrence, **einmal** 'once' is used, which is also found at the beginning of fairy-tales:

> *Es war einmal* ein alter König.
> There was once/Once upon a time there was an old king.

> Da bin ich *einmal* allein im Wald spazierengegangen.
> Once I went walking alone in the woods.

> *Eines Tages* kam der Gerichtsvollzieher zu ihm.
> One day the bailiff came to him.

(See **20.6**A for this use of the genitive)

(d) At some (unknown) time

> *Irgendwann* kam dann die Gemeindeschwester und schaute nach dem Neugeborenen.
> Some time (we never knew when) the district nurse would come and look in on the new-born child.

> Kannst du mir *irgendwann* den Koffer vom Speicher holen?
> Could you get the suitcase down from the attic for me some time?

(e) 'When I was young'

> *Als ich noch klein war,* wurden die Kinder viel strenger erzogen.
> When I was little, children were brought up much more strictly.

(f) 'A long time ago'

> Es ist *eine Ewigkeit her/schon lange her,* seit wir uns das letzte Mal getroffen haben.
> It's been ages since we last met.

(g) When talking about history, **jung** and **alt** mean respectively chronologically more recent and chronologically more distant:

Die *alten Funde* stammen aus dem zweiten Jahrhundert n. Chr., die *jüngeren* aus dem vierten Jahrhundert.
The older finds are from the second century AD, the more recent ones from the fourth century.

81.6 No longer possible or out-of-date

(See also **70.4e**B for things out-of-date and obsolete)

(a) For things that have ceased to apply or are no longer possible

> **nicht mehr** 'no longer'
> **längst nicht mehr** 'not for a long time'
> **schon lange nicht mehr** 'not for a long time'

Seit seinem schweren Unfall darf er *nicht mehr* radfahren.
Since his bad accident he is no longer allowed to ride a bike.

Nach dem Kurs werden Sie *keine* Angst *mehr* vor dunklen Räumen haben.
After the course you will no longer be afraid of dark rooms.

Orchideen gibt es in dieser Wiese *schon längst nicht mehr.*
There haven't been orchids in this meadow for a long time.

Du hast *schon lange nicht mehr* mit mir Schach gespielt.
You haven't played chess with me for a long time.

(b) For something or somebody that is no longer up-to-date

Dieses Textverarbeitungsprogramm ist (längst) *veraltet/ überholt.*
This word processing programme has been out-dated/obsolete (for a long time).

Er ist *nicht mehr up to date.*
He is no longer up-to-date/familiar with current affairs.

81.7 Yet to occur

Der Film von der Hochzeit *ist immer noch nicht* entwickelt.
The film of the wedding still hasn't been developed.

Schreibt er *immer noch* an seinem Bericht?
Is he still writing his report?

Ist die Umgehungsstraße *immer noch nicht* fertig?
Is the by-pass still not ready/finished?

(See also **70.5**B for cancelled events)

Very soon

> **sofort** 'straight away/without delay'
> **gleich** 'in a minute'
> **bald** 'soon'
> **von nun/jetzt an** 'from now on'
> **sobald** 'as soon as'

(a) Immediately, from now on

sofort implies 'straight away/without delay':

> **Bitte kommen Sie *sofort* zum Chef!**
> Please come to see the boss right away.

ab sofort denotes 'from this moment onwards':

> **Der Vertrag gilt *ab sofort*.**
> The contract/treaty has immediate effect.

(b) **gleich** 'straight away/in a minute' leaves a few moments to finish another job first:

> **Ich komme *gleich*.**
> I'll come straight away/be right there.

(c) **bald** 'soon' reassures someone that something is going to happen, maybe later that day or in the next few days, depending on context:

> **Wann sind wir endlich da? Ganz *bald*.**
> When will we be there? Very soon./Quite soon./Not long.

(d) **von nun/jetzt an** is a slightly pompous way of indicating that from now on things are going to be different:

> **Versprich mir, daß du *von jetzt an* nie wieder die Zunge herausstreckst.**
> Promise me that you will never stick your tongue out again.

(e) As soon as something is done

> ***Sobald* ich das Manuskript erhalten habe, werde ich es überarbeiten.**
> As soon as I have received the manuscript I'll revise it.

81.9 **Eventually**

(a) In the near future

> **in Kürze** 'shortly'
> **demnächst** 'shortly'
> **in nächster Zeit** 'in the very near future/shortly'

But note that **kürzlich** is used to mean 'recently/lately' (see **81.3a**B).

> *In Kürze/Demnächst* **wird in diesem Theater ein neues Musical von Lloyd Webber aufgeführt.**
> There will be a production of a new musical by Lloyd Webber in this theatre soon.

> **Wegen der Sparmaßnahmen wird es hier** *in nächster Zeit* **keine neuen Bücher geben.**
> Because of the economy measures there will be no new books here in the near future.

(b) For longer term planning

> **mit der Zeit** 'with time'
> **irgendwann** 'eventually'
> **allmählich** 'gradually'

> *Mit der Zeit* **werden die Schmerzen vielleicht abklingen.**
> With time the pains may ease.

> **Vielleicht sollten wir** *irgendwann* **einmal eine Party veranstalten.**
> Maybe we should organize/arrange a party some time/eventually.

(See **81.5d**B for **irgendwann** 'some time ago')

> **Wir werden** *allmählich* **immer mehr Computerpapier benötigen.**
> We will gradually require more and more computer paper.

81.10 **A specified time in the future**

(a) The following are used to refer to a specific point in the future:

heute mittag/nachmittag/abend 'this lunchtime/afternoon/evening'
morgen 'tomorrow'
morgen früh/abend 'tomorrow morning/evening'
übermorgen/überübermorgen 'the day after tomorrow/in three days' time'
diesen/nächsten Sonntag 'this (the following)/next Sunday'
Montag in einer Woche 'a week on Monday'
in der kommenden Woche 'next week'
wenn du groß/erwachsen/in der Schule bist 'when you are grown up/an adult/at school'

> *Übermorgen* **fangen die Sommerferien an.**
> The summer holidays start the day after tomorrow.

> *Nächsten Sonntag* **fahren wir in die Berge.**
> Next Sunday we'll take a drive into the mountains.

(b) To express a certain length of time until something is to happen, the following are used:

in acht Tagen 'in a week's time'
in vierzehn Tagen 'in two weeks' time'
in zwanzig Jahren 'in twenty years' time'

> **Die Handwerker werden** *in acht Tagen* **mit den Fenstern fertig sein.**
> The builders will have finished with the windows in a week's time.

81.11   Expressing duration

Addition of the adverb or suffix **-lang** emphasizes the length of time.

lang 'long' (after time expressions)
fünf Jahre lang 'for five years'
stundenlang 'for hours'
jahrzehntelang 'for decades'
eine Zeit lang 'for a while'
tagsüber 'during the day'
an Werktagen/werktags 'on working days'
sonntags 'on Sundays'
an Feiertagen 'on public holidays'

> **Sie hatten** *fünf Jahre lang* **im Chor gesungen, bevor sie austraten.**
> They had sung in the choir for five years before they left it.

Stunden *lang***/Tage** *lang***/Jahre** *lang* **habe ich auf ihn gewartet.**
I've waited for him for hours/days/years.

Jahrzehnte *lang***/Jahrhunderte** *lang* **war dieses Land besetzt.**
This country was occupied for decades/centuries.

Wir werden *eine Zeit lang/eine Zeitlang* **ohne Hausmeister auskommen müssen.**
We'll have to manage without a caretaker/janitor for a while.

81.12 Expressing simultaneous events

gleichzeitig/zur gleichen Zeit 'at the same time/simultaneously'
am gleichen/selben Tag wie (+ nom) 'on the same day as'

Man kann doch nicht *gleichzeitig* **Radio hören und Rechenaufgaben machen!**
But surely you can't listen to the radio and do your maths homework at *the same time*!

Er ist *am gleichen/selben Tag* **in die Schule gekommen wie ich.**
He started school on the same day as me.

(See **76.6**B on 'Simultaneity')

81.13 Before and after

(a) 'Before' is rendered by:

vor 'before'
vor dieser Zeit 'before this time'
vorher/bisher/bis jetzt 'until now'

Bitte nicht *vor acht Uhr* **morgens anrufen.**
Please do not phone before 8am.

Vor dem **Schlafengehen Zähne putzen!**
Before going to bed clean your teeth!

Das haben wir aber *bisher/bis jetzt* **anders gemacht!**
But we did this differently up until now!

(b) 'After' is conveyed by:

nach (+ dat) 'after'
anschließend an etw. (= acc) 'following sth.'

Nach sieben Uhr sind die meisten Leute zu Hause.
Most people are at home after 7(pm).

Nach der Schule sollen gleich die Hausaufgaben gemacht werden.
Homework is supposed to be done straight after school.

Anschließend an den Empfang gab es den lange erwarteten Vortrag.
Following the formal welcome the long awaited lecture started.

Frequency

(a) Doing things very frequently

> **sehr oft** 'very often'
> **öfters/oft** 'often'
> **häufig** 'frequently'

Die Windeln müssen *häufig* gewechselt werden.
The nappies/diapers have to be changed frequently.

(b) Doing things infrequently

> **gelegentlich** 'occasionally'
> **ab und zu** 'infrequently'
> **hin und wieder** 'every now and again'
> **selten** 'seldom'
> **(fast) nie** '(almost) never'

Wir gehen *fast nie* tanzen.
We hardly ever go dancing.

(c) Doing things regularly

> **regelmäßig** 'regularly'
> **jede Stunde/jedes Jahr** 'every hour/every year'
> **einmal/zweimal die Woche** 'once/twice a week' (informal)
> **einmal/zweimal in der Woche** 'once/twice a week'
> **alle vierzehn Tage** 'every fortnight'
> **alle vier Wochen** 'every four weeks'
> **jeden zweiten Tag** 'every other day'

Ich muß mir *jeden zweiten Tag* die Haare waschen.
I have to wash my hair every other day.

Das Gerät sollte *alle vier Wochen* überprüft werden.
The equipment ought to be checked every four weeks.

──81.15── **Punctuality and deadline**

(a) Just at the right time is rendered by:

> **rechtzeitig** 'at the right time'
> **gerade zur rechten Zeit** 'just in time'
> **gerade noch** 'just in time'
> **in letzter Sekunde/Minute** 'at the last minute'
> **mit knapper Not** 'in the nick of time'
> **pünktlich** 'in time'

Die Karte kam *rechtzeitig* zum Geburtstag an.
The card arrived in time for the birthday.

Die Bewerbungsunterlagen wurden *gerade noch* vor Einsendeschluß eingereicht.
The application forms were handed in *just* before the deadline.

Er hat ihn *gerade noch* retten können.
He was able to save him *just in time*.

Wir waren *gerade noch* am Hafen angekommen, bevor das Schiff auslief.
We arrived at the harbour just before the boat left.

Die Hilfe war *in letzter Sekunde* eingetroffen.
Help had arrived at the last minute.

Sie erreichten das Ziel *mit knapper Not*. (informal)
They reached the goal in the nick of time.

Der Zug nach Hamburg kam *pünktlich*.
The train to Hamburg came on time.

(b) Not at the right time is rendered by:

> **zur falschen Zeit** 'at the wrong time'
> **(zu) spät/früh** 'too late/early'
> **verfrüht/verspätet** '(too) early/late'
> **sich (= acc) verspäten** 'to be late'
> **Verspätung haben** 'to be delayed/late'
> **etw. mit Verspätung tun** 'to do sth. with delay'
> **mit zwei Tagen Verspätung** 'two days late'

Du hättest früher kommen sollen, jetzt ist es *zu spät.*
You should have come earlier, now it is too late.

Der Flug aus Moskau *hat zwei Stunden Verspätung.*
The flight from Moscow is delayed by two hours.

Das Dokument hat uns *zwei Tage spät* erreicht. (informal)
The document reached us two days late.

Das Dokument wurde *mit zwei Tagen Verspätung* abgeliefert. (formal)
The document was delivered two days late.

(c) Doing something by a certain time

Das Manuskript muß *bis* (zum) Jahresende abgegeben werden.
The manuscript must be handed in by the end of the year.

(d) Within a certain time

Die Wohnung muß *innerhalb von* 10 Tagen/ *innerhalb* Jahresfrist geräumt werden.
The flat must be vacated within ten days/within a year.

Wir bitten um Ausgleich unsrer Rechnung *in 20 Tagen* nach Rechnungserhalt.
We request settlement of our invoice within 20 days of receipt.

(e) Asking for an extension

Vielleicht sollten wir um eine *Verlängerung/ Gnadenfrist* bitten.
Maybe we should ask for an extension/reprieve.

(See **76.5**B for temporal sequences)

82 *Talking about cause and effect*

82.1

Linking cause and effect
(a) 'If... then...'

Cause and effect can be expressed with the pair of conjunctions **wenn** and **dann**.

wenn is a subordinating conjunction (see **8.3**A), whereas **dann** keeps the verb as second idea (see **6.3**A):

Wenn man auf den Knopf drückt, *dann* spult die Kassette zurück.
If you press the button, the cassette rewinds.

wenn can be omitted and the subject and verb inverted. This results in a more idiomatic style. (See **8.5**A for the omission of **wenn**)

> ***Drückt*** **man auf den Knopf,** *dann* **spult die Kassette zurück.**
> If you press the button, the cassette rewinds.

In this case **dann** can be replaced with **so**:

> **Drückt man auf den anderen Knopf,** *so* **spult die Kassette vorwärts.**
> If you press the other button, the cassette fast forwards.

(b) 'The more, the better'

je..., desto 'the..., the...' (as in 'the more, the better')

> *Je höher* **der Stromverbrauch,** *desto höher* **(ist) die Rechnung.**
> The higher the electricity consumption, the higher the bill.

(See **48**A for comparison of adjectives and **51**A for comparison of adverbs)

(c) **zu... sein, (um) zu...** 'to be too... to do sth.'

> **Du** *bist* **jetzt** *zu* **groß,** *um* **im Sandkasten** *zu spielen.*
> You are too big now to play in the sand-pit.

(d) **sobald** 'the moment/as soon as'

> *Sobald* **der Kontakt unterbrochen wird, ertönt die Alarmanlage.**
> As soon as the contact is broken, the alarm system sounds.

(e) **..., so daß, so..., daß...** 'so... that...'

> **Der Zug hatte Verspätung,** *so daß* **wir den Anschluß verpaßten.**
> The train was late so that we missed the connection.

> **Sie sprach** *so* **leise,** *daß* **sie niemand verstehen konnte.**
> She spoke so quietly that no one could understand her.

N.B. **so daß** refers to result, whereas **damit** (see **79.2b**B) refers to purpose.

> **Sie brüllte,** *daß* **das Zimmer bebte.**
> She yelled so loudly that the room trembled/shook.

— 82.2 —

Cause

(a) General causes

> **-e Ursache** 'cause'
> **verursachen** 'to cause'
> **hervor*rufen** 'to bring about'
> **-r Anlaß** 'occasion'
> **veranlassen** 'to cause'
> **jmdm. Schwierigkeiten bereiten** 'to cause sb. difficulties'
> **aus*lösen** 'to trigger (bad things)'

> **Die Luftverschmutzung wird als *Ursache* aller Übel angesehen.**
> Air pollution is seen as the root of all evil.

(See **23.1**A for omission of the definite article in German)

> **Der Unfall *war* durch fahrlässiges Handeln *verursacht worden.***
> The accident had been caused by negligence.

> ***Anlaß* der Unruhen war eine Preissteigerung.**
> The occasion/cause of the unrest/riots was an increase in prices.

> **Ein Attentat in Sarajewo *löste* den ersten Weltkrieg *aus.***
> An assassination in Sarajewo caused/set off the First World War.

(See also **110.10**B for 'Passing on disease')

(b) Causing danger

> **gefährden** 'to endanger'
> **jmdn. in Gefahr bringen** 'to get sb. into danger'
> **gefährlich sein für** 'to be dangerous for'

> **Die Gesundheitsminister warnen: Rauchen *gefährdet* die Gesundheit.**
> Health ministers warn: smoking endangers/(English: damages) health.

(warning on cigarette packs.)

(c) Encouraging

> **fördern** 'to encourage/promote/foster' (not of children!)
> **-e Förderung** 'promotion/fostering'
> **jmdn. für etw. loben** 'to praise sb. for sth.'

> **Gelegentliches Loben *fördert* den Leistungswillen.**
> Occasional praise encourages the desire to do well.

Das Austauschprogramm *dient der Förderung* der englisch–deutschen Beziehungen. (formal)

The exchange programme serves to promote/foster Anglo–German relations.

Lob sie doch mal für ihre Arbeit!

Do praise her for her work!

82.3 — Effect

Effect in general

-e Wirkung 'effect'
wirken 'to work/have an effect'
seine Wirkung (nicht) verfehlen '(not) to fail to have the desired effect'
bewirken 'to cause/produce an effect'
-r Effekt 'effect'
-e Folge 'consequence'

(a) Having an effect

Der Beschwerdebrief hatte seine *Wirkung nicht verfehlt.*

The letter of complaint did not fail to have the desired effect.

Neben*wirkungen* sind keine bekannt.

There are no known side effects.

Höhere Temperaturen *bewirken* ein schnelleres Wachsen der Bakterien.

Higher temperatures cause germs/bacteria to grow more quickly.

Das Medikament *wirkt* innerhalb von 20 Minuten gegen Kopfschmerzen.

The medicine is effective/works against headaches within 20 minutes.

(b) Special effects

wirkungsvoll 'effective'
-r Effekt 'effect'

Die Hintergrundbeleuchtung war besonders *wirkungsvoll.*

The background lighting/illumination was especially effective.

-r Effekt is used to designate well-known (scientific) effects:

-r Treibhauseffekt 'greenhouse effect'
-r Teepoteffekt 'teapot effect'
-r Verfremdungseffekt 'alienation effect'

> **Brecht benutzte den *Verfremdungseffekt*, um seine Zuschauer zum Denken aufzurütteln.**
> Brecht used the alienation effect in order to rouse his audience and make them think.

(c) Consequences

> **-e Folge (-n)** 'consequence'
> **in Folge (+ gen)/in Folge von/als Folge von** 'as a result of'
> **zur Folge haben** 'to have as a consequence'
> **daraus folgt/folglich** 'consequently'
> **infolgedessen/demzufolge** 'consequently'
> **folgenschwer** 'having serious consequences/momentous'

> ***In Folge der* langwierigen Reparaturarbeiten muß die Wiedereröffnung des Theaters verschoben werden.**
> As a result/consequence of the long-drawn-out repair works the reopening of the theatre has to be postponed.

> **Die *Folge*erscheinungen des Industrieunfalls sind schwer abzuschätzen.**
> The consequences of the industrial accident are difficult to estimate.

> **Wenn Wasser gefriert und sich ausdehnt, *hat* das oft einen Rohrbruch *zur Folge*.**
> If water freezes and expands, the consequence is often a burst pipe.

daraus folgt is usually an expression reserved for logical deductions and gives the following statement an air of rationality:

> **Wir haben weder Bargeld, noch Immobilien oder Aktien. *Daraus folgt*, daß wir ein regelmäßiges Einkommen verdienen müssen./*Folglich* müssen wir ein regelmäßiges Einkommen verdienen.**
> We have neither cash, nor real estate, nor shares. From that it follows that we have to earn a regular income./Consequently we must earn a regular income.

> **Er mußte die *folgenschwere* Entscheidung treffen, ob er auswandern solle oder nicht.**
> He had to take a momentous decision/a decision with serious consequences – whether he should emigrate or not.

82.4 Tracing events back to their causes

(See also **76.1**B on 'Basic words for actions and processes' and **79.1–79.4**B on reasons and purpose)

> **etw. auf jmdn./etw. zurück*führen** 'to trace sth. back to sb.'

**Der Absturz des Airbusses wurde *auf* menschliches Versagen
zurückgeführt.**
The crash of the Airbus was traced back to/explained by human error.

Interdependence

> **es liegt an** (+ dat)/**es liegt bei jmdm.** 'it is up to sb.'
> **es hängt von etw. ab** 'it depends on sth.'

**Es *liegt* ganz *an dir*, ob du diese Verantwortung auf dich nehmen willst
oder nicht.**
It is entirely up to you whether you take on this responsibility or not.

**Ich weiß noch nicht, ob wir am Familientreffen teilnehmen können. *Es
hängt davon ab*, wieviel Zeit wir haben.**
I don't know yet if we can take part in the family reunion. It depends how
much time we have.

(For further expressions see **78**B on origins)

83 *Drawing conclusions*

Concluding from evidence

(a) Evidence is rendered by nouns such as:

> **-r Fund** 'finding'
> **-r Befund** 'finding(s)/data'
> **-r Beweis** 'proof'
> **-s Beweismaterial** 'evidence'
> **Daten** (plural) 'data'
> **Fakten** (plural) 'facts'
> **-e Fundstelle/-r Fundort** 'place of discovery'

An der *Fundstelle* wurde eine Untersuchung vorgenommen.
An investigation was carried out at the site (of the find).

Das *Beweismaterial* der Kriminalpolizei ist noch unvollständig.
The CID's evidence is still incomplete.

Die *Daten/Fakten* müssen überprüft werden.
The data/facts have to be double-checked.

> **Was war *der Befund* der (klinischen) Untersuchung?**
> What were the findings of the (clinical) examination?

> ***Kein Befund./Ohne Befund.***
> (There are) no significant findings.

(See also **110.8c**B for the use of **Befund**)

(b) Drawing conclusions from a source

(aus etw.) einen Schluß ziehen 'to draw a conclusion (from sth.)'
etw./ (aus/von) etw. entnehmen 'to infer sth. from sth.'
etw. aus etw. ersehen 'to see/conclude sth. from sth.'
aus etw. hervor*gehen 'to emerge from sth.'
aus etw. folgt etw. 'sth. follows from sth.'
folglich 'consequently'

> **Anhand der gesammelten Daten kann man *den Schluß ziehen*, daß hier eine Siedlung gewesen sein muß.**
> From data collected one can conclude that there must have been a settlement here.

> **Ich habe *(aus) den Unterlagen entnommen*, wie viele Landarbeiter damals ausgewandert waren.**
> I have inferred from the documents how many agricultural workers emigrated at the time.

> ***Aus* den Anschuldigungen *geht hervor*, wie sehr sie ihrem Mann mißtraut hat.**
> It emerges from the accusations how much she mistrusted her husband.

83.2

Talking about consequences

(See also **82.3c**B on 'Consequences')

---

folglich 'consequently'
damit 'therefore'
deshalb/darum/daher/deswegen/also 'that's why/for that reason/so/therefore/thus'

(a) For things that follow necessarily, **folglich** 'consequently' and **damit** 'therefore' are employed:

> **Er hatte seine Studienbewerbung zu spät abgeschickt. *Folglich* wurde er nicht mehr zugelassen.**

He sent off his university application too late. As a result he was refused entry (to the course).

(b) To explain a previous statement, use **deshalb/daher/deswegen** (or, more informally, **darum**), all meaning 'that's why/for that reason':

> **Er wollte seinen Bruder nicht belasten.** *Deshalb/Daher/Deswegen/Darum* **verweigerte er die Aussage.**
> He didn't want to incriminate his brother. That's why he refused to give a statement.

(c) To infer from a previous statement, **also** 'so/therefore' is inserted:

> **Sie haben** *also* **noch nie an einer Safari teilgenommen?**
> So you have never taken part in a safari?

> **Im Labor war er auch nicht zu finden,** *also* **suchten wir ihn in der Kantine.**
> He wasn't to be found in the lab either, so we looked for him in the canteen.

84 *Referring to sources of information*

84.1 Written/literary sources of information

In academic resesarch, sources of information are referred to as **-e Quelle (-n)**.

> **-e Quellenangabe (-n)** 'reference'
> **-r Quellennachweis (-e)** 'reference in footnote'
> **-s Quellenverzeichnis (-se)** 'bibliography/list of works consulted/list of references/acknowledgements'

(a) When citing a source, **nach** or **laut** (+ dat) is used:

> *Nach Goethe* **irrt der Mensch, so lang er strebt.**
> According to Goethe, man errs till his strife is over.

> *Laut Schiller* **kämpfen selbst die Götter vergebens mit der Dummheit.**
> According to Schiller, the Gods themselves struggle in vain with stupidity.

> *Laut* **dem Verkehrsministerium ist die Zahl der Unfälle leicht gestiegen.**
> According to the Department of Transport, the number of accidents has slightly increased.

For further expressions with **nach** and **laut** see below.

(b) Referring to written sources

To give reference to any written source, **stehen** is used:

> ***Steht* das im Text?**
> Is that (written) in the text?
>
> **Das *steht bei* Karl Marx.**
> That is from Karl Marx.
>
> **Das *steht im* Grundgesetz.**
> That's in the (German) Constitution.
>
> ***So steht es* in der Bibel/in der Zeitung/im Lexikon.**
> That's what it says in the Bible/in the newspaper/in the encyclopaedia.

(c) For quoting statements verbatim (formal)

> **lauten** 'to read/say'
> **-r Wortlaut** 'the exact wording'

> **Der genaue Text/Die Stelle *lautet* (wie folgt):**
> The exact text/the passage reads (as follows):
>
> **In dem Testament des Verstorbenen finden wir *folgenden Wortlaut*:**
> In the will of the deceased we find the following (wording):

(See **28.5**A for adjectival nouns)

(d) To introduce a quotation, use **zitieren** 'to quote' or **-s Zitat** 'quotation':

> ***Zitat*/Ich *zitiere*:**
> I quote:

or:

> **Ich *zitiere nach* Böll.**
> I quote Böll./To quote from Böll.
>
> **Wir *zitieren aus* der Textstelle.**
> We quote from the (place in the) text.

(e) The rendering of a lengthy excerpt in an oral presentation is introduced by:

> **(-r) Zitatanfang** 'beginning of quote'

and followed by:

> **(-s) Zitatende** 'end of quote'

(f) For dictation purposes one can use:

> **Anführungsstriche unten/oben** 'quotation marks at the bottom (which is the traditional place for initial quotation marks)/at the top (for the end)'

(g) All of the above are fairly formal and are used in special contexts. It is, of course, also possible to indicate the source of the information very informally:

> **Der Chef hat gesagt/geschrieben, wir müssen länger arbeiten.**
> The boss has said/written that we have to work longer.

Invoking/calling on authority

> **sich** (= acc) **beziehen auf** 'to refer to'
> **bezugnehmend auf** (+ acc) 'with reference to'
> **sich** (= acc) **stützen auf** 'to base oneself on'
> **sich** (= acc) **berufen auf** 'to refer/appeal to'

> **Ich** *beziehe mich auf* **die Verfassung.**
> I refer to/base myself on the constitution.

> *Bezugnehmend auf* **Heidegger möchte ich folgendes erwähnen:**
> With reference to Heidegger I would like to mention the following:

> **Mit dieser Annahme** *stützen* **wir** *uns auf* **die Untersuchungen des Psychologischen Instituts.**
> We base this assumption on the investigations of the Institute of Psychology.

> **Die Finanzminister** *stützen sich auf* **die neuesten Wirtschaftsdaten.**
> The finance ministers base their thinking (etc.) on/are relying on the latest economic data.

> **Er** *hat sich* **nur** *auf* **das Buch seines Professors** *gestützt.*
> He supported what he said by referring only to his professor's book.

sich berufen has the sense of invoking great authority to strengthen one's own position:

> **Er** *berief sich* **ständig** *auf* **Konrad Adenauer.**
> He kept referring to/invoking Konrad Adenauer.

Enquiring about sources

In informal dialogue **haben aus** is used to convey a source of information:

> *Woher hast* **du denn diesen Ausspruch?**
> Where did you get that saying/remark from?

> **Den habe ich *aus* dem S**PIEGEL**.**
> I got it from the S**PIEGEL**.

(See also **85**B on reporting other people's words)

(See also **85**B on reporting other people's words)

84.4 — **Reporting facts**

For reporting facts, **nach**, **laut** and **zufolge** are used. They all translate as 'according to':

> **nach/laut** (+ dat) 'according to'
> **nach Angaben von** (+ dat)/**nach Angaben** (+ gen) 'according to data from' (formal)
> (+ dat) **zufolge** 'according to/following (evidence)' (formal)

> *Nach Angaben vom* **deutschen Wetterdienst/** *Nach Angaben des* **deutschen Wetterdienstes soll es heute kalt werden.** (formal)
> According to information from the German weather service, it is supposed to get cold today.

> *Laut Fahrplan* **müßte der Bus eigentlich gleich kommen.**
> According to the timetable, the bus should be here/be coming quite soon.

> **Augenzeugenberichten** *zufolge* **soll der Täter über die Mauer geflohen sein.** (formal)
> According to eye witness reports, the culprit/perpetrator (is supposed to have) fled over the wall.

(See **35.6b**A for the use of **sollen**)

(See **35.6b**A for the use of **sollen**)

> *Ihrem* **Bericht** *zufolge* **hatte dieses Gespräch gar nicht stattgefunden.**
> According to her report, the conversation didn't take place at all.

zufolge is preceded by the dative.

84.5 — **Writing footnotes**

> **-e Fußnote** 'footnote'
> **-e Anmerkung** 'remark'

(a) For conventions on academic referencing see:

> Fred Becker, *Anleitung zum wissenschaftlichen Arbeiten, Wegweiser zum Anfertigen von Haus- und Diplomarbeiten* (Bergisch Gladbach/Köln, 1990).

or for UK:

Joseph Gibaldi & Walter Achtert, *MLA Style Sheet. Handbook for Writers of Research Papers* (known as *MLA Manual*) (MLA, New York, 1988, 3rd edition). ISBN 0873523792.

for USA:

Chicago Manual of Style (University of Chicago Press, London, 1993, 14th edition). ISBN 0226103897

(b) Selection of useful abbreviations

a.a.O.	**am angegebenen Ort**	'in the place cited'	'loc. cit./op. cit.'
Anm.	**Anmerkung**	'note/footnote/annotation'	
Bd./Bde.	**Band/Bände**	'volume/volumes'	'vol./vols'
ebd.	**ebenda**	'in the same place'	'ibid.'
f./ff.	**und die folgende(n) Seite/Seiten**	'and the following page/pages'	'f./ff.'
Hrsg.	**Herausgeber**	'editor(s)'	'ed./eds'
o.g.	**oben genannt**	'mentioned above'	
s.	**siehe**	'see'	'see/cf.'
s.a.	**siehe auch**	'see also'	
s.o./s.u.	**siehe oben/siehe unten**	'see above/see below'	
u.a.	**und andere**	'and others'	'et al.'
Verf.	**Verfasser**	'author'	
vgl.	**vergleiche**	'compare'	'comp./cf.'

85 *Reporting other people's words and claims*

For reported speech the subjunctive is usually used (see **39**A for Subjunctives I and II). In what follows 'speaker' denotes the user of both spoken and written language.

> *Er sagt, er habe kein Geld/er habe angerufen.*
> He says he has no money/he phoned.

85.1

Questioning the truth of what someone said

There are several ways of implying that the speaker doubts the truth of what has been said:

> **gesehen haben wollen** 'to claim to have seen'
> **angeblich** 'supposedly'
> **behaupten** 'to claim'

(a) **wollen**

(See **35.6b**A for this special use of **wollen**)

> **Der Alte *will* das Opfer zum letzten Mal *gesehen haben*.**
> The old man claims to have seen the victim for the last time.

(b) **angeblich** 'supposedly' adds a note of disbelief:

> **Der Angriff auf die Demonstranten war *angeblich* von der Polizei ausgegangen.**
> The attack on the demonstrators was supposedly initiated by the police.

(c) **behaupten** can imply that the speaker is not telling the truth:

> **Er behauptet, nichts (Alkoholisches) getrunken zu haben.**
> He claims to have drunk nothing (alcoholic).

(d) In order to imply severe doubts about the truth of what has been said, Subjunctive II may be employed:

> ***Er sagt, er hätte* kein Geld/angerufen.**
> He says he has no money/he called (but I don't believe it).

(See **39.6b**A for this use of the Subjunctive II)

85.2

Reaffirming the truth of what someone has said

> **tatsächlich** 'indeed'
> **wirklich** 'really'
> **eigentlich/in der Tat** 'actually/really' (contrary to expectations)

(a) To imply that the speaker believes what he or she has heard, **tatsächlich** 'indeed' or **wirklich** 'really' are used:

> **Es ist kaum zu glauben, aber das neue Ausstellungsgebäude soll *tatsächlich* sieben Millionen Mark gekostet haben.**
> It is hard to believe, but they say the new exhibition hall really did cost seven million marks.

> **Die Flüchtlinge waren *wirklich/in der Tat* mit dem Schlauchboot über die Grenze gekommen.**
> The refugees really *had* crossed the border/frontier in a rubber dinghy.

(b) To imply that something was the case contrary to expectations, **eigentlich** 'really' is used:

Eigentlich war er der Besitzer der Bar, aber als die Polizei kam, wollte er das nicht zugeben.

He really was the owner of the bar, but when the police came he wouldn't admit it.

85.3

Passing on messages

(a) The passing on of verbal messages is conveyed by:

> **wieder*geben** 'to convey/repeat'
> **etw. an jmdn. weiter*leiten** 'to pass sth. on to sb.'
> **jmdm. etw. aus*richten** 'to pass on a message/tell sb.'

Können Sie mir die genauen Worte *wiedergeben,* die der Anrufer benutzt hat?

Can you repeat the exact words that the caller used?

Ich habe Ihr Anliegen *an den* Personalchef *weitergeleitet.*

I have passed on your request to the Personnel Manager.

Ist irgendetwas für mich *ausgerichtet* worden?

Have any messages been left for me?

Kannst du *ihr* etwas *ausrichten*?

Can you give her a message?

(b) For recorded messages

Bitte *hinterlassen* Sie Ihre *Nachricht* auf dem Band.

Please leave your message on the tape.

(See **61.7e**B for messages on telephone answering machines)

(c) For writing messages, notes and memos

Bitte *notieren Sie sich* diesen Termin.

Please make a note of this appointment.

Habt ihr bei der Exkursion auch genügend *Notizen gemacht?*

Did you take enough notes during the field trip?

85.4

Second- and third-hand knowledge

To report rumours, hearsay and general gossip, the following are used:

(a) In order to indicate that the speaker distances himself or herself from what he or she is reporting, **sollen** is employed (see **35.6b**A for this special use of the modal verb):

> **Der Abgeordnete *soll* schon vor der Trennung untreu *gewesen sein*.**
> The MP is said to have been unfaithful even before the separation.

(b) To report gossip

> **Es hat *sich herumgesprochen*, wie schnell die Firma Pleite gemacht hat.**
> Word has spread about how quickly the company went bust.

(c) For rumours

> **Ich halte die Sache mit der Brandstiftung für *ein Gerücht*.**
> I consider this thing about the arson attack to be a rumour.

(d) Reporting things from hearsay

> **Das weiß ich nur *vom Hörensagen*.**
> I only know this from hearsay.

85.5 — **Not naming sources**

In order to avoid naming the person one has information from, the following are used:

> **sich** (= dat) **etw. sagen/raten lassen** 'to have sb. tell/advise one sth.'
> **sich** (= acc) **(in etw.) beraten lassen** 'to seek advice on sth.'
> **sich (etw./zu etw.) raten lassen** 'to seek advice on sth.'

> **Ich habe *mir sagen lassen*, daß die Hormontherapie doch unbekannte Nebenwirkungen haben könnte.**
> I have heard that hormone therapy could have unknown side effects after all.

> **Wir haben *uns* ärztlich/juristisch *beraten lassen*.**
> We have sought medical/legal advice.

(See also **84**B on sources of information)

86 *Expressing necessity*

86.1 — **Commands, instructions and public notices**

Instructions and notices are usually phrased in a neutral and impersonal style. They can occasionally sound off-putting and hence most of the constructions to be discussed in this section are for understanding rather than speaking. They are mostly found in written form, e.g. on noticeboards or in written communication from the authorities.

(a) Personal instructions tend to be given in the imperative (see **41**A):

> *Nehmen Sie* **die Tabletten dreimal täglich.**
> Take the tablets three times a day.

(b) General instructions and formal public notices often use impersonal infinitive constructions (see **33.7**A for parts of the verb):

> **Hier** *nicht parken.*
> Do not park here./No parking.

> **20 Minuten bei mittlerer Hitze** *backen.*
> Bake in a medium oven for 20 minutes.

> **Skier nur im Skiraum** *abstellen.*
> Skis must only be kept in ski room.

A number of these instructions also use a participle:

> **Parken** *verboten.*
> No parking./Parking prohibited.

> **Zutritt nicht** *gestattet.*
> Access not permitted./No access.

(c) Instructions which demand some form of action frequently use **ist** (etc.) + infinitive with **zu**:

> **Die Fahrkarten** *sind* **unaufgefordert** *vorzuzeigen.*
> All tickets must be shown (without being demanded). (On a train or bus)

> **Der Anspruch auf Arbeitslosenunterstützung** *ist nachzuweisen.*
> The right to unemployment benefit must be demonstrated.

(d) Instructions which are issued emphatically can also be expressed by means of the passive. Such instructions are likely to be used by someone in a position of authority.

> **Hier wird nicht geschlafen!**
> No sleeping allowed here!

With the emphasis on **wird**, this can sound much more forceful and unforgiving than the equivalent imperative construction (see **41**A for imperatives). It indicates a *general* restriction for everyone.

(e) Commands and instructions can be expressed more politely by using the modal verbs **dürfen**, **sollen** and **müssen**:

Use the modal verb + infinitive in the active:

> **Hier darf man nicht parken.**
> You must not park here.

> **Der Brief soll heute noch weggehen.**
> The letter is to go off today.

Or use the passive with a modal verb (see **40**A for the passive). This tends to sound more formal:

> **Hier darf nicht geraucht werden. (Hier darf man nicht rauchen.)**
> Smoking is not allowed here.

> **Die Papiere müssen an der Grenze vorgezeigt werden. (Man muß die Papiere an der Grenze vorzeigen.)**
> Documents must be shown at the border.

> **Der Kuchen muß bei 200 Grad gebacken werden. (Man muß den Kuchen bei 200 Grad backen.)**
> The cake has to be baked at 200 degrees.

86.2

Expressing and enquiring about obligation

(a) The most straightforward way of expressing obligation is to use **müssen** and **sollen** together with a full verb (see **35**A for modal verbs):

> **Du** *mußt* **heute noch den Brief** *fertigschreiben.*
> You still have to finish the letter today.

> **Ich** *soll* **heute länger im Büro** *bleiben.*
> I am supposed to work late at the office today.

> **Du** *sollst* **deinen Nächsten** *lieben* **wie dich selbst.**
> Thou shalt love thy neighbour as thyself. (Matthew 23.39)

müssen as used in the first example expresses an obligation which has to be met. **sollen** in the second example leaves room for a different course of action; the speaker could still decide to go home at the usual time. In the third example, **sollen** has a moral implication. It only acquires this meaning in a formal context, especially in the Bible.

(b) To express fulfilment of duty, use the following expressions:

> **-e Pflicht** 'obligation'
> **Pflichten haben** 'to have obligations'
> **die Pflicht haben, etwas zu tun** 'to have the obligation to do sth.'
> **meine** (etc.) **Pflicht sein, etwas zu tun** 'to be my (etc.) duty to do sth.'
> **seine** (etc.) **Pflichten** (+ adv) **erfüllen** 'to fulfil one's duties'
> **-e Verpflichtung** 'obligation/(professional) engagement/commitment'

> **Eltern** *haben* viele *Pflichten.*
> Parents have a lot of duties.

> **Ich** *habe die Pflicht*, Sie darüber *zu* **informieren.**
> I have the duty to inform you about this.

> **Es** *ist meine Pflicht*, Sie *zu* **warnen.**
> It is my duty to warn you.

> **Es** *ist unsere* traurige *Pflicht*, **den Tod unseres Mitarbeiters, Karl Otto, anzuzeigen.**
> It is our sad duty to announce the death of our colleague, Karl Otto.

(See also **65.3**B for 'Bereavement')

> **Er** *erfüllte* **immer** *treu seine Pflichten.*
> He always carried out his duties loyally.

Verpflichtung also means 'duty' but in the sense of 'committing oneself to sth.' **eine Verpflichtung** is not as unavoidable as **eine Pflicht**. In elevated style it is often found with the verb **nach*kommen** (+ dat) 'to fulfil':

> **Wegen Krankheit ist er leider verhindert, seinen** *Verpflichtungen* *nachzukommen.*
> Because of illness he is unfortunately unable to honour his commitments.

> **Die Charta von Helsinki beinhaltet die** *Verpflichtung zur* **Achtung der Menschenwürde.**
> The Helsinki Charter contains a commitment to respect the dignity of man.

(c) When somebody is relieved of their duties, use **von seinen** (etc.) **Pflichten entbunden werden**:

> **Alle leitenden Angestellten der Werft** *wurden* **zum 1. Dezember** *von ihren* *Pflichten entbunden.* (formal)
> All the shipyard managers were relieved of their duties from 1 December.

(d) The verb derived from **Pflicht** is **verpflichten** 'to oblige sb./place sb. under an obligation'. There are a number of structures and also fixed idiomatic expressions which use **verpflichten** in its participial form, i.e. **verpflichtet** (see **49**A):

> **sich verpflichtet fühlen, etw. zu tun** 'to feel obliged to do sth.'
> **verpflichtet sein, etw. zu tun** 'to be obliged to do sth.'
> **zu etw. verpflichtet sein** 'to be obliged/committed to sth.'

> **Ich** *fühle mich verpflichtet,* **ihm** *zu* **helfen.**
> I feel obliged to help him.

> **Wir** *sind verpflichtet,* **Sie vor den Konsequenzen Ihrer Handlung** *zu*
> **warnen.**
> We are obliged to warn you of the consequences of your action.

> **In diesem Fall** *sind Sie* **nicht** *zum* **Handeln** *verpflichtet.*
> In this case you are not obliged to act.

Note that in the above three patterns **verpflichtet** may be replaced by **sich gezwungen fühlen; zu etw. gezwungen sein; gezwungen sein, etw. zu tun. Gezwungen** implies an obligation that cannot be refused.

(e) **verpflichten** can also be used as a full verb with personal endings. There are a number of different constructions:

> **etw./jmd.** (nom) **verpflichtet jmdn. zu etw.** 'sth./sb. forces sb. to {do} sth.'
> **sie** (= nom) **verpflichtet sich** (= reflexive, acc) **für etw./zu etw.** 'she commits herself to sth.'
> **jmdn. zu etw. verpflichten** 'to commit sb. to sth./to book sb. for sth.'

> **Die Lage** *verpflichtet uns zu*m **Handeln.**
> The situation forces us to act.

> **Sie** *verpflichtete sich,* **zwei Jahre als Entwicklungshelferin nach**
> **Lateinamerika** *zu* **gehen.**
> She signed up to go to Latin America for two years as a development aid worker.

> **Wir** *verpflichten uns für/auf* **zwei Jahre** *zur* **Bundeswehr.**
> We are signing on with the (German) army for two years.

> **Es gelang uns, den berühmten Musiker zu einem Konzert** *zu verpflichten.*
> We managed to book the famous musician for a concert.

(f) Different types of obligation

Liability is commonly expressed using **haften für** (+ acc) 'to be liable for' and **-e Haftung für etw./jmdn.** 'liability for sth./sb.':

> **Eltern** *haften für* **ihre Kinder.**
> Parents are legally liable for their children.

> **Wir** *übernehmen* **keine** *Haftung für* **Feuerschäden.**
> We do not accept liability for fire damage.

There are many compound nouns based on **-pflicht-** and these are used in formal or official contexts, e.g. in a legal text. Where an adjective ending in **-pflichtig** exists, this is shown below:

> **In manchen Seminaren *herrscht Anwesenheitspflicht/ Präsenzpflicht.***
> Attendance is obligatory in some seminars.

> **Jeder Autofahrer muß mindestens *eine Haftpflichtversicherung* für seinen Wagen *haben/ haftpflichtversichert sein.***
> Every driver has to have third party insurance at least.

> **Widerrechtlich geparkte Fahrzeuge werden *kostenpflichtig* abgeschleppt.**
> Cars parked illegally will be towed away at the owner's expense.

> **Jeder Bürger in Deutschland *unterliegt der Meldepflicht* (= dat)/ *ist meldepflichtig.***
> Every German citizen is obliged to register at a public registration office. (In Germany this is called **Einwohnermeldeamt**).

> **Eltern *sind schadenersatzpflichtig/ müssen Schadenersatz leisten,* wenn ihre Kinder etwas angestellt haben.**
> Parents are liable for damages if their children get into mischief.

> **Die Untersuchungsergebnisse *unterliegen der Schweigepflicht* (= dat).**
> The results of the enquiry are subject to the rule of confidentiality.

> **Wir *haben* als Gewerkschaftsvertreter eine *Solidaritätspflicht* gegenüber den Streikenden.**
> As union representatives we have a duty to show solidarity with the people on strike.

> **Alle Instrumente sind auf dieser Reise *versicherungspflichtig.***
> On this journey all instruments must be insured.

> ***Zahlungspflicht besteht,* wenn Sie die Ware länger als 14 Tage behalten./Sie *sind zahlungspflichtig,* wenn Sie die Ware länger als 14 Tage behalten.**
> You are liable for payment if you retain the goods longer than 14 days.

> ***Zollpflichtige* Waren sind anzumelden.**
> Goods subject to duty have to be declared.

(g) The perception of obligation may be stronger in one language than the other. The idea of being bound to something and being liable can be expressed in a number of ways:

> **binden, bindend, gebunden sein** 'to bind, binding, be bound/be obliged'
> **ungebunden sein** 'not to be bound/be free'
> **jmdm. verbunden sein** 'to be obliged to sb.'
> **jmdn. in etw. ein*binden** 'to commit sb. to sth.'
> **verbindlich, unverbindlich** 'binding, not binding/without any obligation'

Viele Eltern möchten nicht, daß ihre Kinder sich zu früh *binden.*
Many parents don't want their children to tie themselves (i.e. get married) too early.

Der Vertrag ist *bindend.*
The contract is binding.

Das Team ist vertraglich an die Bedingungen *gebunden.*
The team is bound by contract to the conditions.

Sie ist noch *ungebunden.*
She is not yet committed (meaning in most contexts: she is not married yet).

Wir sind Ihnen für Ihre Hilfe sehr *verbunden.*
We are much obliged to you for your help.

Soll man die ehemaligen Ostblockstaaten *in* das Westliche Bündnis *einbinden*?
Should one allow the former Eastern Bloc states to join (and be committed to) the Western Alliance?

Darf ich Ihnen ein *unverbindlich*es Angebot machen?
May I make you an offer without any obligation on your part?

(h) Expressing legal or contractual obligation

All of the following are inherently formal:

> **-r Vertrag, vertrag-** 'contract, according to contract'
> **vertraglich/laut Vertrag/vertragsgemäß** 'according to contract'
> **gesetzlich** 'by law/lawful/statutory'
> **nach dem/laut Gesetz** 'by law'
> **jmdm. Rechenschaft (über etw.) schuldig sein** 'to be accountable to sb. (for sth.)'

Er ist *vertraglich verpflichtet/gebunden*, die Arbeit zu beenden.
He is contractually obliged to complete the work.

Die Höhe der Steuern wird *gesetzlich* festgelegt.
The level of taxes is set by law.

Nach dem Grund*gesetz* herrscht in der Bundesrepublik Pressefreiheit.
According to the German Constitution there is freedom of the press in
the Federal Republic.

Ich bin Ihnen *über* meine Freizeitaktivitäten überhaupt keine
Rechenschaft schuldig.
As far as my leisure activities are concerned, I am not accountable to you
at all.

(i) Commitment of a less binding nature can be expressed by using **fest*legen**. Its
literal meaning is 'to tie down' and it is used in two principal patterns:

---

sich (= acc) **auf etw.** (= acc) **fest*legen/jmdn. auf etw. fest*legen** 'to commit
oneself/sb. to sth.'
etw. (= acc) **fest*legen** 'to lay down/stipulate sth.'
jmdn. fest*nageln 'to commit sb. to sth./to pin sb. down' (colloquial)

Wir hatten *uns darauf festgelegt,* am Wochenende nach Paris *zu* fahren.
We had committed ourselves to going to Paris at the weekend.

Der Chef *legte* seine Mitarbeiter *auf* diese Vorgehensweise *fest.*
The boss committed his staff to this way of proceeding.

Sie *legte fest, daß* nur sechs Teilnehmer in einer Gruppe zusammen sein
sollten.
She stipulated that there should only be six participants in one group.

Es *wurde* ein Kostenbeitrag *festgelegt.*
The contribution to the cost was determined.

The first three examples above place the emphasis on the doer, whereas in this last
example, which employs the passive voice, the doer remains anonymous.

(See **42.3g**A for the dummy subject **es**)

Als er mich traf, hat er *mich* gleich *festgenagelt,* ihm bei seinem Umzug zu
helfen.
When he met me he immediately made me (firmly) promise to help him
move house.

Sie *läßt sich* nicht *festnageln,* ob sie nächstes Wochenende kommt.
She won't be pinned down as to whether she is coming next weekend.

86.3 Acting contrary to obligation

All of the following are inherently formal:

> **(s)eine Pflicht/Verpflichtung verletzen/vernachlässigen** 'to neglect/act contrary to one's/a duty'
> **pflichtvergessen sein** 'to neglect one's duties'
> **gegen eine Pflicht verstoßen** 'to fail to carry out a duty'
> **gegen ein Gesetz verstoßen** 'to break/contravene a law'

> Er *vergißt seine* (etc.) *Pflichten/*ist *pflichtvergessen.*
> He forgets his duties.

> Sie *vernachlässigt/*verletzt *ihre Pflichten.*
> She neglects/acts contrary to her duties.

> Ihre Handlung *verstößt gegen* Paragraph 221.
> Your act contravenes paragraph 221.

Actions contrary to contracts, duties or laws can be described in the following way:

gesetzes*widrig*	'contrary to (the) law/illegal'
vertrags*widrig*	'in breach of contract'
sitten*widrig*	'against good manners/immoral'
vertrags*brüchig* werden	'to default on one's contract'
der Vertrags*bruch*	'breach of contract'
einen Vertrag *brechen*	'to break a contract'
gegen einen Vertrag *verstoßen*	'to break/contravene a contract'

86.4 Absence of obligation

> **nicht verpflichtet sein, etw. zu tun** 'to not have to do sth.' (formal)
> **nicht gezwungen sein, etw. zu tun** 'to not be forced to do sth.'
> **etw. nicht zu tun brauchen** 'to not need to do sth.'

The expressions **nicht verpflichtet sein**, **nicht gezwungen sein** and words ending in **-pflichtig** tend to be rather formal:

> Ich *bin nicht verpflichtet,* mir das anzuhören.
> I don't have to listen to this.

> Sie *waren nicht gezwungen,* mir zu helfen.
> You were not forced to help me.

> Diese Waren *sind nicht* zoll*pflichtig.*
> These goods are not dutiable.

A common way of expressing that there is no obligation is to use **nicht brauchen** (see also **35.7**A):

> **Du *brauchst* den Artikel heute *nicht* mehr fertigzuschreiben.**
> You don't need to/don't have to finish the article today.

> **Ich *brauche* heute *nicht* länger im Büro *zu* bleiben.**
> Today I don't need to do overtime at the office.

nicht müssen is ambiguous, and depending on context can imply either the absence of obligation or an obligation in the negative. Which meaning is implied becomes clear from the context and, in the spoken language, from the tone of voice:

> **Du mußt das Referat heute nicht mehr fertigschreiben.**
> You don't need to/don't have to finish the paper today.

Here, we are dealing with an absence of obligation.

> **Ihr müßt nicht immer zu spät kommen.**
> You *mustn't* always be late.

In this example a clear obligation is implied (compare: **Ihr dürft nicht immer zu spät kommen**), although it is expressed indirectly.

86.5 Freeing somebody from obligation

> **jmdn von etw. frei*stellen** 'to exempt sb. from sth./to second sb.'
> **jmdm. etw. (= acc) erlassen** 'to let sb. off sth./waive sth.'
> **jmdn. von etw. befreien** 'to free sb. from sth.'

For military service and jobs:

> **Er *wurde* vom Militärdienst *freigestellt*.**
> He was exempted from military service.

For tasks, sins, debts where exceptional concessions are implied:

> **Sie *haben mir* die Hausaufgaben *erlassen*.**
> I was let off the homework.

Where a formal act by somebody in authority is required:

> **Die Schülerin war für Donnerstag vom Unterricht befreit.**
> The pupil was excused from school for Thursday.

87 *Expressing ability to do something*

(See **74.5**B on 'Capabilities and talents', **101.1**B for **wissen/kennen** and **35**A for modal verbs)

Physical and mental ability

(a) These can both be expressed by using **können** and **-s Können**:

> Er *konnte* schon mit sechs Jahren Flöte spielen.
> He could already play the recorder when he was six.

> Das große *Können* des Geigers beeindruckte die Zuhörer.
> The violinist's great skill impressed the audience.

In some instances, **können** has no accompanying verb where it must take one in English:

> *Kannst* du jetzt das Zehner Einmaleins?
> Can you do the ten times table now?

> Ich *kann* das Stück jetzt.
> I can play the (musical) piece now.

> Sie *kann* Spanisch.
> She can speak Spanish.

(b) Sensual ability is expressed using **-s -vermögen**

> **-s Sehvermögen/Hörvermögen/Sprechvermögen** '(physical) ability to see/hear/speak'

(c) Expressing stamina

In this context, **-s -vermögen** is occasionally used in a figurative sense:

> **-s Stehvermögen, Standvermögen** 'staying power'
> **-s Durchhaltevermögen** 'endurance'

Where means or power to bring something about rather than physical or mental ability are to be stressed, the following expressions can be used for precision:

> Die Familie *war* nicht *in der Lage*, das Haus zu kaufen.
> The family was not in a position to buy the house.

> Er *wäre imstande*, so eine Dummheit zu begehen. (formal)
> He would be capable of such a blunder.

> Sie *erklärten sich außerstande*, einen Kompromiß zu finden. (formal)
> They said that they were not in a position to find a compromise.

—— **87.3** —— When the result of an effort is referred to, the verb **schaffen** (**schaffte, geschafft**) 'to get done' is used:

> **Die Läuferin** *schaffte* **einen neuen Weltrekord über 100 Meter.**
> The sprinter achieved a new world record over 100 metres.

> **Die Kinder konnten ihre Hausaufgaben kaum** *schaffen.*
> The children could hardly manage their homework.

Alternatively, **etwas fertig*bringen** and **etwas gelingt jmdm.** emphasize that something has been achieved against odds or expectations:

> **Die Vierjährige** *hatte* **es doch** *fertiggebracht,* **die ganze Tapete in ihrem Kinderzimmer bunt zu malen.**
> The four-year-old managed to paint all the wallpaper in her room.

> *Es gelang uns,* **den Kaufpreis um 10% herunterzuhandeln.**
> We managed to negotiate the purchase price down by 10%.

—— **87.4** —— ## Skills and ability

(a) Where skills which result from training are emphasized, **fähig** 'able' and its derivatives are employed:

> **Sie ist eine unserer** *fähigsten* **Mitarbeiterinnen.**
> She is one of our most capable employees.

> **Er war so schockiert, daß er** *unfähig* **war, etwas zu tun.**
> He was so shocked that he was incapable of doing anything.

(b) **Fähigkeiten** and **Fertigkeiten** are often mentioned together and it is difficult to distinguish the two terms. **Fertigkeiten** may, depending on context, refer to manual skills, whereas **Fähigkeiten** can be of a more complex nature. **handwerkliche Fertigkeiten** are the skills the craftsman (**der Handwerker**) needs to handle the tools. However, his **Fähigkeiten** consist in planning, carrying out, finishing and checking the job. A few compounds where the distinction is less clear cut are given below:

> **-e Schreibfertigkeit** 'ability to produce a letter physically'
> **-e Schreibfähigkeit** 'ability to think out a text and write it down'
> **Lesefertigkeiten** 'basic reading skills': the operation of putting letters together and the ability to recognize a word and its sense
> **Lesefähigkeiten** 'higher reading skills': the skill to differentiate the visual and acoustic shape of a letter; the ability to recognize the structure of a text and, for example, read it out loud in a meaningful way.

88 *Conveying doubt and certainty*

88.1 Defining the degree of certainty

Adverbs can qualify the degree to which something is certain (here arranged in approximate order of increasing probability):

> **auf keinen Fall, in keinem Fall, keinesfalls, keineswegs** 'no way, on no account'
> **kommt nicht in Frage** 'out of the question'
> **kaum, unwahrscheinlich** 'hardly, unlikely'
> **ungewiß** 'uncertain'
> **unklar** 'unclear'
> **einigermaßen wahrscheinlich** 'quite possible'
> **(ziemlich) wahrscheinlich** '(quite) probable'
> **wahrscheinlich** 'probable'
> **fast sicher** 'nearly certain'
> **bestimmt** 'certain'
> **sicher, gewiß** 'certain'
> **klar** 'clear'
> **auf jeden Fall, in jedem Fall** 'most certainly'

Accordingly, predictions can be made:

> **etw. mit ziemlicher Wahrscheinlichkeit an*nehmen** 'to assume sth. with reasonable probability'
> **etw. mit ziemlicher Sicherheit/ziemlich sicher wissen** 'to know sth. with reasonable certainty'
> **etw. mit Bestimmtheit/bestimmt wissen** 'to know sth. for certain'

88.2 Disclaiming personal responsibility and authenticating information which is passed on

(See **84**B and **85**B for further functions in this context)

(a) Personal responsibility can be disclaimed by using the subjunctive mood (see **39**A). Thus the newscaster will report:

> **Die Politikerin meinte, daß die Regierung die Steuern jetzt senken müßte.**
> The politician said that the government should lower taxes now.

(b) A further way of distancing oneself is to use the modal verb **sollen** (see **35.6b**A). Compare the following pairs of examples, those on the left expressing certainty, those on the right expressing doubt:

Er *ist* ein fanatischer Fußballfan.	**Er *soll* ein fanatischer Fußballfan *sein*.**
He is a football fanatic.	He is supposed to be a fanatical football fan.
Sie *war* eine berühmt-berüchtigte Frau.	**Sie *soll* eine berühmt-berüchtigte Frau *gewesen sein*.**
She was a notorious woman.	She is said to have been a notorious woman.

(c) Particularly when you want to repeat something that has been stated as a fact but for which there is no real proof, you may want to use the modal verb **müssen** (see **35.6b**A). The insertion of **wohl** 'probably' emphasizes that an assumed fact is being reported:

Dieser Historiker *hat* einen klaren Verstand.	**Nach dem, was man hört, *muß* dieser Historiker (*wohl*) einen klaren Verstand *haben*.**
This historian has a clear mind.	Going by what one hears, this historian must have a clear mind.
Die Königin *war* eine stolze Frau.	**Nach Presseberichten *muß* die Königin eine stolze Frau *gewesen sein*.**
The queen was a proud woman.	According to press reports the queen must have been a proud woman.

(d) Direct responsibility for information or opinions given can also be avoided by showing that one's knowledge is limited or by giving the source of the information. The indicative usually follows:

> ***Soweit mir bekannt ist*, wußte sie nichts von dem Plan.**
> As far as I am aware she didn't know anything about the plan.

> ***Nach Augenzeugenberichten* hat der Fahrer des Wagens die Ampel bei Rot überfahren.**
> According to eye witness accounts the driver of the car jumped the lights.

> ***Den Berichten zufolge* muß man sich auf einen längeren Eisenbahnstreik einrichten.**
> According to the reports people have to prepare themselves for quite a long railway strike.

> ***Man sagt allgemein*, daß es eine Krise in der Europapolitik gibt.**
> It is being said generally that there is a crisis in European politics.

> ***Wir wissen aus sicherer Quelle*, daß alle Passagiere die Notlandung unverletzt überstanden haben.**
> We know from reliable sources that all passengers have survived the emergency landing unhurt.

88.3

Expressing surprise at something improbable or unexpected

(See also **114**B for expressing surprise)

Formal expressions include:

> **Das kommt völlig überraschend für mich!**
> It comes as a total surprise to me!

> **Ich kann das kaum glauben!**
> I can hardly believe it!

> **Das ist doch einfach nicht zu fassen/zu glauben!**
> It is simply unbelievable!

More informally the following expressions are useful without causing offence:

> **Das gibt es doch nicht!/Das darf doch nicht wahr sein!**
> It cannot be true!/Oh no!

> **So etwas darf es doch einfach nicht geben!**
> Something like this is simply not supposed to happen!

> **Er hat *sage und schreibe* 500DM für vier Stunden Arbeit verlangt.**
> He charged, would you believe, 500DM for four hours work.

89

Expressing assumptions, discussing possibility, probability and conditions

89.1

Simple assumptions can be introduced in a number of ways:

> ***Es könnte sein,* daß er nichts über den Plan gewußt hat.**
> It could be that he didn't know anything about the plan.

> ***Ich nehme an,* daß er davon weiß.**
> I assume that he knows about it.

> ***Es ist/wäre möglich,* daß er nichts von der Affäre gewußt hat.**
> It is conceivable that he knew nothing of the affair.

These introductory clauses can be avoided by using the future or future perfect (see **34.3–34.4**A). There is no particular difference in stylistic level; the degree of certainty about the assumption made is introduced by inserting adverbs such as **sicher** 'certainly', **wohl** 'probably', **möglicherweise** 'possibly' or **vielleicht** 'perhaps':

> **Er *wird* vielleicht nichts über den Plan *gewußt haben*.**
> He may perhaps not have known about the plan.

> **Er** *wird* **wohl davon wissen.**
> He will probably know about it.

> **Er** *wird* **möglicherweise nichts von der Affäre** *gewußt haben.*
> He may possibly not have known anything about the affair.

A statement such as

> **Am Sonntag wird es ja wieder regnen.**
> On Sunday it is bound to rain again.

is an expression of resignation (emphasized by **ja** and **wieder**) – in the context here this means that the following Sunday is expected to be as rainy (and hence as boring and uneventful) as all the previous ones.

89.2 Assumptions in a scientific context are conveyed by Subjunctive I or II, depending on the construction (see **39.4b**A for this use):

> **'A'** *sei* **die Länge einer Seite im Dreieck.**
> Let 'A' be the length of one side in a triangle.

Such a hypothesis, particularly where it is not strictly scientific, can also be introduced as follows:

> *Gesetzt den Fall,* **die Theorie stimmt/stimmte, dann** *würde sich* **die Erde jedes Jahrzehnt um ein paar Grad** *erwärmen.*
> Assuming the theory is correct, the earth would get a few degrees warmer every decade.

> *Angenommen,* **er hat alles gewußt, dann** *hätte* **er ihr** *Bescheid sagen müssen.*
> Assuming he knew everything he should have let her know.

The conclusion deduced from the assumption must be in the conditional. Instead of a conclusion there may be a question:

> *Angenommen,* **sie hat recht mit ihrer Behauptung, was** *würdest* **du ihr** *raten?*
> Assuming she is right in her assertion, what would you advise her to do?

89.3 **Expressing a condition when it can and is likely to be fulfilled**
A condition which can be fulfilled is expressed by using a **wenn** clause. In English, such a condition could be introduced by either 'if' or 'when':

> *Wenn* **es regnet, gehen wir nicht in die Berge.**
> If it rains we don't go walking in the mountains.

> **Wenn sie den Manager ruft, kommt er sofort.**
> When she calls for the manager he comes immediately.

(See also **82**B for cause and effect)

wenn can be avoided by beginning the subordinate clause with the verb and introducing a **so** at the beginning of the main clause. This results in a much more formal style which tends to be found in written German:

> **Regnet es, so gehen wir nicht in die Berge.**
> **Ruft sie den Manager, so kommt er gleich.**

(See also **8.5**A for this construction)

89.4 Making hypotheses

Hypotheses fall into two categories:

(a) about an event which may or may not take place, using Subjunctive II with present or future reference (see also **39.2–39.3**A):

> **Wenn sie mich *liebte, würde* sie mich heiraten.**
> If she loved me she would marry me.

> **Wenn er in der Stadt *wäre, würde* er uns besuchen.**
> If he was in town he would visit us.

> **Wäre er in der Stadt, so würde er uns besuchen.**

It is probable that she *doesn't* love him and that he *is not* in town, but in principle these conditions *could* be fulfilled or the event *could* still happen.

(See **8.5**A and **89.3**B for the construction without **wenn**)

(b) about an event which can no longer take place using the Subjunctive II in the past with past reference (see also **39.2–39.3**A):

> **Wenn sie mich *geliebt hätte, hätte* sie mich *geheiratet.***
> **Wenn sie mich *geliebt hätte, würde* sie mich *geheiratet haben.***
> If she had loved me she would have married me.

> **Wenn er in der Stadt *gewesen wäre, hätte* er uns *besucht.***
> **Wenn er in der Stadt *gewesen wäre, würde* er uns *besucht haben.***
> If he had been in town he would have visited us.

> **Wäre er in der Stadt *gewesen, so würde* er uns *besucht haben.***

The conditions under which a certain (desired) event could have taken place (i.e. a wedding and a visit) were not fulfilled at the time and hence the event did not happen.

The verb of the **wenn** clause needs to be in the past tense of the second subjunctive. In the main clause there is a choice between either another second subjunctive in the past tense (e.g. **hätte gemacht**, **wäre gewesen**), or **würde** with the past participle of the main verb plus **haben** or **sein**.

(See **8A** for word order in subordinate clauses)

XIII *Transactions: getting things done*

90 *Attracting attention*

(See also **61.1**B on 'Making initial contact')

Attracting attention in a dangerous situation

Hilfe!
Help!

Feuer!
Fire!

Vorsicht!
Be careful!

Hallo!
Hello!

(**Hallo!** is not necessarily understood as a request for rescue but as a casual greeting. Only when shouted out with a prolonged **a** does it mean a call for help in dire circumstances.)

(See also **60.2a**B)

Achtung!
Beware!/Watch out!

Attracting someone's attention when he or she is busy

Darf ich mal kurz stören. (polite)
May I interrupt you for a moment.

Entschuldigen Sie bitte. (polite)
Excuse me, please.

Hallo, Sie da!/He, Sie da! (rude)
Heh, you there!

> **Sie, hören Sie mal!** (rude)
> You, listen!

Requests for attention using the Subjunctive II are particularly polite though not deferential (see **39.2b**A):

> *Dürfte* **ich mal kurz stören.**
> If I might interrupt you for a moment.

> **Wenn Sie einen Moment Zeit für mich** *hätten.*
> If you could spare me a moment.

> **Wenn ich Sie mal gerade unterbrechen** *dürfte.*
> If I could just interrupt you for a moment.

> **Entschuldigen Sie, ich** *hätte* **eine Frage.**
> Excuse me, I'd like to ask a question.

90.3 Turning one's attention to somebody

(a) In order to help

> **Ja, bitte?**
> Yes? (How can I help you?)

> **Was kann ich für Sie tun?**
> What can I do for you?

> **Worum handelt es sich?** (formal)
> What is it about?

> **Worum geht es?** (informal)
> What is it about?

> **Worum geht's?** (very informal)
> What is it about?

> **Was gibt es?** (can be impatient)
> What is it?

> **Womit kann ich (Ihnen) dienen?** (very formal, in a shop or an office)
> How can I help/serve you?

> **Was darf's sein?** (in shop or restaurant)
> What would you like?

> **Was möchten/wollen Sie?** (can easily sound off-putting)
> What do you want?

Was ist denn nun wieder los? (when you are annoyed about repeated disturbance)

What is wrong *now*?

(b) In order to send somebody away

Nicht jetzt, bitte.
Not now, please.

Bei mir sind Sie da falsch. (this can be indifferent or rude, depending on tone)
I am not the person you need to see (about the matter).

Ich bin (leider) nicht für Sie/dafür zuständig.
(I'm sorry but) I am not the person responsible (for you/for the matter).

90.4 **Requesting patience**

(See also **103**B and **81.8–11**B for expressions of time referring to future intentions)

(a) **der Augenblick/der Moment** 'moment' suggest a wait of a few minutes:

Einen Moment/Augenblick, bitte.
Just a moment, please.

Wenn Sie bitte einen Augenblick warten würden. (very polite)
If you wouldn't mind waiting for a moment, please.

Moment noch! (fairly informal)
Just another moment! – I won't keep you much longer.

Bitte nehmen Sie im Wartezimmer Platz. (at the doctor's)
Please have a seat in the waiting room.

(b) Requesting more patience

-e Geduld, sich gedulden 'patience, be patient' (formal)

Darf ich noch *um* ein paar Minuten *Geduld* bitten.
May I ask you to be patient for just a few more minutes.

Sie müssen *sich* leider noch ein wenig *gedulden.*
You'll have to be patient a little longer, I am afraid.

Putting in **leider** 'unfortunately' makes the request for patience sound more polite:

Es dauert (leider) noch ungefähr eine Stunde.
It'll take about another hour, I am afraid.

> **Ihr Wagen ist (leider) erst in etwa einer Stunde fertig.**
> Your car will not be ready for about an hour, I am afraid.

90.5

Non-verbal ways of attracting attention

(a) When you are about to propose a toast or make a speech before or after dinner it is common to clink a spoon against your glass, thus attracting everybody's attention.

(b) When you want to attract a waiter's/waitress's attention in a restaurant, lift your hand when the waiter/waitress next comes by your table. She or he will probably say **Sofort** 'I'll be right there' or **Einen Moment, bitte.** 'Just a moment, please'.

(c) When you want to stop a bus at a request stop (**-e Bedarfshaltestelle**), lift your arm vertically and show your palm in the direction from which the bus is coming or simply wave.

91 Helping and advising

91.1

Asking for help

> **jmdm. helfen** 'to help sb.'
> **jmdm. bei/mit etw. helfen** 'to help sb. with sth.'
> **jmdm. helfen, etw. zu tun** 'to help sb. to do sth.'
> **-e Hilfe** 'help'
> **Hilfe leisten** 'to help' (formal style, see **91.5**B)

As in English, you can ask for help by using a modal verb in the indicative or, more politely, in the Subjunctive II (see **39.2b**A). Inserting **bitte** 'please' in a request is always a good idea:

> **Könn(t)en Sie *mir* bitte *bei/mit* diesem Problem *helfen*.**
> Can/Could you please help me with this problem.

> **Würden Sie *mir* bitte *helfen*, den schweren Karton in meinen Wagen *zu* heben.**
> Would you please help me to lift this heavy box into my car.

> **Darf/Dürfte ich Ihre *Hilfe* in Anspruch nehmen.** (very formal)
> May/Might I make use of your help.

> **Wenn Sie einen Unfall sehen, müssen Sie Hilfe leisten.**
> If you see an accident you must assist.

(b) To request a favour rather than help, use **jmdm. einen Gefallen tun**:

Kannst/Könntest du mir bitte *einen Gefallen tun* und heute einkaufen gehen.
Can/Could you please do me a favour and do some shopping today.

(c) **bitten** 'to ask' can be used as a stylistically versatile introduction to requests:

> **(jmdn.) um etw.** (= acc) **bitten** 'to ask (sb.) for sth.'
> **jmdn. bitten, etw zu tun** 'to ask sb. to do sth.'
> **(jmdn.) um Hilfe** (etc.) **bitten** 'to ask sb. for help' (etc).

Darf ich *um* Ihren Beitrag *bitten*?
May I ask for your contribution?

Darf ich Sie *bitten*, unsere Partei bei den nächsten Wahlen *zu* unterstützen?
May I ask you to support our party in the next elections?

Darf/Dürfte ich Sie *um* Hilfe *bitten*?
May/Might I ask you for help?

(d) Although requests using the Subjunctive II are already very polite and leave the addressee a sufficient amount of 'breathing space', you may feel you want to be even less direct. This can be done by introducing your request with a variety of **würde** constructions:

Würde es Ihnen etwas ausmachen, wenn ich heute erst später käme?
Would you mind if I came later today?

Würde es Ihnen etwas ausmachen, heute später zu kommen?
Would you mind coming a little later today?

Würden Sie bitte so freundlich sein, und mir beim Ausfüllen dieses Formulars behilflich sein.
OR *Würden Sie bitte so freundlich sein, mir beim Ausfüllen dieses Formulars zu helfen.*
Would you be so kind as to help me fill in this form.

Würdest du bitte so nett sein, und meine Mutter anrufen.
Would you be so kind as to ring my mother.

91.2 — **Replying to a request for help**

(a) Positively

As a positive reply to a direct request for help, you might say:

Ja, gerne.
Yes, with pleasure.

Ja, natürlich./Aber natürlich.
Yes, of course.

(Aber) selbstverständlich.
But of course.

Klar doch! (informal)
Of course.

Ja sofort.
Yes, right away.

Ja, ich komme gleich.
Yes, I'm just coming.

In reply to a request asking whether you would mind (doing) something, use:

Nein, das *macht mir* gar *nichts*/wirklich nichts *aus*.
No, I wouldn't mind at all.

Nein, das *mache ich* doch *gern* (für Sie/dich).
No, I'll gladly do it (for you).

doch emphasizes **gern** here.

(b) As a negative reply to a direct request for help, you may say:

Nein, ich *kann* Ihnen *leider nicht helfen*.
No, unfortunately I cannot help you.

Nein, *im Moment nicht*.
No, not right now.

Es *tut mir leid, aber* ich kann Ihnen da nicht helfen.
I am sorry, but I cannot help you there.

Leider *weiß* ich *selbst nicht*, wie man das Formular ausfüllt.
Unfortunately I don't know how to fill in the form myself.

Tut *mir leid, aber* ich habe selbst keine Ahnung.
I am sorry, I haven't got a clue myself.

To give a negative reply to a request asking whether you would mind (doing) something, you might say:

Nein, das *ist* leider (heute) *nicht möglich*./Nein, das geht (heute) leider nicht.
No, it is unfortunately not possible (today).

> **Nein, das *ist mir* im Moment *nicht recht.***
> No, it's a little inconvenient at the moment.

> **Nein, das *paßt mir* heute *nicht/schlecht.***
> No, it's inconvenient today (lit. suits me badly today).

Note that in German you need to be more direct than in English to be understood.

91.3 **Offering advice**

Advice and suggestions can be offered bluntly by using the indicative or, more sensitively, by employing the suggestive mode of the Subjunctive II (see **39.2bA**). Alternatively, a rhetorical question may be used; this would be less formal.

Compare:

> **Wir *raten* Ihnen *zu* diesem Kauf.**
> We advise you to accept this deal.

> **Wir *würden* Ihnen zu diesem Kauf *raten.***
> We would advise you to accept this deal.

> ***Warum* kaufen Sie *nicht!*?**
> Why don't you accept the deal!?

As it is polite not to force one's own views on a stranger or semi-stranger, a structure involving the Subjunctive II would normally be the most appropriate:

> **jmdm. raten** 'to advise sb.'
> **(jmdm.) von etw. ab*raten** 'to advise (sb.) against sth.'
> **(jmdm.) zu etw. zu*raten** 'to advise (sb.) to do sth.'

> **Ich würde Ihnen *raten*, das Angebot an*zu*nehmen.**
> I would advise you to accept the offer.

> **Wir würden (Ihnen) *von* diesem Angebot *abraten.***
> We would advise (you) against this offer.

> **Unser Anwalt würde (Ihnen) nicht *zu* diesem Vorgehen *zuraten.***
> Our solicitor would not advocate this procedure.

Further introductory phrases include:

> ***In Ihrer Situation/In Ihrem Fall* würde ich erst mal abwarten.**
> In your situation/case I would wait and see.

> ***Ich würde sagen*, da muß man einen Fachmann fragen.**
> I would say you ought to ask an expert in this matter.

An Ihrer Stelle **würde ich jetzt kein großes Risiko eingehen.**
If I were you I would not take any big risks now.

Wie wäre es, wenn **Sie doch noch einmal mit Ihrer Chefin sprächen?**
How about talking to your boss again?

Alternatively, start your question with a modal verb in the Subjunctive II (see **39.2b**A and **39.3d**A) and use **nicht**:

Sollten **Sie nicht erstmal mit Ihrem Rechtsanwalt sprechen?**
Shouldn't you talk to your solicitor first?

Könnten **Sie nicht mit der Bahn fahren, wo Ihr Auto kaputt ist?**
Couldn't you take the train as your car has broken down?

Dürfte **das nicht etwas teuer sein?**
Might that not be a little too expensive?

Müßten **Sie da nicht erst eine staatliche Genehmigung haben?**
Wouldn't you have to have/Shouldn't you have a state permit first?

Möchten **Sie nicht doch lieber warten, bis Sie mit Ihrer Frau gesprochen haben?**
Wouldn't you rather wait until you have talked to your wife?

91.4 — **Accepting help or advice**

(See **67.1–67.5**B on thanking for help and declining help as well as responding to thanks)

Comments on advice offered in approximate order from slight hesitation to enthusiastic approval:

Hm, das wäre vielleicht möglich.
Hm, that might be possible.

Ja, das könnte gehen.
Yes, that could work.

Danke, daß Sie mich darauf aufmerksam machen. Daran hatte ich noch gar nicht gedacht.
Thank you for drawing my attention to this. I hadn't thought of that at all.

Das ist eine gute/eine prima/keine schlechte Idee.
That is a good/an excellent/not a bad idea.

Ja, stimmt, da haben Sie völlig recht.
Yes, true, you are quite right there.

Mensch, daß ich darauf nicht selbst gekommen bin. Du liegst da genau richtig! (informal, between good friends).
(Oh) yes, I wonder why I didn't think of that myself. You are spot on there!

Different types of help and support

The English term 'help' and its partial synonyms 'aid' and 'support' have quite a wide range of German equivalents:

(a) Financial support

-e Arbeitslosenhilfe money received by people who no longer qualify for 'unemployment benefit' (**-s Arbeitslosengeld**)
-e Sozialhilfe 'income support'
Sozialhilfe beziehen 'to be on income support'
-e Hilfe, -e Unterstützung beantragen 'to claim benefits'
-e Beihilfe financial contribution paid, for example, by the state on civil servants' health insurance
-e Starthilfe 'jump start/pump priming' (either of a car or a business venture)
-e Unterstützung, unterstützend 'support, supporting'
-e Arbeitslosenunterstützung 'unemployment benefits' (in general)
unterstützende Maßnahmen treffen 'to take measures in order to support sth.'
-e Subvention 'subsidy'
jmdn./etw. subventionieren 'to subsidize sb./sth.'

Er bezieht jetzt schon seit drei Monaten *Sozialhilfe*.
He has been receiving income support for three months now.

Hast du schon *Beihilfe* für deine letzte Arztrechnung beantragt?
Have you already claimed for your last doctor's bill?

Die osteuropäischen Länder brauchen bei der Umstellung ihrer Wirtschaft *Starthilfe* vom Westen.
The countries of Eastern Europe need pump priming to reform their economies.

Wenn keine *unterstützenden Maßnahmen* für die Kohleindustrie *getroffen werden*, ist sie in Deutschland bald tot.
If no measures are taken to support the German coal industry it will soon be dead.

Sollte man die europäische Stahlindustrie *mit* Steuergeldern *subventionieren*?

Should one subsidize the European steel industry by means of tax payers' money?

(b) Providing moral support

> **-r Beistand** 'support'
> **jmdm. bei*stehen** 'to support sb.'

Ich bin nur mitgekommen, um meinem Sohn *moralischen Beistand* zu leisten.
I've only come along to give my son moral support.

Danke allen, die *mir* nach meinem schweren Verlust so treu *beigestanden* haben.
Thank you to all those who have supported me so loyally after my tragic loss.

(c) Promoting or supporting somebody

> **-e Erste Hilfe** 'First Aid'
> **jmdn./etw. fördern** 'to promote/give special attention to sb./sth.'
> **-e Förderung** 'promotion/support'
> **Förder-** 'promoting...'
> **fördernde Maßnahmen** supportive measures designed to help a person, a region, a company, etc. which has difficulties coping or deserves encouragement
> synonyms: **-e Förderungsmaßnahme, -e Fördermaßnahme** (bureaucratic)

Jeder sollte wissen, wie man *Erste Hilfe leistet*.
Everybody should know how to administer First Aid.

In Deutschland muß man einen *Verbandskasten* im Wagen haben.
In Germany you have to have a First Aid kit in your car.

Elite*förderung* ist für manche politischen Gruppen ein rotes Tuch.
Measures to further an elite are anathema to some political groups.

Das BaföG (Bundesausbildungs*förderung*sgesetz) sollte Chancengleichheit für alle Studierwilligen schaffen.
The BaföG (federal law guaranteeing financial aid to financially worse-off students) was intended to provide equal opportunities for all those who wanted to study.

Welche *fördernden Maßnahmen* sind in dieser Schule für lernschwache Kinder vorgesehen?

Which supporting measures are provided for children with learning difficulties in this school?

92 *Asking for something to be done*

Errands and similar activities
(a)

> Specific terms:
> **etw besorgen** 'to go on an errand (in order to get sth.)/to acquire sth.'
> **etw. erledigen** 'to get sth. done (possibly on an errand)/carry out sth.'
> **eine Erledigung/Besorgung machen** 'to go on an errand'
> General terms:
> **tun, machen** (and other verbs) 'to do'

Requests for errands are best made with a polite question using the subjunctive:

> *Würden Sie das bitte für mich tun/erledigen.*
> Would you please do this for me/attend to this for me.

> *Könnten Sie bitte die Post erledigen.*
> Could you please deal with the post.

> *Würden Sie mir bitte noch Schweizer Franken besorgen./Würden Sie bitte noch Schweizer Franken für mich besorgen.*
> Would you please also get me some Swiss francs.

> *Könnten Sie den Brief bitte noch heute für uns schreiben?*
> Could you please write the letter for us (as early as) today?

(b) Giving someone responsibility for doing something

> **zuständig sein für etw.** 'to be responsible for sth.'
> **zu*sehen, daß etw. geschieht** 'to ensure that sth. gets done'

> **Herr Kleinschmidt, Sie *sind* heute *für* den Empfang der ausländischen Gäste *zuständig*.**
> Mr Kleinschmidt, you are responsible for welcoming the foreign guests today.

> **Er kann das nicht unterschreiben. Das *liegt* nicht *in* seinem *Zuständigkeitsbereich/Kompetenzbereich*.**
> He cannot sign this. It is not within his remit/authority.

Bitte *sehen* Sie *zu, daß* der Kostenvoranschlag bis morgen beim Kunden ist.

Please see to it that the estimate is with the client by tomorrow.

Emphasizing the importance of a task

Wir *wären dankbar, wenn* Sie sich den Fehler gleich ansehen könnten.

We would be grateful if you could look at the fault immediately.

Es *ist für uns wichtig, daß* dieser Auftrag noch heute ausgeliefert wird.

It is important for us that this order goes out today.

Der Kunde *legt großen Wert darauf, daß* wir die Anleitung in Deutsch, Englisch und Französisch liefern.

It is very important for the client that we deliver the manual in German, English and French.

Es ist *unabdingbar/unerläßlich, daß* die Qualität bei jedem Einzelstück überprüft wird.

It is essential that the quality of every single item gets checked.

Refusing something which you have no authority to grant

All of the following are fairly abrupt:

Das müssen Sie (selbst) wissen.

You should know (not me)./That is your concern, not mine.

Da mußt du selbst zusehen.

You'll have to take care of that yourself.

Sehen Sie erstmal selbst zu, wie Sie zurechtkommen.

First see how you manage on your own.

Dafür sind wir hier nicht zuständig.

We don't deal with that here.

Die Entscheidung liegt nicht bei mir.

The decision is not up to me.

They can be toned down by introducing **leider**, **doch** and/or **aber**:

Das müssen Sie doch aber selbst wissen.

Da mußt du leider selbst zusehen.

Sehen Sie aber doch erstmal selbst zu, wie Sie zurechtkommen.

92.4

Asking somebody else to do something

The most common way of saying that somebody else is charged with something is to use **lassen** as a modal verb:

(See also **35**A and **77.4a**B for other uses of **lassen**)

(a) Having something done to oneself:

> Er *läßt sich* die Haare jede Woche *schneiden.*
> He has his hair cut every week.

(b) Having something done by somebody else:

> Sie *ließ* die ganze Geschichte von einem Journalisten *ausarbeiten* und *veröffentlichen.*
> She had a journalist write up and publish the whole story.

(c) Ordering somebody else to do something:

> Die Polizei *ließ* alle Papiere *überprüfen.*
> The police had all documents checked.

(d) Letting somebody else do something (without interfering):

> Wir *ließen* den neuen Chef mal *machen.*
> We let the new boss get on with it (without giving him support).

A more bureaucratic way of asking somebody to do something is implied when using **an*weisen** 'to instruct':

> Sie *wies* das Personal *an,* die Kunden freundlicher *zu* behandeln.
> She instructed her personnel to treat the clients in a more friendly manner.

The verb **instruieren** for **an*weisen** does exist but is now rarely used. Rather more common would be **Instruktionen geben/hinterlassen** 'to give/leave instructions':

> Ich hatte *Instruktionen hinterlassen,* daß das Essen um 1 Uhr fertig sein sollte.
> I had left instructions that lunch was to be ready at 1 o'clock.

93   *Expressing needs, wishes and desires*

(See **104**B for expressing likes and preferences; **113**B for conveying hopes, wishes and disappointment)

93.1

The obvious verbs to express needs and wishes are **brauchen** 'need', **möchte** 'would like (now)', **mögen** 'to like to (generally)' and **sich** (= dat) **wünschen** 'to wish (for)'. Both **möchte** and **mögen** can be reinforced by using **gern(e)** 'a lot':

> **In Deutschland brauchen Sie im Winter Winterreifen.**
> In Germany you need winter tyres in winter.

> **Ich mag am liebsten arabischen Kaffee.**
> I like Arabian coffee best.

> **Jetzt möchte ich gerne eine Tasse Kaffee.**
> Now I'd love a cup of coffee.

(See **104**B for further examples with **möchte** and **mag**)

> **Zum Geburtstag wünsche ich mir eine Überraschung.**
> I'd like to have a surprise on my birthday.

Where one has a justified claim on something, use:

> **-r Anspruch** 'claim'
> **einen Anspruch auf etw.** (= acc) **haben** 'to have a claim on sth.'
> **einen Anspruch auf etw.** (= acc) **geltend machen** 'to lay claim to (and get) sth.'
> **etw. beanspruchen** 'to claim sth.'

> **Er *hat* dieses Jahr noch *Anspruch auf* zwei Wochen Urlaub.**
> He still has two weeks holiday left this year.

> **Die Nachbarn *machten ihre Ansprüche auf* Schadenersatz *geltend*.**
> The neighbours claimed damages.

> **Sie *beanspruchte* die Hälfte des Hauses.**
> She claimed half the house.

bedürfen 'need' takes the genitive. It tends to be found only in formal letters or reports as well as in the quality press:

> **Diese Gründe sind nicht stichhaltig. Sie *bedürfen der näheren Erklärung*.**
> These reasons are not valid. They need a more detailed explanation.

> **Es *bedurfte aller Überredungskünste*, um die Koalitionspartei zum Zustimmen zu bewegen.**
> It took all manner of persuasion to get the coalition party to agree.

93.2

Different types of need

(See also **112.1**B and **112.2**B for satisfying needs and demands)

Common words include:

> **-bedürftig**
> **hilfsbedürftig** 'in need of help'
> **ruhebedürftig** 'in need of rest/quiet'
> **anlehnungsbedürftig** 'in need of (sb.) to lean on'
> **reparaturbedürftig** 'in need of being repaired'
> **-r Bedarf an** (+ dat) 'need for'
> **-r tägliche Bedarf an Brot** 'daily requirement for bread'
> **Lebensmittel** (= plural) **des täglichen Bedarfs** 'staple foods'

> **Wir bekamen das Haus zu einem guten Preis, da es stark**
> *reparaturbedürftig* **war.**
> We got the house at a good price as it was badly in need of repair.

> **Kennen Sie Ihren täglichen** *Kalorienbedarf?*
> Do you know how many calories you need daily?

sein Bedürfnis verrichten 'to go to the toilet' is today only found in literary contexts. Where it occurs in spoken language, it is probably meant jokingly.

> **-r Anspruch** 'claim'
> **Anspruch auf etw.** (= acc) **erheben/haben** 'to lay claim to sth.'
> **Anspruch auf jmdn. erheben/haben** 'to lay claim to sb.'
> **-r Rechtsanspruch** 'legal (right to) claim'
> **-r Unterhaltsanspruch** 'legal right to maintenance'
> **anspruchsvoll** 'demanding'
> **anspruchslos** 'undemanding/modest'
> **-s Anspruchsdenken** critical word in contemporary German referring to the younger generation's claim on rights and wealth without working hard for them

> **Ich** *erhebe Anspruch* **auf das gesamte Vermögen.**
> I lay claim to the entire assets.

> **Es gibt manchmal Kinder, die ihren** *Unterhaltsanspruch* **an die Eltern vor Gericht einklagen.**
> Sometimes there are children who take their parents to court over their right to maintenance.

> **Der Vortrag war geistig** *anspruchsvoll.*
> The talk was intellectually demanding.

93.3

Wishes and desires

(See also **113.2**B for wishes)

> **-r -wunsch** 'wish'
> **-r Heiratswunsch** 'desire to get married'
> **-r Kinderwunsch** 'desires which children have' OR 'wish of a couple to have children'
> **-s Wunschdenken** 'wishful thinking'
> **-e Wunschvorstellung** lit. 'wishful idea/dream'
> **wunschlos glücklich** lit. 'happy without any further needs/blissfully happy'
> **wunschgemäß** 'according to plan/wish'
> **wünschbar/wünschenswert** 'desirable'

Viele Ehepaare *können sich* ihren Kinder*wunsch* nie *erfüllen*.
Many couples can never fulfil their desire to have children.

Bei der Partnersuche *hat* er eine ganz bestimmte *Wunschvorstellung*.
When looking for a partner he has a certain ideal in mind.

Eine schnelle Erholung der Wirtschaft *ist* jetzt *wünschenswert*.
A quick economic recovery is now desirable.

93.4

Enquiring after need

(See also **113.1**B for hopes and **90.3**B on 'Turning one's attention to somebody')

Note the following for polite inquiries where a positive answer is often expected:

Question	Reply
Darf ich Sie heute abend zum Essen einladen?	**Es tut mir leid, aber heute paßt es leider nicht.**
May I invite you to dinner tonight?	I'm sorry, unfortunately it isn't convenient tonight.
	Ja, gerne.
	Yes, thank you.
Möchten Sie noch ein Glas Wein?	**Ja, gern./Nein, danke.**
Would you like another glass of wine?	Yes, please (Thank you)./No, thank you.
Noch Käse?	**Danke, ich bin schon ganz satt.**
More cheese?	No, thank you, I am already quite full.

N.B. Do not use **voll** instead of **satt** as that can either mean you have had too much to drink or it implies that you didn't enjoy what you have been eating.

(See **67.1–67.4**B for thanking somebody; **112.2**B for satisfying needs and demands; **112.4**B for saying that something is sufficient; and **112.5**B for saying you have had enough to eat)

94 *Expressing objections and complaints*

94.1
Putting somebody right in a polite way

Germans may sound less apologetic than many British speakers when they put somebody right about something. Although they can therefore sound rude to the faint-hearted Briton abroad, this is merely a cultural phenomenon and not meant to give offence. If you have reason to complain, do so in a straightforward manner or you won't be understood.

The most common polite introduction is:

> **Entschuldigen Sie bitte,. . .**
> Excuse me. . .

This can be followed by:

> **. . ., aber ich sehe, daß hier etwas *nicht stimmt.***
> . . . but I can see that something is not right here.

> **. . ., aber Sie *müßten sich dies* hier, glaube ich, *nochmal ansehen.***
> . . . but I think you should have another look at this.

> **. . ., aber ich glaube, hier *liegt ein Irrtum vor.***
> . . . but I think there is a mistake here.

> **. . ., aber hier *ist Ihnen* wohl *ein Fehler unterlaufen.***
> . . . but I think you've made a mistake here.

In turn, you can then add:

Wenn Sie. . . machen wollen/würden 'if you'd do. . .':

> ***Wenn Sie* das bitte noch einmal *überprüfen wollen.***
> If you would please check this again.

> ***Wenn Sie* dies hier bitte noch einmal *durchgehen würden.***
> If you would please go through this again.

(See also **63.4**B on 'Dealing with problems')

94.2
Making complaints

(a) If something is not right and you want to complain without giving offence, use **das geht nicht** 'it is not on':

> ***Das geht doch nicht, daß* Sie einfach vor meiner Garagenausfahrt parken.**
> You can't just park in front of my drive (like that).

Was, du hast in der Klassenarbeit von deinem Nachbarn abgeschrieben? Das *geht wirklich nicht*!
What, you copied from your neighbour in the test? That's simply not on!

(b) If something has not been satisfactory:

---

sich (bei jmdm.) (über etw./jmdn.) beschweren 'to complain (to sb.) (about sb./sth.)'
sich (bei jmdm.) (über etw./jmdn.) beklagen 'to complain (to sb.) (about sb./sth.)'
-e Beschwerde '(official) complaint'
Beschwerde ein*legen 'to make a(n official) complaint'
(über etw. (= acc)/jmdn.) klagen 'to complain (about sth./sb.)'
Note that **klagen** cannot take an accusative object.
(über etw./jmdn.) meckern 'to complain/moan (about sth./sb.)' (often used in casual situations when a complaint is felt to be unfair)

Er *beschwerte/beklagte sich über* den Krach im Hotel.
He complained about the noise in the hotel.

Die Reisegruppe *beschwerte/beklagte sich beim* Reiseleiter, weil das Hotel nicht dem Standard entsprach, den sie erwartet hatte.
The tourist group complained to the courier because the hotel was not up to the standard they had expected.

Wir haben Ihre *Beschwerde* vom 15. Juli erhalten.
We have received your complaint of July 15th.

Sie *klagten*, daß das Essen meistens kalt war.
They complained that the food was mostly cold.

Warum müßt Ihr eigentlich immer *über* das Essen *meckern*?
Why do you always have to go on/complain about the food?

(c) Complaining rudely (informal, potentially offensive)

The following expressions have a varying potential for offence, depending on the geographical region where they are used, the tone of voice and the speaker's general characteristics.

-e Sauerei lit. 'sth. of a sow' can refer to dirt or to treatment which is perceived to be unfair. **-e Schweinerei** lit. 'sth. of a pig' has the same meaning. **-r Mist!** 'damn!' means literally 'manure' and is not particularly offensive in public usage. **Scheiße!** 'shit!', on the other hand, is genuinely vulgar, though an extremely common expletive:

Was ist denn das für eine Sauerei!
What a bloody mess!

Unerhörte Schweinerei!
It's a bloody disgrace!

So eine Scheiße!
Oh, shit!

Da haben Sie einen Riesenmist gebaut!
You have made a right ruddy mess of this.

Das ist doch eine bodenlose Frechheit!
What an incredible disgrace!/You've gone too far!

Das ist einfach unverschämt!
That is simply outrageous!

Unverschämtheit, Sie!
What an outrage!

(d) Taking a complaint to court or other official authorities

The formalities:

-e Anklage 'accusation'
jmdn. an*klagen 'to charge sb.'
jmdn. (bei Gericht) verklagen 'to press (legal) charges against sb.'
gegen jmdn. (eine) Anzeige erstatten 'to report sb.'
eine Klage ein*reichen 'to institute/start legal proceedings'
eine Klage vors Gericht bringen 'to take a matter to court'
jmdn. vors Gericht ziehen 'to take sb. to court'
einen Verteidiger bestellen 'to appoint a defence lawyer'
eine Vorladung (vor Gericht) erhalten 'to receive a summons (to appear in court)'
-e Verhandlung/-r Prozeß 'trial/hearing'
Widerspruch (gegen etw.) ein*legen 'to protest (against sth.)'
Berufung (gegen ein Urteil) ein*legen 'to appeal (against a verdict)'
in die Berufung gehen 'to appeal'

Die Nachbarn hatten *bei Gericht eine Klage eingereicht*, weil der Hund immer die ganze Nacht bellte.
The neighbours had started legal proceedings because the dog always barked all night long.

Die Eltern wollten eine offizielle *Beschwerde beim Direktor einlegen*, weil ihre Tochter in der Schule ungerecht behandelt worden war.
The parents wanted to lodge an official complaint with the head teacher as their daughter had been unfairly treated in school.

Sie *legte bei* der Zeitung *Widerspruch gegen* den Abdruck der privaten Bilder *ein.*

She protested/made an official complaint to the newspaper about the publication of the private photographs.

Der Anwalt des Angeklagten *legte Berufung gegen das Urteil ein.*

The defendant's solicitor appealed against the verdict.

More informal ways of talking about legal proceedings include:

Ich bringe Sie deswegen vors Gericht (formal)/vor den Kadi (informal).

I am going to take you to court for that.

Dafür mache ich Ihnen einen Prozeß.

I'll take you to court for that.

Er hängte ihm einen Prozeß an den Hals. (informal)

He took him to court. (lit. He hung a trial round his neck.)

The parties:

-r Angeklagte 'accused'
eine Aussage zu etw./über etw. (= acc) machen 'to give evidence on sth.'
-e Aussage zu etw./über etw. verweigern 'to refuse to give evidence on sth.'
-e Anklage verlesen 'to read out the charges'
Anklage wegen (+ gen) (gegen jmdn.) erheben 'to bring charges of... (against sb.)'
jmdn. zu etw. befragen 'to ask sb. about sth.'

Die Zeugen sollten *Aussagen zum* Tathergang *machen.*

The witnesses were supposed to give evidence about what happened.

Der Angeklagte *verweigerte die Aussage.*

The accused refused to give evidence.

Die Zeugen *machten* widersprüchliche *Aussagen.*

The witnesses gave contradictory evidence.

Der Staatsanwalt *verlas die Anklage.*

The prosecution read out the charge.

Der Staatsanwalt *erhob Anklage wegen* Mordes.

The public prosecutor brought a charge of murder.

Die Verteidigung *befragte* die Zeugen *zum Tathergang.*

The defence counsel asked the witnesses about the events.

Diese Anwaltskanzlei *übernimmt* hauptsächlich Scheidungs*fälle.*

This solicitors' practice deals mainly with divorce cases.

Der Richter *verkündete* schließlich *das Urteil.*
The judge finally pronounced judgement.

The sentence:

---

jmdn. einer Tat schuldig sprechen 'to find sb. guilty of a crime'
lebenslänglich/fünf Jahre bekommen 'to receive life/five years'
das Urteil lautet auf (+ acc) 'the sentence is for...'
auf Bewährung entlassen 'to suspend the sentence'

Die Geschworenen *sprachen* den Angeklagten (*des Mordes*) *schuldig.*
The jury found the accused guilty (of murder).

Der Angeklagte *bekam lebenslänglich.*
The accused received life.

Das Urteil lautete auf 2 Jahre Freiheitsentzug mit Bewährung.
She/he got a 2-year suspended sentence.

Sie *wurde auf Bewährung entlassen.*
She was released on probation.

94.3

Demanding one's rights

-s Recht 'right'
sein Recht verlangen 'to demand one's rights'
sein Recht bekommen 'to get one's rights'
recht*haben 'to be right'
im Recht sein/im Unrecht sein 'to be right/wrong'
rechtens sein 'to be legal'
auf etw. (= dat) **bestehen** 'to insist on sth.'

Ich *verlange mein Recht*/mein Geld zurück.
I demand my rights/my money back.

Wenn ich *mein Recht* nicht sofort *bekomme,* gehe ich mit Ihnen vor
Gericht.
If I don't get justice immediately I'll take you to court.

Natürlich *hat* sie wieder mal *rechtgehabt.*
Of course she was right again.

Das ist *mein gutes Recht.*
That's my right.

Ich bin *im Recht* und Sie sind *im Unrecht*.
I am right and you are wrong.

Das *ist* nicht *rechtens*, daß Sie uns ständig nachts mit Ihrer Musik belästigen.
You have no right to bother us continually with your music at night.

Er *bestand auf seinem Recht*, die Kinder regelmäßig *zu* sehen.
He insisted on his right to see the children regularly.

94.4
Different types of rights

(a) Speaking about rights in general terms

> **sein Recht auf etw.** (= acc) **aus*üben** 'to exercise one's right to sth.'
> **ein Recht auf etw.** (= acc) **haben** 'to have a right to sth.'
> **ein Vorrecht genießen** 'to enjoy a privilege'

Sein *Wahlrecht* sollte man unbedingt *ausüben*.
One should really exercise one's right to vote.

Ich habe auch *ein Recht auf* ein bißchen Freizeit.
I also have a right to some leisure time.

Wer *Vorrechte genießt*, hat oft auch viele Pflichten.
Those who enjoy privileges often also have many obligations.

(b) Human and civil rights and liberties

> **-e Menschenrechte** (plural) 'human rights'
> **Bürgerrechte** 'civil rights'
> **-s Recht auf freie Entfaltung der Persönlichkeit** 'right to develop freely as a person'
> (i.e. choose work, place of residence. . .)
> **-s Asylrecht** 'right of asylum'
> **-e Freiheit** 'freedom'
> **-e Bewegungsfreiheit** 'freedom to move/of movement'
> **-e Pressefreiheit** 'freedom of the press'
> **-e Meinungsfreiheit** 'freedom of speech'
> **-e akademische Freiheit** 'academic freedom' (to teach, research and publish freely)
> **-e Versammlungsfreiheit** 'freedom to gather' (as a group or party)

(c) Parental rights

> **-s Elternrecht** 'parental right'
> **-s Sorgerecht (für jmdn.)** 'custody (of sb.)'
> **-r/-e Erziehungsberechtigte** person responsible for bringing up a child and taking decisions on their behalf
> **-r Vormund** 'legal guardian'
> **-e Vormundschaft** 'guardianship'

94.5

Finding a solution
(For opinion, agreement and disagreement, see **107–109**B)

(a) Looking for a solution

> **sich um etw. bemühen** 'to make an effort to do sth.'
> **etw. vor*schlagen** 'to suggest sth.'
> **nach etw. suchen** 'to search for sth.'

Alle Delegierten *bemühten sich um* **die Lösung des Konflikts.**
All the delegates made an effort to solve the conflict.

Der französische Delegierte *schlug* **eine Kompromißlösung** *vor.*
The French delegate suggested a compromise solution.

Auf der Konferenz *suchte man nach* **einer Einigung in der Frage der Urwaldnutzung.**
At the conference an agreement was sought on the use of the tropical forest.

(b) Arriving at a solution

> **zu einer Einigung über etw. (= acc) kommen** 'to come to an agreement about sth.'
> **sich auf etw. (= acc) einigen** 'to agree on sth.'
> **etw. akzeptieren/an*nehmen** 'to accept/adopt sth.'

Der Vorstand *kam* **erst um Mitternacht** *zu einer Einigung.*
The board only came to an agreement at midnight.

Man *einigte sich darauf,* **den gegenwärtigen Vertrag zu verlängern.**
Agreement was reached that the present treaty should be extended.

Der Vorschlag **des Präsidenten** *wurde (einstimmig/mehrheitlich) angenommen.*

The suggestion of the president was accepted (unanimously/by a majority).

Der Einigungsvorschlag wurde schließlich *akzeptiert.*
The agreement/compromise was finally accepted.

95 *Giving and seeking promises and assurances*

95.1 Assurance of services

An assurance of service will usually take place in a fairly formal setting. Short exchanges are given here to cover a variety of common situations:

(a) At a garage

> **selbstverständlich** 'of course'
> **das geht** 'it's OK/that will work'
> **ist** (etc.)**fertig** 'is (etc.) ready'
> **geht in Ordnung** 'right you are'

Query

Ich möchte meinen Wagen nächsten Dienstag zum großen Kundendienst bringen. *Geht das?*

I'd like to book my car in for a major service next Tuesday. Would that be OK?

Wann kann ich den Wagen abholen?/Wann ist er fertig?

When can I pick the car up?/When is it going to be ready?

Reply

Ja, *selbstverständlich, das geht.* **Bringen Sie ihn gegen 8.30 Uhr.**

Yes, of course, that's OK. Bring it in about 8.30 am.

Er ist gegen 16 Uhr fertig./Wir haben ihn gegen 15 Uhr für Sie bereit.

It will be ready around 4 pm./We will have it ready for you around 3 pm.

(See **34.2**A for use of the present tense)

(b) When ordering something from stock

(See **71**B and **72**B for availability and non-availability)

etw. vorrätig haben 'to have sth. in stock'
etw. bestellen 'to order sth.'
etw. für jmdn. zurück*legen 'to put sth. aside for sb.'
jmdm. etw. liefern 'to deliver sth. to sb.'
etw. liefern lassen 'to have sth. delivered'
etw. für jmdn. bereit*halten 'to have sth. ready for sb.'
jmdm. etw. zu*sichern 'to assure sb. of sth.'
jmdm. etw. zu*sagen 'to promise sth. to sb.'

Query
Haben Sie Modell 453 *vorrätig?*

Have you got model 453 in stock?

Könnten Sie das *für mich zurücklegen/*
***bestellen/**bis zum 15. *liefern?*

Could you put it to one side for me/order
it for me/deliver by the 15th?

Könnten Sie mir das nach Hause
liefern?/Kann ich mir das liefern lassen?
Can you deliver this to my home
address?/Can I have this delivered?

Reply
Ja, das *ist da.*/Nein, das *müßten wir*
bestellen.

Yes, we've got it./No, we'd have to order it.
Selbstverständlich, wir *halten es für Sie*
zum Abholen *bereit.*/Wir *rufen Sie an,*
sobald es eintrifft./Ja, wir *können Ihnen*
das *zusichern/zusagen.*
Of course. We will have it ready for you to
collect./We will call you as soon as it
arrives./Yes, we can assure you (of that).

Ja, selbstverständlich.

Yes, of course.

(c) Warranties

Talking about guarantees:

-e Garantie, -e Garantiezeit 'warranty (period)'
Garantie auf etw. (= acc) **haben** 'to have a warranty on sth.'
etw. gewährleisten 'to guarantee sth.'
Gewähr/Haftung für etw. übernehmen 'to guarantee sth./accept liability for sth.'

Wie lange läuft die *Garantiezeit* bei diesem Föhn?/Wie lange habe ich
***Garantie* auf diesen Föhn?**
How long is the warranty period on this hair dryer?

Sie haben ein Jahr *Garantie* auf alle Teile und zwei Jahre auf Wartung.
You have a one-year guarantee on parts and two years on labour.

Können Sie mir die höchste Qualität *gewährleisten?*
Can you guarantee me the highest quality?

> **Wir können keine *Gewähr* für dieses Produkt übernehmen.**
> We cannot accept liability for this product.

(d) Declining responsibility, withholding a guarantee (formal)

> **Die *Angaben erfolgen ohne Gewähr.***
> No responsibility is accepted for the accuracy of this information.

> **Wir *übernehmen* keine *Haftung.***
> No responsibility is accepted.

> **Die *Garantie* ist doch schon voriges Jahr *abgelaufen.***
> The warranty period ran out last year.

95.2 Promises between people

For binding promises, such as those concerned with getting married, use the verb
versprechen 'to promise' and its derivatives:

> **sich einander die Treue versprechen** 'to promise to be faithful to each other'
> **das Eheversprechen** 'marriage vows'
> **-s Heiratsversprechen** 'engagement'
> **-s Eheversprechen** 'marriage vows'
> BUT **sich mit jmdm. verloben** 'to get engaged to sb.'

Further promises can be made by using:

> **jmdm. etw. versprechen** 'to promise sth. to sb.'
> **jmdm. ein Versprechen geben/jmdm. sein** (etc.) **Ehrenwort geben** 'to give sb. a
> promise/give sb. one's word of honour'
> **jmdm. das Blaue vom Himmel versprechen** 'to promise sb. the earth' (lit. 'the blue
> from the sky')
> **sein** (etc.) **Versprechen halten/brechen** 'to keep/break one's promise'

versichern means 'to promise' in the sense of assuring, insuring or confirming:

> **(jmdm.) versichern, etw. zu tun** 'to promise (sb.) that you will do sth.'
> **(jmdm.) etw. versichern** 'to assure (sb.) of sth.'
> **etw. versichern** 'to insure sth.'
> **eine Versicherung ab*schließen** 'to get an insurance'
> **eine Versicherung kündigen** 'to cancel an insurance'

> **Er *versicherte (ihr)*, pünktlich zu kommen.**
> He promised (her) to be on time.

Sie *versicherte ihm, daß* sie es ernst meinte.
She assured him that she was serious about it.

Sie *versicherten ihnen* ihre Unschuld.
They assured them of their innocence.

Ich habe gestern meinen neuen Wagen *versichert.*
I insured my new car yesterday.

Haben Sie schon eine Hausrats*versicherung abgeschlossen*?
Have you already got a home contents insurance?

Hiermit möchte ich meine Gebäude*versicherung* zum 1. März *kündigen.*
I hereby wish to cancel my building insurance as of 1 March.

> **(jmdm.) etw. beteuern** means 'to promise (sb.) sth.' in the sense of 'to protest' where the sincerity of the assurance is in doubt

Er beteuerte ihr seine Unschuld.
He protested his innocence/promised her that he was innocent.

Alle Beteuerungen seines guten Willens halfen nichts.
All protestations of his good will were to no avail.

Sie beteuerte, ihn nie belogen zu haben.
She assured (him) that she had never lied to him.

Note the expression **ein Geschäft mit Handschlag ab*machen** 'to shake hands on a deal'.

96 *Issuing, accepting and declining invitations and offers*

96.1

Issuing invitations

(See also **60.6**B for 'Welcoming', **61**B on 'Making introductions', **63**B 'Eating and drinking' and **66.7**B 'Congratulating')

(a) Inviting

More informal invitations are extended over the phone:

Wir *wollten* euch *fragen, ob* ihr nächsten Samstag zu einem Glas Wein zu uns kommen wollt.
We wanted to ask you whether you would like to join us for a glass of wine next Saturday.

Formal invitations may be printed or issued in a handwritten letter:

> *Hiermit möchten wir* **dich und deinen Mann** *zu* **Pauls fünfzigstem Geburtstag** *einladen.*
> We'd like to invite you and your husband to Paul's fiftieth birthday.

> **Wir würden uns freuen, wenn du und Hannelore zu Peters Taufe kämt.**
> We would be glad if you and Hannelore could come to Peter's christening.

Printed invitations often have the abbreviation **u.A.w.g.** printed in the left-hand bottom corner. Fully spelt out this is **um Anwort wird gebeten** 'RSVP' and requires a written reply.

(b) Occasions

If the invitation is **zu einem Glas Wein** 'for a glass of wine', it is more than likely that there will be other drinks and snacks, but your hosts won't serve dinner. This is a very common form of invitation in Germany.

zum Abendessen 'for dinner' means that there will be a meal, but not necessarily a hot one.

zum Kaffee 'for coffee' means that you should come between 3 and 4 o'clock in the afternoon. There will be coffee, tea and cakes. You will probably be expected to leave around 6 o'clock at the latest.

zum Geburtstag 'for a birthday' is probably a bigger occasion with food and drinks served.

zu einer Party 'for a party' is probably an occasion for the younger generation, including music and a larger number of guests but probably not much food.

zu einer Disco 'for a disco' is a party given by hosts as young as 10 or 11 years old, probably with quite a number of friends and including music.

For all other occasions of a more personal nature the invitation will give some indications what to expect.

(c) Presents

Among student friends, simply bringing along a bottle to a party may be in order. For all other occasions you might bring a bottle – this needs to be wrapped. If bringing flowers, you should give them to the 'lady of the house', having first partially taken the paper off (but not the transparent foil!). Cards are not very common.

When presenting the present or flowers, you might say:

> **Hier ist eine Kleinigkeit für Sie.**
> Here is a little gift for you.

Darf ich dir/Ihnen diesen Strauß geben.
May I give you this bunch of flowers.

Hier ist etwas für die Kinder.
Here is something for the children.

Bitte schön!
Here you are.

Appreciative replies can be phrased in the following way:

Vielen Dank, aber das war doch wirklich nicht nötig.
Many thanks, but that was really not necessary.

Danke, das ist sehr nett von dir/Ihnen.
Thank you, that is very kind of you.

To which very polite people might reply:

Gern geschehen.
You are welcome.

Nichts zu danken!
Not at all.

(See **67**B on giving and receiving thanks)

(d) At a dance

In the ballroom one could say:

Darf ich bitten.
lit. May I ask you (for a dance).

If you want to decline, you say:

Ich tanze leider nicht.
I am afraid I am not dancing.

If, as a woman, you don't take up the offer to dance or if you reject a date, the comment may be:

Sie hat mir einen Korb gegeben.
She has turned me down.

Making an offer

(a) To buy or sell something

Common ways of talking about offers include the verb **an*bieten** 'to offer' and its noun **-s Angebot**:

> **Wir können *Ihnen diesen Farbfernseher* zu einem besonders günstigen Preis *anbieten.***
> We can offer you this colour TV at a particularly favourable price.

> **Können Sie uns Ihre *Angebot*e zeigen?**
> Can you show us what you have on offer?

> **Wir möchten ein *Angebot auf* dieses Grundstück *machen.***
> We would like to put in an offer for this plot of land.

> **Der potentielle Käufer *bleibt bei seinem Angebot/ erhöht sein Angebot/ senkt sein Angebot.***
> The potential buyer is sticking to his offer/is increasing his offer/is reducing his offer.

> **Sie *nahmen das Angebot* von 500.000 DM *an/ lehnten das Angebot ab.***
> They accepted the offer of 500 000 DM/rejected the offer.

(b) Special offers

> **-s Sonderangebot** 'special offer'
> **-s Schnäppchen** 'good buy/bargain (informal)'

> **Gurken *sind* heute *im Sonderangebot.***
> Cucumbers are on special offer today.

> **Im Sommerschlußverkauf habe ich heute ein wirklich gutes *Schnäppchen* gemacht.**
> I got a really good bargain in the summer sales today.

(c) Offering to do something

In the form of a question:

> **Möchtest du, daß ich heute auf deine Tochter aufpasse?**
> Would you like me to babysit your daughter today?

> **Soll ich für dich einkaufen gehen?**
> Should I go shopping for you?

> **Kann ich dir etwas aus der Stadt mitbringen?**
> Can I get you something from town?

> **Was kann ich für Sie tun?**
> What can I do for you?

(See also **63.6d**B for offering to prepare food)

With an introduction:

> *Es macht mir wirklich nichts aus,* **für dich miteinzukaufen.**
> I really don't mind doing your shopping as well.

> *Melde dich/ Laß es mich wissen,* **wenn ich dir irgendwie helfen kann.**
> Let me know if I can help you in any way.

> *Sagen Sie mir, was* **ich für Sie tun kann.**
> Tell me what I can do for you.

> *Ich helfe dir gerne,* **den Rasen** *zu* **mähen.**
> I am quite willing to help you mow the lawn.

(See **42.3f**A for verb completion by an infinitive clause with **zu**; see also **8.7**A for word order)

96.3 **Accepting and declining an invitation or offer**
(See **111.2c**B for looking forward to something)

(a) Accepting

Informally:

> *Das ist nett von euch,* **wir kommen gern.**
> That is nice of you. We'd like to come.

More formally:

> **Wir** *nehmen* **Ihre freundliche Einladung zum Faschingsball gerne** *an.*
> We would like to accept your kind invitation to the carnival ball.

> **Ich** *komme gerne* **zu Peters Taufe.**
> I'd be glad to come to Peter's christening.

(b) Declining

(See also **67.5**B on 'Declining help and offers')

Informally:

> *Leider geht es* **am nächsten Freitag** *nicht.* **Wir haben schon etwas vor.**
> Unfortunately, we cannot make it next Friday. We've already got
> something else on.

More formally:

> **Wir *können* Ihre freundliche Einladung zur Jubiläumsfeier *leider nicht annehmen,* da wir an diesem Wochenende schon Gäste eingeladen haben.**
> We can unfortunately not accept your kind invitation to the anniversary celebration as we have already invited some guests for that weekend.

> **Danke, *aber wir sind leider schon verabredet.***
> Thank you but we already have a previous engagement.

> **Ich komme gerne, *aber* mein Mann *hat leider Dienst* und *kann* daher *nicht (mit)kommen.***
> I'd be glad to come but my husband is unfortunately on duty/at work and will therefore not be able to come (along).

Very formally:

> **Es tut uns leid, Ihnen mitteilen zu müssen, daß wir Ihr *Angebot nicht annehmen können.***
> We are sorry to have to tell you that we are unable to accept your offer.

> **Er hat *das Angebot abgelehnt/ ausgeschlagen.***
> He rejected the offer.

> **Wir haben Ihr Angebot reiflich erwogen, *können* Ihnen aber *leider nicht zusagen.***
> We have seriously considered your offer but are unfortunately unable to accept it.

97 *Seeking, granting and denying permission*

97.1

Seeking permission

The most common way to seek permission is to use **dürfen** 'may'. As in English, this is often replaced by **können** 'can' in everyday conversation even though strictly speaking this expresses ability rather than permission.

(See **35**A for modal verbs and **39.2b**A for the use of the subjunctive to make requests for permission more polite)

> **Darf/Dürfte ich mal kurz telephonieren?**
> My I make a brief phone call?

> **Kann/Könnte ich vielleicht Ihr Fahrrad ausleihen?**
> Could I possibly borrow your bicycle?

Another way of asking for permission involves **es geht** lit. 'it goes, it is OK':

> **Geht es, daß/wenn ich heute länger wegbleibe?**
> Is it OK that/if I stay out a little longer today?

> **Ginge es, daß Sie mir die Zahlungsfrist um einen Monat verlängern?**
> Would it be possible for you to extend the repayment period by a month?

Informal replies are normally quite idiomatic:

Limited consent:

> **Na gut./Also gut.**
> Well, OK then.

> **Wenn es (denn) sein muß.**
> If it has to be.

> **Also, ich bin (nicht) dagegen.**
> Well, I am (not) against it.

Consent	Refusal
Ja, das geht.	**Nein, das geht nicht.**
Yes, that's OK.	No, that's not OK.
Ja, das geht auf jeden Fall.	**Nein, das geht auf keinen Fall.**
Yes, that's certainly OK.	No, that's certainly not OK.
Das paßt mir (gut).	**Das paßt mir (gar) nicht.**
That suits me (fine).	That doesn't suit me (at all).
Das ist mir (sehr) recht.	**Das ist mir (gar) nicht recht.**
That's (certainly) OK with me.	That's not (at all) OK with me.
Gut, einverstanden.	**Nein, das kommt überhaupt nicht in Frage.**
OK, agreed.	No, that is out of the question.
Ja, ich bin einverstanden damit.	**Nein, das geht wirklich nicht (an).**
OK, I agree.	No, that is really too much.

97.2   Granting and denying permission when an authority or somebody in a superior position is involved

> **(jmdm.) etw. genehmigen** 'to permit sb. to do sth.'
> **jmdm. etw. erlauben** 'to allow sb. to do sth.'
> **-e Erlaubnis** 'permission'
> **verbieten** 'to forbid'
> **-s Verbot** 'ban/prohibition'
> **zu*lassen** 'to allow (to happen)/register'

genehmigen and its derivatives imply permission or consent of an official nature:

> **Der Direktor *hat* schließlich die Versetzung des Schülers *genehmigt*.**
> The headmaster finally permitted the pupil to move up to the next class.

> **Habt ihr schon die Bau*genehmigung* für euer Haus?**
> Have you already got planning (lit. building) permission for your house?

erlauben and its noun **-e Erlaubnis** refer to permission given or denied to somebody by a person or institution in authority. The opposite of **erlauben** is **verbieten**, together with its noun **-s Verbot**:

> **Wenn ich abends ausgehen will, muß ich *mir* erst *die Erlaubnis* meiner Eltern *holen*.**
> When I want to go out in the evening I first need to get permission from my parents.

> **Wer *hat ihm* denn *erlaubt*, einfach aus der Schule weg*zu*bleiben?**
> Who allowed him simply to stay away from school?

> **Es ist streng *verboten*, in den Klassenräumen *zu* rauchen.**
> It is strictly forbidden to smoke in the classrooms.

> **Meine Eltern *haben es mir* (= dat) *erlaubt*/verboten, in diese Disco *zu* gehen.**
> My parents allowed/forbade me to go to this disco.

> **Sie *haben ihm* (= dat) *ihr Haus* (= acc) *verboten*.**
> They forbade him to enter the house.

zu*lassen has both a very restricted meaning of 'to register' and a more general meaning of 'to permit/let happen'. It is more often used with **nicht** and can imply intolerance:

> **Das Auto war *nicht* einmal *zugelassen*.**
> The car wasn't even registered.

> **Ich kann es *nicht zulassen*, daß so ein Lehrer meine Kinder unterrichtet.**
> I cannot allow a teacher like that to teach my children.

A number of near synonymous expressions fall into the same category of formal permitting or empowering:

> **jmdn. zu etw. ermächtigen** 'to empower sb. to do sth.'
> **jmdm. die Befugnis zu etw. geben** 'to give sb. permission to do sth.'
> **jmdm. die Befugnis zu etw. entziehen** 'to withdraw permission for sb. to do sth.'
> **jmdm. sein Einverständnis zu etw. geben** 'to give one's approval/consent to sb. doing sth.'
> **jmdm. sein Einverständnis zu etw. verweigern** 'to deny one's approval to sb. doing sth.'
> **(-e) Vollmacht über etw. (= acc) erhalten** 'to be granted authority to do sth./receive probate'

Du *bist* **gar nicht** *dazu ermächtigt/bevollmächtigt,* **so eine Entscheidung** *zu* **treffen.**
You haven't got the authority to take such a decision.

Ich *gebe* **dir die** *Befugnis,* **den geheimen Raum zu betreten.**
I'll give you permission to enter the secret room.

Er *hat* **gar keine** *Befugnis,* **diesen Computer zu benutzen.**
He does not have permission to use this computer.

Sie *hat* **das** *ohne mein Einverständnis/mit meinem Einverständnis* **getan.**
She did this without my approval/with my approval.

Zu diesem Vertrag *verweigere* **ich** *mein Einverständnis.*
I refuse to approve this treaty/contract.

Die Erben haben *Vollmacht über* **die Geldangelegenheiten der Großmutter** *erhalten.*
The heirs have been granted power of attorney for their grandmother's financial affairs.

98 *Making, accepting and declining suggestions*

There are three basic ways of expressing suggestions:

(a)

> **jmdm. etw. vor*schlagen** 'to suggest sth. to sb.'
> **-r Vorschlag** 'suggestion'

Ich *schlage vor,* **daß wir uns nächste Woche wieder treffen.**
I suggest that we meet again next week.

> **Er *schlug vor*, den Plan an*zu*nehme*n*.**
> He suggested that they adopt the plan.

(See **42.3f**A for verb completion by infinitive clauses with **zu**; see also **8.7**A for word order)

> **Darf ich mal einen *Vorschlag machen*?**
> May I make a suggestion?

> **Wie *lautet* Ihr *Vorschlag* denn?**
> And what is your suggestion?

> **Sie müssen Ihre *Vorschläge* bis zum Ende des Monats bei uns *einreichen*.**
> You have to submit your suggestions to us by the end of the month.

(b) Being for or against a suggestion

> **etw. (einstimmig) an*nehmen/ab*lehnen** 'to accept/refuse sth. (unanimously)'
> **für/gegen etw. sein** 'to be for/against sth.'
> **sich für/gegen etw./jmdn. aus*sprechen** 'to speak for/against sth./sb.'

> **Der *Vorschlag* des Vorsitzenden *wurde* einstimmig**
> ***angenommen/abgelehnt*.**
> The chairman's suggestion was unanimously accepted/rejected.

> **Die Mehrheit *war für/gegen den* Plan.**
> The majority was for/against the plan.

> **Nur eine Minderheit *sprach sich für/gegen das Projekt aus*.**
> Only a minority spoke in favour of/against the project.

(c) Making a suggestion

> **Wie wäre es, wenn. . .?** 'How about if. . .?'
> **Wie wäre es mit. . .?** 'How about. . . (+ noun)?'

These constructions require Subjunctive II or a conditional (which may make the suggestion sound a little more formal):

> **Wie *wäre* es, wenn wir erst einmal einen Spaziergang *machten/machen***
> ***würden*?**
> How about if we went for a walk first?

> **Wie *wäre* es, wenn du schon heute zu uns *kämest*?**
> How about if you came to us today?

> **Wie *wäre* es jetzt mit einem Kaffee?**
> How about a coffee now?

Appropriate replies to such a suggestion are:

> **Das wäre eine gute Idee/wäre toll!**
> That would be a good idea/wonderful!

> **Ich glaube, das wäre nicht so sinnvoll/keine gute Idee.**
> I think that wouldn't be sensible/such a good idea.

(d) Suggestions in the form of a question using a modal verb:

> ***Könnten wir nicht* schon morgen in die Ferien fahren?**
> Couldn't we go on holiday tomorrow?

> ***Sollte er nicht* erst den Professor fragen?**
> Shouldn't he ask the professor first?

> ***Müßte man nicht* mehr Geld mitnehmen?**
> Wouldn't one have to take more money?

> ***Laß* uns doch mal in die neue Boutique gehen.**
> Let us have a look at the new boutique.

99 *Issuing and responding to warnings*

99.1

Public and semi-public warnings

(a) Weather warnings

> -e **Hochwasserwarnung** 'flood warning'
> -e **Sturm-/Gewitterwarnung** 'storm/thunderstorm warning'
> -e **Schlechtwetterwarnung** 'severe weather warning'
> **jmdn. warnen, etw. nicht zu tun/jmdn. davor warnen, etw. zu tun** 'to warn sb. not to do sth./against doing sth.'

> **In den Nachrichten wurde gerade eine *Sturmwarnung***
> ***gesendet/durchgegeben.***
> A storm warning has just been broadcast on the news.

> **Der ADAC hat gerade bekanntgegeben, daß wir *mit* schlechtem Wetter**
> ***rechnen* müssen.**
> The ADAC (Allgemeiner Deutscher Automobil-Club, similar to the AA) has just announced that we have to reckon with bad weather.

Laut Wetterbericht sollen wir *uns* auf Hochwasser *gefaßt machen*.
According to the weather forecast we should prepare ourselves for flooding.

Die Medien *warnen vor* den schlechten Straßenzuständen.
The media are warning of bad road conditions.

Wegen der Lawinengefahr *werden* alle Gäste *gewarnt, nicht* abseits der Pisten ski*zu*fahren.
Wegen der Lawinengefahr *werden* alle Gäste *davor gewarnt*, abseits der Pisten ski*zu*fahren.
Because of the danger of avalanches all guests *are warned not to* ski off piste.

(See **42.3f**A for verb completion by infinitive clauses with **zu**; see also **8.7**A for word order)

(b) Warnings and alarms in emergencies and wartime

Die *Flutwarnung* wurde sechs Stunden vor der Springflut durchgegeben.
The flood warning was broadcast six hours before the spring tide.

Heute morgen gab es wieder einen *Tieffliegeralarm*.
There was another low-flying aircraft alarm this morning.

Die Bevölkerung war ständig *in Alarmbereitschaft*. (formal)
The population was continuously in a state of alert.

Sogar in London gibt es manchmal einen *Bombenalarm*.
Even in London there is occasionally a bomb scare.

In einem Notfall muß man *die Polizei/die Feuerwehr alarmieren*. (formal)
In an emergency you must call the police/the fire brigade.

Bei einem *Unfall* muß man, wenn möglich, die *Warnblinkanlage* einschalten.
In case of an accident you must, if possible, switch on hazard lights.

Wenn der *Notdienst* mit *Blaulicht* und *Martinshorn* kommt, muß man die Straße räumen.
When the emergency vehicle arrives with lights flashing and its siren sounding, you must get off the road.

(c) Warnings of further potentially unsafe conditions

> **jmdn. verwarnen** 'to warn/caution sb.'
> **jmdn. ermahnen, etw. zu tun** 'to urge sb. to do sth.' (formal)
> **-e Ermahnung** 'exhortation' (formal)
> **sei vorsichtig** 'beware/be careful'
> **paß auf/aufgepaßt** 'beware/watch out'
> **es besteht. . . Gefahr** 'there is a danger of. . .'
> **es gibt Gefahren** 'there are dangers'

Alle Autofahrer *wurden von der Polizei gewarnt, nicht* mit Alkohol im Blut *zu* fahr*en*.

All motorists were warned by the police not to drink and drive.

Vor Taschendieben *wird gewarnt!* (formal)

Beware of pick-pockets.

Der Fußgänger *wurde von der Polizei verwarnt,* weil er bei Rot über die Straße gegangen war.

The pedestrian was given a warning by the police because he had crossed the road when the lights were on red.

Er kam mit einer *Verwarnung* weg.

He got off with a caution.

Sie *ermahnte* den Fahrer immer wieder, langsamer *zu* fahr*en*, weil die Straßen vereist waren.

She urged the driver again and again to go more slowly, as the roads were icy.

(See **42.3f**A for verb completion by infinitive clauses with **zu**; see also **8.7**A for word order)

Vorsicht, Baustelle! Eltern haften für ihre Kinder.

Caution, construction site. Parents are legally liable for their children.

Vorsicht, bissiger Hund./Cave canem. (Latin)

Beware of the (lit. biting) dog.

Seid vorsichtig, es könnte glatt sein.

Be careful, it could be slippery/icy.

Achtung aufgepaßt, da kommt ein Wagen!

Watch out, a car is coming.

Es *besteht* Explosions*gefahr*/Feuer*gefahr*.

There is a danger of explosion/fire.

> **Für kleine Kinder *gibt* es in der Küche viele *Gefahren*.**
> There are many dangers in the kitchen for small children.

(d) Warnings in games and at school

-e gelbe Karte 'yellow card/ (soccer)
-e rote Karte 'red card' (soccer; also used in a metaphorical sense)
einen blauen Brief bekommen 'to receive a letter (in a blue envelope)' from school indicating to parents that their child is in danger of not moving up to the next grade/year.

(e) Reacting to warnings

---

eine Warnung befolgen 'to heed a warning'
eine Warnung mißachten/aus*schlagen 'to ignore a warning'
eine Warnung (nicht) ernst nehmen 'to (not) take a warning seriously'
sich vor*sehen, etw. nicht zu tun 'to be careful *not* to do sth.'
auf etw. (= acc)/jmdn. auf*passen 'to pay attention to sth./sb.' OR 'look after sth./sb.'
auf etw. (= acc) achten 'to pay attention to sth.'
etw. beachten 'to respect sth.'
sich (= acc) vor etw. hüten/in acht nehmen 'to beware of sth.'
auf etw. (= acc) acht*haben 'to pay attention to sth.'

> **Der Skifahrer hatte die *Warnung* nicht *befolgt*.**
> The skier had not heeded the warning.

> **In den Bergen sollte man *Warnungen* von Einheimischen *ernst nehmen/ nicht ausschlagen*.**
> In the mountains one should take seriously/not ignore the locals' warnings.

> **Ich sah mich vor, nicht zu schnell zu fahren.**
> I took care not to drive too fast.

> **Sie *paßten auf* die Kinder *auf*.**
> They looked after the children/paid attention to the children.

> **Ich kann jetzt nicht erzählen, denn ich muß *auf* die Straße *achten*.**
> I cannot chat now because I have to concentrate on the road.

> **Die Familie *beachtete* die Sturmwarnung nicht.**
> The family didn't heed the storm warning.

> **Vor großen Hunden sollten sich besonders Kinder *in acht nehmen*.**
> Children especially should beware of big dogs.

Beim Nähen mußt du *auf* die Nadel *achthaben*. Sonst kannst du dich in den Finger stechen.

When you sew you need to be careful with the needle. Otherwise you might prick your finger.

(See **37**A for the use of reflexive verbs)

99.2

Threat-like warnings

wenn... nicht, (dann)... 'if... not, (then)...'
jmdn. warnen 'to warn sb.'
jmdm. drohen 'to threaten sb.'
eine Drohung wahr*machen 'to carry out a threat'

Wenn **du das nicht bis nächste Woche kannst, bekommst du Probleme.**
If you cannot do it by next week you will have problems.

Ich *warne Sie*, bringen Sie die Sache jetzt in Ordnung oder sie wird Folgen für Sie haben.
I warn you, deal with this matter now or it will have serious consequences for you.

Ihm drohte **eine Haftstrafe.**
He was in danger of receiving a prison sentence.

Er nahm die *Drohung* nicht ernst.
He didn't take the threat seriously.

Du willst es nicht anders. Ich muß meine *Drohung wahrmachen*.
You leave me no choice. I shall just have to carry out my threat.

Jetzt gibt's aber Krach!/Jetzt schlägt's aber dreizehn! (very informal)
That's the limit! I won't put up with this any longer!

XIV Conveying attitudes and mental states

100 Asserting and denying the truth of something

100.1

Commenting on the truthfulness of something

> **Das ist ganz/völlig richtig/falsch.** 'That's entirely correct/completely wrong.'
> **Das stimmt (eigentlich)./Das stimmt (eigentlich) nicht (ganz).** 'That is (in fact) correct./That isn't (really) (quite) correct.'
> **Das ist (wirklich)/(eigentlich) (nicht) wahr.** 'That's (really)/(actually) (not) true.'
> **So ein (völliger) Unsinn/Blödsinn** (very derogatory)/**Schwachsinn!** (probably insulting) '(That's) (total) nonsense/rubbish!'

A dictionary will provide further reference for expressions with:

> **wahr sein** 'to be true'
> **-e Wahrheit/Unwahrheit** 'truth/untruth'
> **gelogen** 'lied/a lie'
> **lügen** 'to lie'
> **-e Lüge** 'lie'

100.2

The most common way to express belief or disbelief involves **jmdm. etw. glauben** 'to believe (sb.) sth.', and **an jmdn./etw. glauben** 'to believe in sb./sth.'

(See **12A** for the order of noun and pronoun objects; and **42.3a–42.3b**A for verb completion with one or two elements)

> **Ich *glaube* ihm seine Ausrede.**
> I believe (him) his pretext/excuse.

> **Ihr *glaubt an* Gott.**
> You believe in God.

> **Sie *glaubt* fest *an* sie.**
> She firmly believes in her.

> **Sie *glaubt an* seinen Erfolg.**
> She believes in his success.

> **Seine Erklärung war nicht sehr *glaubwürdig/glaubhaft.***
> His explanation was not very credible.

> **Die *Glaubwürdigkeit* ihrer Geschichte wurde angezweifelt.**
> The credibility of her story was doubted.

-r Glaube refers to 'belief' in a general sense, whereas the much less common
-r Glauben is used particularly when referring to 'faith'. **-r Unglaube** means 'lack of faith'.

100.3 For saying that something is neither completely true nor untrue there are a number of idiomatic expressions:

> **Das war nur *die halbe Wahrheit.***
> That was only half the truth.

> **Er verbreitete *das Gerücht*, daß sie heute käme.**
> He spread the rumour that she was to arrive today.

> **Diese Behauptung ist völlig *an den Haaren herbeigezogen/aus der Luft gegriffen.***
> This claim is extremely far fetched. (lit. This claim has been pulled by its hair/grasped from the air).

> **Die Antwort ist nur *teilweise richtig.***
> The answer is only partially correct.

100.4 ## Declaring something solemnly

> **etw. (be)schwören** 'to swear sth.'
> **jmdn. beschwören, etw. zu tun** 'to plead with sb. to do sth.'
> **sich (= dat) schwören, etw. zu tun** 'to be resolved to do sth.'
> **einen Schwur leisten** 'to swear an oath'
> **einen Eid ab*legen** 'to swear an oath'

> **Sie *beschwor* ihre Unschuld.**
> She swore she was innocent.

> **Sie *beschwor* ihn, die Sache ernst zu nehmen.**
> She pleaded with him to take the matter seriously.

> **Er *schwor sich*, diesen Fehler nicht noch einmal zu machen.**
> He swore/was resolved not to repeat this mistake.

> **Er *leistete einen Schwur*, nicht eher zu ruhen, bis er dem Geheimnis auf die Spur käme.**
> He vowed not to rest until he had unveiled the mystery.

Alle Angeklagten müssen vor Gericht *einen Eid ablegen/leisten*, die Wahrheit und nichts als die Wahrheit zu sagen.
All defendants have to swear an oath in court to tell the truth and nothing but the truth.

(See **42.3f**A for verb completion by an infinitive clause with **zu**; see also **8.7**A for word order)

101 *Expressing knowledge*

101.1

German has two verbs for 'to know': **wissen** (which usually refers to facts) and **kennen** (which refers to people and places). There are many derivatives which have precise meanings in German, but often have no exact equivalents in English (see also **87.1**B).

(a) **erkennen** and **wissen**

> **jmdn./etw. kennen** 'to know sb./sth.'
> **jmdn./etw. erkennen** 'to recognize sb./sth.'
> **-e Erkenntnis** 'finding/insight'
> **-e Kenntnis** 'knowledge'
> **-r Kenntnisstand** 'level of knowledge'

Er *erkannte* seinen Bruder nach den vielen Jahren kaum noch.
He hardly *recognized* his brother after all those years.

Sie mußte *erkennen*/mußte *zu der Erkenntnis kommen*, daß sie in diesem Fall nicht helfen konnte.
She had to realize/understand that she could not help in this case.

Und er *erkannte*, daß es gut war.
And he saw that it was good. (Bible: Genesis)

Die Forschung bringt uns viele *Erkenntnisse*, die für die Bekämpfung von schweren Krankheiten nützlich sind.
Research produces many findings which are useful for fighting serious diseases.

Es ist gar *keine* so neue *Erkenntnis*, daß der Mensch für seine Umwelt mitverantwortlich ist.
It is not such a new finding/insight that man shares responsibility for his environment.

Die *Kenntnis* dieses Buches ist für die Prüfung unbedingt wichtig.
It is essential to know this book for the exam.

Sein *Kenntnisstand* entspricht dem eines Fünfjährigen.
His level of knowledge is equivalent to that of a five-year-old.

---

etw. wissen 'to know sth.'
von etw. wissen 'to know of/about sth.'
um etw. wissen 'to know about sth.'
das Wissen 'knowledge'
meines Wissens/seines Wissens 'as far as I know/he knows', etc. (lit. 'according to my/his knowledge') (only used in these two persons)
Kenntnisstand and **Wissensstand** are used interchangeably

Er mußte doch *wissen*, daß sein Fahrstil gefährlich war.
He must have known (after all) that his driving was dangerous.

Die Parlamentarier *wußten* schon lange *von* der Affäre.
The members of parliament had known about the affair for a long time.

Wir *wissen um* deine Geldsorgen und möchten dir gerne helfen.
We know about your financial worries and would like to help you.

Trotz unseres großen medizinischen *Wissens* können wir noch nicht alle Krankheiten heilen.
Despite our vast knowledge of medicine we still cannot cure all diseases.

Meines Wissens wurde dieser Punkt schon in der letzten Sitzung behandelt.
As far as I know/am aware, this point was already dealt with at the last meeting.

Der heutige *Wissensstand* wäre vor fünfzig Jahren undenkbar gewesen.
The present state of knowledge would have been unthinkable fifty years ago.

101.2 Talking about arts and sciences

(a) die Wissenschaften

-e Geisteswissenschaften (plural) 'humanities'
-r Geisteswissenschaftler, -e Geisteswissenschaftlerin 'person working in the field of the humanities/arts'
-e Gesellschaftswissenschaften (plural) 'social sciences'
-r Gesellschaftswissenschaftler, -e Gesellschaftswissenschaftlerin 'person working in the field of social sciences'
die Naturwissenschaften (plural) '(natural) sciences'
der Naturwissenschaftler, die Naturwissenschaftlerin 'person working in the field of the (natural) sciences'

(b) Care needs to be taken when using **akademisch**, **der Akademiker**, **die Akademie**:

> **Da Japan schon ein Patent für unser neues Motorenmodell hat, ist unsere Entwicklungsarbeit *akademisch*.**
> As Japan already has a patent for our latest engine model our development work has become academic (i.e. superfluous).

> **Das Diplom wurde ihr mit allen *akademisch*en Würden verliehen.**
> The diploma was given to her with full academic ceremony.

> **In Deutschland gibt es seit Jahren eine hohe *Akademiker*arbeitslosigkeit.**
> In Germany there has been high *graduate* unemployment for years.

Note also: **-e Akademie** 'academy/school/college'. The **Akademie der Wissenschaften** is a German institution similar to the Royal Society (in the different academic disciplines), but a **(Sommer)Akademie** is a '(summer) conference'.

102   *Remembering and forgetting*

102.1

The verb **erinnern** 'remember' and its derivatives can be used in a number of ways:

> **etw. erinnern** 'to remember sth.' (emphasizes the process of deliberately trying to recall sth.)
> **sich an etw./jmdn. erinnern** 'to remember sth./sb.' (emphasizes that a certain piece of information comes to mind – this is the standard verb for 'to remember')
> **-e Erinnerung** 'memory/memories'

> **Er *erinnerte* bestimmte Kindheitserlebnisse, die jetzt eine neue Bedeutung für ihn annahmen.**
> He recalled certain childhood events which were now taking on a new meaning for him.

> ***Erinnerst du dich* noch *an* den schönen Abend neulich im Löwen?**
> Do you remember the lovely evening we had in the *Löwe* (pub) recently?

> **Die *Erinnerung an* ihre Tage in Wien bedrückte sie.**
> Memories of her days in Vienna depressed her.

102.2

Commemoration

> **gedenken (gedachte, gedacht)** (+ gen) 'to remember respectfully'
> **etw./jmdn. ehren** 'to honour sth./sb.'

> **1995 *gedachten* wir *des* Kriegsendes vor fünfzig Jahren.**
> In 1995 we commemorated the end of the war fifty years ago.

> **Wir *ehren das Gedenken* der Toten.**
> We honour the memory of the dead.

Other useful expressions are:

> **-e Gedenkfeier** 'commemoration'
> **-e Gedenkminute** 'minute's silence'
> **-e Gedenkstätte** 'memorial'
> **-r Gedenktag** 'commemoration day/day of remembrance'
> **-e Gedenktafel** 'memorial plaque'

102.3　The (imaginary) place where memories are stored is **das Gedächtnis** 'memory':

> **(klar/deutlich) im Gedächtnis sein/haben** 'to be remembered (clearly)'
> **etw. im Gedächtnis behalten** 'to keep sth. in one's memory'
> **etw. aus dem Gedächtnis verlieren** 'to forget' (lit. 'to lose sth. out of one's memory')
> **an Gedächtnisschwund leiden** (often used jokingly among younger people) 'to suffer from loss of memory'

> **Mir *ist* doch *deutlich im Gedächtnis*, daß wir uns heute treffen wollten.**
> I remember clearly that we wanted to meet today.

> **Das war mir total (aus dem Gedächtnis) *entfallen*.**
> I had completely forgotten about it.

In connection with **Gedächtnis**, other expressions are also common:

> **jmdm. gegenwärtig sein** 'to remember' (lit. 'to be present in one's memory')
> **etw. parat haben** 'to remember off the cuff'/'have a piece of information to hand'
> **in den Sinn kommen** 'to remember' (lit. 'to come into one's mind')
> **etw. im Kopf haben/etw. behalten** 'to remember sth.' (and know by heart)
> **etw. auswendig wissen** 'to remember sth.' (without looking it up)

> **Die Reise *war ihm* noch ganz klar/gar nicht mehr *gegenwärtig*.**
> He still clearly remembered the journey/didn't remember the journey at all any more.

> **In ihrem Physikexamen *hatte* sie alle mathematischen Formeln *parat*.**
> In her physics exam she was able to remember all the mathematical formulas.

Ihm war wieder *in den Sinn gekommen* (literary)/*eingefallen* (neutral)**, daß er heute abend Besuch bekäme.**
He remembered that he was going to have visitors this evening.

Hast du **Marias Telefonnummer** *im Kopf/behalten***?**
Do you know Maria's telephone number (by heart)?/Can you remember Maria's telephone number?

Stell dir vor, er *weiß auswendig,* **wann seine Kollegen Geburtstag haben.**
Imagine, he knows all his colleagues' birthdays by heart.

N.B. A computer's memory is **-r Speicher.**

Acquiring and forgetting knowledge and skills
Lernen, verlernen, vergessen

(a) **lernen** is used for the process of acquiring knowledge as well as for the result:

Lernst **du schon eine Fremdsprache?**
Do you already study a foreign language?

Haben Sie die Geheimnummer (auswendig) *gelernt***?**
Have you learnt your personal number (by heart)?

(b) German makes a distinction between **vergessen** and **verlernen** lit. 'to de-learn'. **vergessen** is used when one has forgotten information that has been learnt. Acquired behaviour, skills and attitudes cannot be forgotten in the same way, and **verlernen** is used in these instances:

Fahrrad fahren *verlernt* **man nie.**
You never forget how to ride a bicycle.

Distinguish **-e Vergeßlichkeit** 'forgetfulness' and **-e Vergessenheit** 'oblivion', which is only used in a few set phrases:

Diese Episode der Geschichte *fiel der Vergessenheit anheim/geriet in Vergessenheit.*
This historical episode sank into oblivion.

103 *Expressing future intentions*

Future intentions can be expressed by **werden** or a modal verb (**möchte, wollen,** see **35**A):

Wir *möchten/wollen* **nächsten Sommer nach Italien** *fahren.*
We'd like to/want to go to Italy next summer.

The future tense with **werden** often implies a particularly firm intention or even a threat:

> **Ich *werde* ihm *zeigen*, was wir leisten können.**
> I'll show him what we can achieve.

> **Er *wird* das nicht noch einmal *machen*.**
> He won't do that again.

103.2 There are other verbal expressions implying intention. Where they are followed by a clause, an infinitive + **zu** construction is required (see **42.3f**A):

---

etw. planen/vor*haben 'to plan/intend to'
etw. im Auge haben lit. 'to have one's eye on sth.'
etw. (für...) ins Auge fassen 'to intend to do sth. (for...)'
sich (= dat) **etw. vor*nehmen** 'to have the intention of doing sth.'

> **Wir *haben* nächsten Sommer eine Reise *vor*.**
> **Wir *haben* nächsten Sommer *vor*, eine Reise *zu machen*.**
> We intend to go on a trip next summer.

> **Ich hatten mir *vorgenommen*, dort nie mehr *hinzufahren*.**
> I had resolved never to go there again.

> **Für die kommenden Ferien *haben* wir noch *nichts Bestimmtes ins Auge gefaßt*.**
> We haven't made any concrete plans for the next vacation.

104 *Expressing likes and dislikes: people, things and situations*

Praise and criticism
(See also **112**B for satisfaction and dissatisfaction)

In German, neither understatement nor exaggeration are taken as a serious comment and can at best disorientate. To some extent what is appropriate depends on the situation. For example, imagine you have just booked into a hotel, and reception has asked whether everything is OK:

(a) Satisfaction – expressions ranging from indifference to high praise:

> **Ja, danke. (Das Zimmer ist in Ordnung).**
> Yes, thank you. (The room is OK).

Ja prima. (Das Zimmer gefällt mir).
Yes, very good. (I like the room).

Danke, alles bestens. (this can occasionally sound a bit short)
Thank you, fine.

Danke, es ist sehr bequem.
Thank you, it is very comfortable.

Danke, es ist wunderbar. Mir gefällt besonders die Aussicht.
Thank you, it is wonderful. I particularly like the view.

(b) Dissatisfaction – expressions reaching from slight dismay to complete dissatisfaction and anger:

Es ist leider ein *bißchen* kalt/*nicht ganz* sauber...
It is unfortunately a little cold/not quite clean...

Es *läßt* (doch) einiges *zu wünschen übrig*.
It leaves something to be desired.

Es ist (einfach) *unmöglich*.
It is (simply) unacceptable.

So ein Zimmer *können Sie unmöglich* Gästen *anbieten*.
How can you possibly offer such a room to your guests?

So ein Lärm/Dreck... *ist einfach unzumutbar*.
Such noise/dirt... is completely unreasonable/just too much.

104.2 Expressions for likes and dislikes can be classified according to whether they are used only for people or for people and things.

(a) People and things

With the accusative:

> **mögen (mag), mochte, gemocht** 'to like'
> **etw./jmdn. (sehr) gern mögen** 'to like sth./sb. a lot (very much)'
> **etw./jmdn. nicht gern mögen** 'to not like sth./sb.'
> **etw./jmdn. so gern mögen** 'to like sth./sb. so much'
> **(nicht) gern(e) etw. tun** 'to (not) like doing sth.'

Sie *mochte* ihn, aber heiraten wollte sie ihn nicht.
She liked him but didn't want to marry him.

Ich *mag* Rosenkohl *überhaupt nicht.*
I don't like sprouts at all/hate sprouts.

Meine Schwester wäscht *gar nicht gerne* ab.
My sister hates doing the washing up.

Im Sommer fahren wir immer *gerne* ans Meer.
In summer we always like to go to the seaside.

With the nominative:

---
gefallen 'to please'
etw./jmd. gefällt jmdm. 'sb. likes sb./sth.' (but not for food and drink)
etw./jmd. gefällt jmdm. gut 'sb. likes sb./sth. a lot'
etw./jmd. gefällt jmdm. sehr (gut) 'sb. likes sth./sb. a lot'
etw./jmd. gefällt jmdm. nicht 'sb. does not like/dislikes sth./sb.'

Die Frau *gefällt mir*!
I like that woman!

Die Musik heute abend *gefällt uns* besonders *gut*.
We particularly like the music tonight.

(b) People only

---
jmdn. lieben 'to love sb.'
jmdn. gern(e) mögen/haben 'to like (but not to love) sb./feel affection for sb.'
jmdn. hassen 'to hate sb.' (conveys a much stronger feeling in German than in English and is therefore to be used with discretion)

Werther *liebte* Charlotte, aber sie war schon verheiratet.
Werther loved Charlotte but she was already married.

Er *mochte* seine älteste Schwester besonders gern.
He particularly liked his eldest sister.

Die Schweiz ist ein gutes Beispiel für ein Land, wo sich Völker verschiedenen Ursprungs nicht *hassen*.
Switzerland is a good example of a country where peoples of different origin do not hate each other.

Note the way **mögen** can be 'graded' in the positive and in the negative:

Positive:

mögen
gern(e) mögen
sehr gern(e) mögen/besonders mögen

Negative:

> **nicht so (gern(e)) mögen**
> **nicht (gern(e)) mögen**
> **gar nicht/überhaupt nicht (gern(e)) mögen**

Significantly, there seem to be more expressions for dislike than for like:

> **jmdn. nicht (so gut) leiden können** 'to not like sb./not be able to bear sb.'
> **jmdn. nicht ausstehen können** 'to not be able to bear sb. at all'
> **nichts für jmdn. übrig haben** 'to not care for (i.e. about) sb.'

> **Für solche arroganten Verkäufer** *habe* **ich** *überhaupt nichts übrig.*
> I don't care at all for such arrogant sales persons.

> idiom: **Du kannst mich gernhaben.**
> Get lost.

N.B. **Du gefällst mir nicht** refers to someone's health and indicates that the speaker is concerned that you are looking ill. Similarly **deine heiße Stirne gefällt mir nicht** is not a comment on your (lack of) beauty but implies that you may be running a temperature.

(See **110.8e**B for temperature)

105 Indicating preferences

—105.1— There is a simple gradation pattern for stating degrees of preference:

Positive: **gern – lieber – am liebsten**

Wir gehen gern in die Oper.	We like to go to the opera.
Wir gehen lieber ins Konzert.	We prefer to go to a concert.
Wir gehen am liebsten ins Schauspiel.	We most enjoy going to the theatre/a play.

Negative: **nicht gern – weniger gern – am wenigsten gern/gar nicht gern/überhaupt nicht gern**

Wir gehen nicht gern in die Oper.	We don't like going to the opera.
Wir gehen weniger gern ins Konzert.	We are less keen on going to concerts.
Wir gehen am wenigsten gern ins Schauspiel.	We like going to the theatre least of all.
Wir gehen gar nicht gern/überhaupt nicht gern ins Schauspiel.	We don't like going to the theatre at all.

105.2

Making comparisons

(a) Where two things are equally liked: **genauso** (+ adverb)... **wie** 'as... as'; **nicht so** (+ adverb)... **wie** 'not as... as' (see also **48.6a**A for the comparative)

> **Ich gehe *genauso gerne* ins Theater *wie* ins Konzert.**
> I like going to the theatre (just) as much as to a concert.

> **Mein Bruder trinkt Rotwein *nicht so gern wie* Weißwein.**
> My brother does not like red wine as much as white wine.

(b) Expressing a preference: comparative + **als**

> **Wir arbeiten *lieber* im Büro *als* auf der Baustelle.**
> We prefer working in the office to working on a construction site.

> **Sie trinkt *lieber* spanischen *als* portugiesischen Rotwein.**
> She prefers (drinking) Spanish red wine to Portuguese red wine.

> **Er hat seine Kinder *lieber als* seinen Hund.**
> He likes his children more than his dog.

(See **48.6a**A for the case after **als**)

(c) The prefix **vor-** can often express a preference:

> **eine Vorliebe für etw./jmdn. haben** 'to have a preference (taste) for sth./sb.'
> **mit Vorliebe etw. tun** 'to particularly like doing sth.'
> **etw./jmdm. den Vorzug vor etw./jmdm. geben** 'to prefer sth./sb. to sth./sb.' (formal)
> **etw./jmdn. bevorzugen** 'to prefer sth./sb.' (may imply unfair preference)
> **es vor*ziehen, etw. zu tun** 'to prefer doing sth.'
> **jmdn./etw. jmdm./etw. vor*ziehen** (formal, mostly written language) 'to prefer sb./sth. to sb./sth.'

> **Er hörte *mit Vorliebe* nachts Musik, wenn alle anderen Hausbewohner schlafen wollten.** (formal)
> He particularly liked to listen to music at night, when all the other tenants wanted to sleep.

> **Ruhigere Schüler *werden* von Lehrern leicht *bevorzugt*.**
> Quieter pupils are easily preferred by teachers (i.e. get better treatment).

> **Er *zog* den alten Shakespeare dem Romantiker Wordsworth *vor*.**
> He preferred the old Shakespeare to the romantic Wordsworth.

> **Wir *ziehen* unser altes kleines Haus dem großen neuen *vor*.**
> We prefer our small old house to the big new one.

Sie *zogen es vor,* kein Risiko einzugehen.
They preferred not to take any risk.

106 Expressing indifference

German is not rich in expressions of indifference:

Das *ist mir* (völlig) *gleich/egal/wurst* (informal)/*scheißegal* (rude).
It's all the same to me./I couldn't care less./I couldn't give a damn.

Das *schert mich* nicht/einen Teufel (rude).
That doesn't concern/bother me at all.

Um solche *Gerüchte schere* ich mich nicht.
I don't bother listening to such rumours.

Das *interessiert* mich *nicht die Bohne.*
I couldn't give a damn.

If you want to leave the decision to someone else or have to concede victory to someone else, you might also say:

Ganz wie du meinst/Sie meinen.
Just as you think.

Das überlasse ich dir/Ihnen.
I'll leave that to you (to decide).

Machen Sie das, wie Sie wollen (potentially impatient).
Do as you please.

Machen Sie, was Sie wollen.
Do as you please.

107 Voicing opinion

The most common words and constructions involve the verb **meinen** 'to think':

Ich meine, das sollten wir machen.
I think we should do it.

Welcher (= gen) Meinung sind Sie?/Was meinen Sie dazu?
What is your opinion?/What do you think about that?

Wessen Meinung sind Sie?
Of whose opinion are you?/Who do you agree with?

A number of verbs can be used with **-e Meinung** (see also the following section). **Meinung** can be replaced by **-e Ansicht** 'view' and often by **-e Position** 'position' as well as by **-r Standpunkt** 'point of view'.

(s)eine Meinung/Ansicht/Position vertreten 'to be of an opinion/to hold/defend a view/position'

(s)eine Meinung/Ansicht/Position verfechten/verteidigen 'to defend one's/an opinion/view/position

(s)eine Meinung/Ansicht zum Ausdruck bringen 'to express one's/an opinion/view'

(s)einer Meinung/Ansicht (= dat) **Ausdruck verleihen** 'to express one's/an opinion'

bei (s)einer Meinung/Ansicht/Position bleiben (also **auf etw.**(= dat) **beharren**) 'to stick to one's guns'

(s)eine Meinung/Position ändern 'to change one's/an opinion/position'

(fest) hinter einer Meinung/Ansicht stehen 'to back (firmly) an opinion/view'

zu einer Meinung/Ansicht stehen 'to support an opinion/to defend an opinion/view'

seine eigene Meinung/eigenen Ansichten (in einer Sache) haben 'to have one's own opinion/views (in a matter)'

eine vorgefaßte Meinung gegenüber etw./jmdm. haben 'to be prejudiced against sth./sb.' (lit. 'to have a preconceived opinion')

der festen Meinung/Überzeugung (= gen) **sein, daß. . .** 'to be firmly convinced that. . .' (lit. 'be of the firm opinion that')

sich (= dat) **eine Meinung über etw.** (= acc) **bilden** 'to come to an opinion about sth./form a view on sth.'

> **Viele Politiker *vertraten die Ansicht*, daß Korruption von Ministern nur die Ausnahme sei.**
> Many politicians were of the view that ministerial corruption was exceptional (lit. the exception).

> **Rechtsextremisten *haben eine vorgefaßte Meinung gegenüber* Ausländern.**
> Right-wing extremists are prejudiced against foreigners.

(See **85.1**B for the mood of verbs when expressing opinion rather than fact)

For compound words with **-meinung-**, consult your dictionary:

> **-e Meinungsverschiedenheit** 'difference of opinion/argument'
> **-r Meinungskonflikt** 'conflict of opinions'
> **-e Meinungsmache** 'manipulation of (public) opinion', e.g. by the media or by political groups
> **Eltern-, Lehrer-, Schülermeinung** 'opinion of parents, teachers, pupils', etc.

Other verbs expressing opinion are **finden** 'to find', **glauben** 'to believe' and **denken** 'to think'. However, **denken** is far less frequently used than **meinen** and **finden**:

> **Ich *glaube* nicht, daß du in diesem Buch eine Antwort auf deine Frage findest.**
> I don't think you will find an answer to your question in this book.

> ***Finden* Sie auch, daß man etwas gegen die zunehmende Umweltverschmutzung tun muß?**
> Do you too think something must be done about the increasing environmental pollution?

> **Er *dachte* nicht, daß seine Abwesenheit solche Konsequenzen haben würde.**
> He didn't expect his absence to have such consequences.

108 *Expressing firm convictions*

Some believe that **Meinung** is an attitude based on emotions rather than reason. In order to stress conviction, **halten von** 'think of/have an opinion about' may be used:

> **Was halten Sie von der neuen Regierung? – Ich halte nicht viel von ihren wirtschaftlichen Plänen.**
> What do you think of the new government? – I don't think much of their economic plans.

-e Haltung 'attitude' or, alternatively, **-e Einstellung** 'view/attitude' refer to something deeper than **Meinung** or **Ansicht**:

> **Die Schule hat die Aufgabe, Schüler zu einer demokratischen *Haltung* zu erziehen.**
> It's the school's task to educate pupils to a democratic attitude.

Haltung can also refer to behaviour:

> **Während der Beerdigung haben die Familienangehörigen *Haltung* bewahrt.**
> During the funeral the family maintained their composure.

Compare also the participle **eingestellt** 'orientated/biased':

> **In den siebziger Jahren galt es als modern, links *eingestellt* zu sein.**
> In the seventies it was considered fashionable to be leftist.

-e **Überzeugung** 'conviction'/**überzeugt** 'convinced', can be an even more deeply rooted attitude, often founded on moral grounds:

> **Sie waren *aus Überzeugung* Christen./Sie waren überzeugte Christen.**
> They were devout Christians (lit. out of conviction).

> **Sie brachte ihren Standpunkt *mit Überzeugung* vor.**
> She presented her point of view with conviction.

109 *Expressing agreement and disagreement*

(See also **119**B for 'Shaping the course of a conversation')

109.1

Many constructions expressing agreement or disagreement centre around **-e Meinung**, **-e Ansicht**. **-e Position** 'position' is also possible in some combinations (as shown below):

(a) Agreement

> **für etw. sein** 'to be for/in favour of sth.'
> **der gleichen/gleicher Meinung/Ansicht sein** 'to be of the same opinion'
> **sich** (= acc) **einer Meinung/Ansicht/Position an*schließen** 'to (come to) back an opinion/position'
> **zu der Meinung von jmdm. stehen** 'to support the opinion of sb.'
> **mit der Meinung/Ansicht/Position von jmdm. überein*stimmen** 'to agree with the opinion/position of sb.'
> **mit jmdm. einer Meinung/Ansicht sein** 'to agree with (the opinion of) sb./be of the same opinion as sb.'

> **In der Frage der Kinderbetreuung war das Ehepaar *der gleichen Ansicht*.**
> As far as childcare was concerned the couple were in agreement.

> **Ich *stimme mit* deiner Meinung in der Frage der Rentenfinanzierung *überein*.**
> I agree with you on the issue of how to finance the pensions.

(b) Disagreement

---

doch! 'not at all!/Yes, it is!/Yes, they are!', etc. (i.e. contradicting a negative)
gegen etw. sein 'to be against sth.'
etw. ab*lehnen 'to refuse sth./be opposed to sth.'
anderer Meinung/anderer Ansicht/einer anderen Meinung/einer anderen Ansicht über etw. (= acc)/**in etw. sein** 'to be of a different opinion about sth.'
unterschiedlicher/verschiedener Meinung/Ansicht über etw. (= acc)/**in etw. sein** 'to be of a different opinion about sth.'
über etw. (= acc) **geteilter Meinung sein** 'to have differing opinions/be in two minds about sth.'
eine Meinungsverschiedenheit über etw. (= acc) **haben** 'to be of a different opinion about sth./have a dispute about sth.'
Differenzen (plural) **zwischen** 'differences of opinion between'

A common way of indicating disagreement with what someone has said is **doch**, but it is only used to contradict an actual or implied negative (see **117.1**B). **doch** can be the first word of the response, or it may be used later in the sentence:

> **Du hast wohl kein Geld.** > *Doch,* **ich habe zwanzig Mark./Ich habe** *doch* **zwanzig Mark.**
> But you haven't got any money. > Yes, I have. I've got twenty marks.

> **Manche Eltern** *sind dagegen,* **ihre Kinder von fremden Leuten betreuen zu lassen.**
> Some parents are against having their child minded by strangers.

> **Wir** *lehnen* **solche Privilegien grundsätzlich** *ab.*
> We are fundamentally opposed to such privileges.

N.B. Use **unterschiedlich** or **verschieden** when at least two different opinions are being discussed; use **ander-** when a second opinion is being introduced.

> **Sie war für den Kauf des Hauses. Er war aber** *anderer Ansicht.*
> She was in favour of buying the house but he disagreed (i.e. was of a different opinion).

> **Premierminister und Schatzkanzler sind in finanzpolitischen Fragen oft** *verschiedener/unterschiedlicher Meinung.*
> The Prime Minister and the Chancellor often differ over questions of finance policy.

> **In finanzpolitischen Fragen** *gibt es* **oft** *Differenzen* **zwischen den beiden.**
> In matters of finance policy there are often differences between the two of them.

Ich *bin geteilter Meinung darüber, ob* wir mit den Kindern wirklich eine so
große Reise machen sollten.
I am in two minds about whether we should really go on such a big trip
with the children.

Wir *waren geteilter Meinung* über das Wahlergebnis.
We couldn't agree on the outcome of the election.

(c) **Meinung**, **Ansicht** and **Position** can be characterized further by the following verbs:

(stark/weit) (voneinander) divergieren 'to diverge (significantly) (from each other)'
auseinander*gehen 'to diverge'
auseinander*klaffen 'to diverge widely'
jmdn. mit etw. überzeugen 'to convince sb. because of sth.'
etw. richtig*stellen 'to correct sth.'

Während der Waffenstillstandsverhandlungen wurde klar, daß die
Ansichten der beiden Verhandlungspartner *stark (voneinander)*
divergierten.
During the cease fire negotiations it became apparent that the views of
the two sides diverged significantly.

Bei der Frage, ob Kinder schon mit vier Jahren in die Schule gehen sollten,
gehen die Meinungen der Eltern total *auseinander.*
On the question of whether children should start school as early as age
four, parents' opinions differ widely.

Er ist ziemlich unpopulär, *überzeugt* aber *durch* seine feste Haltung/*mit*
seiner festen Haltung.
He is rather unpopular but convinces people through his firm stance.

Lassen Sie mich die Ansicht, hier sei nur der Staat verantwortlich, mal
richtigstellen.
Allow me to correct the opinion that only the state is responsible (in this
matter).

(d) **Meinung**, **Ansicht** and **Position** can also be:

kontrovers 'controversial'
unvertretbar 'indefensible'
unhaltbar 'untenable'
klug 'intelligent/smart'
überzeugend 'convincing'
entscheidend 'decisive'

109.2 Constructions with **einigen** 'to come to an agreement' and **-e Einigung** 'agreement/process of agreeing':

> **sich auf (eine Lösung) einigen** 'to come to agree on (a solution)'
> **Einigung (in einer Frage) erzielen** 'to reach agreement (on a question)'
> **-r Einigungsprozeß** 'process of agreeing'; in German politics, process of Unification

The participial form of **stehen** 'to stand' as well as the derived noun form **-ständnis** are often used figuratively and can have different meanings in conjunction with different prefixes:

> **mit etw. *einver*standen sein** 'to agree with/give one's consent'
> **sein *Einver*ständnis zu etw. geben** 'to agree/consent (in a formal context, e.g. marriage) to sth.'
> **über eine Frage im *Einver*ständnis sein** 'to be agreed on a matter'
> **jmdm. (widerwillig) etw. zu*gestehen** 'to concede sth. reluctantly to sb.'
> **ein *Zuge*ständnis machen** 'to make a concession'
> N.B. **jmdm. etw. ein*räumen** 'to concede sth. to sb.'

> **Die Verhandlungspartner *waren* über das Problem der FCKW Emissionen im *Einver*ständnis, wollten sich aber bei der Lösung gegenseitig *keine Zugeständnisse einräumen.***
> The partners in the negotiations about CFC emissions were agreed on the problem but did not want to make any unilateral concessions.

109.3 There are many constructions involving the verb **-stimmen** and the noun **-e Stimmung**. They can occur with a number of prefixes, and the meaning is determined by the respective prefix.

> **für etw. stimmen** 'to vote in favour of'

> **Die Mehrheit *stimmte für* eine Kabinettsumbildung.**
> The majority voted in favour of a cabinet reshuffle.

> **mit jmdm./etw. *überein**stimmen** 'to agree with sb./on sth.'
> **mit jmdm. in einer Sache *überein**stimmen** 'to agree with sb. on sth.'
> ***Überein*stimmung erzielen** 'to reach (an) agreement'
> **zur *Überein*stimmung bringen** 'to bring to an agreement' (also in a mathematical sense)

> In der Frage der Obdachlosen *stimmen* wir mit Ihnen *überein.*
> We agree with you on the question of the homeless.

---

jmdm./einer Sache *zu**stimmen 'to agree with sb./on a matter'
einer Sache die *Zu*stimmung verweigern 'to refuse to agree to sth.'
einer Sache die volle *Zu*stimmung geben 'to agree totally on a matter'
***Zu*stimmung finden** 'to meet with approval'
nur teilweise *Zu*stimmung finden 'to meet with partial approval'
***Zu*stimmung zu einer Sache erhalten** 'to receive/achieve approval in a matter'

> Der Gesetzesvorschlag *fand die* volle *Zustimmung* der Abgeordneten.
> The bill was approved by all the members of parliament.

über eine Sache *ab**stimmen 'to take a vote on a matter'
eine Sache zur Abstimmung bringen 'to put sth. to the vote'

> Der Gesetzesvorschlag über die Mineralölsteuererhöhung sollte noch vor
> der Sommerpause *zur Abstimmung gebracht* werden.
> The bill on the increase in fuel tax was to be put to the vote before the
> summer recess.

N.B. **über etw.** (= acc) **überein*kommen** 'come to an agreement about sth.',
-s Abkommen 'agreement/treaty':

> Man *kam* schließlich *überein,* sich noch einmal in der folgenden Woche zu
> treffen.
> It was finally agreed they would meet again the following week.

110 *Talking about physical well being*

Feeling and looking well

(a) Physical well being is usually expressed by means of **fühlen** or **gehen**.

fühlen is used reflexively: **sich fühlen**, the reflexive pronoun being in the accusative.

(See **37**A for reflexive verbs; and **110.8a**B for feeling unwell)

To express how well you are feeling, the following adverbs can be used:

> **gut** 'well'
> **prima** 'splendid'
> **bestens** 'very well'
> **gesund** 'healthy'
> **wohl/wohlauf** 'well'
> **pudelwohl** (lit. 'as well as a poodle') 'feeling on the top of the world'
> **ausgezeichnet** 'splendid'

> **Bei diesem warmen Wetter** *fühle ich mich* **so richtig** *wohl.*
> In this warm weather I feel really well.

> **In diesem gemütlichen Ferienhaus mit dem köstlichen Essen und netter Gesellschaft** *fühlten wir uns pudelwohl.*
> We felt on the top of the world in this cosy holiday home with its splendid food and nice company.

gemütlich, incidentally, is difficult to translate. It is inherent to the German mentality, and suggests a mixture of cosiness, informality and friendliness.

Another way to express well being is **jmdm. geht es gut** 'someone is well'.

(See **110.2**B for **gehen** + dat)

> **Er fühlt sich ausgezeichnet, besser** *könnte es ihm gar nicht gehen.*
> He feels great, he couldn't feel any better.

(b) Looking well

(See **74.3**B for physical appearance and looks; and **110.8a**B for looking unwell)

> *Du siehst* **gut/gesund/blühend** *aus.*
> You look well/healthy/radiant.

110.2

Enquiring about someone's health and responding

To enquire after physical (and general) well being, the question **Wie geht es Ihnen?** 'How are you?' is used.

(See **60.5**B for 'Enquiring about well being')

This is usually meant as a real, not a rhetorical question and requires a true answer.

The answer would also use, or at least imply, **gehen** with the dative:

> *Wie geht es Ihnen?* – (Mir geht's) Gut, danke.
> How are you? – Well, thank you.

To elaborate on this:

> *Mir geht es prima/recht gut/den Umständen entsprechend gut.*
> I feel great/quite well/well, under the circumstances.

Germans don't tend towards understatements as much as Anglo-Saxons. Therefore **nicht schlecht** literally implies 'not ill', etc. rather than 'really quite well'.

If worried that someone might look unwell, ask:

> *Fehlt dir etwas?/Was fehlt dir denn?*
> Is anything wrong/the matter?

110.3 Talking about health

Health is referred to as:

> **-e Gesundheit** 'health'
> **sich** (= acc) **bester Gesundheit erfreuen** 'to be in the best of health'
> **bei bester Gesundheit sein** 'to be in the best of health'
> **gesund sein** 'to be healthy'

(a) Saying that someone/something is healthy

> *Er ist bei/Er erfreut sich bester Gesundheit.*
> He is in/enjoys the best of health.

> *Er ist gesund/kerngesund.*
> He is healthy/really healthy/fit as a fiddle.

> **Wandern an der frischen Luft** *soll* besonders *gesund sein.*
> Walking in the fresh air is supposed to be especially healthy.

(b) Wishing someone good health when he or she sneezes

> *Gesundheit!*
> Bless you! (lit. Good health!)

110.4 Healthy lifestyle

(a) Exercising and keeping fit

> **sich** (= acc) **(körperlich und geistig) fit halten** 'to keep fit (physically and mentally)'
> **fit sein** 'to be fit'
> **Sport treiben** 'to play sports'
> **sich bewegen** 'to exercise' (lit. 'move oneself')
> **regelmäßig** 'regularly'

> **Mit seinen 45 Jahren** *ist* er noch richtig *fit.*
> At 45 he is still really fit.

Wir wollen *regelmäßig* schwimmen/joggen gehen.
We want to go swimming/jogging regularly.

(b) Keeping a balanced diet

---

sich (= acc) **ernähren** (lit. 'to nourish oneself') 'to eat'
(-e) Diät halten 'to be on/keep to a diet'
etw. zu sich nehmen 'to eat'
eine Kost zu sich nehmen 'to keep to a diet'

Man soll *sich* vernünftig/gut *ernähren*.
We should eat sensibly/well.

-e Diät traditionally means a medically prescribed special diet. The meaning of low-fat/low-calorie diet is more recent:

Sag bloß nicht, du *mußt* schon wieder *Diät halten/machen*!
Don't say you are on a diet/following a diet again!

-e Kost is a more general term for 'diet':

Die Weltgesundheitsorganisation empfiehlt, daß wir eine ausgewogene/fettarme/kalorienarme/vitaminreiche/ballaststoffreiche *Kost zu uns nehmen*.
The World Health Organization recommends keeping a balanced/low-fat/low-calorie vitamin-rich/high-fibre diet.

(c) Gaining and losing weight

-s Gewicht 'weight'
ab*nehmen 'to lose weight'
zu*nehmen 'to gain weight'

Er *hat* trotz der vielen Medikamente *sein Gewicht* (niedrig) *halten können*.
Despite the numerous medicines he had to take he was able to keep his weight down.

Bis zu meinem Strandurlaub *muß* ich unbedingt zehn Pfund *abnehmen*.
I must definitely lose ten pounds before my beach holiday.

Sie *dürfen* auf keinen Fall mehr *zunehmen*.
You mustn't gain any more weight, whatever happens.

--- 110.5 ---

Prevention of disease and accidents

> **etw.** (= dat) **vor*beugen** 'to prevent sth.'
> **vorbeugende Maßnahmen treffen** 'to take preventative measures'
> **vor*sorgen** 'to make provisions'
> **-e Vorsorge** 'precaution/provision'
> **sich vor etw.** (= dat) **schützen** 'to protect oneself from sth.'

(a) Taking precautions

> *Vorbeugen* **ist besser als heilen.** (proverb)
> Prevention is better than cure.

> **Wenn man mit Feuer umgeht, sollte man immer** *vorbeugende*
> *Maßnahmen treffen.*
> You should always take precautionary measures when dealing/working
> with fire.

(b) Preventing disease

> **Die Krankenkassen empfehlen regelmäßige** *Vorsorge***untersuchungen zur**
> **Früherkennung von Krebs.**
> The health insurance companies recommend regular preventative
> check-ups for the early diagnosis of cancer.

> **Er soll** *einem* **Herzinfarkt** *vorbeugen,* **indem er täglich 50mg Aspirin**
> **nimmt.**
> He is supposed to prevent a heart attack by taking 50mg of aspirin a day.

(c) Protecting oneself

> **Es ist notwendig, daß man sich auch im Winter** *vor starkem Sonnenlicht*
> *schützt.*
> It is important to protect yourself from strong sunlight even in winter.

> **Diese Sonnenmilch hat einen Licht***schutz***faktor von 8.**
> This suntan lotion is factor 8.

--- 110.6 ---

Habits

(a) Getting used to something

> **sich** (= acc) **an etw.** (= acc) **gewöhnen** 'to get used to sth.'

Wir *müssen uns* erst an die neue Umgebung *gewöhnen*.
First of all we must get used to the new environment.

Die Augen *müssen sich an die* Dunkelheit *gewöhnen*.
The eyes must adapt to the darkness.

(b) Giving up (bad) habits

sich (= dat) **etw. ab*gewöhnen** 'to kick the habit (of sth.)'

Er *will sich* das Rauchen *abgewöhnen*.
He wants to stop smoking.

(c) Addictions

-e Sucht 'addiction'
-e Nikotin-/Alkoholsucht 'nicotine/alcohol addiction'
die Anonymen Alkoholiker (plural) 'AA/Alcoholics Anonymous'
-wütig/-süchtig '-aholic'
arbeitswütig/arbeitssüchtig 'workaholic'

Mein Mitarbeiter is *arbeitswütig*.
My colleague is a workaholic.

(d) Starving/stuffing oneself

-e Magersucht 'anorexia'
magersüchtig 'anorexic'
-e Freßsucht '(morbid) craving for food/gluttony'
ab*magern 'to become thin'
ab*specken 'to slim down'

Die Schulleitung will etwas *gegen Magersucht* unternehmen.
The school management is trying to do something about anorexia.

Sie *sieht* total *abgemagert aus*.
She looks really emaciated.

Vor der Operation *muß* er erst einmal *abspecken*. (informal)
He must slim down before the operation.

110.7 **Relaxation and stress**

(a) Resting and getting sufficient sleep

> **sich** (= acc) **aus*ruhen** 'to rest'
> **sich** (= acc) **entspannen** 'to relax/unwind'
> **relaxieren/relaxen** 'to relax'
> **schlafen** 'to sleep'
> **sich** (= acc) **aus*schlafen** 'to have a lie-in/to sleep until you wake naturally'
> **etw.** (= acc) **aus*schlafen** 'to sleep sth off.'

Nach dem heißen Bad *sollten Sie sich* **richtig** *ausruhen.*
After a hot bath you should have a proper rest.

Es ist sehr wichtig, daß *die Frau sich* **während der Schwangerschaft** *entspannt.*
It is very important that a woman relaxes during pregnancy.

Im Urlaub möchte er nur in der Sonne liegen und *relaxieren/relaxen.*
In the holidays he only wants to lie in the sun and relax.

Ich möchte mich **mal wieder so richtig lange** *ausschlafen.*
I would love to have a really good lie-in again some time.

Er mußte *seinen Rausch* **erst** *ausschlafen.*
He had to sleep it off (i.e. the drink).

Getting things off your chest:

Sie fühlte sich erleichtert, nachdem *sie sich* **mit ihrem Hausarzt über das Problem** *ausgesprochen hatte.*
She felt relieved after she had talked frankly with her GP about the problem.

Feeling (psychologically) balanced:

Trotz der vielen Sorgen *scheint* **er doch recht** *ausgeglichen.*
Despite the many worries he does seem to be quite well balanced.

Selbst die ernstesten Erwachsenen *können* **manchmal ziemlich** *ausgelassen sein.*
Even the most serious adults can sometimes be rather boisterous/high-spirited.

Recovering from something:

Er brauchte lange, bis *er sich von dem* **anstrengenden Semester/der Virusinfektion** *erholt hatte.*
It took him a long time to recover from the exhausting term/the viral infection.

(b) Stress

---

nicht ein*schlafen können 'not to be able to fall asleep'
nicht durch*schlafen können 'not to be able to sleep through the night'
gereizt sein 'to be irritated'
aufgeregt sein 'to be excited'
etw. nervt jmdn. 'sth. irritates sb.'
stressig sein 'to be stressful'
jmdm. auf die Nerven gehen 'to get on sb.'s nerves'

Es wundert mich nicht, daß Sie bei Ihren Sorgen *nicht einschlafen können*.
I am not surprised you can't go to sleep with all your worries.

Während der Zeit, als sein Haus gebaut wurde, *war* er besonders *gereizt/ aufgeregt*.
During the time when his house was being built he was particularly irritable/excited.

Der ständige Lärm *hatte ihn* total *genervt/ war ihm* sehr *auf die Nerven gegangen*.
The constant noise had been completely wearing on his nerves/had got on his nerves.

Sie *findet* die Situation am Arbeitsplatz äußerst *stressig*.
She finds the situation at work terribly stressful.

110.8 Ill health

-e Krankheit 'illness'
krank sein 'to be ill'
es geht jmdm. schlecht 'sb. is unwell'
an etw. (= dat) erkranken 'to fall ill with sth.'
sich (= acc) erkälten 'to catch cold'
-r Befund/-e Diagnose 'diagnosis'
eine Diagnose stellen 'to diagnose'
leiden an (+ dat) 'to suffer from'
seekrank sein 'to be seasick'
sich (= acc) mit etw. quälen 'to struggle with/be plagued by sth.'
(-s) Fieber haben 'to run a temperature'

(a) Feeling unwell

There are several expressions indicating ill health that use the dative of disadvantage (see **19.3**A) with an optional **es** and a form of **sein**.

Feeling sick:

> *Es ist mir nicht gut./Mir ist (es) nicht gut.*
> I am not well.

> *Ihm ist schlecht/ übel.*
> He is sick. (meaning he is about to vomit)

Feeling cold:

> *Ist dir kalt/heiß?*
> Are you cold/hot?

(The above could just refer to the air temperature but quite often means body temperature.)

Feeling dizzy:

> *Mir schwindelt.*
> I am dizzy.

Looking unwell:

> **Du** *siehst schlecht aus.* **Bist du krank?**
> You look unwell. Are you ill?

(b) Falling ill

> **Er** *ist an* **Gelbsucht/Hepatitis/** *einer* **Halsentzündung** *erkrankt.*
> He has fallen ill/come down with jaundice/hepatitis/a throat infection.

> **Zieh dich warm an, damit** *du dich nicht erkältest.*
> Dress warmly so that you don't catch cold.

(c) Medical results are referred to as **-r Befund (e)**:

> **Der** *medizinische Befund* **im Urin ist negativ.**
> The urine results are negative.

> **Die Leber des Patienten** *war ohne Befund.*
> The liver of the patient was clear.

(d) Suffering is rendered by **leiden** and **sich quälen**:

> **Der Patient** *leidet an* **Herzrhythmusstörungen.**
> The patient is suffering from disturbances of the heart rhythm.

> **Sie *quält sich* schon seit Jahren *mit* ihrem Rheumatismus.**
> She has been struggling with/suffering from rheumatism for years.

(e) Running a temperature

Temperature in German-speaking countries is measured in degrees Celsius: **Grad Celsius**. Normal body temperature would be about 37°C (~ 98.4°F); 39°C (~ 102°F) would be considered **hohes Fieber**, a 'high temperature':

> **Nach der Impfung *hatte* der Kleine *hohes Fieber*.**
> After the inoculation the little boy had a high temperature.

110.9 — Death

-r Tod 'death'
-e Todesursache 'cause of death'
tot sein 'to be dead'
sterben 'to die'
verunglücken 'to have an accident'
tödlich verunglücken 'to be killed in an accident'
ums Leben kommen 'to die'
um*kommen 'to die'

(a) Dying

Dying of something is rendered by **sterben an** (= dat):

> **Das Unfallopfer *war* an den Folgen seiner Verletzungen *gestorben*.**
> The accident victim had died as a result of his injuries.

> **Die Skifahrer *waren* bei einem Lawinenunglück *ums Leben gekommen*.**
> The skiers were killed by an avalanche.

> **Der Popstar *ist* am Nachmittag *tödlich verunglückt*.**
> The pop star was killed in an accident in the afternoon.

(b) Dead

> **Er wurde noch am Unfallort *für tot erklärt*.**
> He was pronounced dead at the scene of the accident.

(c) Fatal consequences

> **Sie hat *tödliches* Gift geschluckt.**
> She has swallowed deadly poison.

> **Er war bei der Schlägerei *tödlich verwundet* worden.**
> He had been fatally injured during the fight/punch-up.

(See **65.3a**B for expressing sympathy)

—110.10— ## Passing on disease

> **sich** (= acc) **bei jmdm. an*stecken** 'to catch (a disease) from sb.'
> **jmdn. an*stecken** 'to infect someone'
> **sich bei jmdm. mit etw. an*stecken** 'to catch sth. from sb.'
> **ansteckend** 'contagious'
> **übertragen** 'to transmit'
> **sich** (= acc) **mit/an** (+ dat) **etw. infizieren** 'to infect oneself with sth.'
> **verunreinigen** 'to contaminate/pollute'
> **hervor*rufen** 'to cause/bring about'

(a) Catching a disease

> ***Er hatte sich* bei seinem Klassenkameraden mit den Masern *angesteckt*.**
> He had caught measles from his classmate.

> ***Sie hatte sich an* einer Spritze *infiziert*.**
> She had infected herself with a syringe.

(b) Transmitting a disease

> **Eine Infektionskrankheit *kann* durch die Luft oder durch Wassertröpfchen *übertragen werden*.**
> An infectious disease can be transmitted via the air or water droplets.

> **Eine *ansteckende* Krankheit *wird* durch Körperkontakt *übertragen*.**
> A contagious disease is transmitted by bodily contact.

> **Halte die Hand vor den Mund, wenn du hustest, damit du *niemanden ansteckst*.**
> Cover your mouth when you cough so that you don't infect anybody.

(c) Contamination

> **Der Durchfall war durch das *verunreinigte* Wasser *hervorgerufen* worden.**
> The diarrhoea had been caused by the contaminated water.

Pain

> **... tut mir weh** 'my... hurts' (informal)
> **Schmerzen haben** 'to have pains'
> **-s -weh** '-ache'
> **sich** (= dat) **(an etw.** = dat) **weh*tun** 'to hurt oneself (on sth.)'
> **-s Leid(en)** 'suffering'
> **leiden an** (+ dat) 'to suffer from'
> **Schmerzen lindern** 'to alleviate/relieve pain'
> **-e Linderung** 'alleviation/relief'

(a) The main way of referring to pain is by using **Schmerzen haben** 'to have pain' (lit. 'pains').

To indicate the exact place of pain, point to it and say:

> **Ich habe** *Schmerzen am Rücken/***an der Hand/im Unterleib.**
> I have a pain in my back/on my hand/in my lower abdomen.

Schmerzen (always plural) is usually the last component in a compound, following the part of the body that is causing pain.

(See **54.2**A for the formation of compounds)

> **Ich** *habe* **Magen***schmerzen/***Kopf***schmerzen/***Zahn***schmerzen.**
> I have stomach pains/a headache/toothache.

(b) In informal speech, **Schmerzen** is often replaced by **(sich) weh*tun** or by **-s Weh** 'ache' which is used in the singular:

> **Ach, mein Arm** *tut mir weh.*
> Oh, my arm hurts.

> **Mutti,** *ich habe Bauchweh.*
> Mummy, I have a tummy ache.

> **Vati, ich habe** *mir am Zaun wehgetan.*
> Daddy, I've hurt myself on the fence.

(c) Suffering

> **Er** *litt an einer* **schweren Lungenentzündung.**
> He suffered from severe pneumonia.

(See **23.2**A for the use of the German article. See also **110.8d**B on the use of **leiden**)

(d) Alleviating pain

> **Zur *Linderung* des Juckreizes wird ein Kamillenbad empfohlen.**
> A camomile bath is recommended to alleviate the itching.

110.12 Doctors, treatment and medication

(a) Doctors

A medical doctor is usually referred to as **-r Arzt**, a female doctor is **-e Ärztin**.

In informal speech **-r Doktor** is also used. A patient would address his doctor as **Herr/Frau Doktor** or the professor in a hospital as **Herr/Frau Professor** (normally without a surname).

Patients are normally registered with their 'General Practitioner' (**-r Hausarzt/ praktische Arzt**), although they could, theoretically, choose a new doctor every three months by taking their 'health insurance card' (**-r Krankenschein**) to someone else. This card could also be taken directly to a 'specialist' (**Facharzt**) but the 'patient', **-r Patient (-en)**, would be better advised to get a 'transfer note' (**-e Überweisung**) from his/her doctor and take it to the recommended consultant.

Consultants usually work in their own practices and one would arrange for 'an appointment' (**-r Termin**) directly with his 'secretary' (**-e Sekretärin**) or 'doctor's receptionist and nurse' (**-e Arzthelferin**).

The official titles for consultants are:

> **-r Facharzt für Allgemeinmedizin** 'specialist for general medicine/GP'
> **Facharzt für Kinder-/Frauen-/Nerven-/Lungenheilkunde** 'specialist for paediatrics/gynaecology/neurology/lung diseases'

N.B. **-r Kassenarzt** 'doctor who treats members of health insurance schemes'.

(For further specialist areas refer to a dictionary.)

In informal speech, compounds are preferred:

> **-e Kinderärztin** 'paediatrician'
> **-e Frauenärztin/Gynäkologin** 'gynaecologist'
> **-e Nervenärztin/Neurologin** 'neurologist'

Other medical staff include:

> **-e Krankenschwester** 'nurse'
> **-e Stationsschwester** 'ward sister'
> **-e Gemeindeschwester** 'district nurse'
> **-r Sanitäter (-)** 'first-aid attendant'
> **-e medizinisch-technische Assistentin (MTA)** 'medical laboratory assistant'
> **-r Heilpraktiker** 'non-medical practitioner'

(b) Treatment

> **jmdn./etw. heilen** 'to heal sb./sth.'
> **heilbar** 'curable'
> **jmdn./etw. behandeln** 'to treat sb./sth.'
> **-e Behandlung (en)** 'treatment'
> **sich (= acc) behandeln lassen** 'to be treated'
> **-e Heilung** 'healing/cure'
> **-s Heilverfahren** 'course of treatment'
> **-e Heilkunde** 'medicine'

Krebs ist oft *heilbar*, solange er frühzeitig erkannt wird.
Cancer is often curable, as long as it is diagnosed early.

Er ist seit drei Jahren bei einem Psychiater *in Behandlung*.
He has been treated by a psychiatrist for three years.

***Sie läßt sich* lieber von einer Frau *behandeln*.**
She prefers to be treated by a woman.

(c) Medical investigation

> **-e Untersuchung durch*führen** 'to do an investigation/a medical'
> **jmdn. untersuchen** 'to examine sb.'
> **sich (= acc) untersuchen lassen** 'to (let oneself) be examined'
> **sich (= acc) röntgen lassen** 'to have an X-ray'
> **ärztlich** 'medical/by the doctor'

Vor der Weltreise müssen *wir uns* noch ärztlich *untersuchen lassen*.
Before the round-the-world trip we have to undergo a medical examination.

Die Infusion darf nur unter *ärztlicher* Aufsicht gegeben werden.
The infusion may only be given with medical supervision/in the presence of a doctor.

(d) Medication

-e Medizin/-s Medikament 'medicine'
-e Pille 'pills' in general
BUT **die Pille** (= **Antibabypille**) 'the (contraceptive) pill'
etw. zu etw. brauchen 'to need sth. for sth.'
-s Heilmittel(-) gegen 'remedy for'
-s Schmerzmittel 'painkiller'
-s Rezept 'prescription'
verschreiben 'to prescribe'
-e Dosis (Dosen) 'dose'

Baldrian ist ein gutes (Heil-)*mittel gegen* **Stress.**
Valerian is a good remedy for stress.

Ich brauche *etwas zur Beruhigung.*
I need something to calm (my nerves).

Prophylaktisches Aspirin wird *in sehr kleinen Dosen*/**Mengen eingenommen.**
Prophylactic aspirin is taken in very small doses/amounts.

To get a prescription:

Ich *möchte mir ein Rezept für Antibiotika verschreiben lassen.*
I would like to have a prescription for antibiotics.

Dieses Medikament ist *rezeptpflichtig.*
This medicine is available only on prescription.

Medically tested medication:

Diese Salbe wurde *medizinisch geprüft.*
This ointment was medically tested.

(e) Operations

jmdn. an etw. (= dat) **operieren** 'to operate on sb.'s sth.'

Meine Nachbarin *wird* **morgen an der Galle** *operiert.*
My neighbour is having an operation on her gall-bladder tomorrow.

(See **66.2a**B for expressing good wishes for health and speedy recovery)

111 *Expressing happiness, fear and sadness*

111.1 Describing mood in general

> -e Stimmung/Laune 'mood'
> guter/schlechter Laune sein 'to be in a good/bad mood'
> gut gelaunt sein 'to be in a good mood'

> **Heute war mein Fahrlehrer** *besonders gut gelaunt.*
> My driving instructor was in a particularly good mood today.

-e Laune (n) also means mood, but has a slightly negative connotation:

> **Er** *hat* **seine** *Launen.*
> He has his moods.

> **Er** *ist* **meistens recht** *launisch.*
> He is quite bad tempered most of the time.

The idiomatic expression **vor lauter** indicates that someone does something 'for sheer ...' **vor lauter Freude/Ärger/Schreck** 'for sheer joy/out of sheer annoyance/fright':

> **Die Kellnerin ließ** *vor lauter Schreck* **die Weingläser fallen.**
> The waitress dropped the wine glasses out of sheer fright.

111.2 Positive moods: joy and happiness

Many expressions of positive mood are based on **freuen** and **Freude**:

> sich (= acc) freuen 'to be pleased'
> -e Freude 'joy'
> sich über etw. (= acc) freuen 'to be glad/happy about sth.'
> erfreulich 'pleasing/gratifying'
> glücklich 'happy'
> sich auf etw./jmdn. freuen 'to look forward to sb./sth.'
> jmdm. eine Freude machen 'to bring joy to sb./make sb. happy'
> Freude an etw. (= dat) haben 'to enjoy/get pleasure from/take pleasure in sth.'
> -s Glück 'happiness/luck/fortune'
> zum Glück 'fortunately'
> glücklicherweise 'fortunately/happily'
> Glück haben 'to be lucky/fortunate'
> Glück im Unglück haben 'to be lucky under the circumstances'
> jmdm. den/die Daumen halten/drücken 'to keep one's fingers crossed for sb.'
> (colloquial)

(a) Being pleased

> **Es freut mich, dich wiederzusehen.**
> I am pleased to see you again.

> **Wir würden uns ganz besonders über Ihren Besuch freuen.**
> We would be very pleased if you came to visit (us).

> **Sie freute sich darüber, ein Schnäppchen gemacht zu haben.** (informal)
> She was pleased to have got a bargain.

> **Der Sieg seiner Mannschaft war besonders für den Trainer erfreulich.**
> The team's victory was especially pleasing for their manager.

(b) Being happy and showing joy

> **Sie war so glücklich wie noch nie.**
> She was happier than she had ever been.

> **Der Teenager war im siebten Himmel.**
> The teenager was on cloud nine.

> **Als sie das gute Zeugnis bekam, ist sie vor Freude in die Luft gesprungen.**
> When she received her good report she jumped with joy.

> **Sie ist ihm vor reiner Freude um den Hals gefallen.**
> She embraced him with sheer joy.

> **Er hat einen Freudenschrei ausgestoßen.**
> He gave a shout of joy.

The happy ending of a fairy-tale is rendered as follows:

> **Sie lebten glücklich und zufrieden bis ans Ende ihrer Tage.**
> They lived happily ever after.

(c) Looking forward to something

> **Ich freue mich auf meine Geburtstagsparty.**
> I am looking forward to my birthday party.

> **Er freut sich darauf, mit ihr auszugehen.**
> He is looking forward to going out with her.

(See **42.3e**A for completion by a clause)

(d) Pleasing someone

> **Ich würde euch gerne eine Freude zum Hochzeitstag machen.**
> I would like to treat you for your wedding anniversary.

(e) Enjoying something

> **Die beiden *haben eine große Freude an* ihrem Garten.**
> The two of them get a lot of pleasure out of their garden.

(f) Being lucky

Glück can mean both 'happiness' and 'luck' in English. Its exact meaning has to be gleaned from context. When used with a form of **haben**, **Glück** means 'to be lucky':

> **Mit dem guten Wetter *haben wir* wirklich *Glück gehabt.***
> We were really lucky with the (good) weather.

> **Unser Auto war total ausgeraubt worden. *Zum Glück* hatten die Kinder noch etwas Geld dabei.**
> Our car had been completely cleaned out./Everything had been taken/stolen from our car. Fortunately the children had some money with them.

> **Der hintere Wagen war auf unseren draufgefahren. *Glücklicherweise* ist uns nichts passiert.**
> The car behind ran into ours. Fortunately we were all right (lit. nothing (bad) happened to us).

(See **76.1g**B for **passieren**)

Hoping for luck:

> **Drücke mir den Daumen, wenn ich meine Fahrprüfung mache.**
> Keep yours fingers crossed for me when I take my driving test.

111.3 **Negative moods**

(a) Negative moods can be expressed in terms of positive ones by negating them:

Positive	Negative
-e Freude 'joy'	**-s Leid** 'sorrow'
freudig 'joyful'	**freudlos** 'without pleasure'
Glück haben 'to be lucky'	**Pech haben** 'to be unlucky'
über etw. (= acc) **froh sein** 'to be happy about sth.'	**über etw.** (= acc) **traurig sein** 'to be sad about sth.'
	über etw. (= acc) **deprimiert sein** 'to be down about sth./be depressed/feel down'

(b) Sadness

> **über etw.** (= acc) **traurig sein** 'to be sad about sth.'
> **über etw.** (= acc) **betrübt sein** 'to be grieved/sorrowful about sth.'
> **über etw.** (= acc) **weinen** 'to cry about sth.'

Sie *war* in tiefster Seele *betrübt* über die Scheidung ihrer Enkelin.
She was deeply grieved about the divorce of her granddaughter.

Sie *weinte*, als ihr Hund starb.
She cried when her dog died.

(c) Yearning

> **Sehnsucht** (f) **nach jmdm./etw. haben** 'to have a yearning/longing for sb./sth.'
> **Heimweh nach etw. haben** 'to be homesick for sth.'
> **Fernweh haben/vom Fernweh gepackt werden** 'to feel wanderlust/yearning to wander'
> **Lust auf etw.** (= acc) **haben** 'to fancy sth.' (colloquial, informal)

Als er in Amerika war, *hatte* er solche *Sehnsucht* nach deutschem Brot.
When he was in America he had such a yearning for German bread.

***Hat* dich das *Fernweh* wieder *gepackt*?**
Have you been caught by the wander bug again?

Manche Schüler *haben* schon in der ersten Nacht *Heimweh* nach Hause.
Some pupils are homesick on the very first night.

Ich habe Lust auf ein Stück Kuchen/auf Volleyball.
I fancy a piece of cake/playing volleyball.

(d) Suffering

> **leiden an/unter** (+ dat) 'to suffer from/under'

Er *hatte* sehr *unter* seinem strengen Vater *gelitten*.
He had suffered greatly under his strict father.

See **110.8** for suffering from a medical condition.

(e) Feeling down or depressed

deprimiert sein 'to be depressed'
sich (= acc) **überflüssig fühlen** 'to feel superfluous'
sich (= dat) **wie ein Versager vor*kommen** 'to feel a failure'
keinen Sinn mehr im Leben sehen 'to see no more sense/point in life'
keinen Lebenssinn/Lebensinhalt mehr haben 'to have no more meaning/raison
d'être in life'
sich (= acc) **einsam fühlen** 'to feel lonely'
ein trostloses Dasein führen 'to lead a wretched/bleak existence'

> Sie *hat* immer wieder einmal *Depressionen.*
> She does suffer from depression every now and again.

> Er *hat sich* als Arbeitsloser *überflüssig gefühlt.*
> He felt superfluous as an unemployed person.

> Viele Menschen *führen* im Altersheim *ein trostloses Dasein.*
> Many people lead a bleak existence in an old people's home.

(f) Sorrow

-r Kummer 'grief/sorrow'
jmdm. Kummer machen/bereiten 'to cause sb. grief/sorrow'

> Das Schicksal ihrer einzigen Tochter *bereitete ihr* großen *Kummer.*
> The fate of her only daughter caused her much grief.

> *Vor Kummer* konnte sie kaum denken.
> She could hardly think with all her sorrow.

(g) Worry

-e Sorge 'worry'
sich (= dat) **um etw.** (= acc) **Sorgen machen** 'to worry about sth./sb.'
sich (= dat) **Sorgen machen wegen** (+ gen)/**um** (+acc) 'to worry because of'
sich (= dat) **um etw.** (= acc) **Gedanken machen** 'to worry about sth.'
sich (= acc) **um etw./jmdn. sorgen** 'to worry about sth./sb.'
etw. macht jmdm. zu schaffen 'sth. worries sb.'
jmdm. am Herzen liegen 'to be important to sb.' (lit. 'to lie close to sb.'s heart')
jmdm. schwer auf der Seele/dem Gewissen liegen 'to weigh heavily on sb.'s
mind/conscience'

Er *machte sich Sorgen um* seine Frau, die bei Nacht und Nebel alleine unterwegs war.

He was worried about his wife, who was out on her own at night/in the dark.

Wir *machen uns große Sorgen* wegen unsrer unbezahlten Rechnungen.

We are very worried about our unpaid bills.

Der Schulwechsel *macht vielen Kindern zu schaffen.*

Many children are worried about changing school.

Wir *machen uns Gedanken/Sorgen über* das Drogenproblem an der Schule.

We are worried about the drugs problem at the school.

Ich *sorge mich um* deine Gesundheit.

I worry about your health.

Es lag ihm sehr am Herzen, daß seine Eltern sich wieder versöhnten.

It was very important to him that his parents should become reconciled.

Der Streit in seiner Abteilung *lag ihm schwer auf der Seele.*

The argument in his department weighed on his mind.

(h) Fear

> **sich (= acc) vor etw./jmdm. fürchten** 'to be afraid of sth./sb.'
> **etw. (= acc) befürchten** 'to fear sth.'
> **Angst haben vor etw./jmdm.** 'to be afraid of sth./sb.'

Being afraid of specific things:

Ich *fürchtete mich vor* einer Begegnung mit seiner Freundin.

I was afraid of a (chance) meeting with his girlfriend.

Sie *fürchtet sich vor* Spinnen/der Fahrprüfung.

She is afraid of spiders/the driving test.

Das schlechte Ergebnis *war zu befürchten.*

The bad result was to be expected/feared.

Er *hatte Angst vor* der Abschlußprüfung.

He was afraid of the final exam.

General feeling that cannot be pinpointed to a specific fear:

Er *hat Angst,* im Beruf *zu versagen/vor der Zukunft.*

He is afraid of failing in his profession/of the future.

(i) Frustration

> **-e Frustration** 'frustration'
> **etw. frustrierend finden** 'to find sth. frustrating'
> **frustriert sein über** (+ acc) 'to be frustrated about'
> **auf etw.** (= acc) **einen Frust haben** (only in spoken language) 'to be frustrated about sth.'

> *Frustrationen*, **die nicht ausgedrückt werden, können leicht zu Aggressionen führen.**
> Frustrations that are not expressed can easily lead to aggression.

(j) Grief and mourning

> **-e Trauer** 'sorrow/mourning'
> **um jmdn./etw. trauern** 'to mourn for sb./sth.'
> **in stiller/tiefer Trauer** '(much loved and) sadly missed'
> **jmdn. vermissen** 'to miss sb.'

> **Sie** *trauerte um ihren* **verlorenen** *Sohn.*
> She grieved for her lost son.

> *Wir trauern um unsre Toten.*
> We mourn our dead.

> **Seit seinem Tode** *wird er* **schmerzlich** *vermißt.*
> He has been sadly/sorely missed since his death.

> **Ihr Witwer** *vermißt* **sie.**
> Her widower misses her.

Black is the colour for mourning in German-speaking countries and is still widely worn at a 'funeral' (**-e Beerdigung**) or less commonly at a 'cremation' (**-e Feuerbestattung**). 'Widows', **-e Witwe (n)**, of the older generation tend to wear dark colours for a suitable period of time, and obituary notices and responses to them usually carry a black edging.

(See also **65.1–65.3**B for expressing commiseration, and **110.9**B on death and dying)

(k) Shock and fright

> **jmdn. schockieren** 'to shock sb.'
> **erschrecken (erschrickt, erschrak, erschrocken)** (intransitive) 'to be shocked/frightened'
> **jmdn. erschrecken (erschreckte, erschreckt)** (transitive) 'to frighten sb.'

Die traurige Nachricht *hatte uns* sehr *schockiert.*
The sad news shocked us very much.

Bei dem nächtlichen Schuß *erschrak sie furchtbar.*
She was terribly frightened by the shot in the night.

Der plötzliche Aufschrei *hat sie erschreckt.*
The sudden cry shocked/frightened her.

(See **114.6**B for more expressions of shock)

(l) Anger

> **wütend sein auf** (+ acc) 'to be angry/furious'
> **zornig sein auf** (+ acc) 'to be angry'
> **vor lauter Zorn** 'in a fit of anger'
> **sich** (= acc) **über etw./jmdn. ärgern** 'to be annoyed about sth./sb.'
> **über etw./jmdn. verärgert sein** 'to be annoyed about sth./sb.'

Er *war* immer noch *wütend auf* **den Dieb, der ihm sein Filofax gestohlen hatte.**
He was still really angry with/furious with the thief that had stolen his Filofax.

Er ist *zornig auf* **seinen Bruder, der ihn beim Lehrer verpetzt hat.**
He is angry with his brother for telling on him to the teacher.

Sie *ärgerte sich über* **die hohe Telefonrechnung.**
She was annoyed about the high phone bill.

Sie waren sehr *verärgert über* **die mißlungene Darbietung.**
They were very annoyed about the failed presentation.

Vor lauter Zorn **warf sie ihm den Teller an den Kopf.**
In a fit of anger she threw the plate at his head.

(m) Feeling insulted

> **beleidigt** 'insulted'
> **gekränkt** 'hurt/insulted'
> **jmdn. kränken** 'to hurt sb.'
> **verletzt** 'hurt/insulted'

Obwohl er versucht hatte, das Mißverständnis zu beseitigen, *war sie* **doch noch stark** *beleidigt.*

Even though he had tried to clear up the misunderstanding, she was still very offended/insulted.

Daß du nicht gekommen bist, *hat deine Mutter* **sehr** *gekränkt.*
Your mother was very hurt that you didn't come.

(n) Saying that one has had enough

---

die Nase voll haben 'to be fed up' (colloquial, informal)
die Schnauze voll haben 'to be fed up' (very informal)
es reicht/langt 'that's enough'

Jetzt *habe ich* **aber** *die Nase voll***!**
Now I am really fed up.

Das *reicht/fehlt mir* **gerade noch.** (ironic)
That's all I need.

Jetzt *langt/reicht es* **aber!**
That's enough now!

111.4 **Sharing feelings**
Making people feel something:

---

jmdn. zum Lächeln/Lachen/Weinen/Verzweifeln bringen 'to make someone
smile/laugh/cry/despair'
jmdn. auf*heitern 'to cheer sb. up'

Er kitzelte sie, um sie *zum Lachen* **zu** *bringen.*
He tickled her to make her laugh.

Wir erzählten uns Witze, *um* **uns gegenseitig** *aufzuheitern.*
We told each other jokes in order to cheer each other up.

112 *Expressing satisfaction and dissatisfaction*

112.1 **Being satisfied and dissatisfied**
The main word for expressing satisfaction is **zufrieden** 'satisfied' and its derivatives:

> **mit etw./jmdm. zufrieden sein** 'to be satisfied with sth./sb.'
> **unzufrieden** 'dissatisfied'
> **sich (= acc) mit etw. zufrieden*geben** 'to accept sth.'
> **-e Zufriedenheit** 'satisfaction'

(See also **104**B for more expressions of satisfaction)

> **Er *ist mit* seinem Leben völlig *zufrieden*.**
> He is completely satisfied with his life.

> **Der Manager *war mit* seiner Sekretärin *unzufrieden*.**
> The manager was dissatisfied with his secretary.

> **Sie *wollte sich nicht mit* der Antwort *zufriedengeben*.**
> She would not accept the answer.

> **Er *fand die schönste Befriedigung darin*, seine Rosen für den Wettbewerb *zu* züchten.**
> He derived the greatest satisfaction from growing his roses for the competition.

112.2 — **Satisfying needs and demands**

> **(Ansprüche/Bedürfnisse) befriedigen** 'to satisfy (demands/needs/expectations)'
> **-e Befriedigung** 'satisfaction/gratification'
> **-e Befriedigung (von Bedürfnissen)** 'satisfaction/gratification (of needs)'
> **-e Neugierde/-s Verlangen/Hunger/Durst stillen** 'to satisfy a curiosity/a desire/hunger/thirst'

> **Seine hohen Ansprüche an seine Mitarbeiter sind kaum zu *befriedigen*.**
> His high demands/expectations of his colleagues can hardly be satisfied.

> **Zur *Befriedigung ihres Heißhungers* wollte sie unbedingt den ganzen Kuchen essen.**
> To satisfy her ravenous hunger she was determined to eat the entire cake.

> **Zur *Befriedigung deiner Neugier* kannst du ja mein Tagebuch lesen.**
> To satisfy your curiosity you can always read my diary. (could be ironic)

> **Ihr großes *Verlangen nach* Sonnenuntergängen konnte an der Westküste *gestillt* werden.**
> She was able to satisfy her great desire for sunsets on the west coast.

(See **112.5**B on **stillen**)

112.3

Satisfactory achievements

(a) Describing someone's achievements as satisfactory, i.e. acceptable without being outstanding

> **befriedigend** 'satisfactory'
> **zur vollen Zufriedenheit** (+ gen) 'to the full satisfaction (of)'
> **zufriedenstellend** 'satisfactory'
> On a scale from least to most satisfactory, the following adverbs are used
> with **zufrieden sein mit**:
> **einigermaßen** 'somewhat'
> **ziemlich** 'rather'
> **recht** 'quite/pretty'
> **sehr** 'very'
> **äußerst** 'extremely'

> **Die Lehrerin *ist* mit seinem Fortschritt *äußerst zufrieden*.**
> The (female) teacher is most satisfied with his progress.

> **Der Lehrling hatte seine Probezeit *zur vollen Zufriedenheit* seines Meisters abgeschlossen.**
> The apprentice had finished his probationary period to the full satisfaction of his boss/foreman.

(b) Achievements are expressed by:

> **-r Fortschritt** 'progress'
> **-e Leistung** 'achievement'
> **-s Ergebnis** 'result'

> **Seine *Leistungen* waren stets befriedigend.**
> His performance was always satisfactory.

> ***Das Ergebnis* der Untersuchungen *war äußerst zufriedenstellend*.**
> The result of the investigations was extremely satisfactory.

(c) Official grades at school are usually scaled as follows (from best to worst):

1 (eins)	sehr gut	'very good'
2 (zwei)	gut	'good'
3 (drei)	befriedigend	'satisfactory'
4 (vier)	ausreichend	'adequate'
5 (fünf)	mangelhaft	'defective/fail'
6 (sechs)	ungenügend	'unsatisfactory/fail'

In Mathematik hat er "*befriedigend*" bekommen.
In maths he got a 'C'.

(d) The difference between **Zufriedenheit** and **Befriedigung** is that **Zufriedenheit mit etw.** usually implies satisfaction with the status quo, whereas **Befriedigung von etw.** means satisfaction of needs/desires:

Der Vorarbeiter *ist mit seinem Lohn zufrieden.*
The foreman is satisfied with his wages.

Sein *Bedürfnis an Wärme und Liebe ist unbefriedigt.*
His desire for warmth and love is unsatisfied/has been frustrated.

112.4

Saying that something is sufficient is expressed with **(aus)reichen** and **genügen** (often with the dative of the person concerned):

(aus*)reichen/genügen 'to suffice'
genug/genügend 'enough/sufficient'
nicht genug kriegen können 'to not be able to get enough/to be greedy' (colloquial)
reichlich 'plentiful'
ausreichend 'sufficient'

Die dünne Decke *reicht/genügt mir* völlig.
The thin blanket is quite sufficient for me.

Hast du *genug/genügend* Getränke für unsre Gäste eingekauft?
Have you bought enough/sufficient drink for our guests?

Wir *konnten nicht genug von* dem Sekt *kriegen.*
We couldn't get enough of the sparkling wine.

112.5 ## Saying one has had enough to eat
(See **63**B for further expressions on food and drink)

Möchtest du noch etwas essen? – Nein danke, *ich bin satt.*
Would you like anything else to eat? – No thank you, I've had enough/
I am full.

(See also **67.5c**B and **93.4**B for thanking in response to polite enquiries)

To eat/drink all one wants:

An dem köstlichen Salatbüffet *kann man sich so richtig satt essen.*
You can really eat all you want (your fill) at the delicious salad buffet.

To get enough:

> **Mit dem spärlichen Essen *kann* man nicht *satt werden*.**
> This meagre meal isn't enough (to fill you up).

(See also **93.4**B for the use of **voll**)

Having enough to drink:

gestillt is an alternative to **satt**, also meaning 'satisfied' with food or drink. It is derived from **stillen** which primarily means 'to quench (a thirst)' and 'to breast-feed':

> **Auf der Wanderung *konnte* er seinen starken *Durst* am Brunnen *stillen*.**
> On the walk he was able to quench his thirst at the spring/well.

112.6 Coming to terms/putting up with things that are unsatisfactory

> **sich** (= acc) **damit ab*finden, daß** 'to put up with the fact that/reluctantly acknowledge'
> **sich** (= acc) **mit etw. zufrieden*geben** 'to accept sth./go along with/acquiesce in sth.'

> **Er *hat sich* immer noch *nicht damit abgefunden*, daß seine Villa in Mecklenburg jetzt jemand anderem gehört.**
> He has still not come to terms with the fact that his villa in Mecklenburg now belongs to someone else.

> **Du *mußt dich mit* dem geringen Taschengeld *zufriedengeben*; mehr gibt es nicht.**
> You'll have to make do with the small amount of pocket money you get; you are not getting any more.

113 *Expressing hopes, wishes and disappointment*

113.1

Hopes in general are conveyed by the following:

> **-e Hoffnung** 'hope'
> **hoffen auf** (+ acc) 'to hope for'
> **hoffentlich** 'hopefully'

(a) Hoping for better things can be expressed in the following ways:

> **Laßt uns *auf* eine bessere Zukunft *hoffen*.**
> Let's hope for a better future.

> Es *besteht* begründete *Hoffnung*, daß sich diese Vogelart wieder hier einnistet.
> There is justification/good reason for hoping that this type of bird will nest here again.

(b) Hoping for a good outcome, that nothing bad has happened or is going to happen:

> *Hoffentlich* ist ihm nichts passiert/geschehen/zugestoßen.
> Hopefully nothing (bad) has happened to him.

Note here that **passieren**, **geschehen** and **zu*stoßen** have a connotation of something bad happening.

(See also **76.1g**B)

> Wenn das *bloß/nur* alles *gut geht*!
> If only it/I do hope it all goes well!

(c) Hoping to overcome present difficulties

> **etw./jmdn. überleben** 'to survive sth./sb.'
> **etw. überstehen** 'to overcome/get through sth.'
> **etw. aus*halten** 'to stick/endure sth.'
> **etw. überwinden** 'to overcome sth.'
> **etw. durch*halten** 'to endure sth.'
> **zusammen*halten** 'to stick together'
> **-s Durchhaltevermögen** '(power of) endurance'
> **etw. schaffen** 'to manage sth.'
> **über die Runden kommen** 'to manage'

(See **36.2**A for inseparable verbs)

> Wir werden auch diesen Winter *überleben/überstehen*.
> We will survive/get through this winter all right.

(**auch** has a soothing effect. See **117.1c**B)

> Sie brauchen die Schmerzen nicht mehr lange *auszuhalten*.
> You won't have to suffer/bear the pains much longer.

> Wenn alle *zusammenhalten*, sind diese Schwierigkeiten zu *überwinden*.
> If (we) all stick together, these difficulties can be overcome.

> Das *schaff* ich/krieg ich schon hin!
> I'll manage that.

Er wird auch mit dem geringeren Gehalt *über die Runden kommen.*
He will manage even on the lower salary.

(d) Hoping against hope

Er darf jetzt auf keinen Fall die *Hoffnung aufgeben.*
He mustn't give up hope now, whatever happens.

(e) Being hopeful and excited

Seid ihr auch so *gespannt darauf,* wie der Wettbewerb ausgeht?
Are you as excited about the outcome of the competition as we are?

113.2

Wishes

The most common way to express wishes involves **wünschen** 'to wish' and its derivatives.

(a) Wishing for things

sich (= dat) **etw. wünschen** 'to wish for sth.'
jmdm. etw. wünschen 'to wish sb. sth.'

Ich *wünschte,* ich *hätte* mehr Zeit zum Klavierspielen.
I wish I had more time for playing the piano.

(See **39.2–39.3**A for Subjunctive II)

Wilhelm *wünscht sich* einen großen Mercedes.
William would like to get a big Mercedes.

Wishing something for someone else on a certain occasion:

Zum Geburtstag wünschen wir dir alles Gute, Gesundheit und Gottes Segen.
For your birthday we wish you all the best, health and God's blessing.

(See **66**B on 'Expressing good wishes')

(b) Granting and denying wishes

jmdm. einen Wunsch erfüllen/versagen 'to grant/deny a wish to sb.'
ein Wunsch geht (nicht) in Erfüllung 'a wish is (not) fulfilled'

Wenn ich *dir* doch nur *diesen Wunsch erfüllen* könnte.
If only I could make this wish come true for you.

Es wäre schön, wenn alle *Wünsche in Erfüllung gehen* könnten.

It would be nice if all wishes could come true.

Ab und zu muß man *den Kindern* auch *einen Wunsch versagen,* sonst werden sie zu verwöhnt.
Every now and again one should refuse/say no to children's wishes, or they'll be spoilt.

113.3

Disappointment

> **-e Enttäuschung** 'disappointment'
> **enttäuscht sein über etw.** (= acc) 'to be disappointed about sth.'
> **verletzt sein** 'to be hurt'
> **leider** 'unfortunately'

(a) These expressions can be modified by the use of adverbs/adjectives such as:

> **furchtbar** 'frightfully'
> **schrecklich** 'terribly'
> **schwer** 'badly'
> **tief** 'profoundly/badly'
> **leicht** 'slightly'

Er wird von ihrer Note in Kunst *schwer enttäuscht sein.*
He will be really disappointed about her grade in art.

Das undankbare Verhalten ihres Sohnes hatte sie *tief verletzt.*
Her son's ungrateful behaviour had hurt her badly.

verletzt sein expresses a much stronger feeling.

(b) Failed hopes

Seine *Hoffnungen* auf einen neuen Lebensanfang hatten sich völlig *zerschlagen.*
His hopes for a new start in life had failed completely.

Seine *Hoffnung,* eine Frau zu finden, die mit ihm den Hof bewirtschaftet, *ging nicht in Erfüllung.*
His hope of finding a wife who would run the farm with him was not fulfilled.

(c) Disappointed expectations

Ihre viel zu hohen *Erwartungen an* das Au-pair Mädchen werden bestimmt enttäuscht.

Her much too high expectations of the au pair girl will certainly be disappointed.

(d) Not having had a chance to do something (on a particular day)

Sie war einfach *nicht dazugekommen,* einmal mit ihm zu tanzen.
She simply didn't get a chance to have a single dance with him.

Not to have the opportunity:

Wir werden *leider keine Gelegenheit zu* einem persönlichen Gespräch haben.
Unfortunately we will have no opportunity to talk in private.

Er *hatte* eben *nicht die Chance gehabt,* schon als Kind eine bessere Allgemeinbildung zu bekommen.
As a child he had simply not had the chance to get a better general education.

(See **117.1c**B for the modal particle **eben**)

(e) Disappointment at failing to do something (correctly) is often expressed through a verb with the prefix **ver-**:

(See **57.2**A for word formation)

> **eine Gelegenheit/einen Bus verpassen/versäumen** 'to miss an opportunity/a bus (by one's own neglect)'
> **einen Namen/einen Jahrestag vergessen** 'to forget a name/an anniversary'
> **einen Verstorbenen/den Geliebten vermissen** 'to miss a dead person/a loved one'
> **einen Ring/den Weg verlieren** 'to lose a ring/the way'
> **ein Buch/eine wichtige Akte verlegen** 'to mislay a book/an important document'
> **(etw./jmdn. mit etw./jmdm.) verwechseln** 'to confuse (sth./sb. with sth./sb.)'
> **sich verirren** 'to lose one's way'

Sie bedauerte, dieses Andenken an ihre Patentante *verloren zu haben.*
She regretted *having lost* this souvenir/memento of her godmother.

Habt ihr uns auch wirklich nicht mit denen aus der anderen Gruppe *verwechselt?*
Are you sure you haven't confused us with (those from) the other group?

114 *Expressing surprise*

Surprise in general

> **überraschen** 'to surprise'
> **jmdn. überraschen** 'to surprise sb.'
> **bei etw. überrascht werden** 'to be surprised/caught doing sth.'
> **jmdn. bei etw. erwischen** 'to catch sb. doing sth.' (usually sth. illicit)
> **von etw./jmdm. überrascht werden/sein** 'to be surprised by sth./sb.'
> **-e Überraschung (en)** 'surprise'

(See **36.2**A for inseparable verbs)

(a) To be surprised

> **Die Kinder *waren überrascht*, wie groß der Spielplatz war.**
> The children were surprised how big the playground was.

(See **40**A for the passive)

> **Wir *wurden* von dem plötzlichen Unwetter *überrascht*.**
> We were surprised by the sudden thunderstorm.

> **Der Einbrecher *wurde* beim Aufknacken des Safes *überrascht*.**
> The intruder was caught (while) cracking the safe.

> **Habe ich dich wieder dabei *erwischt*, wie du in meinen Notizen gelesen hast?** (informal)
> Have I caught you again reading my notes?

> **Alle Dorfbewohner *wurden* von der Flut *überrascht*.**
> All the villagers were surprised by the flood.

(b) Different sorts of surprise

-e Überraschung can be both positive and negative, and also lends itself to the formation of compounds:

> **-e schöne/böse Überraschung (erleben)** '(to have) a nice/bad/nasty surprise'
> **-s Überraschungsgeschenk** 'surprise gift'
> **-e Überraschungsparty** 'surprise party'

> ***Zu meiner* großen *Überraschung* waren auch die Verwandten aus Übersee zu der Familienfeier gekommen.**

> To my great surprise even the relatives from overseas had come to the family celebration.

(c) When visiting someone it is nice to take them a little something as a surprise:

> **Ich habe Ihnen eine *kleine Überraschung* mitgebracht.**
> I've brought you a little something as a surprise.

— 114.2 —

Unforeseen events

To indicate that something was not foreseeable, one of the following expressions is used. These expressions are usually linked to the conditional.

(See **39.7**A for **würde** construction)

> **nicht ahnen** 'to have no inkling'
> **nicht vorher*sehen** 'to not foresee'
> **nicht vorhersehbar** 'not foreseeable'
> **nicht rechnen mit** 'to not reckon with'
> **unerwartet** 'unexpected(ly)'
> **erstaunlicherweise** 'surprisingly'

(a) When there is no idea/inkling of what was going to happen

> **Wir konnten *nicht ahnen*, daß er sich das so zu Herzen nehmen würde.**
> We had no idea that he would take it to heart so much.

(b) If something was not foreseeable

> **Es war nicht *vorherzusehen*, wie schnell sich das Feuer ausbreiten würde.**
> One could not have foreseen how quickly the fire would spread.

For something that was not reckoned with:

> **Wir hatten zwar *mit* dem Abriß der Häuser an der Autobahn *gerechnet*, aber dann geschah es doch *plötzlich und unerwartet*.**
> We had indeed reckoned with/expected the demolition of the houses next to the motorway, but then it happened so suddenly and unexpectedly.

(c) Unexpected events

> **Dem Patienten geht es *unerwartet* gut.**
> The patient is surprisingly (lit. unexpectedly) well.

> **Die Aktien waren *überraschend* gestiegen.**
> The shares had risen unexpectedly.

Die Nachricht von seiner Beförderung kam *überraschend.*
The news of his promotion came as a surprise.

114.3 Hardly believing the news

Expressing pleasant or unpleasant surprise

Er konnte *kaum glauben,* daß er das große Los gewonnen hatte.
He could hardly believe that he had won the jackpot.

Der Krankenwagen kam *unglaublich* schnell zum Unfallort.
The ambulance got to the scene of the accident incredibly quickly.

Es ist *nicht zu fassen,* wie schrecklich abgemagert die Flüchtlinge sind.
It is unbelievable how terribly emaciated the refugees are.

114.4 Astonishment and awe

staunen 'to be astonished', and **jmdn. erstaunen** 'to astonish sb', convey astonishment or even awe about something great or miraculous:

Es *hat mich erstaunt,* daß am Feiertag so wenig Leute im Museum waren.
I was surprised to see so few people in the museum on a public holiday.

Über* die sieben Weltwunder *wird* immer wieder *gestaunt.
The seven wonders of the world never cease to amaze people.

Seine Erfindung hatte das *Staunen* der Nachwelt *erregt.*
His invention had astonished (lit. excited the astonishment of) future generations.

114.5 Incomprehension

(a) **Sich** (= acc) **über etw.** (= acc) **wundern** 'to be surprised about something' is also used for total incomprehension, for something that cannot be understood:

Er *wunderte sich über* ihr eigenartiges Verhalten.
He could not understand her strange behaviour.

(b) Where an interrogative clause follows, **Ich frage mich** is used:

Ich frage mich, ob/warum* hier eine Radarfalle ist.
I wonder whether/why there is a speed trap here.

(c) **verwundert sein** denotes an even more confused state of surprise:

Wir *waren* völlig *verwundert,* wie sehr sie sich zu ihrem Vorteil verändert hatte.
We were completely surprised by how much she had changed for the better.

Shock and dismay

To express shock at an event:

> **Die Gemeinde *war* über die Zahl der Kirchenaustritte *schockiert*.**
> The parishioners were shocked about the number of people leaving the
> church.

> **Die Wanderer *waren* über das Waldsterben sehr *bestürzt*.**
> The walkers were most alarmed about the forest dying.

(See **111.3k**B for more expressions of shock and fright)

Irony

In order to be ironic about a real mess caused by some sort of disaster, **schöne
Bescherung** (lit: 'giving of Christmas presents') 'that's just great' is used:

> **Der Keller steht ein Meter unter Wasser; das ist vielleicht *eine schöne
> Bescherung*.**
> The cellar is under a metre of water; that's just great.

115 *Expressing enjoyment and pleasure*

Expressions of enjoyment and pleasure in general are derived from the following:

> **-r Spaß** 'fun'
> **-s Vergnügen** 'pleasure'
> **-r Genuß** 'enjoyment'
> **-e Freude** 'joy/fun'
> **-e Lust** 'fun'

Giving pleasure

> **jmdm. Spaß machen** 'to give sb. pleasure'
> **es macht jmdm. Spaß, etw. zu tun** 'sb. enjoys doing sth.'
> **erfreulich** 'pleasing/gratifying'
> **über etw. (= acc) entzückt sein** 'to be delighted at/about sth.'

> **Das neue Schweizer Taschenmesser *hatte ihm* wirklich *Spaß gemacht*.**
> The new Swiss Army knife/penknife had really given him pleasure.

> **Es *macht ihm großen Spaß*, beim Regen barfuß über die Wiese *zu laufen*.**
> It gives him great pleasure to run/He gets great pleasure from running
> barefoot across the meadow in the rain.

Die Königin war *entzückt* über die *erfreuliche* Nachricht.
The queen was delighted about the good news.

115.3 **Enjoying things**

> **sich bei etw. vergnügen** 'to enjoy oneself doing sth.'
> **vergnüglich** 'amusing/entertaining'
> **etw. genießen** 'to enjoy' sth.

Er *wollte sich* beim Discotanzen *vergnügen*.
He wanted to have a good time disco dancing.

Wir wollen uns einen *vergnüglichen Abend* auf der Alpenhütte machen.
We want to have a fun evening at the alpine lodge.

Sie hatte den Aufenthalt in den Bergen in vollen Zügen *genossen*.
She had enjoyed the stay in the mountains to the full.

Places where one might enjoy oneself are often expressed using compounds of
vergnügen:

> **-r Vergnügungspark** 'amusement park'
> **-s Vergnügungsviertel** 'pleasure district/entertainment area of a town/red light district'
> **-s Vergnügungslokal** 'night bar/bar providing entertainment'
> **-s Freizeitzentrum** 'leisure centre'

(See **111.2c**B for looking forward to something)

115.4 **Enjoying the taste of things**
(See also **63.6**B and **63.4**B on food and drink)

> **schmecken** 'to taste (nice)'
> **jmdm. schmeckt etw.** (= nom) 'sb. (= dat) is enjoying sth. (= nom)'
> **genüßlich** 'with relish'

Wie hat *Ihnen der Rotwein geschmeckt*?
How did you like/did you enjoy the red wine?

Die vornehme alte Dame konnte so ganz *genüßlich* aus der Meißner Tasse ihren Kaffee *trinken*.
The elegant old lady really relished drinking her coffee out of a Meissen cup.

---115.5---

Being cheerful and having pleasant feelings

Er ist ein besonders *lustiger* Spielkamerad.
He is an especially amusing/funny/cheerful playmate.

Auf seinen Kellerpartys *war* es immer sehr *lustig.*
We always had a lot of fun at his basement parties.

Bei euch scheint es sehr *lustig zuzugehen.*
You seem to be having a lot of fun/really enjoying yourselves.

Dr. Hoffmann hatte sich durch die Einnahme von LSD in einen anfänglich *angenehmen Zustand* versetzt. (formal)
Dr Hoffmann had at first made himself feel quite pleasant by taking LSD.

Mir gefällt die *angenehme Atmosphäre* in einem englischen Pub.
I like the pleasant atmosphere in an English pub.

---115.6---

Doing things for fun/pleasure is rendered by (**so**) **zum Vergnügen/zum Spaß**:

Ich möchte nur einmal *so zum Vergnügen/zum Spaß* mit der Straßenbahn fahren.
I would like to go by tram just once for the fun of it.

Bergsteigen *macht* richtig *Spaß.*
Mountain climbing is really fun.

---115.7---

Feeling like doing something/fancying something is expressed by **Lust haben**:

Lust haben, etw. zu tun 'to feel like doing sth.'
Lust haben auf (+ acc) 'to fancy sth.' (often associated with food)
wanderlustig 'keen on hiking'

Hast du Lust, mit ins Schwimmbad zu *gehen*?
Do you feel like coming to the swimming-pool?

Ich habe *nicht die geringste Lust dazu,* den ganzen Tag lang aufzuräumen.
I don't feel in the slightest like tidying up all day long.

Ich *hätte große Lust* auf eine Grillplatte.
I would really like/I really fancy a mixed grill.

Die Urlauber im Gebirge sind besonders *wanderlustig.*
Holiday-makers in the mountains are especially keen on hiking.

115.8

Treating oneself to something

> **sich** (= dat) **etw. gönnen** 'to indulge in sth./to allow oneself sth.'
> **sich** (= dat) **etw. leisten können** 'to afford sth.'
> **sich** (= acc) **verwöhnen lassen** 'to let oneself be spoiled'
> **jmdm. etw. gönnen** 'not to begrudge sb. sth.'

> **Nach all den Jahren, in denen sie so sparen mußte, sollte *sie sich* endlich *einmal* einen richtigen Urlaub *gönnen*.**
> After all the years in which she had to save so much, she should finally treat herself to a proper holiday.

> **Ich *kann mir* jetzt einen großen Wagen *leisten*.**
> I can afford a big car now.

> **Auf der Schönheitsfarm können Sie sich so richtig *verwöhnen lassen*.**
> At the beauty farm you can really let yourself be spoiled.

Not begrudging something to someone:

> **Ich *gönne ihm* das prächtige Haus.**
> I don't begrudge him the splendid house.

115.9

Joking

> **(einen) Spaß machen** 'to joke'
> **einen Witz machen/erzählen** 'to make/tell a joke'
> **einen guten Witz machen/reißen** 'to make/crack a good joke'
> **eine witzige Bemerkung machen** 'to make a funny remark'
> **jmdn. auf den Arm nehmen** 'to pull sb.'s leg'

> **Er *macht* gerne *Spaß*.**
> He likes to joke.

> ***Machst du Spaß*, oder ist es dir ernst?**
> Are you joking or are you serious?

> **Sie hat wieder einmal eine *witzige Bemerkung gemacht*.**
> She's made a funny remark again.

> **Das hat er nicht so gemeint. Er hat *dich nur auf den Arm genommen*.**
> He didn't mean it. He was just pulling your leg.

XV Communication strategies

116 Using fillers

116.1

Fillers are words or sounds which can be inserted in pauses while the speaker is thinking of what to say next. They have little or no meaning of their own. In German, common 'fillers' include the following:

> **äähm, hmm, nun, und, ja, eben, also, tja, na ja** 'now then'
> **eigentlich** 'actually'
> **sozusagen** 'so to speak'
> **wissen Sie/weißt du** 'you know'
> **sehen Sie/siehst du** 'you see'

> **Das war ... *äähm*... vor vielen Jahren und ... *wissen Sie*... ich habe einiges vergessen, und, *ja, nun*, mein Vater hatte damals eine Stelle bei Siemens, das war ... *also*... in Erlangen, *sehen Sie*,...**
> That was... umm... a long time ago and... you know... I can't remember everything, and, well, now, my father had a job at Siemens at the time, that was... errr... in Erlangen, you see,...

116.2

When searching for the right word, the following can be used:

> **Wie ist... noch?** 'What is... again?'
> **Wie heißt es noch?** 'What is the word again?'
> **Wie war es noch?** 'What was it again?'
> **nicht finden** 'can't find'
> **mir fällt es nicht (mehr) ein** 'it won't come to me'

> **Wie ist das Wort noch?**
> **Wie heißt es noch?**
> **Wie war das noch?**
> What's the word again?
>
> **Ich finde das Wort nicht.**
> I can't find the word.

>**Ach, das Wort fällt mir nicht (mehr) ein.**
>Oh, the word won't come to me.

This could be followed by **Moment noch** or **Augenblick noch** 'just a moment', to signal that the speaker is asking for a little time to think of the word.

(See also **118**B on asking for linguistic cues)

116.3 The following may be useful when pointing to something or describing something for which the speaker does not know the exact word:

> **so ein Ding** 'like that'
> **so aus*sehen** 'to look like that'
> **so machen** 'to go like that'
> **aus*sehen wie** 'to look like'

(a) General words can be used such as **das Ding** 'thing', **die Sache** (which usually refers to a situation or a state of affairs) and **der Ort** 'place'. The meaning of 'like this/like that' is conveyed in German by **so** when one can imitate the thing or point to something by way of explanation.

(See **74**B on 'Describing people' and **75**B on 'Describing objects')

>**Das war** *so ein Ding.*
>It was (a thing) like this (like that).

N.B. **Das ist so eine Sache** as an expression on its own usually means 'It's a bit tricky/It's a complicated state of affairs'.

(b) When describing or imitating the way something looks, **so aus*sehen** can be used (see **75**B):

>**Es** *sieht so aus.*
>It looks like this.

(c) When describing the way something moves or sounds, **so machen** can be used:

>**Es** *macht so.*
>It goes like this/does this.

>**Es** *machte 'brr brr'.*
>It went 'brr brr'.

>**Er** *machte so* **(mit der Hand).**
>He went like this (with his hand).

116.4

When the speaker is able to compare the thing to something for which he or she knows the word, **wie** is used instead of **so**:

> **Es sieht aus *wie* eine kleine Gitarre.**
> It looks like a small guitar.

Alternatively, a relative clause may be used:

> **Das ist das Ding, *das* man mit einem Hammer schlägt.**
> It's the thing you hit with a hammer.

(See **8**A on subordinate clauses)

117 *Keeping the channel open*

117.1

Even when someone carries a conversation for a fairly long time, he or she does not speak in a monologue (see **121**B). There are a number of words and phrases a speaker can use in a conversation to 'keep the channel open': acknowledging the presence of the listener; checking that the listener is following what is being said; and involving the listener in what is being said. Many of the German expressions used for this purpose do not have straightforward equivalents in English.

> **nicht wahr? nicht? gell? was? oder?** 'isn't it? aren't they' (etc)
> **ja, eben, gerade, nun, nämlich** 'you see'
> **sehen Sie? siehst du?** '(you) see?'
> **verstehen Sie? verstehst du?** '(you) understand?'
> **doch** 'surely/after all' (rejecting an actual or anticipated resistance)
> **freilich** 'admittedly' (making some kind of concession)
> **allerdings, immerhin** can function like **doch** or like **freilich**

(a) The commonest of these is **nicht wahr?** 'isn't it/aren't they', etc. This is often abbreviated to **nicht?** or (very informally) in northern Germany to **ne?** In southern Germany **gell?** is common. **Was?** is also colloquial and informal:

> **Komisch, was?**
> Strange, eh?

(b) The slightly more demanding **oder?** usually invites the listener in a fairly direct way to agree with what has just been said:

> **Das ist (doch) unverschämt, *oder*?**
> That is disgraceful, don't you think?

(See **117.1c**B for **doch**)

Wissen Sie? (or **weißt du?**) said like a question is a fairly neutral way of including the listener in what is being said:

>**Sie hat das Examen bestanden,** *weißt du,* **und jetzt geht sie auf die Uni.**
>She passed the exam, you know, and now she's going to university.

It can, however, be quite assertive and challenging, especially when said with a level intonation (i.e. without sounding overtly like a question):

>**Das ist unverschämt,** *wissen Sie!*
>That is really disgraceful!

Other phrases used in this way include **sehen Sie?** or **siehst du?** '(do you) see?' and **verstehen Sie?** or **verstehst du?** '(do you) understand?':

(c) German has a lot of modal particles part of whose function is to 'keep the channel open' to the other person in the conversation. The most common ones are listed below alphabetically:

allerdings introduces a point which re-asserts the validity of an earlier point despite some argument to the contrary. It can thus be used to limit the validity of the speaker's (or the listener's) viewpoint:

>**Das ist** *allerdings* **wahr.**
>That's true, admittedly.

>**Ich muß** *allerdings* **zugeben, daß du recht hast.**
>I have to admit, though, that you are right.

>**Du mußt** *allerdings* **zugeben, daß ich recht habe.**
>You have to admit, all the same, that I am right.

But it can also be used to counter an implied negative:

>First speaker: **Hast du vielleicht seine Telefonnummer?**
>You wouldn't have his telephone number by any chance?

>Second speaker: *Allerdings!*
>I certainly have!

auch can signal the speaker's sympathy for the position of the listener:

>**Das ist** *auch* **nicht dein Problem.**
>That's not your problem.

>**Du konntest es** *auch* **kaum selbst bezahlen.**
>You could scarcely be expected to pay for it yourself.

bloß implies that something is not very important. It can be used to agree with the listener's viewpoint or (with **doch**) to play down something which the listener thinks is important:

> **Das ist *bloß* eine Kleinigkeit.**
> That's not important.

> **Das ist *doch bloß* eine Kleinigkeit.**
> That's really not important.

denn signals some kind of shared relevance between the speaker and the listener. It can express surprise or add a note of informality:

> **Was kann ich *denn* sonst machen?**
> What else can I do, then?

> **Was ist *denn* das?**
> What's this, then?

> **Was machst du *denn* heute abend?**
> So what are you doing this evening?

doch has two main uses, depending on whether it is stressed or unstressed. When unstressed, it adds an emphatic note to what one is saying:

> **Das ist *doch* ganz klar.**
> That is absolutely clear

> **Ich weiß. Du hast es mir *doch* gesagt.**
> I know. You've already told me.

or it can express exasperation:

> **Das gibt es *doch* nicht!**
> I don't believe it!/You must be joking!

and in questions it can express hope for a positive response:

> **Du hast *doch* den Brief abgeschickt?**
> You did send the letter (didn't you?)

When stressed, **doch** can be used to reject an actual or implied negative (see **109.1b**B on expressing disagreement). With even greater emphasis, it can be used to confirm an unexpected turn of events, often with **dann** or together with **noch** (**doch noch**):

> **Trotz der Panne ist der Zug dann *doch* pünktlich angekommen.**
> Despite the breakdown the train still arrived on time.

eben usually highlights a potential problem which the speaker can reasonably expect the listener to understand and sympathize with:

> **Das ist es *eben*.**
> That's just it.

> **Das ist *eben* klar.**
> That is clear, after all (as everyone surely accepts).

freilich signals that the speaker acknowledges the force of some argument that detracts from the argument he or she is making:

> **Die Mitglieder dieser Regierung sind *freilich* keine Engel, aber sie tun ihr Bestes.**
> The members of this government are no angels, admittedly, but they are doing their best.

gerade highlights a particular point, draws the listener's attention to something, and gives it a particular prominence. In a conversation, this may imply that the speaker and the listener need to talk about this further. **eben** can also be used in this way:

> **Das ist *gerade* das Problem.**
> **Das ist *eben* das Problem.**
> That is exactly the problem (which you may not fully appreciate).

halt is used colloquially and generally invites the listener to agree that something is a fact and cannot easily be changed:

> **Es ist *halt* so.** (informal)
> That's (just) the way it is.

> **Heutzutage gibt es *halt* nur Staus.**
> These days there are only traffic jams.

immerhin functions very like **allerdings** (see above):

> **Wir haben das Spiel verloren. *Immerhin* hätte es schlimmer sein können.**
> We lost the game. It could have been worse, though.

> **Mein Deutsch war immer schwach. Ich war *immerhin* der Beste in der Klasse.**
> My German was always weak. I was the best in the class all the same.

ja usually implies that the speaker regards what he or she is saying as self-evident and does not expect the listener to disagree:

> **Das ist *ja* ganz klar.**
> That is absolutely clear (as everyone knows).

mal often implies that the speaker has a strong expectation that the listener ought to or will do what is asked. The effect can be informal and friendly, but it can also be demanding and manipulative. Generally, **einmal** is a slightly more formal version of **mal**:

> **Rechnen Sie *mal* nach!**
> Go on, add it up!

> **Könntest du *mal* für mich anrufen?**
> Could you phone for me (i.e. instead of me)?

> **Geben Sie *mal* zu, daß ich recht habe!**
> Why don't you just admit that I'm right!

> **Lassen Sie mich *einmal* ausreden!**
> Just let me finish, will you?

> **Kommen Sie *mal* her!**
> Come here!

nämlich often signals that the speaker realizes that the listener needs to have something explained a little further. As well as having the sense of 'you see', it usually signals that the speaker is about to elaborate a point:

> **Du hast *nämlich* zwei Möglichkeiten: Entweder... oder...**
> So you have two possibilities. Either... or...

> **Es ist *nämlich* so: Ich habe diesen Monat fast kein Geld.**
> Well you see, it's like this: I have practically no money this month.

nun can be used like **halt** (see above). It can also be used to introduce an idea in such a way that the speaker acknowledges that the listener also has an interest in the matter:

> ***Nun* (ja), das ist eine wichtige Frage.**
> **Das ist *nun* eine wichtige Frage.**
> Well yes, that is an important question.

schon has two main uses. When stressed, it can be used to reject an actual or implied negative. In this usage it is milder than the equivalent use of **doch**:

> **Hier dürfen Sie nicht parken! – Quatsch, hier darf man *schon* parken.**
> You can't park here! – Rubbish, of course you can park here.

Alternatively, it can signal consent or reassurance. In this case it is unstressed:

> **Keine Angst, es wird *schon* gut gehen.**
> Don't worry, it'll be all right.

> **Vati, kann ich mit Elli spielen? – Ja, meine Kleine, das darfst du schon.**
> Daddy, can I play with Elli? – Yes, little one, of course you can.

wohl 'probably' often signals a supposition or expectation on the part of the speaker. It has a wide range of uses, from signalling an awareness that there may be other views on the subject, to an intimidating challenge:

> **Entschuldigen Sie bitte die Störung. Sie haben *wohl* viele wichtige Sachen zu erledigen.**
> Please excuse the interruption. You've probably got a lot of important things to see to.

> **Sie haben *wohl* eine Erklärung?**
> I suppose you have an explanation?

(See also **88.2c**B for **wohl**)

117.2 It is usual for the listener to give little verbal signals to show that he or she is following what the speaker is saying and is involved. In German this can be done using the following expressions. Some of them also express reservation or disagreement:

> **ja, ja/ja, mmm/so, so/ja**
> **ach!** 'oh!'
> **Sagen Sie bloß!** 'You don't say!'
> **tatsächlich? wirklich? echt?** 'really?'
> **(ganz) klar** 'of course'
> **OK alles klar!** 'OK, no problem'
> **eben!/genau!** 'exactly!'
> **richtig!** 'right!'
> **jawohl!** 'yes indeed!'
> **naja, aber...** 'well OK, but...'
> **naja, vielleicht...** 'well, maybe'
> **nein doch!** 'certainly not!'

(a) A fairly low level of interest, without particular involvement, can be conveyed with **ja** (or **ja ja**), **mmm** or **so**, said with a low and slightly falling intonation. Combinations of these are possible, e.g. **so, ja.**

(b) A greater degree of involvement can be signalled by producing the previous set of words with an appropriately emphatic manner, such as a high falling intonation. Alternatively, the use of **ach!** or **tatsächlich!** implies a degree of interest and possibly surprise at learning something. Other responses which could be appropriate here include **Sagen Sie bloß!** and **Was Sie nicht sagen!** 'you don't say!'

(c) To signal explicitly that he or she understands and/or agrees with the speaker, the listener can say **alles klar!** or **OK!** Combinations with the words listed above are also possible, e.g. **so, ja, alles klar!**

(d) Strong agreement can be indicated by saying **genau!** 'exactly' or **richtig!** 'right', **(ja) eben!** 'exactly!', or **jawohl!** 'yes indeed'. Alternatively, one can say:

> **(Das) stimmt (ja)!**
> That's right!

(e) Reservation can be indicated in a variety of ways. In approximate order of forcefulness: **naja, aber...** 'well OK, but...'; **ja, das schon, aber...** 'yes, of course, but...'; **naja, vielleicht** 'well, maybe'; **wirklich?** 'really?'; **tatsächlich?** 'really?' Alternatively, one can say **Meinst du (wirklich)?** 'You really think so?' More abrupt responses include:

> **(Wohl) kaum!**
> Hardly!
>
> **Nein doch!**
> Certainly not!
>
> **Ach was!**
> Come off it!

(See **109**B on expressing disagreement)

117.3 — There are several ways in which the listener can show that he or she has not understood what has just been said:

> **Wie bitte?** 'Could you please repeat that?'
> **Könnten sie bitte das noch mal wiederholen?** 'Could you please repeat that?'
> **Was?** 'What?'
> **etw. nicht verstehen** 'to not understand sth.'
> **etw. nicht mit*bekommen/nicht mit*kriegen** 'to not get/understand sth.'
> **(etw.) kapieren** 'to "twig" (sth.)'
> **schalten, schnallen** 'to catch on, "twig"'

(a) The most common and perfectly polite way to ask someone to repeat what they have just said is **(Wie) bitte?** The following may also be used:

> **Könnten Sie das bitte *wiederholen*?**
> Could you please repeat that?
>
> **Könnten Sie bitte (etwas) *langsamer sprechen*?**
> Could you please speak (a little) more slowly?

> **Was haben Sie gesagt?**
> What did you say?

> *Langsamer, bitte*! (informal, potentially rude)
> Slower, please!

> *Noch einmal* bitte! (informal, potentially rude)
> Again please.

The abbreviated form **noch mal!** is likely to be offensive unless said to a friend, and **Was?** is either very informal or rude. These expressions can of course be accompanied by expressions like **Es tut mir leid** 'I'm sorry' and **Das habe ich nicht mitbekommen** 'I didn't catch that'.

(b) Alternatively, **nicht verstehen** or **nicht mit*bekommen** can be used:

> **(Es tut mir leid.) Das habe ich *nicht verstanden.***
> (I am sorry.) I didn't understand that.

> **Das habe ich *nicht (ganz) mitbekommen.***
> I didn't (quite) get that.

nicht mit*bekommen can also imply that the listener did not properly hear what was said, e.g. because of intruding noise.

(c) In colloquial German **mit*kriegen** is found for **mit*bekommen**; and **schalten**, **schnallen** and **(etwas) kapieren** are also used, with the meaning 'to twig':

> **Hast du das *mitgekriegt*?**
> Did you get that?

> **Ich *kapiere* (*schalte*) (*schnalle*) heute schlecht.** (informal)
> I'm a bit slow today.

> **Das habe ich *nicht kapiert* (*nicht mitgekriegt*).** (informal)
> I didn't get that/I didn't 'twig'.

(d) If the listener realizes that he or she has misunderstood something, he or she can signal this with **Ach so!** or **Ach so, ja!** 'I see!':

> **Er ist krank?** *Ach so*! **Das habe ich nicht gewußt (nicht mitbekommen).**
> He is ill? Oh I see! I didn't know that. (I didn't get that.)

117.4 There are a number of ways in which the listener can check that he or she has understood exactly what the other person means:

> **jmdn. oder etw. richtig verstehen** 'to understand sb. or sth. correctly'
> **Wie meinen Sie das?** 'What do you mean?'
> **Was wollen Sie damit sagen?** 'What are you trying to say?'

These expressions can also be used to challenge or correct what someone has said. The more abrupt and challenging expressions for doing this are listed in points (d) and (e).

(a) Using **richtig verstehen**

> **Habe ich Sie *richtig verstanden*?**
> Have I understood you correctly?

(b) Using a construction with **meinen** 'to mean, intend'

> ***Wie meinen* Sie *das* (genau)?**
> What do you mean (exactly)?

> **Ich weiß nicht, *was* Sie (damit) *meinen*.**
> I don't know what you mean (by that).

(c) Using a construction with **wollen** 'to intend'

> **Was *wollen* Sie *damit sagen*?**
> What are you trying to say?

A slightly more elaborate way of saying this is:

> **Worauf wollen Sie hinaus?**
> What is the point you are trying to make?

These are rather more challenging than **Wie meinen Sie das?**

(d) Where speaker A is implying something about speaker B which speaker B objects to because it is unfair or incorrect, speaker B can object by using the following:

> **jmdm. etw. (= acc) unterstellen** 'to imply (wrongly) sth. about sb.'
> **-e Unterstellung** 'a false or unjustified implication'

> **Was *unterstellen* Sie *mir*?**
> What are you implying (wrongly) about me?

> **Was wollen Sie *mir unterstellen*?**
> What are you trying to imply about me?

> **Nein, das ist *eine Unterstellung.***
> No, that's unjustified.

(e) A very forthright way of challenging what someone has said is:

> **Was soll denn das heißen?** (with the stress on **das**)
> What is that supposed to mean?

118 Asking for spoken linguistic cues

Common expressions include:

> **Wie heißt das auf deutsch?** 'How do you say that in German?'
> **Wie sagt man auf deutsch: hard disk?**
> **Wie sagt man 'hard disk' auf deutsch?** 'How do you say "hard disk" in German?'
> **wiederholen** 'to repeat'
> **langsamer sprechen** 'to speak more slowly'
> **etw. anders sagen** 'to say sth. differently'
> **Wie schreibt man das?** 'How do you spell that?'
> **buchstabieren** 'to spell'
> **A wie Anton?** 'A for Anton?'

118.1 When lost for a word, the help of a German speaker can be sought by asking:

> **Wie heißt das auf deutsch?**
> What is it called in German?

> **(Nun,) (Also,) wie sagt man (auf deutsch) 'hard disk?'**
> (Now then), how do you say 'hard disk' in German?

118.2 Asking someone to reformulate what they have said to make it easier to understand can be done using **anders sagen** or **anders formulieren** (often with an introductory sentence like **Das habe ich nicht verstanden**):

> **Könnten Sie das bitte *anders sagen/formulieren*?**
> Could you please say/formulate that in another way?

118.3 **'Please spell!'**

(a) There may be occasions (on the telephone, writing notes) when it is useful to ask for a word or name to be spelt out. To ask someone to do this, one of the following can be used:

> **Wie** *schreibt man* **das?**
> How do you spell that?
>
> **Wie** *schreibt sich* **das?**
> How is that spelt?
>
> **Könnten Sie (mir) das bitte** *buchstabieren***?**
> Could you please spell that (for me)?

(b) The letters of the alphabet are listed below with an approximate pronunciation in brackets (see also **1.4**A) and the identifying word which most Germans are likely to use. Note that **wie** is used to introduce the identifying word:

> A [ah] **wie Anton**
> B [be:] **wie Bertha**
> C [tse:] **wie Cäsar**
> D [de:] **wie Dora**
> E [e:] **wie Emil**
> F [ef] **wie Friedrich**
> G [ge:] **wie Gottfried**
> H [ha:] **wie Heinrich**
> I [i:] **wie Ida**
> J [yot] **wie Johann**
> K [ka:] **wie Kaufmann**
> L [el] **wie Ludwig**
> M [em] **wie Martha**
> N [en] **wie Nordpol**
> O [o:] **wie Otto**
> P [pe:] **wie Paula**
> Q [ku:] **wie quer**
> R [air] **wie Richard**
> S [es] **wie Siegfried**
> T [te:] **wie Theodor**
> U [u:] **wie Ulrich**
> V [fau] **wie Viktor**
> W [ve:] **wie Wilhelm**
> X [iks] **wie Xaver**
> Y [ipsilon] **wie Ypsilon**
> Z [tset] **wie Zeppelin**

N.B. The letter ß is called **es-tset**.

(c) Note that the following German letters can sound misleadingly like English letters:

[ah] is a German A (not an R)
[e:] is a German E (not an A)
[i:] is a German I (not an E)

(d) If one is in doubt about the exact letter, it can be solicited by asking '**wie** + identifying word?' (or just **wie?** with a level intonation, which invites the other person to supply the identifying word):

> **Das habe ich nicht mitbekommen. *Wie Richard*?**
> I didn't catch that. As in Richard (i.e. R)?

> **Nein, *wie Anton*!**
> No, as in Anton! (i.e. A)

Alternatively, one can leave a pause after **wie** and invite the other person to supply the key word:

> **Es tut mir leid, das habe ich nicht mitbekommen. *Wie. . .*?**
> I'm sorry, I didn't catch that. As in. . .?

> ***Wie Heinrich.***
> As in Heinrich.

119 *Shaping the course of a conversation*

119.1

Developing the current topic

(a) A speaker can use a number of phrases to reiterate and explain what has just been said:

> **das heißt** 'that is to say'
> **mit anderen Worten** 'in other words'
> **anders gesagt** 'in other words'
> **nämlich** 'namely/that is to say'
> **oder besser** 'or more appropriately'

> **Er arbeitet jetzt unter Hochdruck. *Das heißt*, er spielt morgen bestimmt keinen Tennis.**
> He is working under enormous pressure at the moment. In other words, he certainly won't be playing tennis tomorrow.

> **Sabine ist kein Einzelkind. Sie hat *nämlich* einen Bruder und eine Schwester.**
> Sabine is not an only child. You see, she has a brother and a sister.

> **Sie kann nicht morgen.** *Oder besser,* **sie will nicht morgen.**
> She can't make it tomorrow. Or rather, she doesn't want to.

(b) A speaker can use one of the following to expand on what s/he has been saying and to introduce a new point:

> **und zwar** (see **119.5**B)
> **Mehr noch** 'And that's not all'
> **Dazu gehört (auch)** lit. 'to this belongs'
> **Dazu kann man sagen, daß...** 'I can add that...'
> **außerdem, sonst, ansonsten** 'otherwise'
> **In diesem Zusammenhang** 'In this connection' (formal)
> **Hinzuzufügen wäre (noch), daß** 'One could add that...' (formal)
> **Darüber hinaus** 'Over and beyond that/What is more' (formal)

> **Sie heiratet.** *Und zwar* **einen Australier.** *Mehr noch,* **sie wandert nach Australien aus!**
> She's getting married. To an Australian. And that's not all. She's emigrating to Australia!

> **Ja, es gab ein paar kleinere Probleme im ersten Jahr, aber** *ansonsten* **ist alles bestens gelaufen.**
> Yes, there were a few minor problems in the first year, but apart from that everything went smoothly.

> **Ich kann Ihnen ein Anfangsgehalt von 5.000 Mark im Monat versichern.** *Darüber hinaus* **besteht die Möglichkeit, daß Sie ab Januar im Ausland arbeiten könnten.**
> I can assure you of a starting salary of 5,000 marks a month. Also, there is the possibility that you could be working abroad from January.

119.2 Changing the topic

(a) **Übrigens** 'by the way' and **nebenbei (gesagt)** 'incidentally' are useful for introducing a new direction into a conversation. So is the more direct **Wissen Sie was?** 'Do you know what?' A combination of these is possible:

> **... ja, ja.** *Übrigens, wissen Sie was?* **Mein Bruder kommt übermorgen.**
> ... yes, yes. By the way, do you know what? My brother is coming the day after tomorrow.

> *Nebenbei (gesagt),* **wir haben eine Einladung bekommen.**
> Incidentally, we've had an invitation.

(b) Where a speaker does not want to talk about a particular topic any more, he or she can say so explicitly. The following expressions are arranged in approximate order of increasing explicitness:

> **(Aber) reden wir nicht mehr darüber!**
> (But) let's not talk about that any more.

> **Reden wir (aber) von etwas anderem!**
> (But) let's talk about something else.

> **Ich würde lieber über etwas anderes sprechen.**
> I would rather talk about something else.

> **Das hatten wir schon.**
> We've already covered that.

> **Ja, ja, das weiß ich (doch) (alles) schon!**
> Yes, yes, I know all that!

> **(Aber) ich bitte Sie!**
> Please, no more!

> **Das Thema ist geschlossen.**
> The topic is closed.

> **Strich darunter!**
> Matter closed!

119.3 Resisting a change of topic

Where a conversation partner is trying to change the topic or has changed the topic, this can be resisted or registered in the conversation in a number of ways:

(a) By trying to steer the conversation back to the desired topic, using one of the following:

> **(Aber) was wollte ich (gerade) sagen?**
> Now what was I going to say?

> **Aber wie ich (schon) gesagt habe,...**
> But as I was saying (before),...

> **(Aber) wie Sie schon/vor kurzem gesagt haben,...**
> (But) as you were saying before/just now,...

(b) By explicitly pointing out that the topic has been changed without one's agreement, using:

> **das Thema** 'the topic'
> **beim Thema bleiben** 'to keep to the point'
> **vom Thema ab*kommen** 'to get off the point'
> **zum Thema zurück*kommen** 'to get back to the point'
> **zum Thema (nicht) gehören** lit. 'to (not) belong to the topic'
> **mit dem Thema nichts zu tun haben** 'to have nothing to do with the topic'

> **(Aber)** *bleiben* **wir** *beim Thema.*
> (But) let's keep to the point.

> **(Aber) wir** *kommen vom Thema ab.*
> (But) we're getting off the topic.

> **Aber** *zurück zum Thema!*
> *Kommen* **wir aber** *zum Thema zurück!*
> But let's get back to the topic.

> **(Aber)** *das gehört nicht zum Thema.*
> (But) that's not what we're talking about.

> **(Aber)** *das hat mit dem Thema nichts zu tun.*
> (But) that's got nothing to do with it.

More impatiently, one could say:

> **Aber könnten wir jetzt mal endlich zum Thema zurückkommen?**
> But could we now please finally get back to what we were talking about?

119.4 — Broadening the topic

The following are some of the ways in which the topic of a conversation can be broadened, moving from the particular to the general:

> **im großen und ganzen** 'on the whole'
> **in der Regel** 'as a rule'
> **im allgemeinen** 'in general'
> **sonst** 'otherwise/apart from that'
> **solche Dinge/solche Sachen** 'such things'
> **solche Fragen** 'such questions' (etc.)

(a) The expressions **im großen und ganzen** 'on the whole', **im allgemeinen** 'in general', **alles in allem** 'all in all', **in der Regel** 'as a rule' are widely interchangeable:

> *Im großen und ganzen* **kann man sagen, daß die Frauen heutzutage**
> **bessere Berufschancen haben.**

On the whole one can say that women have better career prospects today.

Wir sind diesen Monat überzogen, aber *in der Regel* haben wir genug Geld auf der Bank.
We are overdrawn this month but as a rule we have enough money in the bank.

(b) **sonst** and **im übrigen** (formal) mean 'otherwise, apart from that':

Dieses Bild gefällt mir nicht, (aber) *sonst* finde ich die Ausstellung gut.
I don't like this picture, (but) otherwise I think the exhibition is good.

Sie hat eine leichte Erkältung? Wie geht es ihr *sonst*?
She has a slight cold? How is she otherwise?

Die Regierung hat einige Probleme in der Außenpolitik. *Im übrigen* läuft alles bestens.
The government has a few problems in foreign affairs. Otherwise everything is going smoothly.

(c) With phrases using **solch-** or (formal) **derartig-** 'such a':

Solche (derartige) Dinge **findet man überall. . .**
You find that kind of thing everywhere. . .

Solche Leute **findet man überall.**
You find people like that everywhere.

119.5 Narrowing the topic

The following are some of the ways in which the topic of a conversation can be narrowed, moving from the general to the particular:

(ganz) besonders 'especially/in particular'
insbesondere 'especially/in particular'
vor allem 'above all/especially'
und zwar/nämlich 'to be precise'
(ganz) besonders 'particularly'

Aber was mich *ganz besonders* daran interessiert, ist. . .
But what particularly interests me about it is. . .

insbesondere 'especially/in particular'

Die Elektronik, *insbesondere* die Computerindustrie, erfährt jetzt einen Boom.

Electronics, and in particular the computer industry, is experiencing a boom at the moment.

vor allem 'above all/especially'

> **Mir gefällt das Haus, *vor allem* die Küche und das Wohnzimmer.**
> I like the house, especially the kitchen and the living room.

und zwar and **nämlich** can be used to specify a point of detail:

> **Zwei Leute sind dagegen, *und zwar* der Robert und die Sabine.**
> **Zwei Leute sind dagegen, *nämlich* der Robert und die Sabine.**
> Two people are against – Robert and Sabine.

> **Es gibt ein kleines Problem, *und zwar* ist der Wagen kaputt.**
> **Es gibt ein kleines Problem. Der Wagen ist *nämlich* kaputt.**
> There is a little problem: the car has broken down.

119.6

Requesting more detail

There are several ways of asking for further information or more detail.

(a) By asking **wo?**, **wer?**, **wann?**, **warum?**, etc., often with **genau** 'exactly':

> ***Wo* wohnt er *genau*?**
> Where exactly does he live?

> ***Wann* fährt der Zug *genau*?**
> When exactly does the train leave?

Alternatively, **eigentlich** can be used instead of **genau**:

> **Was macht er *eigentlich*?**
> What does he do exactly?

(b) Using **noch** 'again' with **die Frage**, **die Bitte** or **die Auskunft**:

> **Ich habe (hätte) *noch eine Frage* (*noch eine Bitte*).**
> May I ask another question/make another request?

> **Ich möchte (brauche) *noch eine Auskunft*, bitte.**
> I would like (I need) some more information, please.

(c) When asking for more detailed information about something, the adjectives **weiter** or **näher** are often used:

> **Haben Sie *weitere* Informationen über das Hotel?**
> Have you got further information on the hotel?

>Könnten Sie das Haus *näher* beschreiben?
>Could you describe the house in more detail?

(See also **51**A on comparison of adverbs)

Näheres (über etwas) 'more exact information (about sth.)' is a very useful term for eliciting further information:

>Könnten Sie mir *Näheres* darüber sagen?
>Could you tell me more about that?

>Ich möchte (gern) *Näheres* über diese Wohnung erfahren.
>I would like to find out more about this apartment.

Alternatively **die Einzelheiten** 'details' can be used:

>Könnten Sie mir noch ein paar *Einzelheiten geben/ erklären*?
>Could you give me/explain a few more details?

120 Turn-taking in conversations

120.1 Intonation

Generally, a rising intonation implies that a speaker is intending to continue speaking (unless it is a direct question). A falling intonation implies that the speaker is anticipating the possibility that the other person will say something. In this section, [/] marks the point at which a rising intonation begins, and [\] marks the point at which a falling intonation begins. For example:

>Wie viele Kinder haben Sie?
>[\]Drei.
>Wie viele Kinder haben Sie?
>[/]Drei. Zwei Mädchen und einen Jungen.
>How many children do you have?
>Three – two girls and a boy.

120.2 'Please don't interrupt me'

There are various ways in which a speaker can signal that he or she does not wish to be interrupted, even though he or she may have paused for a moment:

(a) By using rising intonation (see **120.1**B):

>Ich bin nach [/]Hause gekommen... (und...)
>I came home... (and...)

(b) By starting a sentence with a construction that points forward to a following clause for its completion (see **38.2**A for clause links with **da** + preposition, and **42.3b**A for verb completion with two elements):

> **Das hat [/]** *damit* **zu tun. . .** (*daß* **sie nicht zu Hause war**).
> It has to do with the fact that (she was not at home).

> **[/]** *Damit* **hängt zusammen. . .** (*daß* **die Firma in Helsinki eine Filiale eröffnet**).
> Related to this is the fact (that the firm is opening a branch in Helsinki).

(c) Explicitly, by saying so, perhaps after someone else has started to speak. One of the following might be used:

> **Augenblick noch!**
> **Moment noch!**
> Just a moment!

> **Eine Sekunde noch!**
> Just a second!

> **Kann (darf) ich noch etwas sagen?**
> Can I say something else?

> **Ich bin (noch) nicht fertig.**
> I am not finished (yet).

> **Ich bin gleich (bald) fertig.**
> I'm almost finished.

> **Darf ich noch ausreden?**
> May I finish?

> **Lassen Sie mich bitte ausreden!**
> Please let me finish!

120.3 'Please speak!'

There are various ways in which a speaker can signal that he or she is prepared to be or expects to be interrupted, even though he or she may not have finished what he or she was saying:

(a) By using falling intonation (see **120.1**B)

> **Und dann bin ich nach [/]Hause gekommen und. . . [\]ja**
> And then I came home and . . . yes?

(b) By explicitly telling the other person that he or she can take over the conversation at this point:

> [\]**Bitte!**
> Mmm? Yes?!

A rising intonation here (e.g. [/] **Bitte**) could sound impatient or reluctant. Other possible expressions include:

> **Nein, Sie zuerst!**
> No, you first!

> **Bitte, nach Ihnen!**
> Please, go ahead, after you!

Of course, a direct question is usually an open invitation to respond:

> **Sie langweilen sich, nicht?**
> You are bored, aren't you?

> **Ich komme aus Berlin, und Sie?**
> I am from Berlin, and you?

> **Wann macht die Bank auf?**
> When does the bank open?

120.4 Interrupting someone

Breaking into a conversation when the speaker is not prepared or is not expecting to be interrupted needs to be done with some confidence. Amongst the more explicit techniques there are the following:

(a) Using the inseparable verb **unterbrechen** 'to interrupt', or the more informal **ein*haken**:

> **Darf ich Sie (mal) (kurz) unterbrechen?**
> Can I (just) interrupt you (briefly)?

> **Darf ich einhaken?**
> Can I butt in?

(b) Using a similar construction with another verb:

> **Kann/Darf ich etwas sagen?**
> May I say something?

> **Kann/Darf ich (Sie) etwas fragen?**
> Can I ask you something?

Or, more impatiently:

> **Darf ich jetzt mal etwas sagen?**
> Can I just say something now?

All of the above tend to sound assertive and forthright when said with a falling intonation: **unter[\]brechen**, **[\]sagen**, **[\]fragen**. A rising intonation makes these interruptions seem more polite and tentative: **unter[/]brechen**, **[/]sagen**, **[/]fragen**.

(c) Other ways of interrupting, which do not draw attention to themselves as interruptions, include:

> **Ja, [/]wissen Sie,...**
> Ah, you know...

> **(Ja) dazu kann ich [/]sagen...**
> lit. To that I can say...

With a strong stress on **da-**, this claims a close relevance with what has just been said, and the rising intonation signals that the speaker wishes to continue:

> **[/] *Da*zu kann ich sagen, daß...**
> I can tell you that...

Alternatively, a more assertive intervention uses a falling intonation, inviting the other person to stop and listen:

> **(Ja) dazu kann ich etwas [\]sagen.**
> Ah, I can tell you something on that score.

(d) Where the person interrupting wishes to challenge or amend what has just been said, the following might be used (in addition to those listed above):

> **Aber [/]wissen Sie...**
> But you know...

> **Das [/]stimmt zwar, aber...**
> That's right, but...

A direct contradiction of what has just been said can be achieved by using **Nein!** or (where one wishes to correct a negative assertion) **Doch!** (possibly together with **schon**):

First speaker:

> **Sie machen eigentlich keine Fehler.**
> You don't really make any mistakes.

Second speaker:

> **Doch**, ich mache *schon* Fehler.
> That's not so. I do make mistakes.

121 Delivering monologues (formal speaking)

(See also **60.6c**B on welcoming; **66.5b**B on proposing a toast; **66.7–66.8**B on congratulating and celebrating; **67.1–67.2**B on expressing thanks)

Situations in which a person speaks on his or her own without interruption are usually formal or semi-formal occasions, e.g. giving a speech (**eine Rede halten**), a lecture (**einen Vortrag halten**), a report or 'paper' (**ein Referat halten**). Some of the vocabulary and structures given in this section are found only in such formal or semi-formal contexts, and are identified as 'formal'.

121.1 Formally introducing a speaker

The usual way to hand over formally to a speaker is **jmdm. das Wort geben**. Alternatively, **das Wort haben** can be used:

> **(Damit)** *gebe ich Ihnen*, Herr Johnson, *das Wort.*
> (And with that) I hand over to you, Mr Johnson.

> Herr Johnson, *Sie haben das Wort.*
> Mr Johnson, over to you.

121.2 Opening words

(a) The first word may be an introductory 'filler' (see **116**B) such as **Also**, **Nun**, or even **Ja**.

(b) In a speech this might be followed by **Liebe Freunde!** 'dear friends' or **Meine (sehr geehrten) Damen und Herren!** 'Ladies and gentlemen'. In a lecture or a report, some kind of introductory remark might follow, such as **Thema dieses Vortrags (dieses Referats) ist (lautet)...** 'the subject of this lecture (this paper) is...'

121.3 Closing words

(a) Once again, a simple 'filler' such as **also**, after a pause, could mark the beginning of the conclusion. It is also quite common to mark the final part of a monologue with **schließlich**:

> *Also*, ich komme *schließlich* zu meinem letzten Punkt,...
> *Schließlich also* komme ich zu meinem letzten Punkt,...
> Finally, then, I come to my last point,...

A slightly more formal word is **abschließend** 'in conclusion':

> *Abschließend* **möchte ich sagen, daß...**
> In conclusion I would like to say that...

> **Ich komme** *abschließend* **zu der Finanzfrage.**
> I come finally to the financial question.

(b) More formal expressions meaning 'to summarize' include **zusammen*fasssen**, **Fazit ziehen**, and **Bilanz ziehen**:

> **Ich möchte also jetzt** *zusammenfassen:...*
> So, I would now like to sum up...

(See also **121.4**B)

(c) The speaker can signal that he or she is nearly finished speaking as follows:

> **Ich** *bin gleich am Ende/ gleich fertig.*
> I am almost finished.

> **Ich** *nähere mich dem Ende* **dieses Referats.** (formal)
> I am drawing to a close (coming to the end) of this lecture, etc.

(d) In a formal situation it is customary to finish by thanking the audience for their attention. Possibilities, in rising order of formality, include:

> **Ich danke fürs Zuhören.**
> Thanks for listening.

> **Ich danke Ihnen für Ihre Aufmerksamkeit.**
> Thank you for your attention.

> **Ich möchte Ihnen für Ihre Aufmerksamkeit danken.**
> I would like to thank you for giving me your attention.

Using **sich bei jmdm. für etwas bedanken** gives this a slightly more formal ring, and **danken** can also be expanded by **recht herzlich**:

> **Ich möchte** *mich bei Ihnen* **für Ihre Aufmerksamkeit** *recht herzlich*
> *bedanken.*

(See **67.1**–**67.2**B on thanking somebody)

121.4 Giving an overview

(a) A person delivering a lecture or paper usually provides an outline of the whole (**-e Gliederung**) at the beginning. The following might be used to explain that a talk has three main parts:

> **Mein Vortrag** *befaßt sich mit* **drei** *Fragen.*
> **Mein Vortrag** *hat* **drei** *Teile.*
> **Mein Vortrag** *hat* **drei** *Schwerpunkte.*
> **Mein Vortrag** *ist in* **drei** *Teile unterteilt (gegliedert).*

(b)   There are various ways of talking about the order things will come in:

zunächst 'first of all' could be followed by **zweitens.** . ., **drittens,** . . . **viertens,** . . . **fünftens**, etc. Other words for 'next' are **dann** and **anschließend**. 'Finally' is **schließlich** or **zum Schluß**. A combination of these is possible:

> *Zunächst* **gebe ich einen kurzen Überblick über die Situation in den beiden Firmen.**
> First, I will give a brief outline of the situation in both companies.

> *Anschließend* **werde ich die Logik einer Fusion untersuchen.**
> Following that I will examine the logic of a merger.

> *Drittens* **befasse ich mich mit der Haltung des ABC-Vorstands.**
> Third, I discuss the attitude of the ABC board.

> *Dann* **werden die strukturellen Vorteile einer Fusion erörtert.**
> Then the structural benefits of a merger will be discussed.

> **Und** *schließlich* **komme ich zu der Frage, ob das Hauptquartier der neuen Gruppe in Düsseldorf oder Leipzig sein soll.**
> And finally I come to the question of whether the headquarters of the new group should be in Düsseldorf or Leipzig.

A combination of these is possible:

> **Zunächst.** . ., **dann.** . ., **anschließend.** . ., **viertens.** . ., **und schließlich.** . .
> First. . ., then. . ., next. . . ., fourthly. . ., and finally. . .

(c)   Other ways of saying what will come first are **Als erstes**, **Gleich am Anfang**, and **In dem ersten Teil**. Any combination of the following will say that the first part of the talk discusses X:

> *Zunächst* **kommt X.**
> *Als erstes* **werde ich über X sprechen.**
> *Gleich am Anfang* **werde ich X behandeln (erörtern).**
> *Im ersten Teil* **wird X behandelt.**

(d)   When moving from one part of a talk to the next a speaker might say:

> *Das war also* **der erste Punkt.** *Ich komme* (*wir kommen*) *jetzt zu* **dem zweiten Punkt, der Finanzfrage.** . .

That was the first point, then. I come/we come now to the second point, the financial question...

(See **21.1**A on noun apposition)

> *Soviel (also) zu diesem Aspekt (zu dieser Frage), ich gehe jetzt zu dem nächsten (zweiten, dritten) Punkt über.*
> So much for that aspect (that question), I now come to the next (second, third) point.

More formally:

> *Soweit zu dem ersten Teil. Ich wende mich jetzt dem zweiten Teil zu.*
> So much for the first part. I now turn to the second part.

Expressions which also explain the logical relation of the previous part to the next part include:

> *Während in dem letzten Teil (meines Referats) X im Vordergrund stand, gehe ich jetzt auf Y ein.*
> Whereas the focus was on X in the last part (of my talk), I will now look at Y in some detail.

(See **76.5**B on expressing the next step in a process)

(e) Indicating that something will not be dealt with in a talk can be done as follows:

> *Aus Zeitgründen kann ich (leider) X hier nicht behandeln.*
> There is (unfortunately) not enough time for me to deal with X here.

> *Aus Zeitgründen kann (leider) X hier nicht behandelt werden.*
> There is (unfortunately) not enough time for X to be dealt with here.

> *X zu behandeln, würde über den Rahmen dieses Vortrags hinausführen.*
> To deal with X would exceed the remit of this talk.

> *X muß/ mußte (leider) (aus Zeitgründen) ausgeklammert werden.*
> (Unfortunately) since time is short X could not be included in the talk (lit. has to be (has had to be) excluded from the talk).

Another reason for excluding something is that it is not sufficiently relevant:

> *... weil X hier uns nur am Rande interessiert.*
> ... because X is only of marginal interest here.

121.5 **OHP and slide presentations**

Talks with an overhead projector require the speaker to be able to refer to the material being shown. This may be a table (**die Tabelle**) or some kind of pictorial representation (**die Abbildung, das Schaubild, die Graphik**), which could be a diagram (**das Diagramm**) a matrix (**die Matrix**), a graph (**die Kurve, die Graphik**) or some kind of picture (**das Bild**). Common ways of referring to OHP material include:

> **die Abbildung macht deutlich, daß. . .** 'the illustration clearly shows that. . .'
> **wie die Abbildung** (etc.) **zeigt** 'as the picture (etc.) shows'
> **sich** (= dat) **etw.** (= acc) **an*sehen/an*schauen** 'to look at sth.'
> **etw.** (= acc) **an etw.** (= dat) **sehen** 'to see sth. from sth.'
> **etw.** (= acc) **(von) etw. entnehmen** 'to deduce sth. from sth.'
> **aus etw. hervor*gehen** 'to be evident from'

For example, all of the following could say that the visual aid shows a rise in the rate of inflation:

> **Die Abbildung/Das Schaubild *macht* die steigende Inflationsrate *deutlich*.**
> The diagram shows the rising rate of inflation clearly.

> **Die steigende Inflationsrate *wird in* dieser Abbildung (in diesem Schaubild) *veranschaulicht*.**
> The rising rate of inflation is shown in this diagram.

> ***Wie die Abbildung (das Schaubild) zeigt,* ist die Inflationsrate gestiegen.**
> As the diagram shows, the rate of inflation has risen.

> ***Wie Sie der Abbildung (dem Schaubild) entnehmen können,* ist die Inflationsrate gestiegen.**
> As you can see from the diagram, the rate of inflation has risen.

> ***Wie aus der Abbildung (dem Schaubild) hervorgeht,* ist die Inflationsrate gestiegen.**
> As is clear from the diagram, the rate of inflation has risen.

> ***Wie Sie an der Abbildung (dem Schaubild) sehen,* ist die Inflationsrate gestiegen.**
> As you can see from the diagram, the rate of inflation has risen.

> ***Wenn wir uns* die Abbildung (das Schaubild) *anschauen,* (dann) *wird deutlich, daß (wie)* die Inflationsrate gestiegen ist.**
> When we look at the diagram it becomes clear that (how) the rate of inflation has risen.

Index